KRONSTADT
1917–1921

SOVIET AND EAST EUROPEAN STUDIES

Books in the series

KRONSTADT
1917–1921

THE FATE OF A SOVIET DEMOCRACY

ISRAEL GETZLER

PROFESSOR OF HISTORY AND RUSSIAN STUDIES,
HEBREW UNIVERSITY OF JERUSALEM

CAMBRIDGE UNIVERSITY PRESS

CAMBRIDGE

LONDON   NEW YORK   NEW ROCHELLE

MELBOURNE   SYDNEY

Published by the Press Syndicate of the University of Cambridge
The Pitt Building, Trumpington Street, Cambridge CB2 IRP
32 East 57th Street, New York, NY 10022, USA
296 Beaconsfield Parade, Middle Park, Melbourne 3206, Australia

© Cambridge University Press 1983

First published 1983

Printed in Great Britain at
New Western Printing Ltd, Bristol

Library of Congress catalogue card number: 82–9575

British Library cataloguing in publication data

Getzler, Israel
Kronstadt 1917–1921. – (Soviet and East
European studies)
1. Kronstadt (R.S.F.S.R.) – Politics and
government – 20th century
I. Title   II. Series
947'.40841   DK265.8.K/

ISBN 0 521 24479 X

NWP

Contents

For Dvorah
who lived with it

Ours is a very simple prescription: all one has to do is to take what is here in Kronstadt on a small scale in our Soviet and in the Executive Committee and build it on a large scale, and it will work there too.

Efim Yarchuk, in the Kronstadt Soviet on 29 October 1917

Preface

Kronstadt is best known for its March 1921 uprising, when, with the battle-cry 'All Power to Soviets and Not to Parties', its dis-illusioned revolutionary sailors, soldiers and workers rose against Bolshevik Soviet power, the first and major example of left-wing protest from below against 'the complete dominance' of the Communist party. The revolt was all the more confounding to the Communist leaders since it came from the hard core of their social base, from the men who had been the shock-troops of the October revolution, the standard bearers of Soviet power during the civil war.

The student of the Kronstadt uprising is well served by Russian sources, and by Western and Soviet studies (though the latter are very party-minded and tendentious).[1] A similarly rich literature deals with the 1917 Baltic Fleet, of which Kronstadt formed a major base and training centre.[2]

This book sets out instead to focus attention on what I believe was Kronstadt's forgotten golden age of Soviet democracy in 1917–18. It was then, particularly during the March–October 1917 period of the provisional government with its free, open and multi-party society, that Red Kronstadt stood out as the prime example of Soviet power and democracy, well before the Bolsheviks turned the triumph of 'All Power to Soviets' into the Bolshevik dictatorship and Russia's Soviets into its emasculated instruments. Precisely because local Soviet power had been established there immediately in the wake of the February revolution of 1917, Kronstadt had no local October revolution nor any immediate Bolshevik takeover. Its significant contribution to the victory of the Bolshevik October revolution was in Petrograd and in Russia at large. Internal bolshevization came to Kronstadt only as late as June–July 1918, when the Menshevik-Internationalists and the Left Socialist Revolutionaries were expelled from the Soviet. But until that purge by decree from outside, which marked the end of its golden age of political pluralism and radical democracy, Kronstadt had enjoyed genuine Soviet power and a non-Bolshevik majority.

True, 1917 saw other Soviets assuming local power at some stage. Krasnoyarsk and Shlisselburg were the most notable, but Soviet power also held sway, though for shorter periods, in places such as Tsaritsyn, Reval, Riga, Helsingfors, Ekaterinburg, Lugansk and Ivanovo-Voznesensk, and I shall be examining them in a subsequent work. Yet it is already clear to me that all these 'Kronstadts', as some of them were termed, fell far short of Red Kronstadt's achievement.

Whether because of its island position, strategic importance or formidable internal cohesion and strength, Kronstadt was left alone to enjoy a lengthy period of political and social incubation until the middle of May 1917. Adequately provisioned and financed by the provisional government, its Soviet could thus, happily and undisturbed, build its own system of self-government and administration, creating virtually from scratch a rich and impressive political and social culture, a Russian echo of the Paris Commune.

The inaccessibility of the relevant archives precluded the writing of a fully fledged history of Kronstadt during the revolutionary period 1917–21. But this book is the first attempt to reconstruct and record the evolution and demise of Kronstadt's Soviet democracy and its accompanying perennial debate on power. That story began with Kronstadt's violent and sweeping February revolution and the ensuing transformation of tsardom's notorious 'sailors' Sakhalin' into what was, by May 1917, acclaimed as 'the brightest example of the democratic principle in the Russian revolution'. It was then that proud and confident Kronstadt had its first tussle over sovereignty with the provisional government. That was followed by the 'July Days' confrontation and clash with the leaders of the Petrograd Soviet over coalition government. Yet it was only in the aftermath of that humiliation that Kronstadt voluntarily accepted Bolshevik leadership in the campaign for 'All Power to Soviets', in the October revolution, and in the civil war, trusting that the triumph of Soviet power would turn the whole of Russia into one large Soviet democracy, into a Kronstadt writ large.

In that perspective, the uprising of March 1921 marked the final act in the Kronstadt drama, a desperate attempt to restore and reactivate its radical Soviet democracy of 1917–18.

The search for source materials for this study was hampered by failure to gain access to the archives of the Kronstadt Soviet and its Executive Committee, and it was small comfort to receive official assurances that the relevant files contained 'only a few drafts'. Luckily, the *Izvestiia* of the Kronstadt Soviet for the crucial period March 1917 to July 1918 carried very extensive and, more often than not, verbatim reports of the Soviet's plenary sessions and meetings, as well as shorter summaries of the agenda and resolutions of its Executive Committee, though regrettably little information on the working of the base assemblies and committees and on the fascinating mass meetings and debates in Kronstadt's Anchor Square. It was Kronstadt's *Izvestiia*, together with reports published in the contemporary newspapers of Kronstadt, Petrograd and Helsingfors, which made this study possible.

Unfortunately, the richness of Kronstadt's *Izvestiia* during 1917–18 contrasts painfully with its laconic coverage of the years 1919 to 1920, and that has made a study of the Kronstadt Soviet for the period of the civil war well-nigh impossible. This has also made it more difficult to pursue the task I set myself of establishing a continuity in personnel, ideology and institutions linking the 1917–18 Kronstadt experiment in Soviet democracy with its 'Third Revolution' of March 1921.

This continuity is personified by Kronstadt's central figure, Anatolii Lamanov. A third-year technology student in March 1917, Lamanov served as chairman or deputy chairman of the Kronstadt Soviet and chief editor of its *Izvestiia* for most of that year, and also led Kronstadt's large and self-consciously Non-Party faction which, in August 1917, became the Union of Socialist Revolutionaries–Maximalists. A candidate member of the Communist party since the end of 1919, he was the anonymous editor of the *Izvestiia* of Kronstadt's Revolutionary Committee in March 1921. Identified and denounced as the ideologist of the uprising, he was executed as a 'counter-revolutionary'. The promise of Lamanov's brief career and the sad irony of his tragic end mirror the great hopes and potentialities of the Russian revolution, so brutally shattered in Kronstadt.

Acknowledgements

With all the difficulties involved in the study of Kronstadt, I have been fortunate in having had the generous assistance and advice of many institutions, libraries, colleagues and friends over some ten years.

Work on this book began at La Trobe University, Melbourne, with which I have continued to be associated, and I am grateful to my colleagues in the history department and in the library, notably to Professors Jack Gregory and John Salmond and to Dietrich Borchardt, the chief librarian, for their ever ready and warm response.

I have been particularly fortunate in my colleagues at the Hebrew University of Jerusalem who, in many ways, have made it possible for me to pursue my research, and in the cooperation given me by Binyamin Lubelsky, emeritus librarian of the Russian Studies library.

The Government of Finland awarded me a state scholarship, and I owe a special debt of gratitude to the University of Helsinki and to the Slavonic section of the Helsinki University library for its hospitality and cooperation in 1970, 1976 and 1981.

To the History of Ideas Unit of the Australian National University I am grateful for a research fellowship in 1975, and to its chairman Professor Eugene Kamenka, for his stimulation, comments and hospitality.

My thanks go to the Hoover Institution on War, Revolution and Peace, and to its deputy director, Dr Frederick Starr, for generous access to its invaluable collections and for a research grant in 1976.

Freed of all teaching obligations, I was able to make important additions and revisions to the book during the academic year 1980–1 when, as a Visiting Fellow at St Antony's College, Oxford,

I benefited from the generous cooperation of the Warden, Professor Raymond Carr, of the Fellows there, and of Ms Rosamund Campbell, its librarian. I am particularly grateful to my colleagues Drs Harry Shukman, Harry Willetts, Michael Kaser, and Roy Kindersley for their friendship and patience.

Many colleagues and friends have helped with materials, and have read and commented on all parts of the manuscript. I want particularly to thank Professors Paul Avrich, Reinhard Bendix, Dietrich Geyer, Jonathan Frankel, Evan Mawdsley, John Keep, Alexander Rabinowitch, Harry Rigby, Leonard Schapiro, and the readers of Cambridge University Press for all the trouble they have taken.

On a personal note, my thanks are due to Abner Shavitsky, who saved irreplaceable source material from loss, to Margalit Wasserstein, who deciphered the manuscript, and to Avril and Charles Gilmour for their generous hospitality and friendship.

But most of all, I am indebted to Dvorah who saw this book through and to whom it is dedicated.

I.G.

Note on transliteration

The simplified British system of transliteration from the Cyrillic alphabet is used, and in addition diacriticals are omitted. The soft sign has been dropped and 'ii' has been rendered 'y' in surnames.

I

A sailors' Sakhalin

Kronstadt, fortress, naval base and port town on the island of
Kotlin in the Gulf of Finland, situated some twenty miles from
Petersburg and protecting the capital from the sea, entered the
Russian February revolution of 1917 with a population of some
82,000 (20,000 soldiers, 12,000 sailors and 50,000 civilian inhabitants)[1] and a formidable reputation for severe regimentation,
revolutionary unrest, mutiny and repression, and thorough
disaffection.

While some revolutionary cells seem to have been active in the
Torpedo and Gunnery Training Detachments there since 1902,[2]
Kronstadt's first major flare-up – the mutiny of October 1905 – was
spontaneous, its riotous course and pogrom-like outcome reflecting
its 'elemental' rather than political character.

True, in the background there loomed the shattering news of the
Tsushima Straits disaster of 14 May 1905, when the larger part of
the Baltic Fleet, sent to the Far East as the Second Pacific Squadron,
was sunk by the Japanese with the loss of 4,500 men. Nearer home,
there was the heroic example of the crew's revolutionary takeover
of the battleship *Potemkin* in June and its spectacularly defiant
eleven-day cruise in the Black Sea under the red flag. In the Baltic,
the depots of the naval base of Libau rose on 15 June, while on
4 July there was unrest on the battleship *Slava* at Reval. But the
long-standing and now seething discontent in Kronstadt was
essentially non-political.

Bad food, maltreatment by officers who meted out savage
beatings and harsh punishments for trifling misdemeanours, and
humiliating prohibitions were the lot of the Kronstadt sailors. The
town's parks and public squares, taverns and tea-houses, theatres
and markets, as well as the sunny side of the central boulevards,

were all out of bounds for the lower ranks. In Peer Park, alongside the notice 'Do not bring dogs into the park', hung another, arrogantly proclaiming, 'Soldiers and sailors are strictly barred from entry'.[3]

The accumulated discontent burst into the open in the wake of Tsar Nicholas II's manifesto of 17 October 1905 which, marking the beginning of Russia's short-lived era of semi-constitutionalism, granted an elective Duma and a measure of civil liberties. With the local authorities failing to 'explain to the people the true significance of the conferred liberties' (as the chief naval court put it on 11 January 1906),[4] on 23 October a crowd of some 5,000 sailors, soldiers, high school students and civilians gathered in Kronstadt's vast Anchor Square to hear how the October Manifesto's promised liberties would affect them. Couched in moderate, restrained language, the Petition to the Tsar that they then adopted insisted on their rights as 'Russian citizens' and 'defenders of the fatherland' to assemble and discuss matters of common interest, to spend their free time as they saw fit and not, 'like serfs', to have to 'ask permission for everything', and to purchase wine, since, they argued, 'sailors are not like children under parental supervision'. They also demanded the removal of notices which placed sailors and soldiers 'on a par with dogs', a reduction in the seven-year term of naval service (soldiers served five years), decent food and uniforms, and a rise in sailors' wages.

Politically, the petition sought the abolition of estates, 'so that all be equal', freedom of religion, the right of nationalities and ethnic minorities to 'education in one's own national language', freedom of speech, including the right to speak freely to superiors rather than in the rigid rubrics of 'Yes, indeed', 'No, certainly not', and 'Is present', and personal inviolability, so that 'they cannot simply come and grab a defenceless sailor and jail him'.[5]

The Anchor Square meeting also heard the Bolshevik party worker Iosif Dubrovinsky and the Socialist Revolutionary activist Pavel Tolmachev denounce the Manifesto as a deceit cunningly designed to rescue the frightened and tottering tsarist regime. While Tolmachev called for the overthrow of the autocracy and the destruction of the new constitution, since 'We need a Republic!', Dubrovinsky appealed to the crowd for direct action: 'Comrades, sailors and soldiers! You, who have revolutionary consciousness, you also have battleships, cannons, machine-guns and rifles, therefore –

long live the general armed uprising!'[6] But the meeting dispersed peacefully although, in the evening, some gunners and soldiers smashed up brothels, while others assaulted or threw stones at passing officers.

When Kronstadt's governor and chief commander, Vice-Admiral K. P. Nikonov, made the rounds of the sailors' depots and army units on 24 and 25 October, asking to be told their 'needs and grievances', the demands he heard were invariably for 'decent food' and 'decent outfits' and for 'personal eating utensils', since 'ten people are fed from one pot, the sick together with the healthy, while because of that, some do not eat at all and simply waste away'. However, one sailor, A. Kotlov of the Fifth Naval Depot, having been promised 'complete immunity', took Nikonov at his word and spelled it all out:

We are hurt at every step, your Highness. We are treated like beasts. Our officers never have a friendly word for us but always bark; their rudeness cuts us to the quick, for it is as if they set out deliberately to rob us of our human dignity. Some do not content themselves with merely being rude, but slap our faces and, for good measure, pile on exaggerated punishments. The sergeant-majors have been told, 'Beat those sons of bitches, harder and smartly.'

Kotlov adduced in evidence a considerable number of cases of physical violence by sergeant-majors that had been so severe as to lead to the hospitalization of their victims.[7] Nikonov listened attentively though somewhat incredulously, and finally exhorted the men, 'Don't listen to evil-minded persons who incite you to break your oath and engage in disorders.' Alarmed by what he had heard, he urgently ordered reinforcements from Petersburg. But they arrived too late.[8]

The next day, some fifty soldiers of the Second Kronstadt Infantry Battalion, about to march out to work, insisted first on presenting a statement of their grievances and demands to the regiment commander, Colonel Osipov. Refused permission, they promptly began to riot, shouting, 'Liberty! All are equal now! We need no officers!' Arrested and taken under convoy to the railway station for transport to an outlying fort, they appealed to a crowd of sailors, gunners and civilians who were themselves busy breaking into a wine store: 'Brothers, they are going to slaughter us, help!' When the crowd tried to free them, the guards opened fire, killing one sailor and seriously wounding another. An irate sailor crowd now abandoned all restraint and, raising the sailors of the Third, Fifth and Tenth Naval Depots and the gunners of the Gunnery Training Detachment and seizing all the rifles they found in the arsenal of the Seventh Naval Depot, they stormed into the streets, shouting 'Hoorah!' and singing revolutionary songs. Leaderless, with no plans and encountering no resistance – the police, fearing for their lives, had simply vanished, while the officers made for their homes to take their families to safety on the mainland – they roamed the streets aimlessly. Joined, if not prodded on, by the most dubious civilian elements, they broke into the officers' messes and wine shops, got themselves drunk, smashed street lanterns, set fire to houses and shops and, when the fire brigade arrived, slashed the water hoses. A majority of Kronstadt's garrison of 13,000 sailors and soldiers, seven out of the twelve depots, joined in the arson, pillage and drunken orgy, while the half-squadron of dragoons sent to bring the rampaging crowds to their senses did nothing, their commander, Captain Silman, not daring to order them to open fire lest they disobey his command. Only when the troops that Nikonov had ordered from Petersburg arrived on 28 October was the mutiny suppressed. Sixteen sailors and one civilian lay dead, and seventy-five sailors, twelve soldiers and seventeen civilians were wounded.[9]

Though the majority of the Kronstadt garrison had participated in the mutiny, and some 3,000 had actually been arrested, a mere 208 were brought to trial; of these, eighty-four were acquitted and only forty-one were found guilty of mutiny; but none were sentenced to death and only one to *katorga* (hard labour) for life. One reason for the surprisingly lenient treatment of the Kronstadt mutineers may have been the general strike of Petersburg workers who, on 1 November, protested the courts martial and the death penalty and loudly proclaimed their support for 'the brave soldiers and sailors of Kronstadt who rose in defence of their rights and the people's freedom'.[10] But there was, too, the tsarist authorities' desire to damp down the excitement and the universal discontent in the navy (which even they realized were justified), and, more importantly, to depoliticize them, an aim they sought to achieve by treating the Kronstadt mutiny as a mere drunken riot.

But the men of Kronstadt, too, could learn the lesson of the mutiny. If the few Socialist Revolutionary and Bolshevik activists there, who had been working since the summer of 1905, saw to their horror how a spontaneous and leaderless mutiny could degenerate into an 'imbecile, wild and drunken pogrom',[11] the 'United Committee of the Kronstadt Military-Revolutionary Organization' (which came into being during the early months of 1906 with Socialist Revolutionaries predominating) made sure that the growing resentment and rebelliousness of the garrison would never again prematurely explode or waste itself in brawls between soldiers and sailors or wild raids on wine shops. Indeed, it posted special squads to patrol the major streets on public holidays and keep the peace.[12]

Kronstadt's July 1906 uprising was the work of this United Committee. It was planned to coincide with revolts in the other three Baltic fleet bases, at Sveaborg (Helsingfors), Reval and Libau and, coming in the wake of resentment created by the angry tsar's dissolution of the oppositional First Duma on 9 July 1906, was intended to re-ignite the revolution in Petersburg and then the whole of Russia.

While the leadership of the uprising was Socialist Revolutionary (the Bolshevik minority in the United Committee gave only last-minute support), and its ideology and battle-cry 'For Land and Liberty!', 'For the Motherland and the Peasant Folk!' was clearly populist, its mood was violently anti-officer. Indeed, hatred of officers, castigated as 'dragons' and 'bloodsuckers', was so ferocious that when, a few days before the uprising, the question of the officers' fate was discussed in one of the naval depots, sailors were unanimous: officers must be killed. 'We discussed them one by one, and found none deserving of our confidence or simple mercy', the sailor Nikolai Egorov recorded soon after. In fact, he remembered the 'officer question' being a major and frequent bone of contention between the sailors and their mentors, the SR intellectuals who came to organize them.

We were in agreement and lived in harmony with them, but on this one question we never saw eye to eye. They insisted there was no need to kill the officers, that it would be sufficient to arrest them and thus render them incapable of opposing the uprising . . . But we would not budge and thought that any possible sympathizer would long ago have revealed himself by kindness and would not have remained a true servant of the government. As for those who might come over to our side, they would do this only out of fear. Why bother then about their possible sympathy or assistance. To hell with them all![13]

The debate continued up to the very eve of the uprising when, on 17 July, the navy and army delegates met to discuss 'the plan' and its execution. 'Precious hours were wasted', the sailor A. Piskarev complained, in a debate over whether the officers were to be 'killed or merely arrested', with the 'mankind-loving Mensheviks' incurring the 'displeasure of the sailors and workers' because of their spirited defence of the officers. In the end, a compromise was reached to 'deal with the officers according to circumstances'.[14]

Badly planned and haphazardly prepared, the uprising began at 11 p.m. on 19 July, and was defeated by the next morning. Everything went wrong. The Sveaborg revolt, which began on 17 July, was already put down before the Kronstadters had even moved, while the Reval and Libau bases and the ships of the Baltic Fleet remained altogether quiet, except for a short-lived mutiny on the cruiser *Pamiat' Azova*. Worst of all, the little-propagandized Eniseisk Infantry Regiment stationed in Kronstadt, on which the United Committee had relied for support and very badly needed rifles (sailors were kept unarmed), would not join in. Nor did the band of SR-Maximalist terrorists, who had promised to bring revolvers and bombs, arrive.[15] When the sailors' call, 'Comrades, join us, we stand for Land and Liberty!', was answered by the men of the Eniseisk regiment with a volley of bullets, the fate of Kronstadt's 'unarmed' uprising was sealed, and it was easily and almost bloodlessly suppressed.

Of the nine killed during the uprising, four were officers, one a civilian, and only four were sailors; while of the twenty wounded, at least four were officers. Small wonder that Captain Muravev, a member of an investigatory commission on the uprising, complained: 'One cannot help noticing the pathetically small number of mutineers killed during the suppression of the mutiny. It is an alarming sign: the troops shot into the air and not at the rebels, and mutineers may take advantage of this in the future.'[16]

A series of bloody reprisals began immediately on 20 July, with the summary execution by firing squad of seven torpedo-men who were accused of having shot both their new commander, Captain Vrochinsky, and their former commander, Colonel Alexandrov, together with his mistress. Vice-Admiral A. Adlerberg, the commandant of the fortress, who supervised the execution, is reported to have ordered the torpedo-men to dig their own graves: 'Dig, lads, dig, here's your "Land" for you! And as for "Liberty", you'll find that in heaven!'

In a poem which appeared soon after in *Soldatskaia mysl'*, the organ of the military section of the party of Socialist Revolutionaries, Adlerberg was told:

> Rejoice not yet, perfidious, cruel, old rascal:
> 'Land and People's Liberty!'
> Still resounds our battle-cry!
> This to your bullets is our reply!

For the simple soldiers of the firing squad they had another message:

> Get ready, take aim, straight and true,
> Your years of slavery will soon be through,
> Farewell, lads! Long live Holy Russia!
> Land and the People's Liberty![17]

Another seven torpedo-men and three civilians accused of the murder of officers were court-martialled and executed on 7 August. One of the condemned, the student Aram Ter-Marchiants, an SR activist, died shouting, 'Down with the autocracy! Death to the tyrants!'[18]

But it was the execution of nineteen sailors on 21 September which became a major chapter in Kronstadt's rich revolutionary martyrology. Active leaders of the uprising, the majority refused religious rites and the apposition of the Cross and sang the revolutionary Funeral March while the sentence was read out to them. The firing squad must have faltered: only three or four sailors died in the first volley. Even after the second, there were still some left who had to be shot with revolvers.[19]

A total of some 3,000 sailors, 200 torpedo-men, 100 sappers and 80 civilians were tried in Kronstadt in the wake of the uprising. Of these, 1,451 received various terms of imprisonment, 180 were condemned to various terms of *katorga* and 36 were executed. A total of 2,127 were registered as 'politically unreliable' and were gradually drafted from Kronstadt and the Baltic Fleet into special punitive detachments or army units as far away as Archangelsk, Tambov or the Caucasus. Even the silent majority which had not joined in the uprising, but had done nothing to prevent it, were demoted by two ranks.[20]

Both the scale and the ferocity of the punishments meted out to the Kronstadters in 1906 and 1907 were quite unprecedented and in stark contrast with the mild treatment of the mutineers and pogromists of October 1905. The new policy of ruthless 'pacification', of drumhead court martials and gallows – the notorious 'Stolypin neckties' – adopted by the tsarist authorities after the dissolution of the First Duma on 9 July 1906 may partly explain this turn-about, but more important was their panic-stricken realization that at least three-quarters of Kronstadt sailors were 'seized with the intoxication of the liberation movement, ready for any kind of revolutionary action, and only still afraid because they are not sure of the sympathy of the garrison's soldiers'. Yet Kronstadt soldiers were none too reliable either. A letter which the Minister for War, Alexander F. Rediger, received on 23 July 1906 from 'two hundred and seven class-conscious soldiers', drove the point home:

Listen, Minister Rediger. We, 71 conscious sailors and 136 conscious infantry soldiers, assembled in a forest, have sworn to avenge our seven court-martialled and executed comrades. How shall we avenge them? We will avenge them thus: for every comrade soldier killed, we will hang three officers edgewise, and shoot another five. Report that to the tsar! Yet our superiors regard us as the most reliable![21]

The main lesson which the tsarist authorities characteristically drew from the Kronstadt mutinies of 1905 and 1906 was the need to enlarge and tighten the system of police surveillance still further, 'insulate that stronghold of the capital from agitators and other evil elements', and make sure that 'not one person could penetrate unnoticed into the fortress, the port or the barracks'.[22]

With the appointment in 1909 of Vice-Admiral Robert N. Viren as military governor of Kronstadt and chief commander of its port, Kronstadt's system of strict regimentation, thorough surveillance and brutal punishment reached its apogee. Kronstadt, already in disrepute because of its prison dungeons and punitive detachments, now became known and dreaded as a 'sailors' Sakhalin', a Baltic echo of Russia's notorious penal island in the Far East.

Born in 1856 into a Lutheran, Finno-Swedish family, a hero of Port Arthur and the Russo-Japanese war, by 1907 Viren had already distinguished himself by his relentless and ruthless suppression of subversion as chief commander of the Black Sea Fleet and governor general of Sebastopol. The captain of the destroyer *Novik*, G. K. Graf, who admired him for his courage and dedication to the monarchy, nevertheless remembered him as a martinet of martinets:

He was by nature straight, imperious and courageous, but also boundlessly strict and demanding. He would implacably note trifles and mercilessly scolded anybody and at any occasion. It was quite impossible to please him: this was bad, and that was not much good, one could expect no quarter from him . . . At the very sight of the chief commander, sailors would run for their lives as though possessed and try to hide their caps into the bargain, since for the most trifling dereliction he would demand the man's cap, note the number, and have the culprit found.[23]

While that was the comment of a monarchist officer, to an intelligent and alert sailor such as Grigorii Kononov Kronstadt's 'devilish *katorga*-like regime', over which Viren hovered like an 'evil genius', appeared to have been specially invented to 'humiliate and insult' the lower ranks and 'break their human dignity and self-respect'. The moment Kononov was drafted into the navy and even while he was still in Petersburg on his way to Kronstadt, he was told, 'They'll squeeze your juices out of you there!' 'They'll drill you there all right!', as if he were being drafted into a 'punitive battalion'. In Kronstadt, the 'reality was even worse than his expectations': Viren's wife, 'the *admiralshchina*', not to speak of the senior officers and even some of their wives, too, took delight in pulling up sailors who happened to walk on 'the wrong [i.e. sunny] side of the boulevard' and asking for their names and numbers. Thus 'scoffed at', Kononov remembered 'biting his lips bloody' in impotent rage. Yet with all public places and parks out of bounds and visits to private homes strictly prohibited – the offending sailor was liable to thirty days lockup and his host to three months in prison and deportation from Kronstadt – there was little else that a sailor could do with his leave, according to both Graf and Kononov, except walk the streets.[24]

Small wonder that when the battleships *Imperator Pavel I* and *Andre Pervozvannyi* were moored in the Kronstadt harbour for nearly a week in the spring of 1913, only a very few sailors dared go ashore for fear they might be spotted by Viren and his officers, rebuked and thus lose their shore leave in Reval.[25]

Yet the 20,000 or so soldiers and sailors who constituted the Kronstadt garrison in the years before World War I (by February 1917 their number had grown to almost 20,000 soldiers in the Kronstadt fortress and 12,000 naval forces, of whom no less than 7,100 were in training units and training ships, with 4,800 in shore units)[26] were probably the most literate, technically skilled and modern, the most ethnically Russian, least servile and the most disaffected of all Russia's armed forces.

For, having embarked on a vast and very ambitious naval construction programme with the object of creating, within a decade and almost from scratch, a new, powerful, modern navy, 'of a

strength and power that will befit the dignity and glory of Russia'
and more than match the formidable German navy in the Baltic, the
tsarist authorities faced a recruitment problem and found that 'in
view of the special complexity of the modern battleship, the Russian
peasant, straight from the *sokha* [wooden plough] cannot immediately
become a sailor, while it is the working element that is somewhat
prepared for the handling of machines'.[27]

This 'working element' was found so indispensable for the manning and servicing of Russia's modern navy, notably of its latest
Dreadnought battleships, that of those drafted into the Baltic Fleet
between 1904 and 1916, industrial workers formed the largest group
(31%), workers in building and light industry, unskilled labourers
and boatmen made up 23%, artisans, tradesmen, employees and
miscellaneous groups another 21%, and peasants only 25%. In the
same period, a mere 3.43% of army recruits were factory workers.[28]

But while these working-class naval recruits, 84% of whom were
fully literate, with another 10% semi-literate (in the army call-up
of 1903, 44.5% were illiterate, while in 1913, illiterates were still
32.2%),[29] were regarded as indispensable, they were also suspected
of being politically unreliable, if not disaffected. Indeed the director
of the Police Department advised against 'the recruitment into the
navy of draftees who have completed lower technical schools, factory
and railway schools, as well as former factory workers, locksmiths,
foundry workers, electricians, fitters, telegraphists and other tradesmen who, together with their specialist course, have also gone
through the corrupting school of the factory atmosphere'. For, in his
opinion, such recruits would 'bring into the navy a vast battery of
anti-militarist ideas, contempt for military service, and a hostile
attitude to all authority absorbed from the age of 12–15 since when
they have moved amidst propagandized workers'.[30]

Indeed, with the Kronstadt naval base forming the major training
centre of the Baltic Fleet, most of the new recruits were, after some
six months of infantry drill, assigned to one of the many training
companies or schools to become artificers, stokers, gunners, torpedo-
men, telegraphists, electricians, divers, clerks or medical orderlies.
They attended classes in general studies and Russian language,
arithmetic, physics, mechanics, electro-technology, and radio-tel-
egraphy.[31] Yet, as some Kronstadt naval officers complained in 1913,
training recruits, 'already poisoned with [revolutionary] propaganda', in barracks and classrooms rather than on board ships was

not conducive to their 'education' in loyalty and patriotism; that could only be given by identification with 'the glorious military past', the banners and symbols of a particular ship or regiment, they urged.[32]

Moreover, the ablest and better educated, who were given an additional year of training to qualify as petty-officers and instructors, thus received an education well above average which turned them, as Captain Graf peevishly noted, 'into half-intellectuals'.[33] As for qualified sailors, a significant proportion travelled abroad on the annual summer cruises of the Baltic Fleet to the ports of Western Europe and the Mediterranean, and may well have compared their servile lot and tsarist police state with what they saw there.

Yet this alert, skilled and modern lower deck confronted a caste-like naval officers corps, most of whom were the 'blue-blooded' sons of the hereditary gentry, often of the Baltic German nobility, and graduates of the very exclusive Naval Cadet Corpus in Petersburg.[34] Haughty and educated in unquestioning loyalty to the tsar, they had been trained to demand absolute obedience and subservience from the 'lower ranks'. The contempt and distrust of officers for men was only exceeded by the sailors' bitter hatred for an officer class which they saw as the mainstay of Kronstadt's formidable network of political surveillance headed by Colonel V. V. Trzhetsiak, chief of the Kronstadt Gendarmerie Administration, and the indefatigable captain of the gendarmerie, Vladimir Vladimirovich Vladimirov. As the sailors sneered: 'In the Naval Cadet Corpus they don't train officers for ships, but for the Police Department!' Officers and men were certainly worlds apart and the chasm that divided them reflected the basic dilemma of Russia's modernization under tsarist auspices.

The town itself had a substantial industrial work force of some 13,000 by 1911 (17,000 by June 1917), employed in the shipyards, the huge dry-docks, the steamship plant, the arsenal, the chemical laboratories, the sawmill and the twenty-three workshops of the Naval Administration, the privately owned cable factory, and the numerous workshops producing goods ranging from simple chandlery to sophisticated diving equipment, the large timber and coal yards adjacent to the mercantile port which handled timber exports of more than 10 million roubles a year and coal imports of 1.5 million tons a year (the Petersburg port handled only half a million tons of coal a year), the municipal gas company and electric power station.[35]

Kronstadt's workers were thus, like industrial workers all over Russia,
a primary and attractive target for the SRs, Bolsheviks and Mensheviks, whose success was such that at least 1,000 workers of the
steamship plant were reported and promptly dismissed for celebrat-
ing the first of May in 1907.[36]

But Viren's tight *cordon sanitaire* kept revolutionary agitators out
and effectively silenced all organized revolutionary activity among
Kronstadt's workers. Under a system of registration of workers,
already operating for naval recruits, employers with government
contracts – the large majority of Kronstadt's privately owned sector
– cooperated fully with the political gendarmerie and, with their
help, kept dossiers on the political reliability of workers. Employees
regarded as 'unreliables' were put under surveillance and gradually
made to leave the town.[37]

The Kronstadt system of registration and surveillance of both
workers and naval recruits was, thanks to the close and unprecedented cooperation of Governor Viren and the chief of the gendarmerie, so successful that it was held up as a model for Sveaborg,
Reval and Libau at the January 1913 conferences of gendarmerie
and police chiefs of the Baltic provinces, convened to devise measures
'for the prevention of the penetration of criminal propaganda from
without into the ships of the Baltic Fleet'.[38]

As for the local intelligentsia – the teachers of Kronstadt's four
high schools, the medical personnel of its two hospitals, the numerous
engineers and the student sons and daughters of the large body of
officials of the naval and military establishments and of the Ministry
of Trade and Industry – they were singularly apathetic and apolitical. They were thus perfectly in tune with Kronstadt's dull, stuffy,
very provincial and fragmented society in which Viren's dour,
parsimonious and withdrawn life-style – he held no receptions, did
not mix at balls and soirées, supported no associations and clubs
except some philanthropic and temperance societies – set the tone.
There was no local theatre or opera, the large and impressive naval
library was controlled by the naval establishment and the two local
'navy and town' newspapers (the *Kronshtadtskii vestnik* and the *Kotlin*)
were conservative-loyalist and close to the Naval Ministry, while the
municipal Duma was dominated by merchants of the first and second
guilds, and ennobled citizens and retired army and navy officers and
officials. Small wonder that more alert members of the intelligentsia
and young officials tended to regard their jobs and their stay in

Kronstadt as a temporary necessity, and, as Foma Parchevsky who arrived in 1912 to teach in a local high school observed, spent their time thinking 'how to get out of Kronstadt as soon as possible'.[39] Of the more alienated sons and daughters of officialdom and intelligentsia, the Okhrana (political police) recorded in early 1911 the existence of one radical circle with SR connections which, under the cover of the study of Esperanto, and under close secret police surveillance, existed half-heartedly for a few months.[40]

Colonel Trzhetsiak's report to Governor Viren of 30 October 1910, fully corroborated by Parchevsky's observations, is a fair summing-up of the political facelessness of Kronstadt's 'civil society' in the pre-war period:

Among Kronstadt's permanent inhabitants and workers the mood is quiet. People earlier noticed as politically unreliable, and now under observation, have shown no activity. I relate this to the absence of intelligent, energetic and experienced leaders and also to the cooling off of society towards the revolutionary movement.[41]

With the working class cowed and under close surveillance, and the intelligentsia philistine and apolitical, Kronstadt's revolutionary movement survived during the pre-war years in the small cells of training depots and ships and consisted mainly of sailors, naval petty-officers, instructors and medical personnel – Graf's 'semi-intellectuals' – who engaged in sporadic propaganda work and battled hard to maintain occasional contacts with organizers from Petersburg. They were constantly hounded by Colonel Trzhetsiak's small army of gendarmes, stool-pigeons, provocateurs, and part-time spies, including tea-house owners and publicans, and, driven deep underground, were prevented from organizing into larger units or 'collectives' with regular connections with revolutionary party organizations in Petersburg. It is an index of Trzhetsiak's and Viren's success that the existence and activities of these revolutionary cells are known chiefly from the Okhrana records and the trial reports of those apprehended.

For all that, Viren's system proved powerless to insulate the thousands of sailors who went abroad on the annual summer cruises of the Baltic Fleet. The police agents who tailed them could only notice and meticulously record the eager response of the Baltic squadrons' crews to the agitation of Socialist Revolutionary and Social Democratic activists who followed them from port to port and supplied them there with revolutionary literature.

One police agent's report of 27 April 1913 noted that the crews of the squadron which called in Hull, Marseilles and Alexandria met Russian emigré sailors (among them former crew members of the *Potemkin*) and received from them 'large quantities of party literature', including the SR journals *Za narod* and *Moriak*. [42] Another police spy, who tailed the Baltic squadron that visited Copenhagen in October 1912, defined the general mood of the Baltic Fleet as 'extremely oppositional'; many men, he thought, were 'conscious revolutionaries'. Altogether, he assessed the sailors as affording 'very fertile and responsive soil for propaganda', and noted that they took special interest in the agrarian question and complained of onerous service conditions. Those of the *Poliarnaia Zvezda* said they would have mutinied, if not for the respect and affection they had for their commander, Prince Viazemsky. Yet he found the sailors afraid of organizing because of the many arrests in the Baltic Fleet. [43]

Indeed, only a few months earlier Lenin had complained to Maxim Gorky, 'The Baltic Fleet is seething!' But, 'One could weep, there is no organization!' [44]

With the outbreak of World War I, Kronstadt was put on siege footing and the few civilians who were regarded as politically un- reliable were deported to the mainland. That certainly did not solve the new problem created by the arrival in the Kronstadt First Baltic Depot of many ex-mutineers of 1905 and 1906, together with other 'unreliables', who, now remobilized, had on the orders of the chief commander of the Baltic Fleet, Admiral N. O. Essen, been drafted from their ships as 'depraved and propagandized'. The situation threw Lieutenant-General A. A. Manikovsky, commandant of the Kronstadt fortress, into despair, for now, he protested, 'the young sailors are, as a matter of course and from the very first days of their service, mixing freely with the most propagandized and dissolute men drafted from the ships into the Depot'.

'The rise in the revolutionary mood of the Petrograd working masses' was already being felt, Manikovsky warned, and Socialist Revolutionary and Social Democratic leaflets had been distributed 'calling the navy and the army to put an end to the war and to rise in armed insurrection'.

Viren's solution to the problem posed by the hundreds of political unreliables, among whom he noted many specialists and petty- officers, was to demote them all to the rank of sailors second class, to put the 'politicals' on floating barracks such as the former transport ships *Volkhov* and *Argun*, and to send the rest into labour battalions. Kronstadt must be purged of them.[45]

With the news of the recurrent defeats of the Russian army, the 'great retreat' during the summer of 1915, and especially the fall of Warsaw on 4 August 1915 alarming the Kronstadters, old, anti-officer feelings took on a new, patriotic, anti-German form: the defeats were put down, above all, to the pro-German attitudes of the officers and generals, known as 'Ostzeiskie', many of whom, indeed, had German names.

At the end of August 1915, when the minelayer *Pobeditel* arrived in Kronstadt for the second time to repair damage attributed to the negligence of officers, the crews of the battleships *Gromoboi* and *Rossiia*, as well as of all the Dreadnoughts in the harbour, staged a demonstration against their officers, shouting, 'Down with the Germans!' When Admiral Alexander Kurosh, commander of the squadron, threatened them with the gallows, he was told, 'You can't hang all the thousands, for you'll be hanged first!' And when the crews of the battleships *Imperator Pavel I* and *Rossiia*, protesting against bad food and demanding more humane treatment *and* the removal of all officers with German names, again confronted Kurosh – who this time, revolver in hand, threatened to shoot them summarily – they promptly and fearlessly told him: 'This is not 1905! Sailors have learned their lesson and you cannot frighten us any more! Before your Excellency makes good your threat, you will be thrown overboard!'[46] Sixteen sailors were, however, arrested and tried, including the Bolshevik activist Timofei Uliantsev.

Similarly, when a dispute over watered-down gruel on the battleship *Gangut* turned into mutiny in October 1915, the sailors' battle-cry against their officers was, 'Beat the Germans!' And with ninety-five *Gangut* sailors arrested, Captain Vladimirov noted, on 3 November, that Kronstadt sailors were up in arms, claiming the 'Ganguters' were innocent as they had risen 'against the common enemy of the fatherland – the Russian Germans whose authority neither the Russian navy nor the Russian army accepts. Should the authorities find these ninety-five sailor-patriots, who devotedly love Russia, guilty, then the entire navy and army ought to be put on trial.'[47]

Vladimirov noted with great concern that subversive propaganda had by now spread further than the battleships of the Baltic Fleet, also penetrating the army units of the Kronstadt garrison who sympathized with the sailors of the *Gangut.* Indeed, an agent's report which he received in September 1915 referred specifically to the existence and activity of cells of 'Socialist Revolutionary and Social Democratic tendencies' within the Baltic Fleet.[48] More than that, there were a number of serious and for a short time successful attempts in 1915 and 1916 to bring such revolutionary cells under one roof – an organization called the Collective – and to seek connections with the Bolshevik and SR committees in Petrograd (the new, russified name given to Petersburg upon the outbreak of war).

Thus, with the spontaneous creation in May/June 1915 of a number of Bolshevik cells of some ten to fifteen members on the larger battleships such as *Imperator Pavel I, Petropavlovsk, Gangut* and *Poltava,* the cruisers *Rossiia* and *Diana,* the trawlers *Fita* and *Vzryv,* the Gunnery Training Detachment and the First Baltic Naval Depot in Kronstadt, an 'Initiative Group' was formed. Leading it were the petty-officers Ivan Sladkov and Fiodor Kuznetsov-Lomakin, the artificer Timofei Uliantsev and the sailor Nikolai Pisarev, the aim being the coordination of activities in the cells and the establishment of a link with the Bolshevik party committee in Petrograd. As Kuznetsov-Lomakin remembered: 'Though all of us sympathized with the social democratic Bolsheviks, for the sake of party con-nections we were even prepared to turn to the Socialist Revolution-aries in seeking some thread that would connect us with the rest of the world.'[49]

By the end of the year, the Initiative Group, or Leading Collective, had at last established regular contact with the Petrograd Bolshevik Committee through Kirill Orlov, a party worker and a former *Potemkin* man. It was then that the Kronstadt gendarmerie, which through its agents V. V. Baishev, a gunner on the *Imperator Alexander II,* and the worker V. E. Shurkanov had watched it all along, decided to arrest the Collective. The opportunity came on 28 Decem-ber 1915 when Ivan Sladkov was caught redhanded with a parcel of Bolshevik proclamations which he had just brought back from Petrograd and was about to hand over to Stepan Erokhin, an artificer on the *Tsezarevich.* The arrest of more than twenty sailors and the conviction of the ringleaders spelt the end of the Collective and of most of the Bolshevik cells; but only for a time.[50]

For by July 1916, Colonel Trzhetsiak was already planning to liquidate a newly formed and very active Main Collective of the

Kronstadt Military Organization which consisted exclusively of sailors and was again connected with the Petrograd Bolshevik committee. According to another report (of 27 August) that Main Collective, or some other 'strong military organization' in Kronstadt, consisted of both soldiers and sailors, including 'Social Democrats, Socialist Revolutionaries and anarchists', and regarded itself 'formally as non-affiliated' to any party.

Whatever the reason for the delay, it was not until September that Colonel Trzhetsiak, in consultation with Viren, as last decided to take action.[51] The major police action against the Main Collective during the night of 8 September, though bungled and producing little evidence for proper conviction, seems to have liquidated it for good. But Robert Viren took small comfort in that, for, while he was somewhat slow-witted, he now finally realized that his draconic regime had failed. True, it was still eminently capable of terrorizing and maintaining surveillance over a large and far from servile or ignorant sailor and soldier population, and even of ferreting out and arresting its revolutionary activists and ringleaders, but it had, in the last analysis, proved powerless to prevent the growing and deepening disaffection of the entire Kronstadt garrison.

Viren faced his moment of truth courageously: on 15 September, in a letter to Rear-Admiral Count P. A. Geiden, chief of the tsar's chancellory, and in simultaneous reports to the commander-in-chief of the Baltic Fleet and the Minister of the Interior, he pleaded for nothing less than the disbandment of Kronstadt:[52]

I never hesitate to mete out the most severe punishments, and, when necessary, order the lash rather than the birch, or a week's starvation in jail in place of a one night arrest, but I must confess that I am at the end of my tether . . . the situation is becoming catastrophic. You, Count Geiden, who occupy such an eminent position in the Naval Department and in the tsar's intimate entourage, must know the truth. Under my command at present is an army of 80,000 men under all kinds of weapons, trawlers and anti-gas engineering units included. Kronstadt protects the capital from the sea and is the last stronghold on which our navy can fall back should the enemy capture the Baltic Sea. However, and I say this with my hand on my heart, all that is needed to make Kronstadt, together with the ships presently in the port, rise against me, the officers' corps, the government and everybody, is but a push from Petrograd. The fortress is a veritable powder-keg: its fuse is already burning, and soon it must explode.

Yesterday, I inspected the cruiser *Diana*. The crew answered my greetings formally, but with barely concealed hostility. I scanned the faces of the sailors and talked to some like a father, but, and maybe this is just the imagination and nerves of an exhausted old sea-dog, I felt as if I were on the deck of an enemy cruiser – such was the lasting impression of that nightmarish review. Back in their ward-room the officers said openly that the sailors were all revolutionaries and that surprise searches had revealed the existence of a strong underground organization, but that its hard core had remained undetected.

Thus it is all over Kronstadt. All those that we apprehend, we put on trial; we deport, we execute by firing squad, but it is all of no avail, we cannot put 80,000 on trial. And so it has become my deep conviction that we must disperse the majority of land forces throughout Russia, replacing them with long-service battalions; the technical crews must be completely disbanded and the slightest protest severely crushed; finally, the [crews of] ships listed in my report to the commander-in-chief of the Baltic Fleet should be replaced by crews from the Siberian and White Sea flotillas.

These measures, it is true, may in theory for a time lower the combat capacity of Kronstadt, but they will save the fortress for the government. I regard it as the duty of my conscience, my dear Count, to tell you all this.

While Viren's letter made a 'shattering impact' on Count Geiden, the reply that Viren received from the tsar's chancellory assured him that the Police Department had infiltrated Kronstadt's underground network and was only waiting for an opportune moment to liquidate it; the crews of the run-down Siberian and White Sea flotillas were unfit to replace the Baltic sailors, the reply continued, and the disbandment of the land forces would cause great alarm in the army; technical crews, it was pointed out, were much alike everywhere and equally unreliable and, 'all in all, it makes no sense to spread the Kronstadt disease all over Russia'.[53]

2

The February revolution in Kronstadt

News of the unrest in Petrograd, notably of the mutiny on 27 February 1917, when troops ordered to shoot at the demonstrating crowds and striking workers disobeyed and instead joined the masses, seeped through to the garrison and workers of Kronstadt despite the precautionary measures, including the ban on newspapers, that Viren had taken since 25 February to insulate Kotlin Island from the outside world.[1]

Not surprisingly, Viren did not quite grasp the nature of events and felt duty bound to try to reverse them,[2] only desisting from his plan to use Kronstadt troops to help crush the Petrograd uprising after his officers told him that the lower ranks would 'join the insurgents'.[3]

Nevertheless, determined to hold out and prevent the revolution spreading to Kronstadt, Viren placed field cannons and machine-guns on the pier, aimed at the road leading over the ice to Oranien-baum on the mainland, and he may also have given orders to the officers of the Third Kronstadt Fortress Infantry Regiment to keep their troops on the ready near the Petrograd Gates.[4] At the same time he posted orders throughout Kronstadt, prohibiting gatherings, meetings and speeches, threatened to take reprisals with his 'fatherly hand', and his appeal 'To the Workers and Residents of Kronstadt' handed down the 'fatherly advice' that 'everyone carry on normally' both for 'the general good and for his own personal well-being'.[5] In the same vein, when the workers of the steamship plant went on strike on 28 February and their spokesman, the young worker Tsygankov, presented Viren with their demands and asked him to explain the Petrograd happenings to them, he told them he would address them the next day in Anchor Square, but at the same time gave orders to place machine-guns in the naval cathedral overlooking the square.[6] In his stubborn refusal to allow Kronstadt to fall in line with the revolution in Petrograd, a move which might have somewhat defused the explosive situation, Viren himself may well have been responsible for Kronstadt's own local revolution, possibly the most violent and sweeping of the Russian February revolution.

Kronstadt's revolution began as a 'mutiny against God'.[7] Throughout 28 February, their classes and exercises cancelled, the sailors and soldiers of the Kronstadt garrison were confined to barracks and were busy discussing events. Some activists, as was later claimed, may even have been preparing plans for an uprising which was to begin at 11 p.m.[8] But outwardly the city and the garrison looked calm, and there seemed nothing to belie the report that Vice-Admiral Alexander Kurosh, the newly appointed commandant of the fortress, made late in the afternoon to the Minister of the Navy, Admiral Ivan Grigorovich, that 'all is quiet and order has not been disturbed'.[9] Small wonder that the non-commissioned officer Foma Parchevsky, though apprehensive and wondering anxiously why he and his fellow officers had received no orders from their commander, nevertheless went to bed and 'slept as soundly as usual'.[10]

Whatever the role played by the 'workers' delegate' from Petrograd who is reported to have arrived in Kronstadt at 8 p.m. bringing first-hand information on the revolution in the capital,[11] the first clash with the tsarist authorities seems to have taken place in the Torpedo and Mining Training Detachment where instructor Ivan Kolbin and a group of activists had readied sailors to 'come out' during the evening muster. Because of the tense situation, the company commander, Second Lieutenant Rebrov, had himself come, accompanied by Lieutenant Skrydlov, to take the muster, and when all the sailors were lined up, he turned to Sergeant-Major Spiridon Tikhonov asking him to start the anthem. In Kolbin's words:[12]

The Sergeant-Major began the anthem 'God Save the Tsar' but soon fell silent when no one supported him. He tried a second time and, together with the company commander, began to sing 'Save, O Lord, Thy People', but again all stood silent, silent as the dead. Rebrov's elderly voice faltered and broke. There was a burst of restrained laughter. A purple-faced Lieutenant Skrydlov, standing in front of the troops, asked: 'What's the matter?' It was I who answered, saying: 'If the sailors and soldiers refuse to save the tsar, then God will not save him either! We'll not sing any more hymns! Today's anthem is "Down with the autocracy, Long live the revolution!" '

Shouting 'Long live the revolution' the sailors went for their coats and rifles. Skrydlov, handing over his revolver to Kolbin, declared that since the autocracy was already overthrown, he felt he could serve the revolution if they wanted him, and was promptly appointed commander.

Unlike Skrydlov, Second Lieutenant Popov, commander of the Second Company of the First Kronstadt Artillery Regiment, proved a true Viren man. Totally failing to gauge both the disaffected mood and the intelligence of Kronstadt's gunners, he chose as the theme of his address at the evening muster of 28 February – the sanctity of the oath of loyalty. As the muster drew to its close, he issued the customary injunction 'Do your best!' But somewhat to his surprise, only five young soldiers gave the prescribed reply: 'We will do our best, noble Sir', the rest remaining ominously silent. Undeterred, Popov summoned all the junior artillery officers and senior gunners to his office and, after breaking the news of the Petrograd events and declaring that 'the new government will soon be destroyed and order restored', exhorted them to serve as an example to the other ranks and continue to do their duty. What happened then was described shortly afterwards by one of the gunners, Egor Oreshnikov:[13]

Suddenly, at 11.20 p.m. the alarm was sounded. We were lined up, given four clips of bullets each and led into a casemate where, in order to stop us holding a meeting and discussing the burning issue, we were made to listen to a lecture on events at the Caucasian front. But we paid no attention, and, whispering among ourselves, agreed to ignore the order to shoot at the revolutionary troops, and instead, to join them. There were masses of troops near our barracks at that point, but we were not allowed near the windows to identify them. Then, a group of sailors broke in through the opposite doorway, shouting, 'Comrades, come out!' The cry was immediately taken up by the Second Company which burst out of the barracks, ignoring Second Lieutenant Popov who stood in the doorway trying to bar their way with the futile command: 'First Platoon! Shoulder arms!' until a sailor took him by the neck and carried him off to where he was disarmed. All the other companies then followed suit and our entire regiment, the band playing and the men shouting hoorah, marched in the direction of the Second Kronstadt Fortress Artillery Regiment.

Hapless Popov, now disarmed, made one attempt after the other to stop his Second Company and was killed before its men reached the Second Artillery Regiment barracks, there to see that entire regiment, officers, regimental banner, band and all, its commander at the head, marching out of the gates into Pavlovsk Street adjacent to the vast block of military barracks. There the artillery regiments

joined the Torpedo and Mining Training Detachment, led by Ivan
Kolbin and signing,

> Boldly, brothers, together,
> With spirits high for the fray,
> Now to the kingdom of freedom
> Our bodies shall blaze out the way!
>
> Mighty our aim now together:
> To throw off the slave's cursed yoke,
> The red flag of toil our proud banner –
> We'll fly high all over the globe!

Then came the First Infantry Regiment, led by its band playing the
Marseillaise, and, one after the other, the First Baltic Naval Crew,
the Gunnery Training Detachment, the Kronstadt Fleet Half-Crew,
the Artificers' School, the Field Engineers' Company and the Third
Infantry Regiment, this last led by the soldier Stepan Sokolov, 'the
first to march out with a red flag'. While some units marched to the
battleships in the harbour and raised the crews, others opened the
jails and released the prisoners. Finally, they all made their way to
the Naval Manège in Anchor Square where the entire garrison and the
striking workers assembled in the early hours of 1 March to acclaim
the revolution and elect the Kronstadt Committee of the National
Movement as the new revolutionary power. The only exceptions
were the naval cadets and instructor-officers of the Engineers' College
who locked themselves up in the huge building and surrendered
only under threat of artillery fire.[14]

There was surprisingly little resistance. A few officers of the First
Baltic Crew and some battleships tried to prevent their men from
joining the movement, and paid with their lives. The only serious
resistance was that of a group of desperate policemen and political
police who barricaded themselves in the police station of Koz'e
Boloto, the local rag-fair, and preferred to shoot it out. When, at
noon, they came under artillery fire, eight survivors surrendered,
leaving six policemen for dead.[15] Most of their colleagues went into
hiding or were taken prisoner. Before making good their escape
from one of Kronstadt's two gendarmerie stations, the gendarmes
there piled up their sabres, revolvers and bullets on a table and left
a junior gendarme behind who, unarmed and with hands raised,
called in a group of sailors and surrendered the station.[16]

But although the mutinous troops encountered very little resistance and the casualties they suffered were a mere seven killed,

nowhere in the Russian February revolution – not even in Helsingfors and Reval – was there such a bloody squaring of accounts as in the harsh and brutalized 'sailors' Sakhalin'.

The first victim was none other than Admiral Viren, and it was to the governor's villa on the edge of Anchor Square that a large crowd of sailors, soldiers and workers marched 'with malice and fury' from the revolutionary meeting in the Naval Manège in the early morning of 1 March. When asked to come out, Viren appeared dressed only in a white tunic. He stepped onto the footpath and, looking over the heads of the motley crowd of sailors and soldiers assembled there, shouted 'as of old, that powerful, terrifying order: "Attention!" ' but 'this time' he was greeted by a great wave of laughter. Two eye-witnesses, Kolbin and Aleksei Pronin, both instructors in the Torpedo and Mining Training Detachment, recorded the scene: 'Viren looked shrunken, puny and pitiful, changed before our very eyes.' Told that he would be marched to Anchor Square, Viren wanted to step inside to fetch his army-coat; denied that, he was summarily ordered to head the march to Anchor Square, but not before his epaulettes had been ripped from his uniform. There, before a vast crowd, he was read his indictment and sentence: 'Your barbarous, brutal regime has turned Kronstadt into a prison. Did it occur to you yesterday, as you set up machine-guns to shoot at the workers, soldiers and sailors, that you would die today? Now take your deserts.' Viren's reply was dignified: 'I have lived my life in loyal service to tsar and fatherland. I am ready. Now it is your turn to build your life!' Facing death, he turned to say farewell to his chief of chancellory I. F. Pekun, who had also been dragged to the square's Makarov monument to be shot: 'Pekun, let us embrace', he said. But Pekun pushed him aside, shouting that he 'had nothing in common with the enemies of the people', and thus saved his own skin. As for Viren, abandoned now by all, he died bravely. Told to turn his back on the firing squad and face the monument, he refused and met his executioners with open eyes.[17]

There may have been some logic in the executions. The much hated and feared Major-General N. V. Stronsky, commander of the First Baltic Depot, a cruel disciplinarian, notorious for having been in charge of the execution of seventeen mutinous sailors on 5 September 1906,[18] was given short shrift. But Kronstadt's second-in-command, the newly appointed commandant of the fortress, Kurosh, was merely beaten up and imprisoned, and thus survived.[19]

Had it not been for his defiance, Vice-Admiral Alexander Butakov, chief-of-staff of the port, might also have survived. Twice asked to recognize the revolution, he is reported to have replied that he would not betray his oath and sovereign, and 'certainly not to you scoundrels'. And when the first volley missed him, he reaffirmed his loyalty to the tsar and admonished the firing squad: 'Aim better!'[20]

A total of fifty-one officers was killed, the majority of them from the navy. To their number must be added close to thirty gendarmes, policemen and police spies.[21] There seem to have been no civilian casualties. As Parchevsky put it: 'The civilian population neither murdered, nor was it murdered.'[22]

A mere twenty-five to thirty officers who had been popular with the ranks and had immediately joined the revolution were left free, with twelve of them promptly being elected commanders by their men.[23] But the large majority of Kronstadt's officers, some 200 (including 162 naval officers), and thirty-nine ensigns and warrant officers, were arrested and locked up in Kronstadt's notorious dungeons, where they joined more than 250 policemen, plain-clothes men, stool-pigeons, gendarmes and officials.[24] Some may have been placed in jail as much for their own protection as for punishment, for, confronting the irate sailor crowds, swollen in numbers by some just released from the Naval Investigation Prison, and all clamouring for the lives of the 'bloodsuckers', on 1 March Kronstadt's Committee of the National Movement ordered the arrest of all officers and their detention in prison pending trial. That shrewd decree may well have saved many an officer's life, providing that the detachment sent to arrest him was well-disciplined or well-disposed.[25]

One such lucky officer was Parchevsky, who was sufficiently trusted by his men (and shunned by his fellow officers) to be offered the command of his company when his guards called on him in the afternoon of 1 March and marched him from his home, dressed in civilian clothes, to the Naval Investigation Prison at the other side of the town. Yet even he had some terrible moments: trucks with mounted machine-guns swept past, excited crowds argued passionately, heaps of paper went up in flames, and other soldiers marched past with their arrested officers under guard. One such group of men was pushing a middle-aged captain along with their rifle-butts. Before Parchevsky's eyes, they pulled his beard and hit him in the face:

Suddenly some pugnacious-looking sailors holding revolvers in their hands ran up to us and asked: 'Have you caught a police spy?' Even when my soldiers told them that I was their officer, they refused to let go, insisting: 'Why? Is he a good fellow?' and only letting us pass when they had been told: 'Yes, he is a good fellow.'[26]

While the unparalleled violence of the February revolution in Kronstadt initially gave the town a bad name, the night of 1 March, when accounts were squared with the officers, remained a memorable event for the revolutionary Kronstadters. The sailor poet N. Shaposhnikov expressed it in a poem dedicated 'To the Soldiers and Sailors of the First of March':[27]

> Came the hour of revenge, and with the cry:
> 'Out of the way you tsar's vampires!'
> You seized your rifles and administered damnation.
> 'Twas in Russia this miracle was wrought!
> And, as the wave sweeps away the rock,
> So did the soldiers and sailors
> Sweep away for ever and ever
> The rotten throne of Nicholas II.

With Kronstadt's entire command structure eliminated overnight, local power devolved immediately on the Kronstadt Committee of the National Movement.[28] Later called simply the Committee of the Movement, this was a body elected in the morning of 1 March by a mass meeting in the Naval Manège on the motion of A. Khanokh, a twenty-two-year-old student with an SR background who, having arrived in Kronstadt on the eve of the revolution, is reported to have been one of the main speakers at the meeting. Consisting of seven military members (three sailors, an infantry petty-officer, a senior naval lieutenant, an artillery petty-officer, and a soldier) and three civilians (a civil engineer, a worker and a student), including the chairman Khanokh,[29] the Committee of the Movement clearly reflected the military preponderance and character of the revolution in Kronstadt. So too did the Assembly of Delegates from the army and the navy, elected on 2 March by Kronstadt's army and naval units which the Committee of the Movement had asked to send one delegate each. By 3 March, this assembly had already joined the Committee of the Movement in its daily sessions in the hall of the Naval Assembly, Kronstadt's former officers' club. In that first meeting, the Assembly of Delegates decreed that the existing military and naval units, and their divisions into regiments, depots, battalions and ships, be retained, but that henceforth they be under commanders 'elected from among the people who enjoy trust and are known for their experience', and that all units elect committees responsible for 'internal life', and, finally, that neither the army nor the navy disarm 'until the convocation of the constituent assembly'.[30] Together, the Committee of the Movement, acting as an executive, and the Assembly of Delegates, acting as supporting legislature, constituted Kronstadt's first revolutionary organ of power. Their new status was given immediate recognition by the municipal Duma, by Kronstadt's Soviet of Workers' Deputies, elected on 5 March, by the town's merchants and traders, who decided to assemble on 6 March to 'elect their representative to the Committee of the Movement', and by the commissar of the provisional government, Pepeliaev.[31] Appointed on 3 March, Victor Pepeliaev turned to the Committee of the Movement as early as 6 March, with the request that it 'confirm' the establishment of a town militia and 'authorize' the junior officer Filipenko (himself a member of the Committee of the Movement) to organize it.[32]

The immediate and primary concern of the Committee of the Movement, however, was to put an end to violence and bloodshed and to make sure that the very occasional robbery and pillaging of shops and wine stores and the drunkenness that had accompanied the uprising during the night of 1 March should not degenerate into large-scale plundering and pogroms. To that effect, issuing its first appeal to the population and the garrison at 8 p.m. on 1 March, and declaring that it had taken 'the government into its hands' with its first and foremost concern being the maintenance of 'order and tranquility' as well as of 'a proper regime and discipline' among the troops, the Committee of the Movement decreed a curfew as from 10 p.m. and ordered all troops not on patrol duty to return to their barracks.[33] That appeal was followed up the next day by a series of decrees[34] which 'strictly' prohibited and 'mercilessly condemned', as 'actions which bring disgrace on the entire national movement', all unauthorized arrests, searches and requisitions, joy-riding in military trucks and purposeless shooting in the air, and ordered the destruction of all liquor. Apparently realizing how unnatural and absurd this last order would seem, the Committee backed it up with an impassioned plea to 'beware of drunkenness . . . the most dangerous enemy of the dignity of the revolution':

In this historical moment of the revolution, be sober and pure, and promise this, comrades, one to the other, on oath. For a drunk has no control over his own deeds. Do not drink vodka and wine! Do not let others drink them! Destroy all wine and vodka supplies that you have located, and do not leave them untended, for the dregs of society may become drunk and then rob and murder and thus bring great harm to the revolution. Destroy all vodka![35]

By 2 March, order was largely restored; shops reopened, numerous army patrols safeguarded the streets and ensured 'the unhindered sale of newspapers and journals', and whatever drunkenness there had been on the previous night was soon reported as having 'ceased absolutely'.[36]

Thus, that same day, the Committee of the Movement cabled the Provisional Committee of the Duma and the Petrograd Soviet of Workers' and Soldiers' Deputies, offering the 'unanimous and enthusiastic greetings' of the population, workers, garrison, ships' crews and forts of Kronstadt, on the occasion of the formation of the provisional government, 'elected in strict agreement with the Soviet of Workers' Deputies', and reporting with considerable satisfaction that order was being restored and food supplies reorganized. Work, they said, would soon be resumed, and 'the immediate and urgent' arrival of a commandant of the fortress, appointed by the new government, was eagerly anticipated.[37]

While the Committee of the Movement was restoring order and gathering local power into its hands, the Provisional Committee of the state Duma turned its attention to the urgent appeal made on 1 March by Admiral Adrian Nepenin, commander of the Baltic Fleet, who, from his Helsingfors headquarters, noted that 'in Kronstadt anarchy was rampant' and urged that everything possible be done to restore order and 'save all the battleships and supplies'.[38] Thus Pepeliaev, a young Kadet (Constitutional Democrat) Duma deputy from Tomsk, and a former history teacher, was despatched to Kronstadt by Pavel Miliukov to investigate the situation there, together with a fellow deputy, Sergei Taskin. Pepeliaev seems to have had a good reception, until he was seen by sailors of the First Baltic Fleet Depot talking to their arrested officers, whereupon he had a lot of explaining to do before he calmed their tempers.[39] He arrived on 3 March, as commissar of the provisional government in Kronstadt, with the rights of commander of the port. But he soon realized that he had come too late to make any significant change in the already established new order. True, his Order No. 1, in which he announced his appointment and congratulated the Kronstadters on

their 'victory over the old power', also referred to his 'assumption
of the government of Kronstadt'.[40] But he was immediately forced
to accept the Committee of the Movement as the *de facto* power or
'master of the situation' in Kronstadt, and to endorse its principle
that election to all military posts be by the meeting of the rank and
file of army units and from among 'those persons who enjoy trust
and are known for their experience' as proclaimed on 3 March, the
day of his arrival in Kronstadt. As he explained later in May, somewhat apologetically, to his fellow Duma deputies: 'They would not
have recognized anyone appointed from Petrograd.' However, the
main bone of contention between him and the Committee of the
Movement was, naturally enough, the position of the commissar vis-
à-vis the elected military commanders: for his part, Pepeliaev insisted that they be 'subordinate to the commissar', but he was
quickly forced to accept a very much watered down and quite
worthless formula which merely said that commanders were to be
'guided in their activities by the directives of the commissar'. However, since the elective principle enunciated by the Assembly of
Delegates also provided for the election of unit committees to be in
charge of the units' 'internal life', the commanders' authority was
already severely limited, subject both to the rank and file that had
elected them and to the unit committees that watched them, and
both were far more effective than the commissar, who had no way of
checking whether or not a commander took any notice of his
'directives'.[41]

But his set-back did not deter Pepeliaev from making the most of
his ceremonial role as representative of the provisional government
when, on Saturday, 4 March, Kronstadt celebrated the victory of
the revolution. Addressing the Assembly of Delegates, he enjoyed
'noisy and prolonged applause'; he also paid a visit to the municipal
Duma and reviewed the festivities and the parade of naval and
military units which, 'with bands playing, red flags flying, cheered
on by crowds of rejoicing people, greeted "Free Russia" with
enthusiastic shouts of "hoorah" '.[42]

It was his deputy, however, who was sent to the special service of
'solemn thanksgiving for the freedom bestowed on our fatherland'
with which Kronstadt's religious establishment welcomed the
revolution at the naval cathedral on 7 March. After the arch-priest
Sergei Putilin had bestowed his 'pastoral blessings' on the 'long-
yearned-for freedom' that had at last been won by the Russian

people, he went on to offer his 'spiritual counsel' on how this freedom might be maintained for ever. Later, special thanksgiving prayers were recited in all churches, 'offering praise for the liberation of the oppressed people from the hateful yoke of the old power'.[43]

The newly founded Kronstadt teachers' association welcomed the revolution and the provisional government too, and cabled greetings to Minister of Education Alexander Manuilov. Drafted by the chairman, Ivan Oreshin, a history teacher, the cable affirmed the teachers' commitment to the education of all citizens and the formation of 'scientific, enlightened minds'. It also declared their aspiration to the 'renewal of the schools on the foundation of humanism and genuine democracy'.[44]

While the Committee of the Movement, supported by the deliberative Assembly of Delegates, was governing Kronstadt, and the commissar of the provisional government, who merely reigned, was still searching for a suitable power base, a new centre of power came into being in 5 March with the foundation of the Soviet of Workers' Deputies. The Kronstadt Soviet may have been formed with the active encouragement of the Petrograd Soviet, for on 4 March the latter decided to send to Kronstadt two members of its Executive Committee: the Menshevik Mark Broido (representing the workers), and the Bundist Isai Yudin (representing the soldiers), their mission being to explain the Petrograd Soviet's policies, notably its conditional support of the provisional government.

The founding meeting of the Soviet of Workers' Deputies appealed immediately to the garrison to form a Soviet of Military Deputies and work with it 'for the good of the working class and of the troops', and by the next day its call was answered and a Soviet of Military Deputies was founded.[45]

On 7 March the Soviet of Workers' Deputies ordered the resumption of work, decreed an eight-hour day (six hours for youths) and new wage scales. Factory and workshop committees were urged to elect 'work leaders' who, apart from possessing the necessary technical qualifications and experience, should also be endowed with 'satisfactory moral qualities' and enjoy the trust of the majority; and body searches were prohibited in all places of work, this humiliating practice being replaced by the 'collective responsibility' of workers.[46]

Meeting on 8 March, the Soviet of Workers' Deputies elected an additional eight members with a consultative voice to its Executive

Committee of ten for the purpose of liaison with the Committee of
the Movement and with the military bodies.

While the invitation to found a Soviet of Military Deputies came
from the Soviet of Workers' Deputies, its formation on 7 March
proceeded according to instructions issued jointly by the Committee
of the Movement and the Assembly of Delegates, that 'every unit,
regardless of its numbers, elect two delegates and the unit commander from its best and most completely trusted people; these
together will constitute the Soviet of Military Deputies'.[47] Its
Executive Committee was to consist of thirty-six members, elected
by and from the Soviet of Military Deputies, eighteen from the army
and eighteen from the navy. When a considerable number of officers
turned up as elected deputies at the first session of the Soviet of
Military Deputies during the evening of 7 March, rank and file
sailors and soldiers were so resentful that it was decided to 'deprive
unit commanders of the right to participate in the Soviet', while
officers who had been elected as deputies were to have only a
consultative voice.[48]

By 10 March the Soviet of Military Deputies was already so
dominant and confident that it now turned to the Soviet of Workers'
Deputies with an invitation to join it and send eighteen delegates
to its Executive Committee, henceforth to be called the Executive
Committee of the Soviet of Workers' and Soldiers' Deputies and to
have its own elected chairman, the self-educated, highly intelligent
and talented signalman-instructor Artemii Liubovich. Thus they
proposed an Executive Committee of fifty-four, including eighteen
from the navy, five from the artillery, five from the infantry, five
from the sappers, three from institutions and administrative bodies,
and eighteen from the workers.[49] This balance reflected the role
played by the various sections of the population in the Kronstadt
revolution. As the sailor Skobennikov noted, reviewing its first ten
days: 'the military were the vanguard of the revolution', the workers
were 'very weak', 'the intellectual proletariat was nowhere evident'
and 'not one single woman turned up'.[50]

For some time, the two Soviets met separately in the mornings and
jointly in the evenings, the combined session totalling some 280
deputies, including 90 workers.

The Soviet of Workers' Deputies, chaired by Anatolii Lamanov,
a third-year student of technology, who had been elected the delegate
of the port's chemical laboratories, concentrated mainly on matters

normally in the purview of trade unions: working conditions, over-time and labour mobility. Thus, for instance, it fixed the minimum and maximum wages to range from 175 to 225 roubles per month for workers and from 75 to 85 roubles per month for apprentices.[51] The extent to which it followed the lead and guidance of the Petro-grad Soviet can be gauged from its 11 March appeal to all Kronstadt workers endorsing a 'revolutionary defensist' resolution of the Petrograd Soviet, and calling upon them to work harder for defence, to which end it even permitted overtime, provided that the individual workshop committees recommended it to 'raise productivity'.[52]

Real power, however, fell to the Soviet of Military Deputies, which concerned itself with the reorganization and control of Kronstadt's military and naval units. Under the chairmanship of the ambitious and energetic ensign Iosif Krasovsky, elected on 9 March by an overwhelming majority with only three against, and with Senior Lieutenant Glazko as deputy chairman, it gradually took over the Committee of the Movement. Thus, on 13 March, the Soviet of Military Deputies virtually assumed power when it decreed that all orders pertaining to the organization of naval and military forces, the maintenance of order and the defence of liberties were to be 'issued exclusively by the Soviet of Military Deputies' which had taken 'the life and property of all citizens under its protection', and that it alone had the right to 'search, arrest and impose restrictions on the arrested'. Threatening that those who contravened the decree would be 'immediately handed over to the Investigation Commission of the Soviet of Military Deputies', it went on to declare that 'thus, comrades, we shall be united and in solidarity. With serried ranks we shall proceed on the road of great conquests leading to the democratic republic.'[53] So confident did the Soviet feel that on 16 March all remaining curfews were lifted and freedom of movement was restored.[54]

When Commissar Pepeliaev protested against this unilateral re-organization of Kronstadt's military forces, the Executive Committee decided to assert itself. Notifying him that 'in the town of Kronstadt it is the Soviet of Workers' and Soldiers' Deputies that is the govern-ing institution', they then also made him sign that statement.[55] But Pepeliaev refused to give up and instead tried to build himself a supporting power base by organizing a Town Group, consisting of elected representatives drawn from the traders, shopkeepers, house-owners, members of the free professions, carters, civil servants, teachers, independent craftsmen and rentiers. He was too late, however, for by mid-March, when elections to the Town Group had been held and its committee formed,[56] the Executive Committee of the Soviet of Workers' and Soldiers' Deputies was already firmly established as 'the authoritative leader and centre of the entire life of the fortress,' as Mikhail Skobelev, deputy chairman of the Petrograd Soviet, who visited Kronstadt in mid-March, reported.[57] There was little the Town Group could do except send sixty-five new councillors (in addition to the thirty-eight old councillors) to the municipal Duma to broaden its base, and give it further democratic respectability by electing Ivan Oreshin (president of the teachers' union and a member of the Kronstadt Soviet) as chairman.[58] But even that did not strengthen a Duma which, until July when democratic municipal elections were held, continued to be ignored and to be regarded as unrepresentative. Apparently, Pepeliaev went too far in trying to ensure that workers and military personnel and their Soviet would be vastly under-represented in the Duma, sending to it a mere ten councillors, compared with the twenty representing the traders, houseowners, carters and rentiers. Moreover, many municipal functions and services such as food supply and housing had simply been taken over by commissions of the Kronstadt Soviet's Executive Committee.

Pepeliaev's twofold failure was summed up in retrospect by *Kronshtadtskaia iskra*: 'The power of the municipal Duma, like that of the commissar, was nil.'[59]

The cavalier treatment, bordering on contempt, which the Kronstadters meted out to the commissar as an apirant to local political power reflected their attitude to and 'suspicion of the provisional government' which Pepeliaev found there right from the start.[60] Indeed, whether governed by the Committee of the Movement, the Soviet of Military Deputies, or, finally, the united Soviet of Workers' and Soldiers' Deputies, Kronstadt's conditional support of the provisional government followed the lead of the Petrograd Soviet, which was pledged to support that government 'in so far as' it lived up to the declared programme of democratic reforms on which they had agreed during the night of 2 March, and was to last just as long as the Petrograd Soviet 'does not send us a formal notification of its break with the government'.[61] Thus, when on 12 March the Kronstadt Soviet of Military Deputies discussed the provisional government's request to have the garrison swear an oath of loyalty to the new government, it decided to defer the matter until the Constituent Assembly had met[62] and, meanwhile, to tell the provisional government: 'A free people has no need of an oath. It is not for the people to deliver an oath to the government, but rather for the government to swear an oath to the people.'[63] Nor would Kronstadters brook any intercession or interference by the provisional government with regard to the imprisoned officers. Thus, Alexander Kerensky's request to have them transferred to the state Duma building in Petrograd for investigation, thereby removing them from the clutches of the vindictive Kronstadters, was deliberately ignored; and when it transpired that Alexander Guchkov, Minister of War and Navy, was about to lobby the Petrograd Soviet for the release of the officers, he was told, by cable, in no uncertain terms: 'The Kronstadt Soviet of Military Deputies objects to any intercession on behalf of the arrested officers; the Kronstadt Soviet of Military Deputies alone can resolve that question. The officers' lives are in no immediate danger.'[64] One such attempt at intercession, Mikhail Skobelev's impassioned plea during his visit to Kronstadt on 14 March for the 'speediest resolution' of the officers' problem, may well have led to the appointment of an Investigation Commission which, by 25 March, freed ninety-seven officers. However, Skobelev's protest against the officers being kept 'in casemates in a manner resembling the old regime'[65] made no impression whatever on the new regime, and instructions governing the 'maintenance of the arrested officers in the prisons of the Kronstadt fortress' were issued by the Soviet of Military Deputies which laid down that all clearly political criminals were to be separated from the rest and kept under a severe regime. The others were to be treated less severely and, with the special permission of the Executive Committee of the Soviet of Military Deputies, were to be allowed visits, food parcels etc.; comforts such as pillows and featherbeds were absolutely forbidden. Crews and personnel of units whose officers were under arrest were under no circumstances to be admitted to prison buildings without the special permission of the Executive Committee; a commission was to be appointed to ascertain the degree of guilt of those arrested; the appropriate prison regime was to be applied after the degree of guilt had been established; until the degree of guilt was established, no visits were to be allowed.[66]

Defiant gestures apart, the Soviet of Workers' and Soldiers' Deputies, and in particular its Executive Committee, had by mid-

March clearly established itself as the central and sole authority in Kronstadt, with its own excellent newspaper, the *Izvestiia Kronshtadt-skogo soveta rabochikh i soldatskikh deputatove* (edited by a commission chaired by Artemii Liubovich, and with Anatolii Lamanov as secretary), to report its sessions and activities, expound its policies, publicize its decrees and resolutions, and transmit its authority. The Soviet now proceeded to translate that authority into real power by manning Kronstadt's senior military and administrative positions with elected commanders and office-holders who were, in turn, flanked by control commissions. The importance attributed to these commissions by the Soviet from the very beginning can be gauged by examining the appointment of thirty-three-year-old Senior Lieutenant Piotr Lamanov, older brother of Anatolii Lamanov, to the post of commander of the naval forces. A naval officer with long-standing revolutionary credentials – an Okhrana report of July 1911 attributed SR sympathies and connections to him – and a distin-guished record of bravery and concern for his men,[67] Piotr Lamanov was elected on 15 March by a general meeting of the Kronstadt Soviet.

His exemplary past notwithstanding, he was immediately pro-vided with an elected control commission consisting of six members of the Executive Committee. His authorities and duties were care-fully defined and circumscribed.[68] Although all the naval forces of Kronstadt were, 'in matters purely technical and disciplinary', under his command, he and his control commission were, in the teeth of Pepeliaev's protests, responsible and accountable to the Kronstadt Soviet, and 'not to the provisional government or to the commander of the Baltic Fleet'.[69] Further, Lamanov's orders were valid only if endorsed and counter-signed by the duty member of the control commission, and copies had to be filed with the Soviet.

In the same vein, although commanders of naval units and ships stationed in Kronstadt could, 'under the control of the unit's committee', issue orders pertaining to the internal service life of the unit, these were to be in strict accordance with both the decrees of the Soviet and the orders of the commander of the naval forces.[70]

The same principle applied to the appointments on 16 and 17 March of the commandant of the fortress, Major-General Gerasimov, the captain of the harbour, Major-General Ermakov, and the town commandant, Colonel Nikolai Ogarev, who was appointed by 25

March. Elected by the meeting of the Soviet, the first two were provided with control commissions, while Ogarev had 'comrade Aksenov' placed next to him as his 'assistant'. But when his successor was elected on 12 May, he was promptly flanked by a duty member of the Executive Committee with the 'right of control' to ensure that all papers were issued with the 'knowledge of our comrade'.[71]

Pepeliaev summed up both Gerasimov's plight and the effectiveness of the Soviet's control system over Kronstadt's senior military commanders by May 1917: 'His position is desperate and it would be unfair to regard him as responsible for Kronstadt as a fortress. He is tied hand and foot by the control commission. Not one order or piece of paper can he pass through his chancellory unless it has been confirmed by the member of the control commission on duty.'[72] As if such controls were not enough, Kronstadt's senior naval officer, Piotr Lamanov, took advantage of the May Day festivities to address his Kronstadt 'comrades and brothers' thus: 'I assure you, comrades, that to betray you would be tantamount to betraying my very self. I was, am, and shall as long as I live remain on the side of the suffering people . . . I swear to you that no promises or threats will ever bend me towards betrayal and duplicity.'[73] If Piotr Lamanov, with all his revolutionary and democratic credentials, felt it necessary to make such an avowal of loyalty, others, with no such record, all holding their commands by election only and therefore but grudgingly and belatedly confirmed by the provisional government,[74] were even further dependent on and subservient to the Kronstadt Soviet.

Controlling Kronstadt's military and naval forces from above, and wielding additional control from below by the committee system, the Soviet also made sure that its military forces and strength would remain intact and free from outside interference. Thus, on 27 March, a resolution of the Kronstadt Soviet decreed that 'regular units must not be removed [from Kronstadt], so as not to dissipate the military significance of the fortress and of the revolutionary army. This decree is to be brought to the notice of the Ministry for the Army and for the Navy. Training detachments, provided that they are replaced, may, however, be removed.'[75] This decree was reinforced by another, issued on 4 April, whereby each and every transfer of troops was to be 'authorized exclusively by the Executive Committee of the Soviet or by a special session of the Soviet'.[76]

Thus there was no dual power in Kronstadt, for the Soviet and

its Executive Committee reigned supreme and brooked no interference, not even from the provisional government.

As for its relations with Petrograd, like the vast majority of Soviets,
the Kronstadt Soviet regarded itself from the start as 'under the
authority of the Petrograd Soviet',[77] sending it three delegates who
were to serve as permanent Kronstadt representatives. Barring the
officers' problem, Kronstadt basically accepted the Petrograd
Soviet's leadership and policies, at least during the lifetime of
Kronstadt's first Soviet, which was in office until 5 May 1917. This
was partly due to the Kronstadters' natural commitment to Soviet
democracy and power which made them look up to the 'most
authoritative' Soviet, that of the capital, with sympathy and respect,
while such feelings were reinforced by the SR-Menshevik political
complexion of Kronstadt's first Soviet which was very similar to that
of the Petrograd Soviet. It is true that until the elections to Kronstadt's second Soviet, early in May, deputies represented corporate
groups such as sailors, soldiers and workers, rather than parties, and
that they were not as yet organized in political caucuses. But nevertheless, the first Kronstadt Soviet of some 280 deputies has been
estimated as consisting, in March 1917, of some 108 SRs, 72 Mensheviks, 77 Non-Partyists and, initially, a mere 11 Bolsheviks (if not
fewer). Bolshevik numbers rose to some 40 by the end of the month,
and possibly to 60 by late April.[78]

Apart from constituting the largest and dominant political
faction in the Soviet until May 1917, the populist and agrarian-
socialist SRs seem to have had an initial advantage over all other
political parties. Immediately after the revolution, entire army and
naval units joined them, possibly as a result of a long-standing SR
tradition within the Baltic Fleet and of their broad appeal to the
mass of soldiers and sailors with a recent peasant background, which
distinguished them from the narrow and doctrinaire Marxist and
worker-oriented Mensheviks and Bolsheviks. With 4,000 members,
the SRs became Kronstadt's largest, though always amorphous,
party, with comfortable headquarters set up in Viren's villa, and
a large and active Zemlia i Volia (Land and Liberty) club as a
major political and cultural centre. They were led by young and
enthusiastic radicals such as the sailors Alexander Brushvit and
Boris Donskoi, the signalman Konstantin Shurgin, the petty-officers
Fiodor Pokrovsky (signalman) and Mikhail Evstingeev (artificer),
whose revolutionary career as an SR in the Baltic Fleet dated back

to 1911,[79] and the schoolteacher Grigorii Smoliansky, possibly their only party intellectual and perhaps an import. The Kronstadt SRs suffered right from the start from 'a shortage (a real famine) of party workers', as the central SR newspaper, the *Delo naroda* of 30 April noted, appealing to 'opulent Petrograd' to come to the rescue.[80] But no such aid was to be forthcoming, since the Kronstadt SRs – more in tune with Kronstadt's radical mood than with Victor Chernov and the moderate SR leadership – disapproved of SR participation in the coalition government, 'revolutionary defensism' and support for the Liberty Loan that went with it, and – above all – the party's condoning the postponement of agrarian reforms until a Constituent Assembly should be convened. Kronstadt's SRs looked for guidance to the radical minority faction of SR Internationalists or Left SRs led by Boris Kamkov, Mark Natanson and Mariia Spiridonova. Like the Bolsheviks, they called for an active peace policy, 'an armistice on all fronts' and the 'publication of the secret treaties'. But, unlike the Bolsheviks, who aimed at a narrow 'dictatorship of the proletariat and of the poorest peasantry', the Left SRs stood for a broadly based government of the entire 'revolutionary democracy' resting on the Soviets. Yet in practice, by September 1917, the Left SRs had become the Bolsheviks' junior partners in the campaign for 'All Power to Soviets' and the October seizure of power.[81] The weakening position of the SRs in Kronstadt is reflected in the declining number of their deputies in the Soviet, from 108 in March, to 91 in May, and then to 73 in August. Apart from short periods, they could not even sustain their own newspaper, *Za zemliu i voliu*, of which a mere sixteen numbers appeared.

The second largest caucus in the first Soviet was the quaint and self-consciously Non-Party group. Led by two radicals, Anatolii Lamanov and the sailor and poet A. Nemm, and (for some time) the moderate Foma Parchevsky, it rejected party factionalism, stood for pure sovietism and thus fitted admirably into Kronstadt's early revolutionary and markedly soviet landscape before it was ploughed up by party-mindedness. In the first Soviet, the Non-Party group had seventy-seven deputies, in the second, elected on 3 May, it shrank to sixty-eight, but by the third, elected in August, it had climbed to ninety-six deputies (if not more). It was then that the Non-Partyists joined the radical left Union of Socialist Revolution-aries–Maximalists, acquiring in the saintly Grigorii Rivkin and the pugnacious Arsenii Zverin two outstanding leaders who made

Kronstadt into a major centre of SR-Maximalism. Postulating an immediate agrarian *and* urban social revolution, they sought the establishment of a Toiler's Republic based on federated soviets as a halfway house to fully fledged socialism. Deeply committed to soviets, like the French syndicalists they rejected bourgeois parliamentarianism and distrusted political parties, and thus acquired a semi-anarchist image.[82]

The Anarchists proper made their appearance in Kronstadt as a small organized group only in mid-May. They had no deputies in the first two Soviets and, with a mere seven in the third Soviet (elected in August), they were its smallest faction. Deeply split into the more moderate Anarcho-Syndicalists – led by the popular and attractive Efim (Khaim) Yarchuk – and the extremist, terrorist Anarcho-Communists – led by the fierce and unrestrained N. Bleikhman-Solntsev – their impact was particularly felt in Anchor Square. Here they contributed significantly to radicalizing the masses in the latter half of May and throughout June in preparation for the 'July Days'. The Kronstadt Anarchists, each group fired by very different visions of revolution, spoke in two dissonant voices: Yarchuk, in love with Kronstadt's Soviet democracy, sought – with the help of the Bolsheviks to whom he was closely allied – to force the pace of revolution and turn the whole of Russia into one large Kronstadt; Bleikhman, fascinated by Kronstadt's 'Night of the First of March', with its 'permanent fear, eternal spectacle of death and revolution', wanted this 'real revolution' extended to the whole of Russia where the masses, by direct action with 'machine guns and bayonets', would 'seize the mines, factories and plants'.[83]

Furthest to the right were the Trudoviks, led by A. Khanokh. In a Kronstadt which lacked a liberal bourgeois party of Constitutional Democrats, they remained outside the Soviet and its radical socialist consensus. Though they published quite an impressive liberal-democratic newspaper *Trud, zemlia i more* from April to November 1917 and received more than 2,000 votes in the elections to Kronstadt's municipal Duma in July, the Trudoviks never gained so much as a single deputy to the Kronstadt Soviet. Consistent and staunch supporters of the provisional government and its war effort, and advocates of agrarian reforms which included compensation for landowners, the Trudoviks were far too moderate for, if not out of place in, Red Kronstadt. Early in September, having failed three times to gain representation through elections to the Soviet, they applied for representation in that body as a socialist party. This request was overwhelmingly rejected (with six abstentions and only one vote in favour) since Trudoviks did not 'express the will and mind of the revolutionary democracy of the city of Kronstadt'.[84]

The social democratic Mensheviks, with seventy-two deputies in March, were the third largest caucus in the first Kronstadt Soviet. Initial support from Kronstadt workers, notably those in the steam-ship plant, and from soldiers, especially the gunners, and the early prestige of their leaders in the Petrograd Soviet, Nikolai Chkheidze, Iraklii Tseretelli and Skobelev, gave the Mensheviks the better of their Bolshevik rivals. But that head start was squandered when the Petrograd Menshevik leaders joined the second provisional government on 5 May and, becoming the most committed champions of coalitionism, were thus destined for head-on collisions with Kronstadt late in May and during the 'July Days' of 1917.

True, the Kronstadt Mensheviks and their leaders – Pavel Malyshev, a cadet instructor, Piotr Ediet, an artillery petty-officer, Ivan Alnichenkov, a worker in the port's carpentry shop, and V. A. Valk, a sawmill foreman whose revolutionary experience dated to March 1910 when he was a leading member of a short-lived social democratic military organization in Kronstadt[85] – soon turned left to support Martov's small faction of Menshevik-Internationalists. This group vehemently opposed the coalitionism and revolutionary defensism of official Menshevism but, until the eve of the 'July Days', it had no other solution to the question of power than a doctrinaire abstention from power. Unable to dissociate themselves in the public mind from official Menshevism, Kronstadt Mensheviks made no impact on the Soviet or on the Anchor Square crowds. Ediet, who had sufficient prestige to be elected chairman of the Committee of the Kronstadt Artillery Regiment in March 1917 and who became Kronstadt's (third) commissar of the provisional government in August, seems to have taken little note of party discipline.

The Mensheviks' steadily dwindling role in Kronstadt is starkly reflected in the steep decline of their party faction in the Soviet: from seventy-two deputies in March, to sixty-four in May, and a mere thirteen in August 1917. They were also unable to maintain publication of their *Kronshtadtskaia iskra*, of which they put out only four numbers.

Their loss and, to lesser extent, that of the SRs, was certainly the

Bolsheviks' gain. From a faction numbering a mere eleven deputies in the Soviet in mid-March, their numbers grew to ninety-three deputies in the May elections and ninety-six in the August elections, making them the largest and most influential political party in the Soviet and in Kronstadt at large. Even in the municipal Duma, they trailed only slightly behind the SRs after its July elections. The Bolshevik party organization had a stable membership of some 3,000 to 3,500 and was the only one in Kronstadt to produce a regular and vigorous daily newspaper, the *Golos pravdy*, which, appearing first on 15 March, admirably fulfilled the function of party organ and organizer allocated to it in the Leninist organizational scheme.

The success story of Kronstadt's bolshevism from March to May 1917 is particularly impressive, the more so since it began inauspiciously – notwithstanding claims to the contrary by some Soviet historians.[86]

In September 1916, the small Bolshevik party organization (or collective) had been smashed by the Okhrana and, with the arrest and trial of Sladkov, Uliantsev and Semion Pelikhov, its leaders, and of Kirill Orlov, their liaison with the Petrograd committee, the party organization effectively ceased to exist. Consequently, when the February revolution came, the few Bolsheviks and sympathizers who were not arrested (men such as the sailors Dmitrii Kondakov, Grigorii Grebenshchikov and Vladimir Potekhin, petty-officer Stepan Grediushko, and the worker Mikhail Lebedev), and who then participated and even played a leading role in the uprising, did so as individuals or together with the SRs; but 'organizationally they were not connected one with the other and some did not even know one another'.[87]

They still lacked any defined identity when the first revolutionary organizations, such as the Committee of the Movement and its Assembly of Delegates and, soon after, the Soviet of Workers' Deputies and the Soviet of Military Deputies, were formed, and the very few Bolsheviks who were elected as deputies – Stepan Grediushko, Mikhail Lebedev, Vladimir Zaitsev and Fiodor Gromov – represented only the particular unit or workshop that had elected them.[88] Both the initiative and the leadership came at this point primarily from young intellectuals with vague SR or Menshevik allegiances, including the student A. Khanokh, the civil engineer A. Krasovsky and the artillery petty-officers Filipenko and Gudimov in the Committee of the Movement, and the officers Iosif Krasovsky and Glazko, the ensign L. Zhivotovsky, the student Anatolii Lamanov and the signalman-instructor Artemii Liubovich (who only later in March joined the Bolsheviks).

When the Bolshevik sailors Sladkov, Uliantsev and Pelikhov, freed in the February revolution from the transit prison of the Neva Gates in Petrograd, returned to Kronstadt on 2 March, they confronted a Committee of the Movement and a revolutionary Kronstadt that had taken on a general SR-Menshevik complexion. That very night, Pelikhov and Uliantsev hurried despairingly to Petrograd and the radical and very active Bolshevik Vyborg District Committee, where they made an impassioned appeal for reinforcements. About five would-be agitators, including the worker Ilia Gordienko and the student Fiodor Dingelshtedt, arrived in Kronstadt and began to agitate against the war, against the provisional government and, possibly, against the Petrograd Soviet's support of the provisional government – all apparently in line with the radical manifesto of the Bureau of the Central Committee read out to a meeting of 2,000 Bolsheviks in Vyborg District on 2 March. They also argued that the revolution had been left 'incomplete', and they received a very mixed reception, ranging from unfriendly coldness to an outright hostility that included a short arrest.[89] Indeed, some Kronstadt 'army delegates', notably Filipenko, a member of the Committee of the Movement and about to become Kronstadt's chief of the militia, were so incensed that they hurried off to the Executive Committee of the Petrograd Soviet on 4 March to complain about the disruptive agitation of the 'representatives of the [Bolsheviks] from the Vyborg District who had criticized the provisional government and the Soviet of Workers' and Soldiers' Deputies'. The response was immediate, for the next day two emissaries of the Petrograd Soviet, Mark Broido and Isai Yudin, were sent to Kronstadt to counter Bolshevik agitation and rally Kronstadt behind Petrograd.[90] By 7 March the Vyborg District contingent, with the exception of Dingelshtedt, having brought little credit to bolshevism in Kronstadt, returned to its home base.

However, in response to another appeal by the Kronstadt Bolsheviks to the Petrograd Committee some young but experienced party workers were again sent to Kronstadt after 7 March. This group included the twenty-one-year-old student of neurology and firebrand agitator Semion Roshal, the technology students Peter Smirnov and Boris Zhemchuzhin, and the old hand Kirill Orlov, who arrived between 10 and 12 March.[91] But their import, while it helped found the Kronstadt Bolshevik party organization, does not seem to have changed the aggressive and shrill style of early Bolshevik agitation in Kronstadt. One Bolshevik 'orator', fresh from Petrograd but 'completely hoarse', is even reported to have harangued a crowd that 'revolution has broken out in Berlin!'[92]

To cap it all and render Kronstadt Bolsheviks even more odious came Fiodor Dingelshtedt's brash and brazen report in *Pravda* on 11 March. According to his account, on the morrow of the revolution utter confusion had reigned in Kronstadt and it was only thanks to the arrival of the Bolshevik 'delegates' from Petrograd that 'the first fog was dispersed' and 'the cause of the revolution consolidated there'.[93]

It did not take long for the leaders of the Kronstadt Soviet to find out how their revolution had been misreported in *Pravda* and, issuing a special and indignant declaration, to denounce the account as plain 'dishonest'. This document also reaffirmed their policy towards the Petrograd Soviet and the provisional government: Kronstadt had, as early as 1 March (i.e. before the arrival of sundry 'delegates'), become a 'mighty and firm stronghold' of the revolutionary people, and had placed 'all its bayonets, cannons and machine-guns' at the disposal of the Petrograd Soviet, giving its support to the provisional government 'in so far as that body is in agreement with the [Petrograd] Soviet'. As for the claim made by 'the delegates from *Pravda*' that they played a 'leading role' in the consolidation of the revolution, the opposite was true; their 'mass oratory' had 'undoubtedly' hindered and 'put the brakes on the establishment of order and organized work' in revolutionary Kronstadt.[94]

Fresh from the narrow, party-minded, faction-ridden and cantankerous atmosphere of their underground, the first batch of Petrograd Bolshevik party workers who arrived as reinforcements in Kronstadt during the first ten days of March apparently had great difficulty in adjusting to the new conditions of open and legal political activity and propaganda and adapting themselves to the spirit of brotherhood and popular unity that characterized the early period of the February revolution.[95] Keenly aware of the importance of the Baltic Fleet and of its bases, the Petrograd Bolsheviks' immediate response to the difficulties that their comrades had encountered in Kronstadt (reported to them by Kirill Orlov on

18 March) was a prompt decision to send 'more comrades' 'in view of the special importance of the Kronstadt organization',[96] while Kirill Orlov published 'an explanation' to pacify the Soviet there. The second wave was headed by Fiodor Raskolnikov, who arrived in Kronstadt on 17 March to serve as chief editor of the local *Golos pravdy*, set up by Smirnov and Zhemchuzhin and making its first appearance on 16 March. Cultured and, despite his twenty-five years, already a very experienced party worker (he had been the Bolshevik *Pravda*'s secretary from 1912 to 1914) and 'fleet Bolshevik', midshipman Raskolnikov soon became the leader of Kronstadt bolshevism. He was soon followed by a group of quite distinguished and well-educated party workers: they included the naval surgeon Victor Deshevoi; the professional revolutionary and intellectual Ivar Smilga who, aged only twenty-five when the February revolution freed him from exile in the Eniseisk area, could already look back on some five years of exile, with a few arrests and prison detentions thrown in for good measure; Deshevoi's former fellow student, the naval surgeon Lazar Bregman, a dedicated, disciplined, 'rock-hard' Bolshevik; and Solomon Entin, a party worker and intellectual about whom little is known. Working together with the early arrivals (party workers Semion Roshal, Kirill Orlov, Fiodor Dingelshtedt, Piotr Smirnov and Boris Zhemchuzhin), the local veteran Bolsheviks (Ivan Sladkov, Timofei Uliantsev, Vladimir Zaitsev, Efim Zinchenko, Mikhail Lebedev, Stepan Grediushko, Semion Pelikhov, Dmitrii Kondakov and Fiodor Gromov) and a very impressive group of new recruits to bolshevism (Artemii Liubovich, Fiodor Pervushin, Ure Gertsberg, Ivan Kolbin, Nikolai Pozharov and Aleksei Pronin), and aided by the lively and popular *Golos pravdy*, they managed during the latter part of March and into April to forge the Kronstadt party organization into a formidable political instrument.

They were in close contact with the Bolshevik leaders in Petrograd, particularly with Lev Kamenev who, since his return to Petrograd in mid-March, had become editor of *Pravda* and a leading member of the Russian Bureau of the Central Committee. Fiodor Raskolnikov and Semion Roshal used to visit him at home every Sunday to report on Kronstadt affairs and receive 'directives for the future';[97] through Kirill Orlov they were also connected with the radical Bolshevik Military Organization in Petrograd and with its leader, Nikolai Podvoisky.

If the unsuccessful Bolshevik debut in Kronstadt was to some extent due to its aggressive, 'maximalist', jarring tone, the moderate, 'minimalist' stance adopted from the latter part of March until the 'April Days' seems to have served well in the building up of the Bolshevik party organization and influence in the base committees, in the Soviet, where Artemii Liubovich was chairman of both the Executive Committee and the editorial commission of *Izvestiia*, and in Anchor Square, Kronstadt's informal popular assembly.

The moderate, 'minimalist' line can be traced both in Bolshevik resolutions and in *Golos pravdy*, which seems to have followed the lead given by the Petrograd *Pravda* and its editors Kamenev and Stalin. Thus, on 29 March a Bolshevik mass meeting in the Naval Manège greeted the Petrograd Soviet as 'the expression of the entire revolutionary people' and adopted such 'minimalist' slogans as 'Long live the Constituent Assembly! Long live the Democratic Republic! Long live Socialism!',[98] while as late as 2 April, Artemii Liubovich, Kronstadt's most impressive local Bolshevik, albeit only of recent vintage, propounded the famous 'in so far as' formula of the Petrograd Soviet at the meeting of the Kronstadt Soviet before a large visiting delegation from the First Army: 'We recognize and support [the provisional government] in so far as it keeps the ship of Russian democracy on course. On the other hand, we, in agreement with the Petrograd Soviet, firmly keep our hands on the helm and, should the need arise, shall sharply change course.'[99]

In a similarly minimalist vein, writing in *Golos pravdy* on 13 April, Raskolnikov reiterated the 'Old Bolshevik' doctrine which, *à la* Kamenev, postulated that 'the present revolution, though achieved by the working class and the soldiers, is bourgeois in character'. This, incredibly, came ten days after Lenin's arrival in Petrograd and the promulgation of his radical and startling April Theses propounding a 'new bolshevism' which, declaring the bourgeois revolution complete, called for the transfer of power to the Soviets and the establishment of a 'commune-state'. Yet for Raskolnikov, as for his mentor Kamenev and the moderate 'Old Bolsheviks' in Petrograd, Russia's 'bourgeois-democratic revolution' had only 'just begun', and its task was still to liquidate Russia's bureaucratic regime and its aristocratic social structure by the 'democratization of the entire government system from top to bottom'. The 'socialist revolution' must therefore wait until the bourgeois-democratic revolution had 'exhausted itself and realized its aims'.[100]

In the same issue of *Golos pravdy*, an early appeal for elections to the Constituent Assembly invested that parliamentary institution – *pace* Lenin's 'commune-state' – with 'unlimited state power', notably as regards decisions concerning 'the most important problems of state and finance' and the election of the government, and further stipulated that this government 'be under the authority of the Constituent Assembly'.[101]

With such moderate policies and relatively restrained rhetoric, the Kronstadt Bolsheviks, under Raskolnikov's leadership, had no difficulty in becoming an increasingly influential and integral part of Kronstadt's 'Soviet democracy' during its halcyon months. Indeed, a mere four weeks after his arrival there, Raskolnikov felt very much at home in Kronstadt, and had already reported to *Pravda* that 'The mood here is good, confident, revolutionary. Workers, sailors and soldiers work amicably together. One's heart truly rejoices in the Kronstadt democratic republic.'[102] His enthusiasm was shared by the *Izvestiia* of the Helsingfors Soviet then under SR control: 'What has been done by the Kronstadt garrison and workers during the five weeks of liberty surpasses all expectations . . . they have already achieved more than during the preceding first two years of the war. The country and the army need not worry; the garrison is unanimous that the combat capacity of the Kronstadt fortress is well up to scratch.'[103]

Incredibly, Kronstadt's commissar, Pepeliaev, reporting back to the provisional government, also added his voice to the chorus of praise for the Kronstadt Soviet's 'great organizational work'. His report was even published in the *Rech'*, the organ of the liberal Party of Constitutional Democrats (Kadets), which never had a good word to spare for Kronstadt:

Life has returned to normal and the confidence of soldiers and sailors in their officers has been restored to such an extent that ordinary constructive work is perfectly possible.

The special defence commision attached to the commandant of the fortress, in which the ranks participate [Pepeliaev's circumlocution for the Soviet's *control* commission *over* the commandant] has had outstanding success in strengthening defence.

The mass of military ranks and workers is closely organized by the local Soviet of Workers' and Soldiers' Deputies and expresses its full confidence in the provisional government.

Pepeliaev reported with special satisfaction that the intractable problem of some eighty officers still under arrest was now being

tackled by a new Investigation Commission chaired by the procura-
tor Pavel Pereverzev and consisting of government lawyers and
representatives of the Kronstadt Soviet, and that a few prisoners had
already been freed (Kronstadt's concession to Alexander Kerensky
and his visit of 28 March).[104]

There can be no doubt that Kronstadt had indeed travelled a long
way since the bloody night of 1 March, yet for all that, Pepeliaev,
possibly anxious to impress the government with his achievement
and to allay its fears for the loyalty and effectiveness of this most
important fortress, may perhaps have overstated the case. In fact,
Captain Arno Almkvist, one of the imprisoned officers whose
release he had acclaimed, was nearly lynched on 8 April when his
men spotted him making his way unguarded to the Petrograd ferry-
boat, while the new Investigation Commission, having been
threatened by crowds of angry sailors and soldiers protesting against
its liberal release of officers, was compelled to return to Petrograd as
early as 9 April, its mission unaccomplished, with over eighty
officers still locked up in the casemates.[105]

With the entire command and administrative structure destroyed
by the revolution, Kronstadt's real and distinctive achievement was
its Soviet democracy which, based on a universal application of the
elective principle, rebuilt institutions and filled all offices, military,
naval and civilian, from top to bottom, by democratic elections in
which all 'toilers', i.e. sailors, soldiers, workers and employees,
participated. Admired by the entire left-wing of the 'revolutionary
democracy' as 'the brightest example of the democratic principle in
the Russian revolution',[106] Kronstadt was equally deeply detested,
feared and slandered by a broad spectrum, ranging from the
moderate socialist but fiercely 'defensist' *Den'* and *Edinstvo*, to the
liberal *Rech'*, and the notorious right-wing *Novoe vremia*, who saw in
it a dangerous stronghold of extremism, violence and triumphant
anarchy.

It was in rejection of such charges that Kronstadt and its *Izvestiia*
proudly and aggressively advertised its elective democracy. An
editorial of 1 April defended election of officers as 'the basic instrument in the complete democratization of the army'; this, and this
alone, would ensure that officers were elected only on the grounds
that 'they really know their business and are truly competent to lead
masses of soldiers'. Indeed, the very hue-and-cry provoked by the
application of the elective principle in Kronstadt even further high-

lighted 'the need to go to the very end of the people's creative
enthusiasm, the democratic transformation of the entire structure
of our life, and the creation of an army that is a permanent bulwark
of freedom'.[107]

When Guchkov, Minister for War and Navy, dared to question
the effectiveness of the elective system in military appointments, the
sailor Skobennikov, a member of the Executive Committee of the
Kronstadt Soviet and the chairman of its food commission, sent him
the following open letter, published in Kronstadt's *Izvestiia* on 12
April:

Why do you, just as in the good old days, so threateningly berate the sailors
and soldiers who have presumed to elect their commanders and who now
accept their authority unconditionally, ready, together with them, to fight
to the death for the people's freedom? Do not you, provisionally entrusted
with the defence of the country as you are, also regard yourself as *elected* to
that post? Perhaps we do choose our commanders badly . . . if so, then it
is your task to teach us how to do it better, since, under the Old Regime,
all that we sailors and soldiers ever learned was how to use our hands and
feet . . . It is only since the First of March that we, the democracy, have
begun to use our heads too, and, half-witted though we are, have begun to
elect all our commanders, including the commander of the fortress . . .
Come and see our new abilities for yourself . . . you will find that the
electing of officers has both democratized the army and raised its combat
efficiency.[108]

This letter was no merely defiant gesture. Early in June, the
Kronstadt Torpedo Reserve Battalion flatly rejected an invitation
by the chief-of-staff of the Petrograd Military District to *nominate*
20% of its men for promotion to officers' rank. Such action, they
said, would 'undermine the might of the revolutionary army by
estranging the best elements from the general mass'. Instead, they
offered to *elect* men who could and would do the job 'without bestow-
ing on them the rank of officers'.[109]

The Kronstadters did indeed use their heads *and* the power and
confidence given them by control over a first-rate fortress, naval
base and well-appointed and well-supplied town to build a Soviet
system of government and administration which, by the beginning
of May, when elections to the second Soviet were about to be held,
was fully formed and effectively at work. 'An example of unity of
purpose and action . . . a model of organized construction' they
called it, and were mightily proud of their achievement.[110] For their
Soviet, and its network of commissions and committees, controlled

and administered all the military and naval forces stationed in Kronstadt and its forts, and ran all its industrial enterprises, the steamship plant, the sawmill, the electrical station, the building industry and the water supply, the military workshops, the arsenal and its stores, the dockyards, the cable factory and the foundries, the food supply, the allocation of raw materials, the fixing of wages and pensions, the cleaning of streets and the maintenance of parks. These enterprises, with the exception of private houses and shops, the cable factory and some workshops, the two film-theatres and the pubs, had previously all been state-owned in Kronstadt, so all that was needed was for the Soviet to take the place of the state. Though Kronstadt was entirely dependent on the provisional government for its finance and provisions, the government, anxious that this key fortress and naval base be kept in good order and repair, never used its power of purse to call Kronstadt to order, but instead swallowed its pride, and its doubts, and footed the bill.

Indeed, when the cable factory was closed by its owner who claimed it was running at a loss, the Soviet requisitioned it and had it managed as a state enterprise. Likewise, after the death of the owner of the Von Shultse diving equipment workshop (possibly the only one of its kind in Russia), his trustee reported a debt of 160,000 roubles; the Executive Committee of the Soviet, jointly with the Divers' School Committee, decided that the workshop's capital equipment amply covered the debt and suggested that the Kronstadt port requisition it, put experienced engineers in charge, keep on existing staff and operate it for the defence effort.[111]

Visitors to Kronstadt were indeed deeply impressed with the 'exemplary order' they found there: the clean, sometimes even washed, streets, the scrubbed floors of the clubs, with never a trace of litter or cigarette butts, and the orderly parks with their notices urging care for trees and flowers.[112]

By the beginning of May the power structure and organizational network of Kronstadt's Soviet system of government and administration was fully working, its practice receiving constitutional definition in two key documents: 'The Statute of the Soviet of Workers' and Soldiers' Deputies' of 3 May, and 'The Instructions regarding the Local Committees' of 4 May 1917.[113]

While the electorate or body politic was defined as 'the workers, soldiers, sailors and the entire organized mass of toilers in the City of Kronstadt' (also including elected officers, their full franchise now restored), their representative organ was the Kronstadt Soviet, elected on the principle of one deputy for every base unit (i.e. ship's crew, company, workshop, plant, enterprise and institution) numbering from 30 to 100 members, two deputies for a base unit numbering from 100 to 300 members, and one additional deputy for every further 200 members. Units of less than thirty members banded together and elected one deputy, and where that proved impractical (e.g. in the case of crews of small ships), then these units elected one deputy each.

In addition, the recognized political parties, SRs, Bolsheviks, Mensheviks and Non-Partyists, sent three deputies each to the Soviet which consisted altogether of some 300 deputies.

This electoral system seems to have been a compromise between the individual one-toiler-one-vote principle and the corporate principle of equitable representation for all base units, an arrangement designed to ensure that all workshops, army units and crews were adequately represented.

For the purpose of discussing matters of professional concern, the military (sailors and soldiers) and worker deputies would also assemble as separate sections of the Soviet, but their decisions would be referred to the Executive Committee, the governing body, for approval and implementation.

The Executive Committee consisted of thirty members elected in the Soviet from among deputies nominated by the 'political groups' or 'factions' (caucuses) in accordance with their numerical strength there. Each faction had an additional member on the Executive Committee. Thus, this latter body was, in effect, a socialist coalition government which, while it had charge of the Soviet's overall 'organizational and political activities', was specifically charged with preparing the agenda and the materials for the general and extraordinary meetings of the Soviet and implementing its resolutions and decisions. Its emergency powers were limited to 'cases that brook no delay', and their use was to be guided by 'the general directives of the Soviet', each and every such use being statutorily reported back to the Soviet.

With the Soviet serving as Kronstadt's parliament and the Executive Committee as its government, Soviet control over Kronstadt's military and civil establishments and their effective administration was ensured by an array of control commissions such as those attached to the commander of the Naval Forces, the commandant of the fortress, the captain of the harbour, the town commandant or the chief of the arsenal. Permanent operational commissions (e.g. for food provisions and finance) and proliferating special *ad hoc* commissions were elected, such as that to set up a ration-card system, that for 'The Struggle against Drunkenness and Prostitution' or the Special Military Commission (elected during the Kornilov putsch and active during the October revolution), to name but a few.

Control commissions had from four to six members, operational and special purpose commissions from four to ten members, the latter elected by and from the plenum of the Soviet, with members of the Executive Committee ineligible for membership. From 3 May onwards, when the principle of 'factional' (i.e. party) representation replaced that of 'corporate' (i.e. sailors, soldiers and workers) representation, the commissioners were both in fact and in principle nominated by party caucuses in the Soviet, in proportion to their numerical strength.

The parties were zealous indeed in watching and insisting on the proportional representation due to them: thus, when the Non-Partyist G. Petrov was, for whatever reason, co-opted to the editorial commission which published the *Izvestiia*, it was immediately stipulated that the other parties be compensated.[114] This same zeal also ensured that commissions were manned, although sometimes only nominally, and there was a shortage of manpower in those commissions where, as Foma Parchevsky complained, it was 'simple, menial work that had to be done'.[115]

The bureaucratization of Kronstad's vast network of commissions, i.e. their transformation into permanent administrative departments, completed by January 1918, was so far advanced by the beginning of August that it was decided to concentrate them all in one building near the Naval Assembly where the Soviet and its Executive Committee were housed, *and* to provide each and every commission with a paid clerk; at the same time military personnel serving as commissioners were issued a tobacco allowance and provision was made for them to have a free lunch, so that they need not run back to their units and thus waste time.[116]

But it was Kronstadt's direct democracy, provided by a multitude of base plenary assemblies in each workshop, army unit or ship's crew, all making up the organized body politic of toilers,[117] that formed the base of the Soviet system of representative democracy. Convened by their own elected committees, these assemblies met

regularly once a week, though extra meetings could be called at the
request of one-third of the membership; two-thirds of the members
constituted a quorum. Each assembly deliberated problems of particular interest to its members, approved or rejected proposals
brought forward by the committee, elected both the committee and
its deputy (or deputies) to the Soviet, could recall and replace the
deputy or appeal to the Executive Committee against the instructions or activities of its own committee. Limited judicial powers
permitted each assembly, sitting as a 'comradely court', to hear cases
of breaches of work discipline and other individual misdemeanours
and any committee incompetence or misdeed.

Committees were elected for three-month terms with two members
for every hundred personnel. Committee men were expected to
'enjoy general confidence and, as far as possible, to be literate'.
They, in turn, elected their chairman and secretary, and allocated
functions subject to the approval of the assembly, and to final
confirmation by the Executive Committee.

The committee was collectively responsible for the good order of
the enterprise or unit, supervised its routine, and controlled its
administrative operations. While its special concern was the improve-
ment of working conditions and efficiency, it was made clear that
this must never be at the expense of 'the interests of the state which
every citizen must defend'. Thus any matter of more than local
importance was beyond its purview, and was to be brought before a
higher body such as the Port Authority, the Artillery Regiment
Committee, or the Executive Committee, in the form of an
'inquiry'.

The committee was charged with preparing and announcing the
agenda three days before convening the assembly, issuing instructions and regulations of a purely local character subject to the
assembly's approval but in accordance with the Soviet's general
rules, granting leaves and work exemptions, supervising the recruitment of new employees through the Bureau of Labour strictly in
accordance with the candidate's number in the unemployed queue
and thus free of 'patronage and friendships', and, as regards incom-
ing letters, 'sending written replies without delay'.

Constant liaison between the committee and the Soviet was maintained by the assembly's Soviet deputy who had to report back on
all decisions taken there, keep a regular journal of Soviet proceedings
for the benefit of the committee and ensure that the Soviet's *Izvestiia*,

which carried verbatim reports of the Soviet's debates and the roll-call of important votes, was received and duly displayed.

Since the Executive Committee was each assembly's final court of appeal against its own committee, enjoying the right to veto its instructions as 'improper' and even disband it and request the assembly to elect a new committee, the assemblies, their committees and Soviet deputies formed together a vast network through which the Executive Committee transmitted its influence and power down to the very grass-roots of Kronstadt's Soviet democracy. But the assemblies and their committees, to whom the Soviet deputies were accountable and reported constantly, could instruct the latter how to vote and could check (in *Izvestiia*) that their instructions had been obeyed. By exercising their right of instant recall, they had the whip hand, and could make their wishes clearly heard in the Soviet.

Although it has proved almost impossible to determine how active the committees were, what is almost beyond doubt is that the ships crews' committees in Kronstadt, and generally in the Baltic Fleet, were highly organized and alert right from the start. Thus as early as 14 March the Naval Command instructed officers to recognize the elected ships' committees and thus 'preserve the combat capacity of the ships'.[118] The artillery committees, however, were criticized (in April) for lacking initiative and relying instead on the well-functioning central Artillery Regiment Committee, chaired by Piotr Ediet, for guidance and instructions.[119] On the other hand, Philips Price, correspondent of the *Manchester Guardian*, visiting Kronstadt in June 1917, was impressed with the 'high state of efficiency' of the dockyards' and foundries' committees,[120] and while the protocols of the Kronstadt Soviet certainly contain complaints about lazy commissions,[121] they are silent about malfunctioning committees.

Yet the hub of Kronstadt's political life was the Soviet and its very active Executive Committee. Nikolai Rostov, an SR and member of the Executive Committee of the Helsingfors Soviet, who came to Kronstadt early in June 1917,[122] found the Soviet well attended – 'they know how to sit it out' – orderly and businesslike, with the speakers facing the chairman as if they had adopted the 'Anglo-Saxon custom'. The agenda was various and wide-ranging. On the issue whether or not 'the *Narodovolets* should put to sea' in compliance with the provisional government's order, a majority voted 'yes' and a deputy was promptly sent to the *Narodovolets* to make sure it did put to sea. The next question revolved around whether wages and salaries in a given workshop or enterprise should be shared and thus equalized, as the small group of Anarchists in the Soviet passionately urged, or whether existing, though small, wage differentials should be maintained. The majority voted 'no' to 'communalization' of wages.

A newspaper vendors' petition complaining of interference with the sale of newspapers led to a debate on whether all, including those that had recently slandered Kronstadt, should be freely sold there. A minority, opposing such freedom, suggested that those wishing to read 'bourgeois' or 'social-patriotic' newspapers such as *Den'*, *Edinstvo* or *Volia naroda* should get them by subscription. However, the majority voted for the free sale of newspapers and thus, as Rostov was pleased to note, 'the Kronstadters retained the right to read whatever newspapers they liked'. And avid newspaper readers they were, as both friendly and hostile visitors alike observed. The same freedom, Rostov noted, extended to the right to stick up posters which appeared in profusion on the trees 'without some Bolshevik tearing them off; apparently the customs of the [Bolshevik] Vyborg District have not yet been imported here'.

The Kronstadt Soviet's social composition and advanced stage of political differentiation was reflected in its appearance in session. A group of veteran Kronstadt Bolsheviks remembered: 'On the right sat the Bolsheviks, on the left the SRs, and in the back the Non-Partyists. The colours sprang to one's eye: the Bolsheviks – blue with sailor blouses (white in summer), the SRs – a mixture of blue, green [soldiers] and black [workers]. Behind the SRs and the Bolsheviks it was all black.'[123] Thus it was that hundreds of quite ordinary, but literate, Kronstadters turned into Soviet deputies, commissioners and committee men, patiently and religiously attending the twice-weekly regular and very numerous extraordinary sessions and meetings, learning to speak in public, to move amendments, to vote, govern and run their complex military and civilian establishments. Apart from some fifteen party activists (mostly Bolsheviks) imported from the mainland, the Kronstadt Soviet was made up of articulate, activist sailors, soldiers and workers, with a thin sprinkling of local teachers and intellectuals, such as Lamanov, Oreshin, Parchevsky, Malyshev, Ediet and Kamyshev, elected by their comrades because of their intelligence and ability, some few also having revolutionary experience.

Contrasting the tension and bustle of the debates and the voting in the Kronstadt Soviet with the sleepy sessions of the Petrograd Soviet which he had just attended, where the real business had been transacted beforehand by the party intellectuals, so that 'the resolutions moved by the speaker were almost automatically adopted', Liubovich, himself a self-educated and very impressive Kronstadt leader, saw Kronstadt's virtue as being 'the promotion, out of its own midst, of activists who became the leaders of the movement, connected with the mass of their comrades by thousands of threads . . . in other words, the soldiers, sailors and workers advanced their own intelligentsia from within their own ranks'.[124] Perhaps it was the home-grown nature of the membership which accounted for the earthy freshness and seriousness of many of the Kronstadt Soviet debates as they discussed a wide range of problems, trifling and weighty, which worried them and their comrades. Thus, they argued about labour mobility, the equality of women, fraternization with enemy soldiers, drunkenness, gambling, dances and pornography, censorship, the treatment of officers, policemen and deserters, agrarian reform and the nationality problem. Above all, they argued passionately and persistently about war and peace, about power and the provisional government.

Recorded verbatim by the wife of Alexander Brushvit, the Kronstadt Soviet protocols were published in its *Izvestiia*, together with a good many articles, reports, letters to the editor and poems written by Kronstadt's leaders, activists, sailor-poets and rank and file. They bear moving testimony both to the humanizing and civilizing effect that the February revolution had on Kronstadt's popular masses, and to the hopes it awakened for an active and better life, for education, self-government and community.

In the centre of the Kronstadt drama stood the earnest, friendly, somewhat enigmatic figure of the student Anatolii Lamanov, the young man with the 'long hair, dreamy eyes, and the far-off look of an idealist', whom Philips Price met in June as the chairman of the Kronstadt Soviet.[125] Son of Lieutenant-Colonel Nikolai P. Lamanov who was, in 1913, the *equipagemeister* in the Kronstadt port,[126] and of a mother with populist sympathies, he was the younger brother of Lieutenant Piotr Lamanov, revolutionary Kronstadt's commander of naval forces. A third-year student of the Institute of Technology at the outbreak of the revolution, Anatolii Lamanov had made a name for himself among workers and soldiers during his frequent war-time visits to Kronstadt as a popular lecturer on natural history, geography and technology; but, unlike his older brother, who was connected with the SRs, he seems to have had no political affiliation.[127] With the outbreak of the revolution, he was elected to the Committee of the Movement by the employees of the Kronstadt port's chemical laboratory. Chairman of the Kronstadt Workers' Soviet in March and April and, from May onwards, of its Workers' and Soldiers' Soviet, leader of its large Non-Party faction, secretary and, since 25 April, chairman of the editorial commission of Kronstadt's *Izvestiia*, Lamanov, with his many public and festive addresses, and his restraining, conciliatory, and civilized 'non-party' chairmanship of its sessions, set the tone for the Soviet's debates and helped shape Kronstadt's ideology and creed, which was simply radical-democratic, very egalitarian, and radically socialist, or, as one Menshevik observer in Petrograd put it, 'neither Leninist nor Anarchist'.[128] Lamanov propounded his democratic *credo* on many occasions. His speech at the opening of the People's Theatre in the Naval Assembly building on 9 April was an early statement. Referring to the profound changes which the revolution had wrought in giving Russia a 'democratic frame', he reminded his audience that:

before the revolution, the walls of the Naval Assembly saw only a select public on theatre nights. True, of late, a democratic element had begun to penetrate it, but it is only now that we see the people here, an undifferentiated people, without distinction of rank or estate, soldiers and sailors for whom this place was once out of bounds. Hand in hand with the democratization of the public has gone a profound change in the character of the plays staged here . . . words such as Liberty, Equality, and Fraternity, never before heard by the masses, resound here now to form and enrich the soul of the people. This democratization of the theatre will have immense consequences, for the theatre complements what we see and hear in life and read about in books; it injects new ideas into the minds of spectators, ideas that are new not because of their content, but because of their embodiment before us on the stage. Long live the democratic theatre.[129]

Lamanov's tireless reiteration of his democratic creed and his steady educational effort, so intimately a part of the organizational–educational atmosphere and trend in the early phase of the February revolution, served as a constant appeal to the humanity and reason of his Kronstadters in making them feel citizens of a Great Free Russia *and* 'citizens of the universe'; his was a constant call for restraint, for close ties with the Petrograd Soviet, for 'the unity of the revolutionary all-national movement', and a voice that spoke always against that 'disunity and party discord' which had 'ruined the revolution of France'.[130]

He was strongly supported by Kronstadt's *Izvestiia* which was filled throughout April 1917 with speeches and articles urging on its readers the virtues of education and enlightenment and appealing to Kronstadt's 'educated citizens' to volunteer as lecturers and teachers and 'work for the good of their brothers in the dark', the slogan being 'Wipe out illiteracy before the Constituent Assembly.' The sailor Skobennikov put his aim higher: his article 'Knowledge is Light' was prefaced hopefully, if wistfully, 'When will the people at last pick up Belinsky and Gogol in the bazaar and take them home to read?' But the sad truth, as he himself well knew, was that 'the liberated people still drink methylated spirits and play cards'.[131]

An editorial, under the heading 'We Must Forge Freedom', appealed to the educated:

The old state power kept us deliberately in darkness . . . now your sacred duty is to help our comrades . . . You few who, at the people's expense, had the chance to receive a good education, must now go to the people: preach the true word of liberty . . . enlighten them . . . this is the shortest route that the Kronstadt officers' corps can follow in drawing close to the soldiers-citizens . . . the common cause: the creation of the All-Russian Democratic Republic.[132]

When the response from the 'educated citizens' fell short and the Lecturers' Bureau managed to put on only a few lectures, an article entitled 'A Strange Phenomenon' reminded the 'better educated' officers that the civilization which the February revolution had brought to the sailors' Sakhalin was – *pace* Lamanov and his *Izvestiia* – still nothing more than a thin veneer:

What did they teach you in the cadet colleges, schools, high schools and academies if you cannot independently prepare an intelligible lecture on some political subject? Must you enlist professors and scholars for such a task? Is the intellectual baggage that you carry with you from the schools of the Old Regime so conservative that you have nothing to talk about and to pass on to your comrades, the workers, soldiers and sailors? If that is so, then why do you still presume to become our commanders, teachers and leaders? Is it the mere word 'socialism' that makes you tremble? We know that mention of 'anarchism' makes your hair stand on end, sends shivers down your spine, and conjures up the abyss and the night of the First of March . . .

If you cannot give us lectures, leave it and be done with it! We will find our own people ready and able to acquaint us with socialism and

anarchism, and with those true sciences of liberty, equality and fraternity
. . . If you think you can just read us tales and novels and thus distract us
from current affairs, you make a big mistake. All we are interested in is
politics, and labour and agrarian problems; but not your stories! To the
very last man, we are preparing ourselves to become builders of the society
of the future; in the meantime we are all getting ready for the Constituent
Assembly. If you continue to drag on with your preparations, you will soon
be left behind, if not thrown overboard. Come boldly then to our socialist
clubs, gatherings and meetings, otherwise we will ignore you altogether.[133]

But unless his revolutionary credentials were as convincing as
those of Piotr Lamanov, Mikhail Evstingeev or Piotr Ediet, it was
obviously only a bold officer or intellectual who was ready to play
an active part in Kronstadt's radical democracy which had, from
the outset, seen itself as turning the tables on the officer class.

If Kronstadt's elected radical elite took so readily to debate and
decision-making in the Soviet, the mass of its sailors, soldiers and
workmen flocked in their thousands to the vast Anchor Square or
(on rainy days or after dark) to the large hall of the Naval Manège.
There, on festive occasions, or in the late afternoons, they heard
many of the Russian revolution's leading orators and tribunes
ranging from Kerensky and Ekaterina Brezhkovskaia, Trotsky,
Chudnovsky and Lunacharsky, Robert Grimm and Angelica Balabanova, to Alexandra Kollontai, Iraklii Tseretelli and Vladimir
Voitinsky. But they gave increasing attention to their own local
talents and firebrand Bolshevik and Anarchist orators, Semion Roshal,
Kirill Orlov, Fiodor Raskolnikov, Ivan Flerovsky, Efim (Khaim)
Yarchuk and I. S. Bleikhman. Anchor Square and its direct, extra-
parliamentary democracy would go into action when radical, sometimes absurd, sometimes sinister, resolutions were adopted after the
crowd had been whipped up by a bout of wild oratory. Thus, they
resolved that the Constituent Assembly be convened soon in Kronstadt and that the tsar and his family be brought there for safe-
keeping. In a more practical and sinister vein, a meeting of some
10,000, mostly sailors and soldiers, assembled in the Naval Manège
on 7 May and resolved that, 'in view of the fact that the yellow
bourgeois and Black Hundred press wages a slander campaign
against the revolution and against revolutionaries and preaches war
until final victory', all their printing presses were to be confiscated
and made available only to socialist parties and trade unions.[134]
Two days later, and after speaking out at a mass meeting against the
blessings of fraternization at the front, the soldier Shchikin was

manhandled by a crowd shouting 'Off to the front with him!' Only the intervention of the Executive Committee rescued him.[135]

Bolshevik orators, supported by Anarchist allies such as Yarchuk, dominated Anchor Square and in time acquired a monopoly there. They thus had the opportunity to stir up and control the masses, using them to put pressure from the outside on the Soviet where these parties were in a minority. It was from a mass meeting in Anchor Square on 25 May that a large crowd marched to the Naval Assembly and forced the leaders of the Soviet to rescind the agreement reached with the leaders of the Petrograd Soviet. This episode had its prelude in a similar, though unsuccessful, attempt made by Semion Roshal during the April Days. Anchor Square meetings were also organized to neutralize the moderating or patriotic effects of festive visits such as that of General Lavr Kornilov, commander of the Petrograd Military District, on 6 April, and that of the veteran SR leader, Ekaterina Brezhkovskaia, the 'grandmother of the Russian revolution' on 8 April. Foma Parchevsky recorded it:

On that day Kronstadt was unrecognizable; it was as if tranquillity had at last come. Marching in serried ranks, the soldiers and sailors filed past the commander-in-chief, amicably acknowledging his salute. After the parade, and to the shouts of hoorah, they bore the gallant general aloft on their shoulders to his car.

Two days later they gave a rousing welcome to E. K. Brezhkova-Brezhkovskaia, applauding stormily when she spoke of her love for the people and the homeland. Yet, only half-an-hour after her departure, a meeting began to assemble in Anchor Square in which a gentleman wearing the uniform of a military surgeon delivered a three-hour speech purposely designed to incite hatred against the officers and the intelligentsia. That meeting all but ended in the lynching of one bystander who dared to voice his indignation at the unscrupulous address.[136]

Kronstadt had but a short time to enjoy the luxury of self-concern. The April crisis of government, sparked off by the Foreign Minister Pavel Miliukov's Note to the allied governments reaffirming Russia's commitment both to the prosecution of the war until final victory *and* to the annexationist provisions of the secret London Treaty of 1915, forced the Kronstadt Soviet to turn outwards and begin to debate the question of power as it pertained to Russia at large rather than to the local scene. It also marked the end of Kronstadt's organizational–educational period of creativity and innocence, and the beginning of its intensive politicization and radicalization.

The Kronstadt Soviet met in extraordinary session in the morning of 21 April after it had been briefed on the government crisis by a special emissary from the Petrograd Soviet, Iu. Vainberg.[137] The chairman, Anatolii Lamanov, set the tone when he denounced Miliukov's Note of 18 April as having 'destroyed' all previous declarations of the provisional government, and then took the lead in trying to turn the debate into a demonstration of solidarity and 'maximum cooperation' with the Petrograd Soviet. Lamanov, and all the Menshevik, Non-Party and SR speakers who supported him (Larionov, Kamyshev, Alnichenkov, Iu. Vainberg, Shurgin, Evstingeev and Brushvit) urged 'calmness' and appealed to the deputies' 'sense of realism' and 'reason', arguing that since the 'democracy' was not yet ready to take power it should, for the time being, be satisfied with 'control over the government'. To demand that the entire government resign and hand over power to the 'revolutionary democracy', rather than force the resignation of Miliukov and Guchkov, would, Lamanov urged, be a 'stupid' move, for it would shift responsibility for Russia's 'economic dislocation' and its hardships onto a socialist government. The immediate task on hand was to make a 'gigantic effort' to organize 'our masses'; only then would the circumstances be ripe to 'overthrow all those who go against the people'. They must not, he said, look at things purely from the narrow 'view-point of Kronstadt', but must give full support to the Petrograd Soviet.

The Bolshevik speakers, with Liubovich giving the lead, were unanimous in denouncing the provisional government as 'having taken the open road of counter-revolution'; it was a government of traitors whom 'we must overthrow', for its policy of 'war until victory' simply 'tightens the noose around our neck'. Such a bourgeois government of Kadets should never have been trusted, said the sailor Baranov, for it was incapable of pursuing 'democratic' policies: 'No bourgeois can become a democrat, for he has received a different education which prevents any quick regeneration. In order to become a democrat one must work and toil with the sweat of one's brow.'

Unanimous as the Bolshevik speakers were about the need to overthrow the provisional government, there seems to have been some confusion among them as to what should replace it. While Gromov would no longer trust even the 'socialist Kerensky' and wanted a government of *narodniki* (men from the people), Lebedev called for the 'overthrow' of the government and its replacement by a 'Kerensky ministry', and Uliantsev, as impatient as ever, called for 'immediate action', warning that 'one must not be sentimental' with a government that deceives the people.

In the end, the debate narrowed down to a point where the moderates warned against a second revolution, while Roshal taunted them: 'You are afraid of power!' When at last the vote was taken, it was the moderate resolution, moved by the SRs and supported by the emissary of the Petrograd Soviet, that won the day by 138 to 36 votes. The Kronstadt Soviet's resolution denounced Miliukov's Note and 'similar criminal steps' of the government, 'energetically' endorsed the Petrograd Soviet's 'protest' and 'fully supported [its] revolutionary pressure on the provisional government and its continuous and relentless control over it in the interests of the revolution'. The Bolshevik resolution, which received a mere thirty-six votes, denounced the provisional government as 'henchmen of the bourgeoisie', 'hostile to the interests of Russian democracy', and promised all-out support 'for the revolutionary actions' of the Petrograd Soviet aimed at defending the interests of the democracy against all encroachments by 'serf owners and capitalists', and at the continuation and consolidation of the revolution 'until power is transferred to the people'.[138]

The surprising thing about the Bolshevik resolution is not so much its solid defeat, which was due more to its merely lukewarm and very conditional support of the Petrograd Soviet than to its outright denunciation of the provisional government, but rather its relative moderation as compared with the radical Bolshevik speeches that preceded it. The resolution was thus more in keeping with the line taken by the *Golos pravdy*, which had warned against the slogan of 'the immediate overthrow of the provisional government',[139] than with the radical stance of the mass meetings organized by the Kronstadt Bolshevik Committee in the Naval Manège and at the Kronstadt steamship plant, where, on 21 April, Kronstadt crowds had resolved to fight with all their strength 'for the overthrow of the provisional government and for the transfer of power to the Soviet of Workers' and Soldiers' Deputies'.[140]

The militant resolution of the Kronstadt Bolshevik Committee (as distinct from that of the Bolshevik Soviet faction and the line of *Golos pravdy*) was very much in tune with the radical wing of Russian bolshevism represented in Petrograd by the Bolshevik Military Organization and the Vyborg District Committee, both regarded as 'more left than Lenin himself'. Indeed, in flagrant disregard of the injunction of the Petrograd Soviet (endorsed and heeded by the Kronstadt Soviet) to 'send no military units and detachments' to Petrograd,[141] the Kronstadt Bolshevik Committee, upon the request of Nikolai Podvoisky, chairman of the Bolshevik Military Organization, despatched a task force of 150 Bolshevik sailors who arrived in the evening of 21 April. As Raskolnikov, its organizer, proudly remembered, that task force was the 'vanguard' of a series of Kronstadt expeditionary forces despatched to Petrograd under Bolshevik auspices.[142]

Smarting under their defeat in the Soviet in the morning and emboldened by their success with the masses outside during the day, the Bolsheviks made a further attempt to have the moderate resolution rescinded when the Executive Committee of the Soviet met in the evening with Artemii Liubovich in the chair; but dismal failure awaited them, and in the course of the debate the radical Bolshevik resolution adopted at mass meetings was denounced as 'foul play and a provocation'. Undeterred, Semion Roshal raised a mass demonstration against the Executive Committee which was then in session; carrying banners bearing the slogan 'Down with the provisional government', the crowd demanded the adoption of the Bolshevik resolution and the 'dismissal' of the provisional government. Resuming its night session after it had adjourned to hear the demonstrators' demands, the Soviet, at the end of a heated debate in which all Bolshevik speakers defended Roshal to the hilt, decided by sixty-five to fifty votes to exclude him from the Executive Committee. Although Roshal (and his Bolshevik witnesses) vehemently denied the charges, and specifically that he had used his position as member of the Executive Committee to raise a crowd and undermine the Committee's authority, he admitted as much when he concluded his defence: 'I cannot do violence to my deep convictions; as long as power is not in our hands, we will not rest.'[143]

Apparently this was not the first time that Bolshevik activists had tried to create the impression in Petrograd that the Kronstadt Soviet, in which they were but a small minority, was not just radical but Bolshevik-dominated. Thus Mikhail Lebedev, one of Kronstadt's two delegates to the All-Russian Conference of Soviets which convened in Petrograd at the end of March, skilfully wrapped up his radical Bolshevik speech in 'greetings from the Soviet of Workers' and Soldiers' Deputies of the city of Kronstadt',[144] and, when taken to task upon his return to Kronstadt by chairman Lamanov and other deputies, defended himself by claiming that 'he had the right to act according to his personal convictions since he had not been given any instructions'.[145] Although the Kronstadt Soviet resolved on 6 April that delegates 'must express and defend the views of the collective that sends them', and declared that in future it would provide its delegates with a mandatory *nakaz* or instruction for the purpose of which a special *Nakaz* Commission was elected,[146] the damage had already been done. Thus at the first major conference of Soviets from all over Russia, Kronstadt was on record (since its second delegate Mikhail Evstingeev did not speak) as having spoken with a militant Bolshevik voice. A series of similar, but less clear-cut, Bolshevik manoeuvres in which Semion Roshal and other activists were allegedly involved was cited by Larionov and Glazko at the Soviet session of 25 April, which debated protests from the crews of the training-ships *Okean* and *Osvoboditel* against the exclusion of Roshal from the Executive Committee and their demands for his reinstatement.[147]

What apparently made the Kronstadt Bolsheviks so angry and pugnacious during the April Crisis (to the point of mobilizing Anchor Square pressure against the Soviet) was not only that they had been balked and solidly defeated there, but also, and perhaps primarily, that the moderate Kronstadt resolution of 21 April had, as Larionov put it, 'exposed the truth' in Petrograd where everyone had previously been convinced that the Kronstadt Soviet was 'under Bolshevik influence'.[148] Indeed Liubovich admitted as much at the Bolshevik April Conference when he complained that the hitherto 'dominating influence of the Bolsheviks in Kronstadt' had been weakened during the April Crisis and that this was due to the 'demoralizing influence' of the Petrograd Soviet which had 'spoilt things for us'.[149]

While the apparent immediate effect of the Bolsheviks' radical agitation and mobilizing effort during the April Crisis was their defeat and isolation in the Kronstadt Soviet, its real and lasting result was their emergence as the party par excellence of Kronstadt radicalism. The exclusion of Semion Roshal, popular with Anchor Square audiences as a passionate speaker and admired by base assemblies and committees as a tireless agitator and organizer making the round of workshops, ships and army units, was used in an intensive campaign to discredit the Soviet as unrepresentative and undemocratic and to demand its immediate reorganization. When that campaign was well under way, Liubovich and his Bolshevik comrades on the Executive Council confronted the Soviet on 2 May with a demand for its 'immediate' reorganization, and when that was voted down by 111 to no less than 76 votes, they forced immediate elections by resigning their posts.[150]

Thus, on the eve of the elections to the Kronstadt Soviet, in which the attitude to the provisional government and to coalition with it was perhaps the major political issue, the Bolsheviks appeared clearly and forcefully as the party opposed to coalition and as the chief advocates of the transfer of power to the Soviets. But their campaign had, in fact, begun earlier. On 28 April, Liubovich, seconded by Lebedev, made the most of the Soviet debate on the Liberty Loan to denounce the provisional government as committed to 'war to a victorious end', and to discredit the Petrograd Soviet for giving that government full confidence, and placing the seal of popular approval on its loan for the 'murder of liberty'.[151]

Two days later, on 30 April, the Bolsheviks gave battle to Vladimir Voitinsky, Menshevik member of the Executive Committee of the Petrograd Soviet, who spoke for coalition at a mass meeting in Anchor Square. They howled him down, but not before adopting a resolution which acclaimed soviets as 'the sole parliament which expresses the will of the entire toiling people of free Russia'.[152]

The battle-royal on coalition was fought in the Kronstadt Soviet on 2 May, on the eve of election day. The occasion was the arrival of Vainberg, sent again to seek Kronstadt's endorsement of the Petrograd Soviet's decision to join a coalition government. Chairman Lamanov again set the tone of the debate when he announced that the Petrograd Soviet had already 'in principle' recognized the need for the formation of a 'coalition ministry', since the terrible crisis which Russia was experiencing required a 'strong united state power which is capable of saving Russia from ruin, yet is a state power which belongs unreservedly to the people'.[153] Vainberg explained why, in spite of the failure of the provisional government, the democracy would not assume 'entire power', since this would turn the bourgeoisie, which was still quite powerful, into an enemy of the revolution precisely at a time of crisis. Realizing that socialism could not yet be achieved, the Petrograd Soviet had decided to join a coalition government with 'revolutionary elements of the bourgeoisie' and thus save the country.

Liubovich, the Bolsheviks' main spokesman, totally rejected Vainberg's 'sweet speech' praising the 'virtues and merits' of the bourgeoisie in order to justify a policy which the Petrograd Soviet had already adopted: 'By refusing power at a moment when only a state power rooted in the people can lead the country out of the blind alley which it has entered, we take upon ourselves a grave responsibility to history.' The provisional government, he argued, was incapable of doing anything without the cooperation of the Soviets who were the real 'sources of strength and power'. Why then should the Soviet not pick up the power which had been 'demonstratively' thrown down, especially now, when the 'bankruptcy' of the provisional government was apparent to all, and its replacement but a matter of course, though it would be far more difficult at a later stage. Such Soviet government would be 'fully authoritative' and would enjoy the confidence of the people, while a coalition government would give the Soviets 'colossal responsibility', but a mere 'fraction of power'. Liubovich then moved a resolution denouncing the provisional government as led by a 'gang of capitalists and landowners', and rejecting coalition as an attempt, by means of the 'partial replacement of a few people', to shift the burden of responsibility on to the Soviets; it demanded, instead, 'the transfer of the entire power to the Soviets'.

Raskolnikov, too, dwelt on the weakness of the provisional government and contrasted it with the real strength of the Soviets: 'The ground is slipping from beneath the very feet of the provisional government: there is not a single cannon, not a single bayonet, not a single armoured car on its side. The entire army is on the side of the Soviet of Workers' and Soldiers' Deputies.' This weak government, he claimed, emulating the example of the Belgian and French governments, had invited the popular leaders of the Soviets to join it and thus prop up its authority. The Bolsheviks were strenuously opposed to socialists entering a coalition government. What was needed was 'not a coalition ministry, but a government of the Soviets of Workers' and Soldiers' Deputies, headed by the people's Constituent Assembly'.

The Bolshevik sailor Pankratov translated Raskolnikov's and Liubovich's political analysis into a homely simile: to him the provisional government 'resembled a gang of skilled cardsharpers who, to gain respectability, have invited some honest players to join them; while they may genuinely prefer an honest game, their passion for money will always get the better of them and the honest players will find themselves cheated'.

The SRs were clearly divided in this debate. While Grigorii Smoliansky could not make up his mind whether a coalition government or what he called a left-wing 'social ministry' was the lesser evil, Alexander Brushvit rejected coalition outright as bound to be 'unpopular' and to 'lead us by the nose'. He presumably favoured a Soviet government when he concluded: 'Long live the Soviet of Workers' and Soldiers' Deputies.' On the other hand, Stepan Sokolov supported a coalition government with the bourgeoisie, even though he knew it was not 'pure of heart', 'for the good of the homeland, for the freedom we have won and for the realization of socialism'. Two speakers representing the Union of Republican Officers of the Army and the Navy, Maikopar and Drutskoi-Lubetskoi, strongly favoured a coalition government: it would, they said, rally all 'the creative forces of the country' and, strengthened by the prestige accruing to it from 'the leaders of the revolution' in the Petrograd Soviet, would become a 'government of popular confidence and revolution'.

In the end, Lamanov moved a resolution endorsing the Petrograd Soviet's decision to join a coalition government:

Recognizing that the salvation of the country and of the revolution demands the participation of representatives of the Executive Committee of the Petrograd Soviet of Workers' and Soldiers' Deputies in the exercise of political power, and that the removal of the progressive strata of the bourgeoisie from the provisional government would undermine the country's power of resistance to economic and military ruin, the Kronstadt Soviet of Workers' and Soldiers' Deputies approves in principle the Petrograd Soviet's decision to send its representatives into the provisional government, where they will remain responsible to the Soviet, and further insists on guarantees and conditions to secure the development of the coalition cabinet's activities as a ministry of struggle for peace and the complete democratization of Russia.

When the resolution was put to the vote it was adopted by ninety-five to seventy-one votes, with eight abstentions. Since at the end of April there were at most sixty Bolsheviks in the first Soviet, some SRs must have voted with the Bolsheviks and others may have abstained.[154]

But that victory of moderation, or rather of solidarity with the Petrograd Soviet, was short-lived. The result of the elections, and the composition of the new (second) Soviet which assembled on 5

May to elect its Executive Committee and chairman, reflected the radicalization of Kronstadt and marked its emancipation from the influence and leadership of the Petrograd Soviet, and certainly from its coalitionism. The Bolsheviks, chief spokesmen against coalition with the bourgeoisie and for a government of the Soviets, had emerged the largest faction, with ninety-three deputies, overtaking the SRs who, with ninety-one deputies, had lost seventeen seats. Next came the Non-Party group who, with sixty-eight deputies, had lost nine seats, and then the Mensheviks who, returning forty-six deputies, had dropped twenty-six.

Lamanov was again elected chairman of the Soviet, the three deputy chairmen being the Bolshevik Fiodor Raskolnikov, the SR Konstantin Shurgin and the Menshevik Ivan Alnichenkov, while Artemii Liubovich was again elected chairman of the Executive Council which now consisted of nine Bolsheviks, nine SRs, seven Non-Party and five Mensheviks; but the complexion of the Soviet had changed. Apart from the large and powerful Bolshevik faction, a substantial majority of the SR and Menshevik deputies were 'Internationalists' and stood on the extreme left wing of their parties, while Lamanov's Non-Party group, too, was moving leftwards, and in August finally joined the extreme SR-Maximalists.

This second Soviet had little understanding or sympathy for Russia's new coalition government formed on 5 May. Small wonder that as early as its 6 May session, which debated the situation in the villages and the landowners' alleged sabotage of grain deliveries to the towns,[155] the Soviet returned to the question of power. This time Brushvit gave the lead when he urged that, in view of the 'incredible' situation in the countryside, 'power must be taken in the villages', and then moved that the matter be put on the agenda of the session as an urgent item. He was promptly supported by Semion Roshal who called for 'taking power into our hands without waiting for the Constituent Assembly', and for 'giving the land to the peasants'. Roshal was, naturally enough, seconded by Mikhail Lebedev who denounced the new coalition government as 'anti-people', and urged that the 'central power' be changed and that the peasant committees take local power into their hands and not wait for the Constituent Assembly.

If Roshal and Lebedev made light of the forthcoming Constituent Assembly as an idea only intended 'to put peoples' minds at rest', Liubovich struck a new note and took liberties with the Bolshevik slogan 'All Power to Soviets' when he declared that only Soviets 'reflecting the mood of the masses' should take power, while the Petrograd Soviet and others were still 'divorced from the masses'. It was, therefore, essential that all Soviets be reorganized to 'really reflect the mood of the people'. He was supported by the Bolshevik Pakallo who had 'ploughed the fields for twenty years', and, knowing 'the aching soul of the Russian peasant', knew too that he could not wait for the Constituent Assembly before receiving the land. The Bolshevik Fiodor Gromov took issue with Brushvit who had thought power must first be taken in the localities and only later in Petrograd: to him, it made no sense to take power 'from below' since it would 'be crushed from the top'; power must be taken 'from the top', and then be given to the Soviets.

While a few speakers did no more than repeat what had been said before, twenty more had put down their names to speak when it was decided to close the debate and put the rival SR and Bolshevik resolutions to the vote. The SR resolution, which received 208 votes, i.e. all the non-Bolshevik votes, demanded as imperative the 'speediest transfer of the land and of the power in the localities to the toiling peasantry'. The Bolshevik resolution, which received ninety-four votes, made no reference to the question of power but advocated 'the confiscation of all land and inventory and their transfer to the authority of the Soviets of Peasants' and Agricultural Labourers' Deputies' as a solution to 'the economic and political crisis' and as conducive to 'rallying the poorest peasantry in the defence of the revolution'.

Both the resolutions and the debate were an early reflection of the radical composition and mood of the new Kronstadt Soviet. More important still, while the question of power had, until the April Crisis, always been viewed and solved in Kronstadt within its local confines, it was now beginning to be seen and debated by Kronstadters, both in the Soviet and in Anchor Square, as a major all-Russian issue of profound concern to them, too. In addition to the Bolsheviks, with their war-cry 'All Power to Soviets', there were now the SRs under the radical leadership of Alexander Brushvit and Konstantin Shurgin who saw a Kronstadt-style 'assumption of power in the localities' as providing the solution to the problem of power which so bedevilled the Russian revolution. As Nikolai Rostov observed, with apprehension: 'Having almost totally uprooted the old regime, and seeing no more enemies before them, they think that such is the position in the whole of Russia! The revolution has turned only its glorious face on them here; they seem almost completely unaware of the difficulties and dangers besetting the mainland.'[156]

That misunderstanding of Russian realities, coupled with pride in their own achievement and a growing suspicion that the comrades in Petrograd who had entered the coalition government were forgetting their revolutionary business, was soon to bring the Kronstadters into head-on conflict both with the provisional government and with the Petrograd Soviet.

3

The Kronstadt Republic

With the formation on 5 May of the first coalition government, 'reinforced' by six representatives of the 'revolutionary democracy', to guarantee its 'fullness of power',[1] Commissar Victor Pepeliaev may have regarded the time ripe to strengthen both his own feeble and largely decorative authority and that of the new government.

His opportunity came when the Kronstadt Soviet, as was its wont, confirmed the appointment, as chief of the Kronstadt militia, of H. I. Orvid who assumed his duties on 13 May with the blessings of the municipal Duma. Pepeliaev had thus been completely ignored in an appointment that he may have had some reason to regard as within his purview.[2] He may also have resented the Kronstadt Soviet's 12 May decision to tighten its control over the town commandant by flanking him with a permanent representative of the Soviet equipped with 'wide plenary powers'.[3] No longer prepared to acquiesce, Pepeliaev remonstrated with the Soviet's Executive Committee, only to be told, 'This is what we have decided and we shall act accordingly, and no one can force us to depart from this decision.'[4] To put Pepeliaev firmly in his place and make sure, once and for all, that there was no doubt that in Kronstadt 'power is concentrated in one body alone', on 13 May the Executive Committee resolved, subject to confirmation by the plenary meeting of the Soviet, as a 'decision of principle', that:

the sole power in the city of Kronstadt is the Soviet of Workers' and Soldiers' Deputies, which in all matters of state enters into direct contact with the provisional government.

All administrative posts in the city of Kronstadt are to be occupied by members of the Executive Committee, while resultant vacancies in the Executive Committee are to be filled by a corresponding number of members of the Soviet of Workers' and Soldiers' Deputies.

Candidates for administrative posts are to be proposed by the [political] factions, who will be responsible for their activities.[5]

The resolution was duly published in the Kronstadt *Izvestiia* on the following day, where it appeared on the front page. Pepeliaev could have left it at that and, as in the past, have allowed the incident and the indignity to be 'hushed up and patched over',[6] but this time he decided to resign, and on 15 May he informed the Executive Committee of the Kronstadt Soviet and the minister-president, Prince Georgii Lvov, that he could no longer regard himself as 'responsible for Kronstadt'.[7] He intended, so he told a conference of former Duma deputies on 27 May, to appeal to 'the public opinion of the entire country' against Kronstadt and in particular to 'contrapose Kronstadt to the Petrograd Soviet' in the hope that this would lead to 'the liquidation of the Kronstadt affair'.[8] If such was his intention, he certainly succeeded in provoking a major conflict between the Kronstadt Soviet on the one hand and the provisional government and the Petrograd Soviet on the other, the bone of contention being the question of sovereignty in Kronstadt. The Kronstadt Soviet played into his hands when it made both its own resolution of 13 May and his letter of resignation the subject of the Soviet's general meeting on 16 May where it became the focus of Kronstadt's major debate on power.

The Soviet deputies were certainly well briefed. Early in May they had discussed the April Crisis at length and many had swallowed their considerable misgivings when, by a small majority, they had endorsed the Petrograd Soviet's decision to join the government. But the new Kronstadt Soviet had many more radicals who were strongly opposed to coalition than the old Soviet had. The majority of the SRs were, together with Alexander Brushvit, committed to 'take power in the villages' and 'in the localities', while the massive Bolshevik faction linked its war-cry 'All Power to Soviets' with contempt for the Petrograd Soviet which had, as Liubovich had sneeringly put it at the session of 12 May, 'refused to take power' during the April Crisis, 'when it was begging to be taken'.[9]

On 14 May, Kronstadt heard the 'internationalists' Trotsky and Grigorii Chudnovsky arguing it out with the Menshevik Mark Broido both in the Soviet and in Anchor Square in a debate[10] that marked Trotsky's debut in Kronstadt and the beginning of that special relationship which made him its tribune and advocate in Petrograd. Trotsky's visit was certainly well timed. He arrived in the morning of 14 May when the front page of Kronstadt's *Izvestiia* carried the Executive Committee's resolution of the previous day, and two days before the plenary meeting of the Soviet was to be convened to debate and confirm it. While it is difficult to assess Trotsky's contribution to that debate, he certainly helped the Kronstadters to clarify and sharpen the issue.

His appearance in the Soviet was a festive occasion. Lamanov, as he was wont to, greeted him and Chudnovsky as representatives of 'the International' just returned from 'far-away exile', and used this as an occasion to proclaim his own internationalist *credo*, perfectly attuned to the sentiments and hopes of his audience, that 'only the unity of the working masses of the entire world will bring about the victory of socialism' when there would be no slaves 'neither political nor economic', when the toilers themselves would rule, and no one would have the power to 'drive one nation against the other into fratricidal war'.

Leaving revolutionary poetry to Lamanov, Trotsky, in acerbic prose, denounced the coalitionist policy of the Petrograd Soviet as 'wrong' and 'terribly mistaken'. If it had not felt strong enough to take power, it should have remained in sharply critical opposition to the government awaiting the moment of 'inevitable crisis', when it could take 'the entire power'. He then lashed out at Victor Chernov, now Minister of Agriculture, who had proved a 'minister of agrarian statistics' when what was needed was a minister of 'agrarian revolution' who would tell the peasants to 'take the land into their own hands under the supervision of the Soviet of Peasants' Deputies' and thus turn each and every one of them, 'even the darkest of yesterday's monarchists', into a 'fervent supporter of the revolution'.

Worse still, Trotsky argued, the Petrograd Soviet had not only failed during the April Crisis and on the agrarian question, but had also joined a government that prohibited fraternization between opposing front-line soldiers when it was this that was the beginning of 'peace-making from below', for, starting in one section, fraternization would spread 'like fire' along the entire front. It would not make for a 'separate peace', as some had argued, but was the 'only road' towards the liquidation of war and militarism.

The task on hand, as Trotsky saw it then, was to prise loose the Petrograd Soviet, 'the supreme institution of the Russian revolution', from the propertied classes by working 'within its framework' to change its composition.

Mark Broido spoke next, reminding Trotsky and the Kronstadters that the Petrograd Soviet's 'political line' enjoyed the overwhelming support both of its own deputies and of the Soviets of Russia at large and that its leadership had been recognized both by the Conference of Soviets (in Petrograd on 1 April), and the Congress of Delegates from the Front (in Minsk on 11 April) alike. To take power now, as Trotsky urged, would mean nothing less than the upheaval of a premature 'social revolution', while the present still called for a 'democratic bourgeois revolution' carried out by the 'democratic masses'. Unperturbed by the whistling and catcalls which greeted this statement, Broido reminded his audience that, as far back as 1905, Trotsky had advocated 'social revolution', and he had been proved wrong then, too. He was also wrong 'now', in a Russia where some 75% of the people were still illiterate and where there was a vast peasant mass not yet ready for the 'kingdom of socialism'. Since Russia was backward and still unprepared for a 'socialist order', it made little sense to form a Soviet government which, 'by the nature of things, and by popular pressure', would be compelled to confiscate 'factories, plants and private property'.

Seeing that his exposition of the Menshevik concept of bourgeois revolution, with its self-denying ordinance extending even to respect for private property, had provoked the crowd to a burst of derisive whistling, catcalls, uproar and even outright hostility, Broido swore that he was no defender of private property, but an 'old social democrat'. True, it would be easy enough to overthrow the government, but it would be quite another thing to cope with the power thus given them, together with the economic dislocation, the war, and possibly even with civil war. 'True, we are afraid, for we feel responsible for the Russian revolution, and we do not want civil war.'

Referring to Trotsky's trust in fraternization and in the imminence of revolution in the West, Broido wondered whether Russia's fate or the question of war and peace should be made dependent on the 'problematic expectation of revolution in other countries'. He felt sure that the forthcoming Zimmerwald conference of the socialist parties of belligerent and neutral countries to be convened in July in Stockholm, which the Bolsheviks had rejected, would provide a far better arena for the search for peace than either fraternization or that conference of small revolutionary groups which the Bolsheviks favoured.

It was Broido's nightmare – a Soviet government which would, in

spite of itself, 'confiscate factories, plants and private property' –
that was Chudnovsky's ready solution to Russia's economic crisis.
Nor did Russian backwardness and illiteracy worry him unduly:
'What percentage of literates is required for the construction of
socialism?' he asked Broido. Like Trotsky, he saw the Russian
revolution's immediate task as endowing the peasants with the land,
whereby 'we prepare the world revolution for those countries which
are already ripe for socialism'. They, in turn, would give Russia 'a
push towards socialism', and thus, 'the wave sweeping from one part
of the world to the other will also lift us up to the highest crest of
socialism'.

Asked how peace would be achieved, Chudnovsky had a ready
answer: 'We shall take power into our own hands and then the
democratic masses of France and England will raise their voice in
defence of the nations' rights against their own bourgeoisie and
governments'; subsequently, the same would happen with the
'German proletarians' and those in other enemy countries. His
admission that these latter might 'not rise tomorrow' was greeted
with angry uproar, whereupon Trotsky jumped to his rescue, lashing
out against all the doubting Thomases, including that anonymous
Kronstadter who interjected that 'there will be no revolution in
Germany!':

I lived in France for two years during the war, and I'm telling you that
France is closer to social revolution than any other country . . . If it's the
fate of the Russian revolution as a whole that concerns you, then you had
better grasp this: whatever turn the war may take, unless there is a social
revolution in Europe, England and Germany will crush us anyway. That is
how the question stands.

With seizure of power by the Russian Soviets being the linchpin
in his scheme of European revolution, Trotsky then appealed to the
Kronstadters:

You yourselves have drafted a resolution about taking power into your
hands! Don't you agree that what is sauce for the goose is sauce for the
gander, and what is good for Kronstadt is also good for any other town?

It is you who stand in the front line, while the others have fallen behind.
It is up to you to call on them to adopt your standpoint. What you have to
say is: we are standing firm as a rock, and you too must stand firm, take
power into your own hands and demand that the central power of Russia be
transferred to the Soviet of Workers' and Soldiers' Deputies.

Since Lamanov cut the debate short so as not to deprive the 'popular
masses' already assembled in Anchor Square of 'the opportunity to

hear our guests',[11] there is no way of gauging the impact made on the Kronstadt Soviet by Trotsky's and Chudnovsky's breath-taking vista of European revolution. The Menshevik P. Ia. Golikov, who happened to be present, thought Trotsky did far better in Anchor Square than in the Soviet.[12] There can be no doubt, however, that Broido's call for self-restraint and his warning against seizure of power both fell on deaf ears.

On 16 May 1917 the Soviet assembled to debate[13] the resolution of 13 May, and it was a great day in the history of Kronstadt. The Soviet's agenda and the business transacted before Lamanov opened the grand debate were fully worthy of the occasion and quite staggering in range. Beginning somewhat festively, with five speeches of welcome (one delivered by Lamanov and four by spokesmen of the various political factions) to Anatolii Lunacharsky, just returned from exile, the meeting went on to hear Lunacharsky's reply and his praise of internationalism and of the Zimmerwald socialist peace movement. With the ceremonial part completed, the 'regular business' began.

Item 1. The 'struggle against drunkenness': the draft decree which declared all drunkards 'enemies of the revolution and liable to deportation to the front-line army' was described by its mover, Alexander Brushvit, as 'brutal' but necessary, since drunkenness was the result of 'extreme irresponsibility and a weakness in the human personality', leading to such 'outrageous' exploits as a recent armed attack on a wine store. Lebedev, seconding Brushvit's motion and speaking on behalf of the Bolshevik faction, concurred that it was 'hard, and even inhuman', but added that drunkenness was nothing less than a 'retreat from the revolutionary movement', to be punished 'mercilessly'. On the motion of the Bolshevik sailor Pankratov it was decided to set up a Commission for the Struggle against Drunkenness and Prostitution consisting of eight members, two from each political faction, to supervise the implementation of the decree which was passed unanimously, and subsequently published in big letters on the front page of Kronstadt's *Izvestiia*:[14] 'All drunkards are herewith declared enemies of the revolution. The property of those observed selling alcoholic and generally intoxicating drinks will be subject to immediate confiscation, while those convicted of drunkenness will be sent to the front immediately.' Armed with this ferocious decree, the commission was expected to succeed where Viren's five temperance societies had failed.

Item 2. A telephonogramme from the Central Committee of the Baltic Fleet was read requesting the despatch of a delegate from the Kronstadt Soviet as 'liaison'. The meeting voted in favour of electing and sending one, who 'must be a sailor'.

Item 3. Lamanov moved the introduction of a system of food rationing to ensure that reserves of bread would last until the new harvest, and that the bread be distributed equitably and not, as in the past, that the ships' crews receive a ration of only 600 grammes of bread per day, while bread was freely sold in the shops. After a short debate which established the principle of the 'equitable distribution of foodstuffs', it was resolved to put 'all town citizens' on a system of food rationing and to instruct the food commission to set up and administer a ration-card system as a matter of urgency.

Item 4. Approval was given for the co-option to the editorial commission of Kronstadt's *Izvestiia*, with full voting rights, of G. Petrov, member of the Non-Party group; but the proviso was made that the party balance on the commission be maintained in accordance with that obtaining in the Soviet.

Item 5. Lamanov complained about commissioners 'whose work is not in evidence' and admonished them to 'start work forthwith' for 'we cannot live by ideals alone, we must also practise them'. Singled out was the estimates commission, whose members were told to start work immediately on the 'standardization of wages'.

Item 6. The setting up of a supreme control commission to supervise all other commissions and committees, including the Executive Committee, was moved. There was some disagreement as to whether its members should be elected from the body of the Soviet or from the Executive Committee. A. Nemm urged that election from the Executive Committee would be tantamount to the latter being given power to 'control itself', whereupon election from the Soviet was decided on by 128 to 98 votes.

Item 7. N. Priselkov, secretary of the Soviet, reported that on the previous day a 'band of armed men' had illegally occupied the officers' wing of the Naval Assembly, named it the Anarcho-Communist club, and only thereafter informed the Soviet's housing commission of their *fait accompli*.

The central issue in the ensuing debate was what to do with the Anarchists who had won recognition as an extreme faction of the 'revolutionary democracy' and were therefore entitled to a 'free existence in Kronstadt', but would not, for their part, and 'on principle', recognize the authority of the Soviet, 'the only real power in Kronstadt'; when reprimanded and told to submit, so the Soviet learned, they had even threatened the Executive Committee with violence. Lebedev made light of this 'ridiculous' threat, since 'we represent the entire Kronstadt garrison', while they are but a 'bunch of some thirty people'. Brushvit, too, tried to play down the incident as 'utterly childish', but thought the Anarchists should be reminded that they were no longer dealing 'with [Governor] Viren, but with the Soviet of Workers' and Soldiers' Deputies'; he recommended asking them to appear before a 'comradely conciliation court' that would deal with the dispute. On the other hand, the Menshevik Glazko thought that in taking the field 'against us' the Anarchists had treated 'our power as we have treated the old power'; thus, they should not be allowed to establish themselves in Kronstadt, otherwise 'we ourselves will not be recognized as a political power'. Alnichenkov, the second Menshevik speaker, had a simple solution: first of all, the Anarchists must be evicted, and only when this had been done could they then be given premises by the housing commission. Eventually it was agreed that the Anarchists must be persuaded, and if need be forced, to accept the authority of the Soviet. But that was precisely what the Anarchist spokesmen, Numtsev and Savich, who proved anything but 'childish' when they appeared in the Soviet, refused to do. Numtsev rejected any 'binding subordination' to the Soviet: 'We, as Anarcho-Communists, can support a power only to the extent that it executes our will', he proclaimed, adding that he and his fellows could not recognize 'a power which contradicts our interests'. Savich, for his part, insisted that they were guided solely 'by our conscience and by the people'. He then taunted Brushvit for having set the example himself by taking possession of Viren's villa and installing both the Zemlia i Volia club and the SR offices there. (Not that Brushvit took this lying down, for, with Lamanov confirming his words, he told Savich that *his* action had been authorized by the Executive Committee.)

At this point, Lunacharsky broke in with a plea for an 'amicable solution', treating his patient audience to an off-the-cuff lecture on the virtues of Anarchism as distinct from the excesses of ignorant Anarchists. Foma Parchevsky then joined in for good measure, offering his own learned and long-winded definition of Anarchism which seems to have clinched the matter, for Lamanov closed the debate and it was decided that the Anarcho-Communists must first accept the authority of the Soviet and only then would they be allowed to retain the club.

Lunacharsky sat it out, witnessed it all and fulsomely thanked the Kronstadt Soviet for the 'shining minutes' experienced in their midst, promising to report them in the socialist press abroad as proof that 'the Russian people was capable of a strictly organized order'. Alas, he then had to rush off to the mass meeting awaiting his distinguished presence in Anchor Square where he treated a very responsive audience to a 'passionate and inspired speech' and to glorious vistas of the future.[15] Thus, he missed Item 8, Kronstadt's major debate on power and 'declaration of independence' which challenged the anything but 'strictly organized' political order established by the February revolution in Russia and brought Kronstadt into head-on conflict with both the provisional government and the Petrograd Soviet.

Opening the debate,[16] Lamanov explained that in adopting the resolution of 13 May, which he now submitted to the general meeting of the Soviet, the Executive Committee had been guided by the idea that 'the aspiration of the democracy leads in the direction of power belonging to the Soviets as the real representatives of the democratic masses.' Nevertheless, he wanted it clearly understood that Kronstadt wished only to solve its own problems and to ensure that there be no interference with the decrees of the Kronstadt Soviet on local matters only. As for matters pertaining to the 'general laws' of Russia, there could be no question of each locality legislating these as it saw fit, for this would be tantamount to making each a 'separate republic'. With this consideration in mind, the Executive Committee had declared that it could not make its own laws on 'matters of state'.

The leaders of the party 'factions', Brushvit for the SRs, Lebedev for the Bolsheviks, Malyshev for the Mensheviks and Parchevsky for the Non-Party group, were the first to speak, with Brushvit and the SRs dominating the debate. Agreeing with Lamanov that there must be a recognized central state power and that Kronstadt must be in contact with it, Brushvit said that on the other hand, as socialists, they stood for 'far-reaching autonomy' and the 'local rights' of every individual territorial unit which should also have its own legislative and executive powers, free from interference by the central state power, except in matters pertaining to the 'state as a whole'. It was on this ground that the Executive Committee had been of the opinion that 'in the city of Kronstadt it is the Soviet of Workers' and

Soldiers' Deputies that is the sole legislative and executive power'. As for the commissar, his presence in Kronstadt was the result of a 'misunderstanding' dating back to the February revolution, when 'propertied Russia', by way of the Duma committee, which defied the tsar's order to disperse on 26 February 1917, had claimed that it too had made the revolution and had then formed the provisional government which, in turn, had appointed the commissars. Now, however, when 'we stand for the transfer of all power to the Soviets', it followed that contact between the central power and the local power, i.e. the Kronstadt Soviet, regarding 'matters of state importance' be by way of a commissar whom the Soviet itself had elected. The question then was where Russia's central power was located:

I am of the opinion that the central power is the Soviet of Workers' and Soldiers' Deputies of the city of Petrograd, since the coalition government is merely its executive organ, a body set up on the basis of a definite platform, which the Petrograd Soviet can remove at any given moment, replacing it with a more suitable executor of its will.

For that reason, and on behalf of the SR faction which had discussed the resolution and found it wanting, he proposed the following amendment: 'The sole power in the city of Kronstadt is the Soviet of Workers' and Soldiers' Deputies which, in matters of state, enters into direct relations with the Petrograd Soviet.' Seeing the Petrograd Soviet as the central state power to which they should address themselves, he thus urged all those who 'correctly understand' the situation in Russia to vote for the amendment.

Mikhail Lebedev, speaking on behalf of the Bolshevik faction, welcomed and supported Brushvit's amendment as reflecting a stance that was close to the Bolshevik's advocacy of 'one single state power of the Soviet of Workers' and Soldiers' Deputies in the whole of Russia', but not before he had patronizingly complimented the SRs for 'acquiring clearer consciousness' and thus, as 'socialists in the full sense of the term', moving closer to the Bolshevik position. Since the Bolshevik leaders Raskolnikov, Liubovich, Roshal and Bregman had gone to Anchor Square with Lunacharsky, it fell to lesser lights such as Nikolai Pozharov and Vasilii Aleshin to denounce coalition as tantamount to giving the capitalists 'the decisive voice' in the government, leaving the Soviets 'responsible but powerless', and this was the Bolsheviks' sole contribution in a debate which was clearly dominated by the SRs.

The opposition to Brushvit's amendment came from the Mensheviks Pavel Malyshev and Piotr Ediet and from the Non-Party spokesman Foma Parchevsky. Malyshev could not resist harking back to the 'bourgeois' character and limitations of the Russian revolution which, he claimed, 'even the Bolsheviks do not deny'; consequently, the proletariat must not seize power yet since, if it did, 'all reproaches will fall on it'. Only then did he take issue with Brushvit: the term 'sole power' used in the amendment made little sense, said Malyshev, when, as everyone agreed, Kronstadt claimed power only with regard to matters of local import. Nor could they, who were all committed to the principle of universal franchise, share Brushvit's view of the Soviets as 'fully democratically elected institutions' when in fact they represented only the 'revolutionary democracy', to the exclusion of the propertied strata of the population. Most important of all, while the Petrograd Soviet controlled the provisional government in all sorts of ways, it had for all that decided against assuming the 'plenitude of power' as this would have burdened it with the entire responsibility for the conduct of the war and would also have provoked civil war. He then moved a resolution on behalf of the Menshevik faction.

Ediet, the other Menshevik speaker, thought that while it made a distinction between matters of local and state importance, the amendment failed to spell out who would decide what was what, and that thus it invited dissension and conflict. Moreover, since the Petrograd Soviet took a very different view of what was, and ought to be, Russia's state power, this amendment, far from bringing Kronstadt closer to the Petrograd Soviet, would rather 'tear us apart'.

Parchevsky, speaking for the Non-Party group which, as he claimed, tried to 'soften party dissensions', moved the original resolution. Professing to adopt a pragmatic view of things, he said that the 'real facts' were that the provisional government, regardless of the 'patent agitation against it', did exist and its existence was favoured by the Petrograd Soviet. There was, therefore, no reason why they in Kronstadt should 'sever contact' with it, and, if they found Commissar Pepeliaev 'undesirable', then they should have their 'own representative'. But he was still not sure that they should really assume 'all administrative power' at a time when there were 'incompetent commissions', few volunteers for 'simple humdrum work', and insufficient people to man all positions.

With the SRs rallying behind Brushvit and dominating the debate, one SR speaker after the other laboured to explain away the paradox in Brushvit's amendment which endowed the Petrograd Soviet with governmental authority, while that body itself would have nothing of the sort, but recognized the supreme authority of the provisional government and was determined to strengthen it.

Stepan Sokolov harped on the distinction between the sovereign legislature and its executive: the Kronstadt Soviet, recognizing the Petrograd Soviet as the 'legislature', would turn to it as to the supreme authority, while the Petrograd Soviet, if it so wished, would refer the Kronstadt Soviet, in matters political, economic and of 'the state as a whole', to the provisional government as the 'executor of its will'. That subtle distinction adduced in solution of the awkward problem was unacceptable to such young SR hotheads as Fiodor Pokrovsky, Boris Donskoi and D. Kalabushev. To them, the real meaning of the amendment was that 'it was desirable that the power at last be transferred to the Soviets' (Pokrovsky), for power, as Kalabushev urged, ought to belong to the majority, i.e. to the Soviets who represented 'almost the entire population', and not to the small group of bourgeois. To the impulsive Donskoi, the amendment was simply a call 'to take power in the localities', a move that would prod the Petrograd Soviet into saying: 'Down with the government!'

Konstantin Shurgin rounded off the debate: there was no need for either a commissar or even a representative of the provisional government since they in Kronstadt had long enjoyed real power, the commissar being merely a 'figleaf' with which they had 'bashfully covered' themselves. In his view:

the cart of the revolution, with the bourgeoisie in harness and the Petrograd Soviet sitting on the coachbox and holding the reins, is now rolling along. This is fair enough as long as the little beast continues to pull, but it is now beginning to stop here and there. So the Soviet must pull hard on the reins and, dismounting from the coachbox, must help the little beast along: should the beast come to a complete stop, the Soviet will have to unharness it and pull the cart on its own. This may prove hard and difficult, but at least the cart will be on the move rather than standing still.

Shurgin's analysis of the situation met with applause and seems to have clinched matters, for when the vote was taken, the amended resolution received 211 votes, including those of the Mensheviks, as against only 41 for the original version. Thus, Russia was told that:

The sole power in the city of Kronstadt is the Soviet of Workers' and Soldiers' Deputies which, in matters of state, enters into direct relations with the Petrograd Soviet of Workers' and Soldiers' Deputies. All administrative posts are to be filled by members of the Executive Committee or by persons so authorized by it.[17]

Naturally enough, both Kronstadt's *Izvestiia* and the Bolshevik *Golos pravdy* fully supported this 'declaration'. However, while Liubovich, writing in *Izvestiia*,[18] played it down as nothing more than a 'formalization of an existing situation' and described Pepeliaev's resignation as the 'timely and painless removal of an appendix', the *Golos pravdy*, in its editorial,[19] held it up as an example to others and as a blueprint for the future:

The Kronstadters have no wish to be the aristocrats of the revolution, the denizens of the only island where the Soviet of Workers' and Soldiers' Deputies has declared itself the revolutionary government. For the Kronstadters fully understand that their own work will only come to full fruition when all power belongs completely and undividedly to the Soviets of Workers' and Soldiers' Deputies both in the localities and in the centre. May the Kronstadt commune serve as an example to others. What is good for us is also good for Petrograd, is also good for Russia as a whole.

The only dissonant voice, and that came from outside the Soviet, was that of A. Khanokh who, writing in Kronstadt's moderate Trudovik newspaper *Trud, zemlia i more*, lectured the Kronstadt Soviet that by treating the provisional government contemptuously it was also 'insulting the Petrograd Soviet which sent its representatives there', and this could not have been its intention. He therefore called for 'more sincerity, equanimity and deliberation!'[20]

Kronstadt's declaration burst like a bombshell in Petrograd, sparking off a gleeful furore among the right and plunging the left into embarrassment and consternation. The moderate and right-wing newspapers, ranging from *Edinstvo, Rech'*, and *Birzhevye vedomosti* to *Novoe vremia*, pounced on it to highlight the need for 'strong government', and to discredit the Soviets and the provisional government as 'impotent' and thus goad them into action against Bolshevik and anarchist Kronstadt.

The *Rech'* saw in the 'triumphant declaration of a Kronstadt republic' the 'crowning' achievement of Kronstadt's two-month-long period of 'separatism',[21] while Plekhanov's *Edinstvo* (edited by the notorious Grigorii Alexinsky) and Potresov's *Den'* published the faked facsimile of a 'temporary voucher', or banknote, allegedly issued by the 'Kronstadt Republic', as incontrovertible evidence of

Kronstadt's 'secession from the All-Russian Republic'. The Executive Committee of the Kronstadt Soviet could only denounce the forgery as a 'dirty lie', threaten legal action, appeal to the First Congress of Soviets 'to refute rumours of Kronstadt's "anarchy" ' and request the provisional government through the commissar to 'reject all rumours regarding a Kronstadt "republic" and Kronstadt vouchers'.[22]

The *Birzhevye vedomosti* carried reports on the 'Kronstadt Republic' as a matter of course and, telling its readers that all power there had passed into the hands of 'Bolsheviks of the most extreme shades', called for action: 'Enough! The moment when action is needed may be very near!'[23]

But it was the *Novoe vremia* that capped it all, with an unsigned *and* unfounded report on Kronstadt drunkenness describing the 'endless numbers . . . of drunken soldiers, sailors and ordinary citizens of the Free City of Kronstadt lying all across the quay and the park, near factories and barracks', and regaling readers with its own 'good-humoured' explanation of the Kronstadt act of secession: 'Kotlin resolved on secession at the very moment when the provisional government decided to lock up all drunkards in jail and send all drunken brawlers off to *katorga*.'[24]

The Kronstadters, who had really gone all out to fight alcoholism and public drunkenness and had initially by and large succeeded, were mightily proud of their achievement and were certainly not amused. 'Peregrinus', a *Delo naroda* reporter, was in Anchor Square on 21 May when, after a memorial procession had filed past and laid wreaths on the tombs of the martyrs of the 1905–6 revolution, a front-line soldier reported what the newspapers wrote about Kronstadt: 'Workers do not work, soldiers refuse to go to the front, there is mutual hatred among the political parties, the town is full of wholesale drunkenness and robberies.' Then, 'Peregrinus' wrote:

Suddenly, as if it were being tossed like a football, one word was taken up by the crowd: 'Confiscate!' Then came the cries: 'A resolution!' Someone with a feverish glitter in his eyes was already on the step of the rostrum scribbling away. When the marshals told the crowd they could disperse, the Kronstadters shouted: 'No! No! First the resolution on confiscation!' One and then another volunteered help in its drafting, within seconds more authors with pencils and pieces of paper squatted at the foot of the rostrum.

'Peregrinus' did not stay and thus could not report whether or not a resolution was eventually adopted, yet he did note that: 'in this categorical demand for the immediate confiscation of all bourgeois newspapers I instantly felt the true pulse of Kronstadt, the heat of that fever which has wholly overcome this peculiar town'.[25]

The press campaign against Kronstadt was backed up by detailed reports on the very depressing, if not outrageous, conditions in its prisons and the callous, almost inhuman, though nevertheless correct, treatment meted out to the officers still kept there without trial.

Disregarding the clearly slanderous and vicious reports of the *Novoe vremia*,[26] the factual and quite fair reports of the Associated Press correspondent, Robert Crozier Young, published in *Rech'*[27] and those by the SR reporter, Evgenii Trupp, appearing in *Delo naroda*[28] both tell a story of institutionalized vindictiveness and cruelty. Worst of all was the frightening uncertainty, in the absence of any formal accusation and trial, surrounding the fate of those officers who knew that they were in the hands of sailors and soldiers who had murdered many of their fellow officers and who, while they controlled their hatred towards the 'class enemy', nevertheless did not disguise it. Even as sympathetic and indulgent a visitor as Philips Price was appalled:

I left the prisons and tried to forget what I had seen. For they contained men who were punished for being agents of a cruel system which was after all their only means of livelihood. There were others who had served that system because they were educated in an atmosphere which made them see nothing but good in it. But these agents of the old regime were now being punished by men who had suffered far more than they were now inflicting.[29]

And, indeed, their hatred was relentless. The protocol of the Soviet debate of 8 May on the petition of the officers' relatives to allow them to visit them twice a week with food parcels, published in the Kronstadt *Izvestiia* on 18 May,[30] must have made very sad reading both to the imprisoned officers and their families. Even Lamanov's and Piotr Ediet's desperate appeals to the prudence of the Kronstadt Soviet at a time when 'we are running short of humane feelings' proved of no avail and was drowned out by the shrill call of the wild Anarcho-Communist Bleikhman to 'throttle and choke them' and to defer 'magnanimity' and 'humanism' until 'after we have seized power and shall then love the whole world'. It was the Kronstadt Soviet, and not some wild sailor crowd in Anchor Square, which, after a lengthy debate in which at least fifteen deputies spoke, rejected both Lamanov's urgent plea and the relatives' petition by 157 to 89 votes with 8 abstentions.

Whatever may have been its effect on the Petrograd Soviet and the government in goading them into action, the press campaign against Kronstadt certainly succeeded in making the fate of the imprisoned officers a public issue.

But even the left was, to say the least, embarrassed by the Kronstadt declaration of power. The independent left-wing *Novaia zhizn'*, while dissociating itself from the slander of the 'bourgeois' press, branded it 'a purely anarchist act' which could be neither justified nor tolerated.[31]

Lev Kamenev, in *Pravda*, played down the Kronstadt affair but at the same time insisted that, contrary to what was generally believed, the Bolsheviks had not masterminded it: they were a minority in the Kronstadt Soviet and in any case, as a party, were generally against local seizure of power; furthermore:

of course, the Kronstadt comrades know perfectly well that there is nothing more dangerous than taking power piecemeal, in different areas, towns and districts. In taking the administration of Kronstadt into their hands, they did not establish a 'Kronstadt Republic' that was separate from Russia . . . but only realized the right of the local population to run their *own local* town affairs.[32]

In a similar vein, Lenin, too, defended the Kronstadters' right to enjoy local autonomy and to elect their own commissar, backing up his case by invoking the principle of 'democratism' and the authority of Engels who, in his critique of the Erfurt programme of German social democracy of 1891, had championed 'complete self-government in the local commune, district and province to be administered by officials elected in general elections'.[33] This tallied with Lenin's own revolutionary strategy as he jotted it down for the April Conference of the Bolshevik Party; he expected the transition to 'the second phase of revolution' to begin with the establishment of local *de facto* revolutionary power rather than by seizure of power in the capitals.[34]

Nonetheless, in private, Lenin severely rebuked the Kronstadt Bolsheviks for having involved themselves in the Kronstadt affair without prior consultation with the Bolshevik Central Committee; this was a violation of 'elementary party discipline' and for actions of this nature, he told Raskolnikov whom he had summoned post-haste to Petrograd, 'We shall shoot!' Moreover, it was both 'utopian and a clear absurdity' to take power in Kronstadt alone, just as it had been bad tactics to advertise that it was the Soviet which controlled Kronstadt by removing the 'harmless' Pepeliaev who had served them so well as an 'umbrella'. Thus rebuked, Raskolnikov promised to report to Lenin daily by telephone on all 'the most important matters of Kronstadt's political life', and it was from then that Lenin 'personally . . . guided the more important activities of our Kronstadt party organization'.[35] So seriously did Lenin view the episode that, only a few days later, he cited it as one which 'has undoubtedly harmed the party', adducing it as proof that central party control was 'indispensable'.[36]

On the radical left, only the SR-Internationalists (later called Left SRs), and Trotsky's own small group of 'Mezhraiontsy' (Inter-Districtites) who soon joined the Bolsheviks, gave the Kronstadters unqualified support. The left SR *Zemlia i volia* complimented Kronstadt on its 'healthy, vigorous process of construction' and congratulated itself on the 'predominating influence' of the SRs there: 'Both socialists and all true democrats, too, must recognize in the "Kronstadt anarchy" that order which we want to achieve, not just for the whole of Russia, but for Europe as well.'[37]

In the same vein, if not in the same words, Dmitrii Manuilsky (Bezrabotnyi) in Trotsky's *Vpered* held up Kronstadt's 'model order' and cultural creativity as worthy even of the envy of 'Europeans who can look back on decades of parliamentary life', and lashed out against the 'bandits of the pen' of the bourgeois press who had exaggerated the 'incident' and used it as a 'provocation' to split the revolutionary democracy.[38]

The notoriously radical and rebellious First Regiment of Machine-Gunners stationed in Petrograd went even further and may have embarrassed the Kronstadters somewhat when, on 28 May, they came out in an armed demonstration in support of Kronstadt's sailors and soldiers and their 'staunch position of non-confidence in the provisional government'.[39]

On 19 May, just after the Kronstadt resolution had burst on Petrograd and as the first reports of the furore and consternation it had caused were filtering back, Kronstadt celebrated the visit of Robert Grimm and Angelica Balabanova, the secretaries of the Zimmerwald movement, as guests of the local SRs. A festive procession complete with flags and two bands led them from the Zemlia i Volia club to Anchor Square and there to the graves of the martyrs of the revolution. After the Funeral March had been played, Robert Grimm, speaking in French, with Angelica Balabanova translating into Russian, addressed a crowd of some 15,000 assembled

there. Grimm spoke of the importance of the Russian revolution for
the rebirth of the International and for its victory over 'our common
enemy – European capitalism'; then, with the crowd growing ever
larger, the procession moved on to the Soviet in the former Naval
Assembly and, there now being over 20,000 people, to the Naval
Manège. Here, in his major speech, Grimm complimented the
Kronstadters on their achievements: 'May God give the entire
world such "anarchy" of liberty, fraternity and justice' as there was
in Kronstadt, he said, for their liberty was greater even than could
be found in the most democratic countries of Europe, including his
own Switzerland. Kronstadt's and Russia's struggle for bread and
peace and the socialization of the land was only 'the first step
towards the emancipation of labour' but it would prove a 'powerful
factor in the social revolution of the West'. For in Kronstadt, that
'world-renowned citadel of the Russian Revolution', he had heard
the still small voice of the socialist internationalism of Zimmerwald
and Kienthal resound in a 'mighty accord' which was bound to
reverberate all over the world. 'Long live the Great Russian Revolution, the beginning of social revolution, the International!' he
concluded, his enthusiasm echoed by the vast crowd which responded
with 'an ovation the like of which had never been heard before'
in Kronstadt.[40]

Sceptical Parchevsky, who was there and could not quite grasp
why these vast crowds were giving so enthusiastic a reception and
hearing to strangers of foreign origin addressing them in French and
in German, asked one 'comrade', whom he had watched all attention
and agog during Grimm's French speech, how he liked it. 'I did not
understand a thing', came the answer, 'but my word, he did speak
well!'[41]

A better explanation was spelt out in the resolution adopted by
the meeting of 20,000 'sailors, soldiers and workers' who assembled
to honour 'comrades Grimm and Balabanova'. The two were
greeted as the 'representatives of the working masses of all countries',
as fighters against 'the imperialist governments', as those champion-
ing a peace which would pave the way both to 'the construction
of a life based on social justice, and to socialism'.[42]

Thus it was that they honoured Zimmerwald and expressed their
hopes for peace and for a better world:

Comrades Grimm and Balabanova were borne aloft on their shoulders with
music and songs all the way from the Naval Manège to the pier where a

special ship awaited them. Never before had Kronstadt witnessed such a send-off. The entire shore and the entire pier were covered with a densely packed mass of people shouting hoorah, waving kerchiefs and trying in every possible way to express that solidarity which unites Kronstadt with the International, and the cries of hoorah echoed back and forth as they were taken up by the crews on the ships.

To Priselkov, secretary of the Kronstadt Soviet, who was present and who reported it for *Zemlia i volia*, 'It was an unforgettable day. A very telling demonstration and full of promise.'[43]

It may well have been Kronstadt's last day of innocent radicalism before it plunged headlong into a confrontation with the Petrograd Soviet. Indeed, the Bureau of the Executive Committee of the Petrograd Soviet, alarmed by the Kronstadt affair, met that very same day and decided to send a high-powered delegation to Kronstadt consisting of the Menshevik Nikolai Chkheidze, chairman of the Executive Committee, and leading members of the Bureau: the SR Abram Gots, the Bundist Mark Liber, and the Menshevik Vasilii Anisimov. They arrived in Kronstadt on 21 May and met the Executive Committee of the Kronstadt Soviet, with a correct and accommodating Lamanov in the chair, for the purpose of obtaining 'comradely information' and eliciting from it an explanation, or 'elucidation', of the Kronstadt resolution which would remove its sting. This achieved, they then addressed the Kronstadt Soviet which would have to confirm the revised formulation.[44]

Explaining the Petrograd Soviet's attitude to the provisional government, Chkheidze pointed out[45] that in the past the Soviet had supported the government only conditionally, 'in so far as it acted in the wake of the revolution', and in accordance with the initial agreement the Soviet had reached with it. The Soviet now had full confidence in the new coalition government in which it was participating and wanted to endow it with 'plenitude of power'. The Kronstadt resolution was at variance with their policy, but they had already ironed out some of the differences with the Kronstadt Executive Committee which had prepared a draft resolution to this effect, and this would now be followed up in discussion in the Petrograd Soviet to which delegates from Kronstadt would be invited.

Abram Gots explained the coalition government's foreign policy, saying that it had already received 'the Allies' agreement, in principle, to review the treaties' and thus revise the war-aims and describing the proposed Stockholm Conference of Socialist Parties as 'the greatest victory of the Russian revolution' in the 'struggle for peace'. The Petrograd Soviet had not taken power all by itself but had entered the coalition government because the masses were still unorganized and the world revolution yet tarried. Even though he knew Kronstadt was critical of this decision, he appealed to the Kronstadt Soviet not to act unilaterally but rather to await the imminent All-Russian Congress of Soviets, the 'united parliament of the toilers', scheduled to convene in Petrograd on 3 June. Mark Liber spoke in the same vein, urging that the authority to decide on the assumption of power belonged only to the Congress of Soviets and not to 'Kronstadt today, and Tula or Moscow tomorrow', while until that Congress convened Kronstadt should respect 'the authority and decision' of the Petrograd Soviet.

Artemii Liubovich, speaking for the Kronstadt Soviet, declared that they had recognized the provisional government 'because there was no other government' but it was 'out of the question' to say that they had 'full confidence' in it.

To the accompaniment of Gots's praise for Kronstadt, the 'vanguard of the revolution', and for the 'spectacle of the consolidated unity of a disciplined army' which had so impressed him there, the Kronstadt Soviet endorsed the 'elucidation' proposed by its Executive Committee with only two dissenting votes. The 'resolution' of 16 May, it said, made official an existing situation whereby the Soviet possessed all the power, while the commissar was redundant. Although the Kronstadt Soviet claimed to be 'the only institution as regards local power', and while, in 'all political questions of state importance', it wanted to deal directly with the Petrograd Soviet, nevertheless this did not preclude certain 'indispensable relations' with the central government: 'We recognize the central state power of the provisional government and shall recognize it as long as the existing government is not replaced by a new government, as long as the All-Russian Central Soviet of Workers', Soldiers' and Peasants' Deputies does not deem it possible to assume central power.'[46]

Pleased with the result, Chkheidze and Anisimov addressed the customary mass meeting in Anchor Square late in the afternoon, but, anxious to return to Petrograd and report to their colleagues, they would not stay for question time. Semion Roshal and Efim Yarchuk (leader of the Anarcho-Syndicalists), apparently disapproving of the amicable spirit in which the incident had been resolved, took advantage of Chkheidze's and Anisimov's departure to incite the crowd against the Petrograd Soviet and to vilify Chkheidze for 'running away' from their questions. Efim Yarchuk, in particular, spat venom about the 'former socialist' Chkheidze who, he alleged, together with Kerensky had called on the army 'to pillage and plunder',[47] and he thus again provided an object lesson in the tactics used by the 'agitators' of Anchor Square in attempting to neutralize whatever favourable impression the moderate Petrograd leaders may have left behind.

As for Chkheidze and the Petrograd delegation, armed with the Kronstadt 'elucidation', on 22 May they reported back to the Petrograd Soviet in the presence of Liubovich, Raskolnikov and Roshal, who had arrived as representatives of the Kronstadt Soviet.[48]

Anisimov argued that the whole 'affair' had been deliberately exaggerated by the bourgeois press; Kronstadt had not turned into a 'republic or an independent state', it had merely decided to give 'juridical expression' to an existing situation and to abolish the position of the commissar. Kronstadt would recognize the authority of the provisional government until such time as the Soviets took power, he said, and when 'we told them that the Soviet was not a state power, they replied that they wanted to set an example for us, in view of our indecisiveness'. This he interpreted to mean that Kronstadt is 'with us in so far as we are with them'. He then proceeded to propose a resolution in the name of the Bureau of the Executive Committee complimenting the Kronstadters on their 'unshakeable devotion and fervent desire to strengthen and broaden democratic liberties', while at the same time regretting that the 'revolutionary energy of the Kronstadt masses had taken the wrong turn', since 'the seizure of power by local Soviets' was a 'flagrant departure' from the policy of the revolutionary democracy which aimed at the creation of a 'strong central revolutionary state power' and which for that reason participated in the coalition government.

The Petrograd Soviet therefore appealed to the Kronstadt comrades' 'devotion to the revolution', trusting that they would 'without delay' return to the ranks of the 'revolutionary democracy of Russia'. It also urged them at the same time to take speedy action in creating municipal organs of democratic self-government based on universal franchise in which 'the entire population' of Kronstadt would be represented.

The Kronstadt delegates were then asked to state their case. Raskolnikov, who may not have been too happy with the 'declaration' even prior to Lenin's rebuke, spoke first and was sweet reason itself;[49] dwelling on the terrible oppression suffered by the 'sailors' Sakhalin' before the revolution, as if pleading this as an extenuating circumstance, he presented a minimalist interpretation of the declaration: Kronstadt was so intent on 'consistent democracy', to the point that even commanders were elected by, and under the control of, their men, that it could not tolerate 'officials appointed from above'. Liubovich, in his laconic way, was more aggressive: sneering at all the uproar created by the resignation of the commissar – 'We had a commissar, and when he left, a room and a chair simply became vacant in Kronstadt!' – he then dealt with the provisional government: 'We soldiers know only two turns, right or left. Should the government turn to the left, then we Kronstadters will march with it, but should it turn to the right, then we, to be frank, will not follow.'

Semion Roshal, as aggressive a demagogue as ever, forgot he was not in Anchor Square and reported that of the 280 officers who had originally been arrested, only 40 were still in prison and, when asked, 'What happened to the others?' would not answer but, after accusing the bourgeois press of scandal-mongering, suggested that the Petrograd Soviet should 'shut up that press'. As for those who condemned the Kronstadt Soviet for assuming power, it had merely followed the example of the Petrograd Soviet which had taken power 'throughout Russia, and not just in Petrograd', and without the population 'having any say in the matter'. True, Kronstadt had gone further, but this was only because 'we are genuinely and truly revolution-minded'.

While Roshal's provocative speech was greeted with 'loud applause' from the Bolshevik benches, Captain Maximilian Filonenko, on behalf of the government, handed a list of officers jailed in Kronstadt to the Executive Committee with the request that 'the honour of revolutionary justice' be restored and the officers be transferred to Petrograd. Roshal's angry retort was: 'The Kronstadters will hand over the arrested officers to Petrograd only when Petrograd collects the arrested reactionaries from the whole of Russia.'

Not surprisingly, Anisimov regarded the Kronstadt delegates' speeches as a provocation, and Tseretelli, too, made it quite clear that Kronstadt would be expected to accept the authority of the provisional government and allow the officers to be put on trial in Petrograd; Mikhail Skobelev, for his part, reminded the Kronstadters that they depended on the state treasury for their money and on the Ministry of Agriculture for their food.

Kamenev, however, speaking for the Bolshevik faction, opposed Anisimov's resolution as 'an insult to the Kronstadters' and, whatever the reason, it was decided to defer both the debate and the vote to the next session.

At the special meeting of the provisional government which began late in the evening of 22 May, Tseretelli and Skobelev reported on their colleagues' findings in Kronstadt. Apparently in the light of that report and of other 'available information', the government declared that it regarded the situation as 'dangerous and intolerable' and, upon Tseretelli's suggestion, deputed him and Skobelev to visit Kronstadt and ascertain 'its attitude to the central power, the state of its defence, local government and justice, and the conditions under which prisoners are kept' and to report back so that appropriate measures could be taken.[50]

For Tseretelli, the acknowledged leader of the Menshevik–SR alliance which controlled the Soviets during the period of the provisional government, March–October 1917, this was the first serious challenge to the power and sovereignty of the newly formed coalition government in which he himself, though holding only the minor post of Minister of Posts and Telegraphs, was both a senior minister and central figure. Kronstadt's maximalism was also an outright attack on the very essence of his policy of socialist self-restraint and cooperation with 'all the living forces of the country', a term he used in season and out to describe the coalition between the Soviets and the liberal, propertied elements, i.e. the Kadets.

As early as the first days of the February revolution, when Tseretelli, hero and martyr of the Second Duma, and a former hard-labour convict and exile in Siberia, became, as a matter of course, chairman of the Irkutsk Committee of Public Organizations, he had congratulated the Petrograd Soviet on the 'decisive role' it and the working class had played in rallying 'all the living forces in the country in the struggle for a new Russia'.[51] Immediately upon his arrival in Petrograd on 19 March, when he found his comrades in the Executive Committee of the Petrograd Soviet unsure of themselves and floundering in their new roles, he presented them with a clear programme of socialist self-restraint in the national-democratic revolution of Russia which, he maintained, was an essential pre-condition for cooperation between the 'revolutionary democracy' and the progressive bourgeoisie.[52] That truly rational and wise policy – 'razum revoliutsii' he called it – continued to guide him as the moderating influence in the period of the first provisional government when, as the leading member of the liaison committee of the Petrograd Soviet, he ironed out its differences with the govern-ment and thus provided that body with more than the conditional support the Soviet had itself promised.[53]

In the April Crisis, albeit after some hesitation, he threw his prestige and weight behind the decision to enter the coalition government and, when drafting the coalition agreement, 'cate-gorically' insisted that the Soviets and the 'revolutionary people' accord the new government 'full and unconditional confidence' and thus guarantee it 'plenitude of power', and this at a time when his own colleagues would have preferred to accord such unconditional support only to the government's socialist ministers.[54]

With his entire policy at stake, he and Skobelev hurried to Kron-stadt on 23 May and immediately presented its Executive Committee with the virtually imperative demands of the provisional govern-ment on recognition of the central government and the commissar, the proper trial of the arrested officers, and the holding of municipal elections. They made it quite clear, particularly in conversations with Raskolnikov and Roshal, that were the demands to be rejected, Kronstadt would be declared a 'rebellious province' and dealt with accordingly.[55] After a long day that drew into the deep night of discussion, negotiations and cajoling, a compromise agreement was hammered out in the morning of 24 May, taking the form of five questions and answers.[56] A special plenary session of the Kronstadt Soviet was then convened later in the morning to debate the agree-ment, point by point, and put it to the vote.[57]

In addressing the Soviet, both Tseretelli and Skobelev insisted that they had come as representatives of the provisional government which viewed the situation in Kronstadt as 'serious, dangerous and intolerable'. The resolution of 16 May, they said, was understood as a 'denial of the plenitude of power granted to the provisional government as the central organ of state power'. True, in its later 'elucidation', the Kronstadt Soviet had stated that it 'fully recog-nized' the central power, but that contradicted the Soviet's claim

to be the 'sole power in Kronstadt' and that claim would debar the
government from exercising its power in Kronstadt as it did in the
rest of Russia. While the coalition government enjoyed the confidence
and support of the vast majority of the revolutionary democracy
which had sent its representatives into the government, it felt it
could not so rely on Kronstadt. Alone in the whole of Russia,
Kronstadt had not been satisfied to criticize the government, as it
both could and should, but it had taken the law into its own hands,
acting unilaterally in administrative, economic and political matters,
as if it were bent on 'breaking with the rest of Russia'.

Anatolii Lamanov, who chaired the session, made a spirited but
conciliatory speech in defence of Kronstadt: the commissar had left
because he was redundant, for 'everything is done by the Soviet
here'. As for the 'resolution', it only gave *de jure* recognition to a
de facto situation: Kronstadt was 'independent' in all local matters;
but even so, they had neither claim nor aspiration to be 'a separate
unit which can just do as it pleases'.

The Soviet was 'trusted by the people of Kronstadt', guarded their
'democratic interests' and had put the fortress into 'excellent military
shape', said Lamanov; at the same time it had always been guided
by that 'spirit of responsibility which every citizen of Russia must
have'.

Greeted by 'warm applause', Lamanov's speech set the conciliatory tone, with the circumspect Mikhail Evstingeev continuing in that
vein but warning against any attempt to undo what had been done:

We cannot just turn back, for life itself has decreed our path. Just to give
you one example: the commander of the Naval Forces came and asked
permission to despatch naval units to the fleet. We agreed, provided that
the units were complemented from Petrograd. Now, you would advise us
to tell him to go away, but that would mean renouncing our previous
freedom, the freedom of the early days [of the revolution] which we have
now written into a resolution.

Moreover, he went on, the whole of Russia was moving towards the
'transfer of power to the Soviets' and that could best be achieved if
the central power could rely on 'organized points' such as Kronstadt:
'We Kronstadters have set an example. What we have said is: here
is the first, small foundation stone, and now we want to tell all the
others to build on that foundation.'

With both Evstingeev *and* Roshal affirming Kronstadt's recognition of the provisional government, its decrees, its judiciary and its

officials, Tseretelli and Skobelev expressed the 'greatest satisfaction' with the assurances they had heard. They certainly would not question Kronstadt's right to propagate the transfer of power to the Soviets. But since 'we think seizure of power is premature, while you think the time is already ripe for it', the imminent Congress of Soviets would debate that question and decide; until then Kronstadt must recognize the provisional government and act accordingly.

On that conciliatory note, the Kronstadt Soviet proceeded to hear, debate and vote the agreement which had been reached between its Executive Committee and the ministers Tseretelli and Skobelev. To ensure that party factions were fully involved and responsible for the agreement, which had been formulated in the form of five questions put by the ministers and answers given by the Kronstadt Soviet, the Soviet adjourned for an hour so that the factions could meet and instruct their spokesmen on how to speak and their members on how to vote.[58]

Stripped of their long-winded, revolutionary, yet face-saving rhetoric, the answers amounted to a promise to recognize the 'plenitude of power' of the provisional government, and to accept its laws and decrees as being as 'valid for Kronstadt as for the rest of Russia'; the commissar, henceforth to be called Director or 'representative of the provisional government in civil matters', would be elected by the Kronstadt Soviet and then confirmed in office by the provisional government; Kronstadt's military and naval commanders would follow the directions of the High Command, while relations with their respective control commissions would remain unchanged; Kronstadt would accept the municipal and judicial arrangements and institutions that applied throughout Russia; and, most problematically, the Kronstadt Soviet undertook to cooperate with the Investigation Commission, to be appointed at the highest judicial level, to which representatives of the local Investigation Commission would be co-opted. Point five provided that preliminary investigations be conducted in Kronstadt, persons found guilty would be committed to trial in Petrograd, with representatives of the interested crew or army unit summoned there to assist in the trial. Those found innocent would be released by the Investigation Commission in Kronstadt and both the Executive Committee of the Soviet and all garrison units would be notified.

Point five, predictably, proved the bone of contention. Unlike the others which had been endorsed by all four factions, it was endorsed only by the Menshevik, Non-Party and SR factions. While no official Bolshevik spokesman is on record as having opposed point five, the two deputies Fokin and Shmelev, and others who warned that 'the crews will not agree with that point', were apparently all Bolsheviks. They were promptly told by the SR Fiodor Pokrovsky that it was not the function of political parties 'to follow the masses', but rather to lead them and 'explain things to them'.

When the vote on point five was taken, it was passed by 160 to 57, with 16 abstentions, i.e. with a substantially reduced majority as compared with points one to four (one: 195 to 22, 26 abstentions; two: 202 to 9, 26 abstentions; three: 213 to 9, 14 abstentions; four: 207 to 7, 18 abstentions).

Lamanov made a final, amicable speech, inviting the Petrograd press and public to come to Kronstadt, visit the prisons and see for themselves, and complimenting Tseretelli and Skobelev on their 'comradely spirit' which had proved that 'the socialist ministers, though they had been co-opted into a bourgeois ministry, nevertheless remained socialists'. We Kronstadters, he reassured them, 'know our responsibility and will not endanger the common cause'. Raskolnikov also took the floor, feeling he must explain that the 'compromise resolution' had been couched in much softer language than they were used to in Kronstadt, out of a desire to find an understanding with the Petrograd comrades.

Though Tseretelli expressed some 'apprehension' that, in the light of the views expressed in the debate, 'they might find it easier to adopt resolutions than to realize them', he seems to have been pleased with the agreement. Indeed, it appeared that the sweet reason of Lamanov had prevailed, until there came a jarring and quite unexpected resolution moved on behalf of the Bolsheviks by the young party worker Piotr Smirnov, which called on 'the socialist ministers to resign from the government or cease calling themselves socialists'. His surprise action provoked 'trampling of feet, whistling and shouts', while Tseretelli's rejoinder that they would regard themselves as 'deserters' were they to leave the government into which they had been sent by the Petrograd Soviet and by the 'will of the revolutionary democracy' was greeted with applause and shouts of 'Bravo!'

So well disposed did the Soviet seem that the customary, but manifestly unfriendly, meeting in Anchor Square which Tseretelli later addressed did not unduly worry him.[59]

His mission concluded, and the five-point agreement in his pocket, Tseretelli hurried back to Petrograd and reported to the provisional government during the 24 May night session. The government seems to have been satisfied, and in implementation of the agreement resolved to suggest to the Kronstadt Soviet that it put forward its own candidate for the post of commissar, or, as it was now to be less offensively known, 'representative of the provisional government in civil matters in Kronstadt'; it was also to be asked to organize elections of councillors for the town Duma in accordance with the municipal elections law of 15 April. For its part, the government resolved to commission the Ministry of Justice immediately to set up an Investigation Commission consisting of six representatives of the Department of Justice, the Bar and the Executive Committee of the Petrograd Soviet; that Commission should then co-opt representatives of the Kronstadt Investigation Commission and investigate the Kronstadt prisoners, dealing with them in accordance with the agreement reached in 'point five'.[60]

Thus it seemed as if the conflict between the Kronstadt Soviet and Petrograd had been resolved, with the two burning issues of the commissar and the arrested officers now about to be settled; but this was to reckon without the last-minute intervention of Kronstadt's Anchor Square 'democracy'.

When on 25 May news of the government was reported in the Petrograd newspapers and spread in Kronstadt, it caused, as some Bolsheviks had predicted (or was it a self-fulfilling prophecy?), great anger. A large, turbulent crowd gathered in Anchor Square and denounced the Soviet deputies for having 'sold themselves to the bourgeoisie', and demanded that Kronstadt break off relations with the provisional government. Some 3,000 sailors then burst into the Naval Assembly where the praesidium of the Executive Committee was meeting and forced the Kronstadt leaders to eat their own words and, without convening and consulting the Executive Committee and the Soviet, to send the following cable to the provisional government:

Since numerous Russian newspapers have today published some 'resolutions' passed by the Soviet, we feel duty-bound to state the following: the replies given in the session of 24 May to the questions put by the ministers Tseretelli and Skobelev to the Executive Committee of the Soviet of Workers' and Soldiers' Deputies are neither resolutions, nor elucidations, but merely answers to questions and nothing more.

We maintain the point of view expressed in the resolution of 16 May and the elucidations of 21 May 1917 which recognize the Soviet of Workers' and Soldiers' Deputies as the sole local power in Kronstadt.

Chairman – Lamanov, Secretary – Priselkov.[61]

While there is no conclusive proof that it was a group of Bolsheviks, in particular Semion Roshal, who had mobilized the sailors against the agreement, there is weighty circumstantial evidence to suggest that they were, in fact, bent on damaging if not destroying it. Parchevsky noted that immediately after Tseretelli and Skobelev had left, the Bolsheviks, who had been surprisingly quiet and restrained during their visit, began to agitate and 'brought the Kronstadt public . . . under the spell of their rhetorical talents and impetuous temperament'.[62] Roshal, both in a statement made to a Petrograd journalist in the evening of 24 May, and in a provocative editorial in *Golos pravdy* of 26 May, trumpeted the 'victory of the Kronstadt Soviet', boasting that its replies had in no way 'gone back on its original position', and that it continued to have 'no confidence in the provisional government and did not support it'; if it maintained relations with it, he added, this was simply because of 'the need for financial means to maintain the crews and the garrison'.[63]

Whatever Roshal's role in the dramatic repudiation of the agreement, he certainly incurred the 'condemnation' of Trotsky[64] and, *mutatis mutandis*, of an anti-semitic leaflet which denounced him, in badly spelt Russian, as 'a mercenary, non-Christian, mangy Yid provocateur' who had, in his Anchor Square speech, 'put us to shame before the ministers Tseretelli and Skobelev and profaned us before the entire Russian people'.[65]

Lamanov's cable to the provisional government was like a bolt from the blue for the leaders of the Petrograd Soviet. Tseretelli was beside himself and made the Kronstadt *volte face* the sole item on the agenda of an extraordinary session of the Petrograd Soviet which assembled in the evening of 26 May. Vladimir Voitinsky, the Petrograd Soviet's trouble-shooter, remembered it as 'one of the most dramatic moments of the year 1917', with Tseretelli cast in the role of chief prosecutor, Trotsky as chief counsel for the defence, and Iulii Martov pleading for patience and delay.[66] Tseretelli denounced Kronstadt as 'a hotbed of anarchy and a disgrace to the revolution' whose destruction it was now preparing; he then moved a resolution which condemned it for 'secession from the revolutionary democracy' and castigated the Soviet for its 'utter inability' to stand up to 'those anarchist elements which it had itself fostered' and for disgracing the revolution by incarcerating hundreds of prisoners 'in the worst tsarist dungeons', without specific accusation and proper trial, in an act of 'unbecoming vengeance and reprisal'. Finally, he reminded the Kronstadters of the exceptional privileges they enjoyed regarding food supplies and demanded that they 'immediately and unconditionally execute *all* instructions of the provisional government, which issued them in the interests of the revolution and the external security of the country'. This resolution was to be broadcast to all Kronstadt forts and garrisons and to all naval crews of the Baltic Fleet and all other Soviets.[67]

Trotsky, in a passionate speech opposing the resolution, argued that the contradictory statements of the Kronstadt Soviet which had given so much offence were, in fact, the natural outcome of 'dual powerlessness', of a situation in which neither the provisional government nor the Soviet had real power; appealing to Tseretelli not to push the Kronstadters too far, he exclaimed: 'Yes! The Kronstadters are anarchists, but when the final battle for the revolution comes, those gentlemen who now incite you to a showdown with the Kronstadters will soap the [hangman's] ropes for all of us, while it will be the Kronstadters who will fight and die with us.'[68]

The resolution was adopted by 580 to 162 votes with 74 abstentions, an unusually small majority by Petrograd Soviet standards, as Voitinsky noted. The substantial minority that voted against further suggests that almost one-third of the Petrograd Soviet saw little wrong with what the Kronstadt speakers in the debate called the 'deepening of the revolution', or with what Liubovich confidently recommended to the Congress of Soviets on 6 June as 'the well-tried method of injecting blood into those areas that suffer from revolutionary anaemia',[69] and, too, that they were certainly opposed to coalitionism.

With their hands strengthened by the Petrograd Soviet's tough resolution, the provisional government, meeting in night session on 26 May, issued an order instructing all Kronstadt citizens to 'unconditionally execute all orders of the provisional government', and, to check its implementation, ordered the commander of the Baltic Fleet to 'pull all training ships out of Kronstadt forthwith and set sail for Biorke and Tranzund for summer exercises', and to report back.[70]

Trotsky must have realized by this time that things had gone too far both for the Petrograd Soviet and for the provisional government and that they had finally decided to take action against Kronstadt's open defiance. Thus, on 27 May he betook himself to Kronstadt and did his best to persuade first Raskolnikov, who had rushed by boat from Kronstadt to intercept and brief him, and then the Kronstadt Executive Committee, to accede to the ultimatum and revoke the cable repudiating the agreement with the provisional government. But at the same time he had to tread carefully, and, in order to make their climb-down palatable to the Kronstadters, issued an appeal presenting it as a mere temporary retreat.[71]

He was strongly supported at the meeting of the Kronstadt Soviet on 27 May[72] by the senior Bolshevik party worker Ivan Flerovsky who had returned from Petrograd to report on the mood of the Soviet there, on its resolution and on the provisional government's order. Denouncing the 'socialist' ministers, and in particular Tseretelli, 'the prosecutor of Kronstadt', for their duplicity, Flerovsky warned against 'premature demonstrations and explosions', and called for restraint: 'Gnashing their teeth, revolutionary Kronstadters will await that moment when, together with the whole of revolutionary Russia, they will raise the banner of the people's full power, the power of the Soviet of Workers', Soldiers' and Peasants' Deputies.' But until this day dawned, they must comply with the ultimatum and, in the first place, recognize the provisional government, but only for as long as 'democratic Russia' did likewise, and on the understanding that such grudging recognition did not necessarily imply 'confidence and support'; and, most important of all, they must keep the agreement reached regarding the imprisoned officers.

Trotsky spelt it out:

If you do not keep the agreement, comrades, this will be a breach of promise, and they will make you comply somehow, I do not know how precisely; I am not saying that they will send troops, but I think they may refuse to supply bread and money. I do not think it is worthwhile squabbling over this matter, and, since an agreement was reached, it must be kept, so that Kronstadt's name remain undefiled.

Trotsky's plea received 'thunderous applause', an index both of his popularity in Kronstadt and of his powers of persuasion. With the matter thus clinched, the Soviet endorsed the 'Appeal from the Sailors, Soldiers and Workers of Kronstadt to the Revolutionary People of Petrograd and to the Whole People of Russia'.[73] Written in Trotsky's fiery prose, it is an impressive hotchpotch of clever half-truths and self-righteous indignation, mind-boggling demagoguery and solemn, revolutionary incantations: 'Do they say it is we who refuse to recognize the authority of the provisional government, we who have seceded from Russia and set up an independent Kronstadt republic? What an inane lie, what pitiful, shameless slander!' Kronstadt had established 'an honest and firm revolutionary order' with the Soviet as the authority in 'all local, Kronstadt matters'; and as for the imprisoned officers, Kronstadt did stand for 'an honest, free, impartial, revolutionary trial of the criminal enemies of the people' and had, to that effect, concluded an agreement with the representatives of the provisional government and would, in fact, stand by it; and as long as the government was recognized by 'the will of the organized revolutionary people', Kronstadt could not but recognize that government's 'central authority' in all matters of state and would, furthermore, stand by that agreement which included the election of the commissar and control over military commanders.

A substantial section of the Appeal related to Red Kronstadt's condemnation of the provisional government which, consisting largely of 'landowners, factory owners and bankers', could not be a 'true government of the democracy', while its policies had already created anarchy and economic crisis. There was also a critique of the Petrograd Soviet and of the many provincial Soviets who had 'mistakenly' given their support to the government against which Kronstadt declared it would fight solely with the 'honest weapon of the revolutionary word'; as for Kronstadt's alleged repudiation of the agreement, that was a 'monstrous misrepresentation' put forward in an atmosphere of 'exaggerated slander and malicious suspicion' artificially created by provocateurs plotting to sabotage it in an endeavour to destroy Kronstadt as a 'revolutionary centre' and thus to assist the counter-revolution. It was therefore a matter for the 'deepest regret' that the socialist ministers and the Petrograd Soviet should have succumbed to that slander campaign and have denounced Kronstadt in 'an unjust and insulting resolution' as 'secessionists from the Russian revolution'.

But, Kronstadters remained 'firmly convinced' that their Appeal would expunge 'all lies, slanders, suspicions and misrepresentations' and thus restore the 'indissoluble links of mutual revolutionary trust'. Meanwhile, 'we Kronstadters will remain at our posts, on the left-wing of the great army of the Russian revolution. We hope, we believe, we are convinced . . . that the hour is near when, with the united strength of the working masses, plenitude of power will pass to the Soviet of Workers' and Soldiers' Deputies.' Kronstadt's final appeal was

to you, brothers in revolution, in Petrograd and in the whole of Russia, we, the sailors, soldiers and workers of Kronstadt, stretch out our hands. Nothing can sever the bonds that link us. Nothing can destroy our unity, for our loyalty is eternal. Down with all slanderers who sow dissension among the revolutionary people! Long live the Russian revolution!

This time, in addition to the endorsement of the Executive Committee and of the plenary assembly of the Soviet, the explicit sanction of 'Anchor Square democracy' was sought for the Soviet's conciliatory policy and its Appeal, and a vast meeting was convened by the Soviet in the Naval Manège late in the evening. The mood was grim and tense, reported Efim Yarchuk:

The Naval Manège was packed. All the windows, each and every possible foothold, even the tops of the ovens, all were densely crowded with excited figures. Through the wide open doors came the din of the overflow crowd straining forward to hear regardless of the rain and foul weather. Reports of the debate inside were passed back from one to another. In an atmosphere of the utmost tension the meeting stretched on from seven in the evening until four in the morning.[74]

Only then, and still grudgingly, did they give their approval.

It was apparently far easier for Trotsky and Flerovsky to roll out a face-saving, yet rousing Appeal, than for the exalted and indignant masses of Kronstadt sailors and soldiers to back out of a head-on collision with the Petrograd Soviet and the provisional government. Indeed Bolshevik agitators, notably Kirill Orlov, worked overtime in Anchor Square calming down the same crowds whom only a week earlier they had incited to 'march on Petrograd', destroyers and all, and force 'the bourgeois government and the Soviet' to accept the Kronstadt position.[75]

Anxious to comply with the provisional government's demands and thus liquidate the conflict as quickly as possible, Lamanov next day requested the Soviet to regard as urgent the election of a 'representative of the provisional government in civil matters'. The Bolsheviks refused to nominate a candidate because it was inconceivable that 'our comrade serve as an official of the coalition government'. The Mensheviks, in line with Martov's Menshevik-Internationalists who strongly opposed 'coalitionism', followed suit, claiming, 'we do not elect, nor do we support an official of the government'. The Non-Party group, together with the SRs, proposed Parchevsky, the man who had, all along, counselled moderation and warned against defiance of the provisional government. He was elected unopposed.[76]

Losing no time, Lamanov, on behalf of the Soviet, accompanied Parchevsky to Petrograd on 30 May and introduced him to Prince Lvov, the minister-president, as Kronstadt's elected nominee for the post. Only after Lamanov's assurance that Kronstadt had complied with the order to send its training ships to Biorke and Tranzund did Lvov propose to the government that it 'confirm the high school teacher Foma Iakovlevich Parchevsky, in accordance with his election by the Kronstadt Soviet of Workers' and Soldiers' Deputies, as the provisional government's representative in Kronstadt in civil matters'.[77] Thus, the government's face was somewhat saved, but at the price of its acquiescence in Kronstadt's virtual autonomy.

On the very same day that the provisional government confirmed the appointment and thus removed one major bone of contention, it also sent an Investigation Commission to Kronstadt consisting of two representatives of the Petrograd Soviet's Executive Committee, two of the Bar and three of the Ministry of Justice, all in accordance with the agreement. After co-opting seven representatives of the Kronstadt Soviet, they fixed the opening session of the Commission for 2 June when the case of the imprisoned officers of the Artificers School was to be heard.[78]

Though the Kronstadt Soviet had ostensibly accepted the compromise terms of the provisional government and had begun to implement them on the two crucial matters of the commissar and the imprisoned officers, it soon demonstrated the very slight respect it had both for the authority of the government and for its own undertaking to observe that body's laws and decrees.

On 7 June, it resolved, by an overwhelming majority (with twenty-one abstentions), to reject 'in its entirety' War Minister Kerensky's Declaration of the Rights of the Soldier (Order No. 8) of 11 May, which strengthened the authority of officers and gave commanders the exclusive right to appoint and dismiss officers. The Kronstadt Soviet's resolution insisted that a new charter of soldiers' rights be worked out by a congress of representatives of all army units, and not by the War Ministry, and that until then Kronstadt would continue to abide by Order No. 1 of 2 March (which had given great power in army matters to elective soldiers' committees and to the Petrograd Soviet).[79] Not surprisingly, Piotr Ediet, who led the minority opposing this defiant resolution, denounced it as a bad 'mistake', for thus 'we openly declare our opposition and insubordination to an official decree of the War Ministry' when only as recently as 24 May they had promised they would respect such decrees as 'extending as much to Kronstadt as to the rest of Russia'. Ediet accused the Soviet of double-talk: 'We either said what we did not want to say, or made promises that we did not wish to keep', and, demanding that Kronstadt speak 'clear revolutionary language', challenged those who wished to fight the provisional government to do so 'openly'. Wisely, he called his protest 'A Personal View-Point'[80] and, though he claimed there were 'many comrades, including some members of the Executive Committee', who shared his views, they were certainly outnumbered. There can be little doubt that the large majority of the Kronstadt Soviet had, in the course of the showdown with Tseretelli and the Petrograd Soviet, become thoroughly alienated from the latter, and that they also deeply resented the provisional government. Their feelings were certainly shared by the mass of sailors and soldiers who, in the evening of 9 June, milled around in Anchor Square where a host of Bolshevik and Anarchist orators harangued them, denouncing 'the government of the bourgeoisie' and inviting them to assemble next morning in Anchor Square, thence to proceed to Petrograd for a demonstration under the Bolshevik slogans 'Down with the Ten Capitalist Ministers' (the first coalition government had ten 'bourgeois' and six 'socialist' ministers) and 'All Power to Soviets'.[81] The initiative for and invitation to the demonstration both came from the Bolshevik Central Committee in Petrograd which that same evening had telephoned its Kronstadt counterpart to send a large contingent.

The response, however, surpassed all expectations, and at a conservative estimate some 15,000 to 20,000 assembled on the bright and sunny morning of 10 June in Anchor Square which soon filled to capacity with 'the black bulk of the workers, the white columns of the sailors and the massed grey-green of the infantry battalions', all complete with their flags and orchestras; even the crews scheduled to attend and testify before the Investigation Commission that morning, made instead for Anchor Square and the session was adjourned.[82] As the vast crowd waited to embark in the barges that stood ready, Artemii Liubovich, just back post-haste from Petrograd, broke the news that the demonstration had been called off in response to the ban imposed on it by the Congress of Soviets which was then in session in Petrograd. He was angrily howled down by the irate crowd and even the old hand Ivan Flerovsky, who jumped to his rescue, fared little better. Explaining that a demonstration held despite the ban would be tantamount to nothing less than 'a military campaign for Soviet power', he asked: 'Are we ready for the fight?' But the unyielding answer came without hesitation: 'Yes, we are ready!' and the vast crowd gave its noisy approval. When he asked, again rhetorically, whether they were sure that 'the Petrograd garrison, the front and the provinces' were ready too, again the answer came: 'Yes! They are ready too . . . and we shall arouse them! They will come with us!''

Even the popular soap-box orator Efim Yarchuk, who mounted the rostrum to come to the aid of his hard-pressed Bolshevik friends, could win no hearing, and his warning that 'without the Bolsheviks' they must not venture forth to Petrograd, since 'without organization and leadership one cannot win', made no impression whatever.

The situation deteriorated still further when an unknown sailor from Reval leaped up before the excited crowd and passionately appealed to it to come to the help of the Petrograd comrades whose demonstration had been shot up so that 'the whole of Mars Fields is sown with corpses'. But the worst moment came when, shouldering his way out of a group of Anarcho-Communists visiting Kronstadt from their headquarters in the Durnovo Villa, the wild and notorious Shlema Asnin appeared on the rostrum, every inch a 'carbonari', a 'conspirator': 'a long black coat, a soft, broad-brimmed hat, his black blouse hanging loose, high hunting boots, a brace of revolvers in his belt, and, in his hand, a swinging rifle on which he leaned . . . a black spade beard'. The crowd fell silent and attentive as he repeated the story told by the Reval sailor and added his call for help. But he proved an awkward and useless speaker, to the great relief of Flerovsky who, seeing this 'splendid specimen of a Durnovets' rapidly losing his hold on the crowd, used the lull to propose that they elect and send a fact-finding delegation to Petrograd and 'should our help be needed there, then we shall always know how to stand together with our Petrograd comrades and if need be, to die together'.

The election of two hundred delegates proved a veritable lightning-conductor, while the final intervention of the Kronstadt Soviet, which the Bolsheviks had deliberately ignored and bypassed in preparing for the 10 June demonstration, put an end to the turbulent anti-climax with which the meeting closed, and the 'tired, disappointed and sullen' crowd dispersed. True, some hooligans later attacked a militia patrol and robbed a money-chest, but Kronstadt as a whole soon quietened down.

The anxious, if not panic-stricken tone of the 10 June appeals by both the Kronstadt Soviet and the Bolshevik party committee, warning against 'unauthorized actions' and calling for 'revolutionary discipline', truly reflected their fears that the excitable Kronstadters, feeling they had been led by the nose, would now escape their control and follow ill-disciplined Bolshevik extremists and wild Anarchists into an untimely confrontation with the provisional government, only to be 'drowned in rivers of blood'.[83] Thus, when Lenin reviewed the 18 June demonstration in Petrograd (which, unlike the cancelled 10 June demonstration, proceeded under the auspices of the Soviets), he was quite startled by the small size of the Kronstadt contingent which marched past behind its cheer-leader, Kirill Orlov, shouting 'Down with the Ten Capitalist Ministers!'[84] The officially sanctioned and expressly unarmed and peaceful demonstration, though endorsed and led by the Kronstadt Bolsheviks, left the vast bulk of the Kronstadters cold.

Yet, a few days later, thousands of sailors and soldiers did respond enthusiastically when Kirill Orlov and some Bolshevik hotheads led them from Anchor Square into a demonstration in front of, if not against, the Kronstadt Bolshevik party headquarters where they demanded that 'our party lead the navy and the Kronstadters to [Petrograd] for the overthrow of the provisional government'. Only after 'all [party] forces' had been mobilized to persuade and sober the impatient crowd in the course of a 'long-drawn-out meeting' would they desist from their 'dizziness'.[85]

Concurrent with such minor explosions, and partly overlapping them, there began a steady build-up of resentment and antagonism towards the leaders of the Petrograd Soviet, notably Tseretelli and the socialist ministers, expressed in *Golos pravdy*, Anchor Square, and, also, in the Kronstadt Soviet itself. Thus, on 9 June, the Kronstadt Soviet espoused the cause of Robert Grimm, expelled from Russia as a 'German agent' who had ostensibly tried to communicate German peace offers. This expulsion, the Kronstadters protested, was a blow against 'the growing liberation movement of the entire world' and an act of 'counter-revolution . . . an All-Russian Dreyfusiade'. They further indignantly rejected Tseretelli's explanation of the deportation to the First Congress of Soviets, castigating it as 'demagogical' and lacking in substance. In a defiant gesture, the Kronstadt Soviet invited Grimm to come and teach them the lessons of Zimmerwald: the way in which international socialists fight for 'truth and the happiness of mankind' against 'the lords and oppressors of all countries'.[86]

On 10 June, as if timed with the abortive demonstration, the *Golos pravdy* ran three separate pieces (one signed article and two letters to the editor) lashing out at the 'socialist ministers' Tseretelli and Skobelev. Since the Kronstadt Bolsheviks were in daily telephone contact with, and under the control of, the Bolshevik leaders in Petrograd, to the point of Raskolnikov reading out *Golos pravdy*'s major editorials to Lenin for his approval before their publication, it is not unreasonable to assume that the attack on the 'socialist ministers' had been similarly approved.

It began with a diatribe against the once 'pristine-pure' socialists who had plunged into the 'dirty pool' of the provisional government, wallowed in its mire up to their necks, and had now finally 'sold out'; in the same spirit was a specific attack on Skobelev, made in a letter signed by no less than seventeen 'engine-drivers of the revolutionary train' belonging to the Kronstadt School of Artificers whose 'sole desire' was to 'push the train of the Russian revolution ever forward'. The climax came in a disguised vilification of Tseretelli, Minister of Posts and Telegraphs, who was charged with being responsible for the military censorship which delayed or confiscated letters and socialist newspapers such as *Pravda* and *Soldatskaia pravda*: 'We curse such erstwhile comrades and erstwhile fighters for the freedom of speech who now fight for the freedom to search and to silence.'[87]

That curse turned into outright incitement in Anchor Square, where Vladimir Voitinsky recorded a middle-aged Bolshevik agitator addressing the crowd:

I will tell you, comrades, who are those that the socialist ministers look after. Look at Tseretelli, Minister of Posts and Telegraphs. Every one of you, comrades, has a brother or some relatives at the front, but do you get letters from them? 'Never!' shouted the crowd. Now, take the noble-born gentlemen, the officers. Not a day passes without them getting letters and telegrams. Why? Because the Minister ordered your letters, the letters of the soldiers and the sailors, to be thrown away; but the letters and telegrams of the noble-born officers are to be delivered, by his order, to their homes.

Is what I'm saying true? 'Right you are!' came the reply. Can you then trust the provisional government? 'Down with the government!' shouted the crowd.[88]

Another Bolshevik agitator, reading from a piece of paper, told the crowd that at the suggestion of Victor Chernov, Minister of Agriculture, the provisional government had decreed that all peasants were to pay one thousand roubles in compensation to the landowners for every *dessiatine* (0.9 hectares, or 2.7 acres) they received in the course of agrarian reform. 'Comrades', he shouted, 'we did not pay such prices even under the tsar!' When Voitinsky asked him from where he had got this stupid fabrication, he replied: 'We know everything!' and, turning to the crowd, he asked: 'Whom do you believe, comrades, me, or those who strip the very shirt off your back?' 'You! We believe you!' roared the crowd.[89] Next to mount the rostrum was a sailor denouncing the war:

We sailors will not wait until the gentlemen officers choose to end this war. What does it matter to them? They receive their salaries and rations come what may; but we, we shed our blood. We've got to put an end to the war by ourselves: let's rivet up the guns and throw the rifles overboard – this is our programme![90]

The anti-war campaign grew in intensity when news reached Kronstadt that Lieutenant Flavian Khaustov, editor of the Bolshevik newspaper for soldiers *Okopnaia pravda*, had been arrested and charged with treason for his articles against the planned Kerensky offensive. A meeting of some 16,000 assembled in Anchor Square on 16 or 17 June to protest his arrest and that of all others who had agitated 'against the war and the offensive' and thereby exposed the 'counter-revolutionary government', and the vast gathering pledged to fight 'with all means and with arms in our hands, against any attack on the freedom and rights of the people, and the freedom of the press, of speech and of assembly'.[91]

Adding to the growing resentment against the provisional government and rendering the socialist Minister of Justice Pavel Pereverzev even more odious was the reprisal raid he ordered against the headquarters of the Federation of Anarcho-Communists at the Durnovo Villa after the group had forcibly freed Khaustov from the Kresty prison. Pereverzev's raid claimed the life of the hapless Shlema Asnin who, holding a bomb in his hand, grabbed a soldier's gun barrel and was promptly shot. Among those arrested and jailed were a group of Kronstadt sailors, including the later

renowned Anatolii Zhelezniakov. Kronstadt's reaction was prompt
and fierce. The next day, on 20 June, the Soviet denounced the raid
as 'a counter-revolutionary act' and a *'direct challenge'* to all revolutionaries, demanding the severe punishment of those responsible, and
the *'immediate release* of the arrested innocents'.[92]

Two days later a protest meeting decided to send a delegation to
Petrograd to secure the freedom of these 'sixty innocent men' and,
meanwhile, to arrest and hold as hostages those members of the
Investigation Commission then in Kronstadt. 'Our sailors lie in
prison while these scoundrels set the bloody executioners free!'
shouted the angry crowd of sailors and soldiers surrounding the
Naval Court, and, had it not been for the Executive Committee of
the Soviet coming to the Commission's rescue and offering themselves as hostages, the crowd would have made good its threat. Even
then, the Executive Committee left nothing to chance and made
sure the Commission was sent safely on its way back to Petrograd.[93]

Nor was this the end of the matter. On 23 June another mass
meeting resolved that if the 'Durnovtsy' were not released, their
Kronstadt comrades would proceed to Petrograd and free them by
force. Indeed, as soon as that same afternoon a Kronstadt delegation
appeared in the Ministry of Justice in Petrograd demanding the
release of the men and threatening, in the name of the 'entire
Kronstadt garrison', to secure their release by force should the
judicial authorities refuse.[94]

Similar threats to use force were made when Kronstadt agitators
were arrested in country centres as far away as the Urals where they
had gone to speed up the agrarian revolution. There they had urged
the immediate 'transfer of the land and the meadows to the peasants',
and they had already made such a name for themselves that, as one
complaint to Kerensky put it, 'They have it in their power to halt or
permit the requisitioning of cattle for the army as they see fit.'[95]

That these threats to free comrades 'in a revolutionary manner'
had no backing from the Kronstadt Soviet is irrelevant, for by mid-
June it was well-nigh impossible to hold back the excited, confident
and armed sailors. Indeed, the members of the Executive Committee
must have realized their helplessness when, during the night of 13
June, they unsuccessfully tried to prevent an irate crowd from meting
out lynch-justice to five armed men who, when caught robbing a
doctor's residence, had shot at a crowd, wounding some. All that
their intervention won them was threats and a lecture by the crowd

on the virtues of summary revolutionary justice: 'Investigations drag on for months, and in the end the criminals are sent off to Petrograd, where, of course, the provisional government releases them, just as it does the officers.'[96]

As one hectic event chased the other throughout the month of June, the Kronstadt Soviet can only barely have managed to ride the tide of Anchor Square's turbulent democracy, as the crowd, no longer content to bask in the glory of internal achievements, instead set course outwards to spread the Kronstadt gospel to the rest of Russia.

To cap it all came the Kerensky offensive which only added to their distrust and their hostility towards the provisional government. The Bolsheviks made the most of it when the Soviet debated the offensive on 23 June.[97] Ivan Flerovsky gave the lead when, in a speech that was certainly most effective for a Kronstadt audience, he linked the question of war and the offensive with the question of power:

We are not opponents of war as such, but what we stand for is a revolutionary war, a liberation war! And we insist that the first precondition for revolutionary war is the transfer of power to the Soviets of Workers' and Soldiers' Deputies! The second – the immediate publication of the bourgeois treaties! The third – an appeal to the nations of the world.

Should there then be no response, and no peace, he continued, only then

will our revolutionary army have the right to take the offensive in a revolutionary liberation war. Only then will our army have the right to say to the democracy of the entire world that the Russian proletarian, the poor Russian peasant, brings you peace! For we wage war only on the bourgeoisie, only on the thrones.

Flerovsky concluded with a quotation from 'comrade Martov's' speech against the offensive: 'Down with this pernicious war! Long live the International!'

The resolution[98] he put forward condemned the offensive as a concession to the 'imperialist bourgeoisie' of England, France, the United States of America and Russia, as 'injurious' to the Russian revolution, a stab in the back of the 'maturing German revolution', and a fillip to 'chauvinistic intoxication' and national hatreds. The 'socialist' ministers were denounced for having given it their 'blessings', and the Mensheviks and the SR-Defensists fared no better, for they had given it their support; the 'imperialism of the offensive' must be answered by the transfer of power to the Soviets, who would immediately propose a 'just peace'. But the immediate and specific tasks on hand were a 'campaign' to ensure the merciless exposure of the provisional government, the Mensheviks and the SR-Defensists; agitation for new Soviet elections so that all deputies who had supported the offensive would be recalled; organizational work in the army; and agitation against the removal of 'the revolutionary regiments' from the interior of the country, so that these men could there 'repulse counter-revolution'.

All this, the resolution went on, was intended to serve the chief task and objective – the 'widening and deepening' of the revolution in preparation for its 'new stage' which would put an end to its domination by the 'petty-bourgeois defensist bloc' of Mensheviks and SRs which had compromised itself by a 'shameful policy' of coalition with the bourgeoisie and support for its 'selfish machinations'.

This aggressive and clearly Bolshevik resolution proved so acceptable to the Kronstadt Left SRs that they withdrew their own, much milder resolution in its favour.[99] Adopting it by 195 votes with 65 abstentions and only one against,[100] the Kronstadt Soviet had voluntarily accepted Bolshevik leadership and its call for a 'new stage' of revolution.

Kronstadt was ready for the 'July Days'.

4

The July Days

It was to Kronstadt, as to its natural ally, that the First Regiment of Machine-Gunners turned on 3 July when it decided to demonstrate and to force the Central Executive Committee of Soviets to assume power. After all, had not the regiment demonstrated, fully armed, on 28 May, in support of Kronstadt and its defiance of the provisional government,[1] and was it too much to ask it now to reciprocate?

Indeed, in the afternoon of 3 July, while the Kronstadt Executive Committee was busy clipping the wings of commissar Parchevsky who had presumed to publish a news-sheet, *Kronshtadt*, without the Soviet's permission, it interrupted its session to summon three emissaries from the First Machine-Gun Regiment who had arrived in Kronstadt and had begun to agitate among the troops of the garrison and call them to Petrograd in their support.[2] Two members of the Petrograd Bolshevik Military Organization, I. F. Kazakov and P. Koshelev, and the Anarcho-Communist Pavel Pavlov, the emissaries in question, duly appeared and immediately appealed for armed support for the gunners *and* the Petrograd garrison which, they claimed, had taken to the streets to urge 'All Power to Soviets'. Told by Pokrovsky, chairman of the Kronstadt Soviet, that this was impossible unless backed by 'directives' from the Central All-Russian Executive Committee of Soviets (elected by the First Congress of Soviets in June), they then accused him of supporting the bourgeoisie and declared that they would take no notice of the Kronstadt Executive Committee, but would appeal directly to the masses.[3] Slipping out before they could be arrested, they made straight for the Infantry Manège where the Anarcho-Syndicalist Yarchuk was just finishing a lecture on war and peace. 'Blood is flowing in Petrograd!' they shouted, interrupting his closing remarks and haranguing the

audience. 'The men have taken to the streets there! And you Kronstadters, good revolutionaries all, indeed, sit around and listen to
lectures.'[4]

The taunt stung, and, amidst shouting and calls for action, the
ever-swelling crowd streamed to Anchor Square, while, on Yarchuk's
suggestion, a delegation made straight for the Executive Committee
in the Naval Assembly building to plead for all-out support for the
First Machine-Gunners. By that time, some time between 7 and 8
p.m., the Executive Committee had already received the news of
the cabinet crisis precipitated by the Kadet ministers' walk-out in
protest against the concessions on autonomy made to the Ukrainian
Rada (Council) by Kerensky, Tseretelli and Foreign Minister
Mikhail Tereshchenko. The Committee had also had confirmation
that the Machine-Gunners had indeed come out. Thus, Raskolnikov,
Roshal, Yarchuk and Brushvit were sent to Anchor Square both to
report the news there *and* to calm down and restrain the crowds.[5]
Raskolnikov, as circumspect as ever, had already managed to telephone Lev Kamenev and report on the 'alarming' excitement of the
crowds that the Gunners' emissaries had caused, and, as he later
claimed, was told by Kamenev that while the Bolshevik leaders in
Petrograd were urging the Machine-Gunners 'to return to their
barracks in a disciplined manner', they in Kronstadt should use all
their 'moral authority' to prevent the masses from coming out.[6]

Arriving in Anchor Square, they found the Machine-Gunners
haranguing the crowd: they, together with other regiments, had come
out to overthrow the provisional government and to transfer all
power to the Soviets. 'We have resolved to pave the streets with our
bones, but to achieve our aim!' Worse still, Bolshevik activists such
as the party worker Iosif Gurvich (Venik), Ensign Afanasii Remnev,
and the sailor Fiodor Gromov supported them enthusiastically, with
Gromov even exhorting the crowd from the rostrum, 'Comrades! We
have been fobbed off long enough! Let us go to the barracks, grab
our arms and embark for Petrograd lest we be taken for traitors and
expunged from the list of revolutionary units!'[7] When Brushvit called
for caution and warned against rash actions 'so as not to shed blood
in vain', he was howled down.[8] Roshal, too, seems initially to have
called for restraint, but in the end, and quite 'unexpectedly', according to one observer, instead of shouting 'Back', 'he shouted
"forward!"'[9] Warned by Raskolnikov, 'And what if the party
decides not to come out?' he is reported to have replied, 'Never mind,

we'll do the forcing from here!' even speaking in that vein while addressing the crowd.[9] Nevertheless, while the meeting voted solemnly to come out, it also resolved that everyone return to his unit, there to be on the ready for the orders of the Executive Committee.[10]

With turbulent Anchor Square thus calmed down and brought under control, the initiative passed to Raskolnikov and his party friends who, returning to the Naval Assembly and to a rump of the Executive Committee in nervous attendance there, henceforth dominated its proceedings. Though a mere deputy chairman of the Soviet and not even a member of its Executive Committee, Raskolnikov quickly assumed the leadership during the July crisis and it was he who made the vital decisions which brought Kronstadt to Petrograd. Anatolii Lamanov, who as chairman of the Executive Committee was Kronstadt's number one and could have thwarted him, was caught unawares and proved no match for such experienced Bolsheviks as Raskolnikov and Roshal, Liubovich and Flerovsky, Bregman and Deshevoi.

Indeed, Lamanov had already shown great weakness during a similar crisis, when, on 26 May, he had given his good name and signature to Kronstadt's notorious cable and *volte face*. His position had since been steadily eroded, so much so that at the end of June he had been taken to task for his accommodating attitude to the town Duma, and the question of his resignation had been raised.[11]

Lamanov was certainly caught off guard on 3 July when, on his own admission, he only learned of the political crisis by chance, meeting Raskolnikov and Roshal en route for Anchor Square as he took his evening walk.[12] True, he immediately betook himself to the Naval Assembly, but there, during a crucial night meeting of a rump of the Executive Committee – apparently most of its Non-Party, Menshevik and SR members stayed away,[13] while the Bolshevik leaders skilfully complemented or stacked it with some thirty unverified representatives of armed units – he failed to use his power to insist on a full meeting, and instead sat by while Kronstadt's intervention in Petrograd was determined. Not that he was entirely quiescent: together with his Non-Party comrades Stepan Bogomolov and Grigorii Kapitonov, he did demand that an extraordinary meeting of the Soviet be convened, but he then allowed himself to be out-voted by a body which, as he himself urged, had no legal standing.[14] All he then did was to refuse to chair the meeting, thus

playing straight into the hands of his deputy, the Bolshevik Lazar
Bregman, who was only too willing to take the chair and thus enable
his comrades Raskolnikov and Roshal, Victor Deshevoi and Afanasii
Remnev, who were all present, and Flerovsky and Liubovich who
were in Petrograd as Kronstadt liaison delegates to the Petrograd
Soviet, to assume leadership of events.

Raskolnikov certainly rose to the occasion. Making the most of the
meeting, which lasted until 3 a.m., he managed to organize, under
Soviet auspices, the mobilization, equipment and transportation of
Kronstadt's armed expedition to Petrograd, hence bringing it under
the control of the Bolshevik Central Committee and Military
Organization there and thus making it serve open-ended Bolshevik
aims. These seem to have ranged from a massive 'show of bayonets', as
Raskolnikov claimed in the Kronstadt Soviet on 7 July (when he was
promptly asked by Lamanov: 'Then what were the bullets for?'),[15]
to the transformation of 'the armed demonstration into an armed
insurrection', as he admitted in 1925, adding, 'We would have been
bad revolutionaries had we not thought of our aim – the overthrow
of the provisional government.'[16]

Since Fiodor Raskolnikov stands out as a key figure in this attempt
at reconstructing Kronstadt's role in the 'July Days' events, his
moves during the night session of the enlarged rump Executive
Committee and in the morning of 4 July have been pieced together
and recorded in some detail.

While it may be true that following his telephone conversation
with Kamenev some time after 7 p.m. Raskolnikov tried to restrain
the expedition-happy crowd in Anchor Square, on returning to the
Naval Assembly and the night meeting of the rump of the Executive
Committee he nevertheless did his best to force a decision in favour
of an armed demonstration. It was he who read out the cable that
Bregman had received from Ivan Flerovsky in Petrograd reporting
that the workers' section of the Petrograd Soviet had 'in view of the
government crisis', i.e. the resignation of the Kadet ministers, resolved to demand the transfer of power to the All-Russian Congress
of Soviets and that it would strive 'with all its strength' to bring that
about; and thus he helped the meeting to make up its mind.[17] Neither
he nor Flerovsky as much as mentioned that this resolution had been
adopted solely by the Bolshevik faction of the workers' section and
only *after* the Mensheviks and SRs had walked out. Yet, rushing from
Petrograd to the meeting in the Naval Assembly with news of the

Central Executive Committee's resolution against the demonstration, the Menshevik Kondratii Sokolov, who only arrived soon after the cable was read, was sharply rebuffed when he asked to speak, and, when he persisted, was brusquely told, 'There's nothing one can do now!'[18]

It was again Raskolnikov who received *and* concealed a phone call from Artemii Liubovich urging him to 'send a demonstration' to Petrograd;[19] some time later, he himself rang Zinoviev to tell him that 'the mood of the Kronstadt masses' was such that a demonstration was 'inevitable' and the question now was whether the Bolsheviks should lead it or wash their hands of it. He thus may have helped Zinoviev, Lenin and the Bolshevik Central Committee and Military Organization, who were then in session and deliberating what to do, to make up their minds, decide on an armed demonstration, and give the Kronstadt Bolsheviks the green light.[20] Raskolnikov's next move was to arrange the technical details of the Kronstadters' disembarkation in Petrograd with Liubovich and Flerovsky to whom he spoke on the telephone, and he was received with 'stormy applause' when he announced the Bolshevik Central Committee's decision to back the demonstration. At this, Fiodor Pokrovsky, the SR chairman of the Soviet, spoke by telephone to Boris Kamkov, receiving the SR-Internationalists' endorsement of the demonstration, this announcement also receiving 'thunderous applause'.[21] These endorsements gave added credence to the impression the Kronstadters had that the Petrograd garrison had indeed come out, especially since an anonymous cable received from Petrograd by midnight and beginning with the war-cry 'Down with the provisional government! Down with Kerensky!' announced that the 'regiments in Petrograd have come out', there was shooting in the streets, trucks were moving up and down and that 'the situation is very similar to what it was during the first days of the revolution'.[22] Thus, on the motion put by Lazar Bregman, the meeting decreed that, 'in view of the possibility of a massive demonstration in Petrograd', adequate transport be provided by 6 a.m. on 4 July and that units having 'surplus weapons' hand them over to those in need of them and that all apply to the artillery store for ammunition.[23] That resolution was opposed only by Anatolii Lamanov, Bogomolov and Kapitonov. The marching route of the demonstration from its point of disembarkation in Petrograd to the Tauride Palace was fixed, and Raskolnikov then composed the following directive to the commander of Naval Forces, Lieutenant Piotr Lamanov, and the chief-of-staff of the Kronstadt fortress, Lieutenant-Colonel Alexander Kozlovsky, for immediate implementation:

The Executive Committee requests you forthwith to inform all units that they are to assemble at 6 a.m. fully armed in Anchor Square in order to proceed in an organized fashion to participate together with the troops of the Petrograd garrison in an armed demonstration under the slogan, 'All Power to Soviets'.[24]

That directive of the Executive Committee, the only Kronstadt body possessing emergency powers, was signed by Raskolnikov who was not even a member of the Executive Committee, and by Liudvik Grimm, its secretary. Duly counter-signed by Kronstadt's senior officers, Piotr Lamanov and Alexander Kozlovsky, who had apparently learned to accept the authority and orders of the Executive Committee unquestioningly, it was then, as a matter of course, transmitted to all military and naval units under their command.

With the mobilization of the Kronstadt garrison thus put in motion and given Soviet legitimacy, Pokrovsky and Grimm sent a cable to the Executive Committee of the Oranienbaum Soviet inviting its garrison too to participate 'with armed force' in the demonstration. At the same time, and on the motion of Raskolnikov, Kronstadt's training-ships anchored in Biorke and Tranzund were ordered to 'get up steam' and to return to Kronstadt as soon as possible, since 'in Petrograd a coming-out has begun. The workers' section of the Petrograd Soviet insists on the transfer of all power to the Soviets by way of the All-Russian Congress of Soviets and the Executive Committee of the Petrograd Soviet.'[25] This order aroused fierce opposition from Alexander Perstnev, chairman of the committee of the Baltic Naval Half-Depot, who pleaded thus:

Comrades, the active navy is deployed in advanced positions where it is needed, and it is not right to order it back. If the Soviet wants state power it needs no armed 'coming-out' in order to take it. It is ridiculous to drag out the entire navy and all the troops against some ten [capitalist ministers].[26]

Raskolnikov had also decided to cable a request to the torpedo-boats in Helsingfors to give armed cover to the motley civilian flotilla put together to transport Kronstadt's contingent to the Petrograd demonstration, and he only desisted after Lieutenant Piotr Lamanov rejected such interference in naval operations as 'amounting to state treason'. Lamanov also vetoed the use of the training-ship *Okean*, the only military vessel moored in the Kronstadt harbour, and countermanded the order recalling the training-ships from Biorke and Tranzund.[27]

Raskolnikov also intended asking the Bolshevik-dominated Central Committee of the Baltic Fleet to despatch armed ships equipped with guns to Kronstadt, but, on second thoughts, did not send off the order which, significantly enough, he had written out and signed on a form bearing the heading and the seal of the Bolshevik Military Organization.[28]

Lazar Bregman, for his part, sent a directive to the commandant of the fortress authorizing him, in the name of the Executive Committee, to issue some 60,000 bullets and 500 revolvers from the artillery store; duly received, these were then stacked in Anchor Square. With a flotilla of private and state-owned ships, tugboats and barges put together and the details of the marching route from the English Quay to the Tauride Palace worked out, a commission to lead the demonstration was elected, consisting of seven Bolsheviks (Raskolnikov, Roshal, Stepan Grediushko, Afanasii Remnev, Mikhail Martynov, Andrei Samoukov and Aleksei Pavlov) and two SRs (Piotr Beliaevsky and Georgii Pupuridi).[29] By 5 a.m. preparations for the expedition to Petrograd were complete.

Thus, when the siren of the steamship plant sounded at 6 a.m. on 4 July, the better part of Kronstadt's naval crews, infantry and artillery units, estimated at some ten to twelve thousand men, assembled in Anchor Square, all armed with rifles, there to receive five to ten bullets each. Adding to their ranks was a contingent of armed workers and a medical platoon equipped with stretchers and commanded by the Bolshevik Dr Victor Deshevoi.[30] At 6.30 a.m., just as they began to board the boats and barges, Piotr Beliaevsky, one of the demonstration's two SR leaders, received an urgent order from the Central Committee of the SRs 'categorically prohibiting' the demonstration; about to announce the order, he was told that since some boat-loads were already on their way to Petrograd, it would be impossible to hold the others back.[31] Grigorii Smoliansky, too, received a similar cable,[32] this time from the Central Executive Committee of Soviets, while the SR Mikhail Evstingeev, the Kronstadt Soviet's third liaison delegate to the Petrograd Soviet's Executive Committee, was simply ignored when, hurrying back on a tugboat to intercept the flotilla, he tried to persuade the Kronstadters to turn back since 'no one has called you to Petrograd, and everything is quiet there'.[33]

The Kronstadters' disembarkation on the Nicolaevsky and University Quays near the Nicolaevsky Bridge at 11 a.m. proceeded smoothly and to the cheers of a procession of workers from the factories of Vasiliev Island who were then on their way to the Tauride Palace. It was only a few older workers who seemed somewhat taken aback at the sight of these men, armed to the teeth, although many spectators also eyed them apprehensively from their windows which they were gruffly and emphatically told to shut.[34] When asked why they had come, some Kronstadters replied, 'To help make order in Petrograd, for the bourgeois here have got out of line.'[35] Two emissaries from the Central Executive Committee, who awaited them with messages urging moderation, were just ignored. But extremist agitators, among them the inevitable Bleikhman, received a sympathetic hearing when they called for the overthrow of the provisional government.[36]

With Raskolnikov and Roshal effectively in charge of the expeditionary force, and Liubovich and Flerovsky awaiting them at the quay, as arranged, with instructions from the Bolshevik Military Organization, the demonstration was taken straight to the Bolshevik headquarters in the Kshesinskaia mansion rather than on the direct route to the Tauride Palace as the marching orders of the Executive Committee prescribed, a change intended to put it under the command of the Bolshevik Military Organization, notably Nikolai Podvoisky and Vladimir Nevsky, and, very likely, to impress Lenin and sway a hesitant Bolshevik Central Committee.[37] The reason given by Liubovich, who ordered the detour, was 'to join some military units waiting for us there', an explanation that eased the minds of Yarchuk and the Left SR leaders who were thus made to believe that they would together make up 'a more impressive force'.[38] But, arriving at the Kshesinskaia mansion to find no military units waiting for them, they soon realized that they had been led by the nose and side-tracked into a Bolshevik mass meeting, with speeches being delivered from the mansion's balcony.

The first to speak was Yakov Sverdlov, the Bolshevik party's secretary, who welcomed them as 'the vanguard of the Russian revolution'; he was followed by Anatolii Lunacharsky, who made a long speech and told the heavily armed Kronstadters to proceed to the Tauride Palace and there pronounce their 'imperious word'.[39] Finally Lenin spoke, greeting them as 'the pride and glory of the Russian revolution'. Proclaiming his confidence in the victory of the slogan 'All Power to Soviets', he then called for 'tenacity, stead-fastness and vigilance'. The assembled Kronstadters responded with a 'rousing ovation' and shouts of 'Long live comrade Lenin!'[40] But Lenin's call for moderation surprised many; certainly Liubovich recalled that neither the impatient Anarchists nor many of the Bolsheviks, all formed up in 'an armed column straining for the fight', could envisage contenting themselves with a 'peaceful demonstration'.[41]

At this point, the SR leaders Grigorii Smoliansky, Boris Donskoi and Alexander Brushvit, their patience exhausted, told Raskolnikov they 'had not come for a meeting here, but for a demonstration in front of the Tauride Palace', and off they walked in angry protest;[42] so did Alexander Baranov, an SR member of the Kronstadt Soviet, who could not stomach being led under the Kshesinskaia balcony to receive 'Lenin's blessings', duped by those who denounced others for 'carrying portraits of Kerensky'.[43] Yarchuk hissed furiously: 'This is scandalous! We have not come to listen to Bolshevik speeches here!' But he nevertheless stayed on even after the Bolshevik leaders finally sealed their party's takeover of the Kronstadt demonstration by placing at its head a huge banner of the Bolshevik Central Committee; his bitter complaint that this was a demonstration which had set out 'led by the Executive Committee [of the Kronstadt Soviet]', and 'under flags which [the Kronstadt garrison] had brought with it', was simply ignored.[44]

The rousing speeches over, the huge procession then crossed the Neva on the Troitsky Bridge and moved through the Mars Fields, Sadovaia Street and the Nevsky and Liteinyi Prospects towards the Tauride Palace, there to make a show of strength in support of Kronstadt's petition to the Central Executive Committee of Soviets to take power.

A strange demonstration it was: a dense forest of rifles and bayonets, but only few flags, and a muted band; the mood was sombre and grim, especially along the Nevsky Prospect, with its shops and banks closing, windows slamming shut, and throngs of well-dressed strollers, silent and aloof, if not hostile, as the Kron-stadters marched through 'veritable enemy country'.[45] They had turned into the Liteinyi Prospect and were just reaching Pantelemon-ovskaia Street at 3 in the afternoon, when what had so far been an orderly, if intimidating, demonstration turned into panic and near-rout. This notorious mêlée has had many chroniclers, including

the Bolshevik Victor Deshevoi who told the Kronstadt Soviet the
very next day that 'everyone saw a different story'.[46] But the SR
Alexander Baranov, a medical orderly in the Kronstadt fortress
hospital, giving his version to the Soviet on 7 July in the critical
presence of Raskolnikov, Yarchuk and Deshevoi, may have provided
an objective and certainly unchallenged account.[47] He left the
demonstration to go and visit his sister in the Liteinyi Prospect:

When I heard the band I went onto the balcony and, from the fourth floor,
saw our huge demonstration stretching from the Pantelemonovskaia to the
Nevsky and beyond. Then the first shot was fired, from a house opposite
Zhukovskaia as could be seen clearly from its flash. Everyone dashed to the
sides. There was pandemonium! It was impossible to control the crowd!
People, though armed, threw away their rifles, broke through the windows
and hid. Not a living soul remained in the street. Some, standing behind
house corners, shot indiscriminately. Mind you, many did not know how to
handle their rifles. I grabbed bandages and went down to treat the wounded.
There were many killed and wounded. Soon the shooting died down, and
only intermittent shots were heard.

Just who fired that first shot has never been established. But if
that was his intention, he could not have wrought more havoc
among Kronstadt's sailors and soldiers, for many of whom this was
their baptism of fire.

After supreme efforts, the Bolshevik leaders Raskolnikov and
Roshal, Flerovsky, Bregman and Deshevoi succeeded in calming
down the panicky and irate demonstrators, some of whom continued
to spray suspect houses with bullets, while others pointed their rifles
at open windows, thus forcing them to be closed.[48] But they failed
to restore the crowd's original well-disciplined appearance. Only
when they were about to reach the Tauride Palace was some
semblance of order restored, as the Kronstadters marched, with the
band playing and the First Machine-Gunners cheering them on, to
join the crowd pressing on the palace.[49]

While the leaders of the organizing commission went inside to
present Kronstadt's petition, a group of sailors banged at the door –
Yarchuk feared they would 'take the whole Tauride to pieces' –
calling for Minister of Justice Pereverzev. In his absence, and disregarding the warning of Tseretelli, Victor Chernov went out to the
sailor crowd. Pandemonium broke loose when he tried to explain
and justify the Soviet leaders' coalitionist policies.[50] One irate worker
is reported to have shaken his fist at him, shouting, 'Take power
when it is given to you, you son of a bitch!'[51] The sailors of Kron-

stadt's radical Artificers' School would sooner have 'wrung the neck of the coalitionist leaders' than have given them power.[52] They promptly grabbed Chernov and pushed him into a car and, had it not been for the intervention of Raskolnikov and Trotsky, and of an alert ship's piper who blew the ship's signal and thus enabled them to make themselves heard in silence, Chernov might well have been lynched. The revolution's chronicler Nikolai Sukhanov's classical account[53] of Chernov's rescue by Trotsky has been repeated many times. Raskolnikov's is less known, though not very different:

Trotsky jumped onto the bonnet of the car and, waving his hand, signalled for silence. The noise died down and there was deadly silence. With his powerful, sharp voice, weighing every word and enunciating every syllable, he said something like this: 'Comrades, Kronstadters, pride and glory of the Russian revolution! I cannot think for a moment that the arrest of the socialist minister Chernov was your deliberate decision! I am convinced that there is not a single person here who stands for his arrest and would lift his hand to disgrace, by this futile and unauthorized act, today's demonstration, our festive day, our solemn review of revolutionary forces. He who stands for violence, let him raise his hand!' Here comrade Trotsky stopped and glared at the crowd as if throwing down the gauntlet to his opponents. Having listened to his speech with great attention, the crowd froze in dumb silence; there was not so much as a whisper of disapproval. 'Comrade Chernov, you are free!' said Trotsky triumphantly, and, with a wave of his hand invited him to leave the car. Chernov was more dead than alive. I helped him get out. Looking withered and tormented and with an uncertain and hesitating step, he went up the stairs and disappeared into the vestibule.[54]

After Chernov's discomfiture, the crowd shouted, 'Tseretelli, Tseretelli!' as if sensing that he was the key figure in the political drama and that it was he who had to be persuaded of the all-power-to-Soviets panacea. Indeed some sailors, among them a few Anarchists, keen to arrest him, had already been searching for him.[55] Though a courageous man, Tseretelli apparently had no stomach for facing an angry Kronstadt crowd and explaining his policy: he had done that before in Anchor Square and had certainly not enjoyed the experience. Thus it was Zinoviev who came out of the Palace, defusing the atmosphere somewhat when he asked, 'Will you have me instead of Tseretelli?' and then proceeding to thank them all for the demonstration and to ask them to disperse peacefully.[56]

At this point even the Kronstadt Bolshevik leaders and Yarchuk realized that they had better wind up the demonstration, and Raskolnikov advised the majority to return to Kronstadt, telling those who wanted to stay overnight to turn for quarters to the Naval

School, the Grenadier Regiment and the Kshesinskaia mansion.
Thus the bulk of the Kronstadters limped home on 4 July as best as
they could. Foma Parchevsky saw them arrive 'after darkness had
set in': 'They who had been straining for a fight looked pitiful,
simply like a beaten army; some without caps, others without
rifles; their uniforms torn and bloodstained; some were seriously
wounded.'[57] Indeed, they were so rapidly discredited that by 5 July
Alexander Baranov reported that it was dangerous for Kronstadters
to show themselves in Petrograd. 'There were instances of Kronstadters returning from furlough who, asked to identify themselves
as they crossed the Palace Bridge, were shouted at by the crowds:
"Throw them into the water!" '[58]

Two Kronstadt sailors, Aleko Fadeev and Mikhail Mikhailov,
who had stayed on in Petrograd, were arrested by a detachment of
military cadets on 7 July as they tried to make their way home, and
a rough time they had of it:

While we were being led through the streets, the intelligentsia pounced on
us, determined to kill us. Some of them said scandalous things about us,
that we were German agents . . . when we passed the Naval Staff building,
even the doorman there begged our guard to line us up on the bank and
shoot us . . .[59]

Flerovsky, too, had a narrow escape. Walking along the Nevsky
in the evening with Lunacharsky, someone with '[a tsarist] Order
of St George in his lapel' recognized him and shouted, 'Here's a
Kronstadter! This one's always there at meetings!' But for his quick
wit, a lucky arrest, and the intervention of SR leader Gots, he would
surely have been lynched.[60]

That Kronstadt's reputation did not greatly improve for some
time can be gauged from the decision of the Kronstadt Executive
Committee to instruct all units to compile lists of demonstrators still
missing and to cancel all leave 'so that comrades will not be subjected to arrest in Petrograd and other places'.[61] Even from as far
away as Arkhangelsk, there came complaints of outright discrimina-
tion against Kronstadters, to the point of their being excluded from
the local Soviet and the Central Committee of the Northern Sea
Flotilla.[62]

With Raskolnikov's election as commandant of the Kshesinskaia
mansion by the Bolshevik Military Organization in the morning of
5 July, it was the 700 or so Kronstadt sailors from the Artificers'
School and the training-ship *Okean* who had remained in Petrograd

who then became its main force in what may have been a mere rearguard action or a desperate last bid for power by that body. Assisted by Roshal and Yarchuk, Raskolnikov readied his sailors for the defence of the Kshesinskaia. True to form, he sent a request (on Military Organization stationery) to the Kronstadt Executive Committee asking for the despatch of four artillery pieces, with the appropriate shells, and a supply of hand grenades. As he explained in the letter which his emissaries, the sailors Nikolai Platonov and Ignatii Selitskii, delivered to the Kronstadt Executive Committee on 5 July, 'This military equipment is required for the self-defence of the units of the Kronstadt garrison in Petrograd against possible attacks by counter-revolutionary forces.'[63] He also sent a request to the Central Committee of the Baltic Fleet in Helsingfors for a gunboat or a torpedo-ship, convinced that 'it would suffice to send one good warship into the mouth of the Neva to make the provisional government significantly less decisive'.[64] Pleading for help before the Kronstadt Soviet, his emissaries made out an eloquent case:

The cossacks and the Preobrazhentsy are moving against us. They have seized and raised the Nikolaevsky Bridge and fortified it with their own machine-guns. The Vyborg District, the Petrograd District and the area of the Tauride Palace are occupied by our troops. During the night the enemy tried to attack the [Bolshevik] Central Committee in the Kshesinskaia, but we beat them off. The larger part of the Kronstadt garrison is in the [Kshesinskaia] and has decided to offer resistance. We have been sent with this plea: if you are in sympathy, give us all-out help!

Afanasii Remnev, who had earlier returned to Kronstadt leaving half of the unit under his command 'surrounded' in the Kshesinskaia, supported them strongly. He proposed returning to Petrograd 'to rescue our comrades, among whom there are many wounded. I must bring my unit back, I shall take a machine-gun and free my unit.'[65]

Remnev's threat to go it alone started a debate in which Victor Deshevoi, spokesman for the Bolshevik faction, urged that the guns be sent since Raskolnikov 'was not the man to request help unless it was needed', but at the same time he also counselled sending a delegation to the Central Executive of Soviets to declare that 'we are against bloodshed and share the view of the Central Executive Committee that the question of power cannot be decided for the time being'. His final proposal was a compromise: to send the delegation and have the guns 'ready' should they be needed. The

Soviet, interested solely in extricating the Kronstadters from Petrograd, thus decided to refuse the guns and send a delegation consisting of two representatives of each of the four political factions to the Central Executive Committee to negotiate the Kronstadters' return home together with their weapons.[66]

It was only after a series of tedious and tough negotiations that the Central Executive Committee finally agreed to give the stranded Kronstadters free passes, provided that they surrender their weapons, and Raskolnikov, Roshal and Yarchuk had no easy task in convincing their hotheads, who 'had a burning desire to join battle with the provisional government' and refused to 'run away', that it would be 'nonsense and madness' to throw themselves into a desperate fight.[67] Finally, however, they accepted the terms offered and returned to Kronstadt late in the evening of 6 July, humiliated, angry and disarmed. As Nikolai Rostov joked, punning on the Zimmerwald formula, they made 'peace without annexations' in evacuating the Petropavlovsk fortress, but, since they had been forced to surrender their rifles, it was not peace 'without contributions'.[68]

Next day the Kronstadt Soviet held a post-mortem debate on the fiasco of the July Days which, far from giving power to Soviets, had greatly weakened them and certainly discredited Kronstadt. The blame was firmly and naturally enough fastened on the Kronstadt Bolsheviks rather than on the demonstration itself, which was seen by both SR and Menshevik critics alike as a well-nigh irresistible act of nature. Brushvit, who both in Anchor Square and the Naval Assembly had tried to prevent the demonstration, expressed the general tenor of feelings:

I cannot condemn anyone. I saw the faces of those who went and they bore not the slightest sign of any wish to go against the will of the people, they were convinced that our will is the will of the entire working people. When they went to seek the truth, they thought that only thus could Russia be saved, and it never occurred to them that they were going against the whole of Russia . . . Kronstadt may have made a mistake, but its intentions were good.[69]

In the same forgiving vein the Mensheviks deplored the 'tragedy and futility' of the 'armed demonstration', but described as 'intrinsically beautiful' the 'enthusiasm which suddenly, and with an elemental force, gripped the masses and brought them armed into the streets of Petrograd'.[70]

Critics such as Bogomolov and Sokolov probed somewhat

clumsily and perhaps half-heartedly into the methods the Bolshevik leaders had employed to promote a Soviet demonstration and then turn it into a Bolshevik venture. Anatolii Lamanov, Raskolnikov's chief critic, returned again and again to the key matter: Raskolnikov, who was not even a member of the Executive Committee, had illegally usurped its authority during the night of 3 July and used the emergency powers vested in it. He had exploited a rump of some eight Committee members and complemented them with representatives of naval and military units whose credentials had not been verified to make the crucial decisions leading to 'the death of many soldiers, sailors and workers'. Raskolnikov, conveniently ignoring the fact that it was his comrades, in particular Victor Deshevoi, who had then prevented the convening of the Soviet, now, in rebutting Lamanov's charges, invested that body, of which he was a deputy chairman, with supreme power. Appealing obliquely to its deputies' sense of importance, Raskolnikov declared:

I reckon the Soviet is the higher institution and has greater authority than the Executive Committee, which is merely its executive organ and formed from within. Whenever an acute problem arises the [Executive Committee] is obliged to appeal to the Soviet. In my view, the chairman [of the Soviet] and his deputy have the right to sign all official documents issuing from the Executive Committee.

Lamanov, refusing to get into a constitutional argument, insisted that Raskolnikov had clearly 'exceeded his competence': 'There must be a strict delimitation between what the one ought to do and what the others ought to do, and even if I am accused of formalism, I still delimit my rights strictly, for I have no right to assert my own will but only to assert the general will.'[71]

Whatever moral satisfaction he may have derived from his denunciation of Raskolnikov – Yarchuk protested vehemently against him assuming the role of 'prosecutor'[72] – it remained but a futile *post-factum* showdown, in no way compensating for Lamanov's pathetic failure to match Raskolnikov's consummate skill and daring during the crucial night of 3 July and thus prevent him from using Kronstadt for Bolshevik ends.

All in all, Kronstadters were in a chastened if not contrite mood in the wake of the July Days. When Grigorii Smoliansky, chairman of the Kronstadt committee of the SRs, appealed to the Soviet to condemn the 'shameful act of violence' perpetrated on Victor Chernov, 'the veteran and honoured revolutionary', and to send its apologies to the Central Executive Committee of Soviets and to the party of Socialist Revolutionaries with an expression of confidence in Chernov as a 'revolutionary political figure', he won virtually unanimous support. The notable exception was Efim Yarchuk who thought they had 'gone overboard'.[73]

In the same accommodating if not submissive mood, on 8 July the Soviet, on the motion of Smoliansky, and with the consent of all political factions, proposed to the Central Executive Committee that in order to dispel 'the suspicions' under which Kronstadt had fallen, it make provision to screen the members of its Soviet and Executive Committee, confident that the leaders of the Central Executive Committee, as 'veteran and honest revolutionaries', could be trusted to administer 'speedy and fair justice'. Proposing his motion Smoliansky struck an optimistic note and predicted that power would 'gradually pass to the Soviets' because the conservative Kadets and Progressists were leaving the government, while those who remained, such as Nabokov and Tereshchenko, had parted company with them, and, in calling themselves 'democratic revolutionaries', had only just stopped short of 'becoming socialists'. In his opinion it would only be a matter of some ten to twelve days before the problem of power was solved 'satisfactorily', and then the Democratic Republic would be proclaimed at last and would take action against counter-revolutionary activities. As an encouraging sign of the times he pointed particularly to the closure of the right-wing *Malenkaia gazeta* and the arrest of its editors.[74]

In the same vein, and very likely in response to Kerensky's angry order of 7 July accusing the Kronstadters of harbouring traitors in their midst, an enlarged meeting of the Executive Committee, in which representatives of all naval units' committees participated, was held on 10 July when it adopted a restrained, conciliatory, though dignified resolution. Inviting an Investigation Commission to ascertain whether there were any 'provocateurs and spies' among them, it promised that if such were identified, they would be handed over. 'Deep regret' at the loss of life of innocent citizens in Petrograd was then expressed, though it was pointed out that this had been caused by the shots and actions of 'unknown and sinister individuals' who had thus 'blackened our idealistic demonstration'; finally, the resolution affirmed Kronstadt's full subordination to the provisional government, acting in agreement with the All-Russian Soviet of Workers', Soldiers' and Peasants' Deputies, as 'the only authoritative organ of the revolutionary democracy', at the same time maintaining its opinion that all power must be transferred to the All-Russian Congress of Soviets. Three delegates from Kronstadt's naval units, together with the commander of the naval forces, were then commissioned to present the resolution to the Ministry of the Navy.[75]

Thus, under the leadership of the SRs Pokrovsky, Smoliansky and Brushvit, Kronstadt demonstrated that not even Kerensky's threatening order of 7 and 13 July could provoke them to abandon their novel, moderate and conciliatory policy.

In his angry, cavalier fashion, Kerensky had accused Kronstadt (rather than its Bolshevik leaders), together with the Baltic battle-ships *Petropavlovsk* and *Respublika*, of having stabbed in the back an army that was fighting the enemy in 'bloody battle'. Demanding that Kronstadt's military forces surrender the ringleaders within twenty-four hours and declare their complete submission to the provisional government, he threatened that otherwise they would be declared 'traitors to the fatherland and to the revolution' and that 'the most drastic measures' would be taken against them. He also ordered the disbandment of the Baltic Fleet's Central Committee, on which Kronstadt was duly represented, and the holding of new elections.[76]

On 11 July, as a follow-up to Kerensky's 7 July order, Deputy Minister for the Navy Boris Dudorov ordered the immediate arrest of Roshal, Raskolnikov and Remnev, the leaders of the 'Kronstadt sailors' demonstration', on a charge of treason against the state, while the Bolshevik *Golos pravdy* was to be closed as an 'accessory to crime' and a search made of its premises.[77]

The Kronstadt Soviet's immediate reply to Kerensky was restrained but firm: Kronstadt had always endeavoured to serve 'the interests of the revolution in the name of the emancipation of the toilers'; it harboured no 'counter-revolutionary ringleaders' in its midst, and therefore could not arrest them; and, finally, 'We assure the provisional government of our subordination, but stand resolute for the transfer of power to the Soviets.'[78] The reply to Dudorov's demands was compliant, but made under protest. In its resolution of 13 July, the Soviet declared that 'in view of the ulti-matum' of the provisional government, it welcomed the decision of Raskolnikov and Remnev to turn themselves in for investigation and declared that it had no knowledge of the whereabouts of Roshal (who had gone into hiding). Denouncing the closure of *Golos pravdy* as an act 'unworthy of the Russian revolution', it said that while it would not resist the closure of the paper, and would allow the commandant of the fortress, General Gerasimov, to search its premises, representatives of the Soviet must be present on that occasion.[79]

Before leaving for Petrograd to turn himself in, Raskolnikov made a farewell speech in the Kronstadt Soviet on 13 July. Opening with a paean of praise to 'the freedom that there is now in liberated Russia' which 'nowhere yet has its equal', he accused the provisional government of trying, by way of arrests and the closure of newspapers, to reduce the country to the war-time levels of France and England with their 'regulations and restrictions'. Exhorting 'Kronstadt's revolutionaries' to refrain from rash actions that could lead to bloodshed, he pleaded for their trust in him as the same 'deeply dedicated and honest man' upon whom they had bestowed 'the exalted title of deputy chairman of the Soviet'. Warm applause greeted his declaration of love: 'The four months which I spent in Kronstadt and in its revolutionary Soviet of Workers' and Soldiers' Deputies will remain the most cherished and joyful of my life. Farewell, comrades!'[80]

Raskolnikov meant what he said. Even Foma Parchevsky, who had no love for Kronstadt's Bolsheviks, had learned to respect him as a 'cultured man and an idealist'.[81] He was certainly that, but he was also a young Bolshevik professional par excellence.

Although *Golos pravdy* was closed down on 13 July, it reappeared the next day as *Proletarskoe delo*, now in an edition of no less than 12,000 copies, since until late July it also served as the organ of the Bolshevik Central Committee in lieu of *Pravda* which had also been closed down.

The Soviet and the military commanders, notably Lieutenant Piotr Lamanov, commander of the naval forces, also complied formally with the orders of the provisional government: they did disband the 'transitory companies' of the First Naval Depot and despatch them to the front, but only a mere handful arrived there, while the rest drifted back; they also lowered the red flags on the ships, replacing them with traditional Andreev naval flags; but it was only in enabling the Judicial Investigation Commission to return to Kronstadt, wind up its affairs and transfer the remaining imprisoned officers to Petrograd that they yielded the provisional government its only major net gain during Kronstadt's brief period of contrite moderation following the July Days.[82]

The Soviet even complied with the provisional government's appointment of Captain N. D. Tyrkov as commandant of the Kronstadt fortress to replace their *elected* commandant, General Gerasimov, and similarly acquiesced in the subordination of the elected commander of Naval Forces, Lieutenant Piotr Lamanov, to Tyrkov's command, all part of Kerensky's plan to free Kronstadt's military and naval establishment from Soviet control.

Captain Tyrkov arrived in Kronstadt on 14 July with a detachment of cyclists commanded by Staff-Captain L. K. Artomonov; by the next day he had already made such a fool of himself when searching for the 'German spies', Roshal and Lenin, on the *Zare svobody* that he had to apologize to its crew. He fared no better the day after, when he reviewed a parade of all naval crews in the Naval Manège, causing great resentment by publicly insulting their commander, the very popular Lieutenant Piotr Lamanov, and being laughed out of court when, at the end of the parade, he suddenly fell on his knees and recited a prayer. By 17 July, commissar Foma Parchevsky and Kronstadt's senior officers were all convinced that Tyrkov was mentally unbalanced, if not quite mad, and they alerted the Assistant Minister for the Navy, Lieutenant Vladimir Lebedev, who arrived post-haste to recall him. Appointed to replace him as commandant of the Kronstadt fortress, Captain L. K. Artamonov made a point of working 'in close contact' with the Executive Committee, but whether he threw in his lot with the Kronstadt Soviet because he read the situation well or because, being of Left SR sympathies, he liked what he saw, is difficult to decide. The cyclists under his command certainly felt very much at home in Kronstadt from the day of their arrival.[83]

Thus Kerensky's attempt to bring the Kronstadt fortress and its military and naval establishments under the control of the provisional government ended in farce. Small wonder that he took no action when General Aleksei Brusilov, the comander-in-chief, suggested in a memorandum of 18 July that he 'finish once and for all with Kronstadt – that nest of bolshevism', disarm it and, should the garrison resist, bombard it.[84] He just did not have the 'two pre-war battalions' that Parchevsky later thought would have been required to do the job.[85]

Though outwardly compliant, internally the Kronstadt Soviet

closed ranks. Even the Mensheviks who had suffered so many ignominies and humiliations at the hands of their Bolshevik rivals in the Soviet, and especially in Anchor Square, jumped to their rescue now that they were under a cloud and subjected to repression. Piotr Kamyshev, speaking for the local Menshevik Committee, declared that 'since the Bolsheviks are baited', the Mensheviks regarded it as their duty to support 'the comrades' and 'this, our duty, we shall fulfil'.[86]

A similar spirit pervaded the 13 July Soviet Appeal 'To all soldiers, sailors and workers of Kronstadt', protesting against the 'unscrupulous and dishonest' slander campaign which accused 'an entire political party or its leaders' of being in the paid service of the Germans. The Appeal reminded Kronstadters that all socialist parties had together fought, suffered repression and overthrown tsarism, and that all had stood together since the revolution, engaged in 'glorious creative work'; anyone who slandered a socialist party or leader was branded 'an enemy of the people'; and, finally, the Appeal called for 'solidarity and unity among all truly revolutionary forces', urging the masses to 'rally closely around the Soviet and the organizations which [they] have created'.[87]

The Kronstadt Soviet also declared its solidarity with the Central Committee of the Baltic Fleet (Tsentrobalt) which had been disbanded by Kerensky, and with its delegates, including its chairman, Pavel Dybenko, who had been arrested in Petrograd for alleged incitement to rebellion during the July Days. It demanded the 'speediest release' of those arrested for holding 'radical left-wing political opinions', unless other charges had been preferred against them; and, finally, it reaffirmed revolutionary Kronstadt's loyalty to the transfer of power to the Soviets as providing the 'only solution' to the national crisis.[88]

Kronstadt's subdued and moderate mood was but short-lived, and on 17 July it gave a hostile enough reception to Vladimir Lebedev when he addressed a meeting of some 10,000, mostly sailors, held in the Naval Manège. Misjudging their mood of outward compliance, he harked back to their exploits in Petrograd during the July Days but condescendingly assured the sailor crowd that 'the revolutionary democracy' did not hold all of them responsible, and was sure that those who were responsible had repented: 'You made a mistake – may this be your last!' This provoked the angry sailors to fire some searching and hostile questions at him, interspersed with 'shouted threats'. Had it not been for Commissar Parchevsky pleading for courteous treatment of a visitor, and then contriving to get him out of the Manège and into the waiting car which took him to the safety of the Soviet in the Naval Assembly, he would have been man-handled, if not more severely beaten up.[89]

A few days later, Anchor Square resumed its daily meetings and, on 20 July, adopted the inevitable radical resolution urging the transfer of power to the Soviets, the abolition of the death penalty for insubordination and mutiny at the front which had been re-introduced by Kerensky, and the despatch of all cossacks, former policemen and gendarmes to the front, as well as the disbandment of the distrusted special 'death battalion'.[90]

On 23 July, the Kronstadt Soviet cabled its protest against 'the destruction of workers' party and trade union organizations' to the Central Executive Committee of Soviets, demanding the final dis-bandment of the state Duma as a 'hearth of reaction and a threat to the revolution'.[91]

A few days later, on 28 July, and in response to the Central Executive Committee's request to join it and give the 'most vigorous support' to the new coalition government formed on 24 July 'in its measures aimed at defending the country and the revolution and at consolidating the revolution on the basis of its programme of 8 July', the Soviet resumed its perennial debate on power.[92] Victor Deshevoi, speaking for the Bolshevik faction, thought the new coalition government no different from the old, indeed worse and more to the right, since its socialist ministers were no longer responsible to the Soviet but only to 'their consciences'; what was needed was a 'firm revolutionary power based on the Soviets'.[93] It was apparently no easy matter for the Bolsheviks in Soviet-run Kronstadt to follow Lenin's example and directives in the wake of the July Days and scrap the 'All Power to Soviets' war-cry, dismissing it, *à la* Lenin, as 'Don Quixotism or a mere mockery'.[94]

Both Anatolii Lamanov, speaking for the Non-Party group, and Piotr Ediet, for the Mensheviks, urged that the new government be given a chance. Ediet noted with satisfaction that it included more socialists than the old one and that it was firmly committed to a far-reaching radical democratic programme; in the given situation, both those on the left who still repeated the slogan 'All Power to Soviets', as well as those on the right who stood for coalition with the bourgeoisie 'at any price', were doctrinaires. Lamanov thought they should support the government in all measures directed towards 'defence against the external enemy and the crushing of counter-revolution' but at the same time they should demand that the Central Executive Committee maintain 'vigilant' watch to ensure that the government's performance accorded with the 8 July programme, and this could only be achieved if they rallied to the Soviets and strove for 'the victory of the toilers'.

Yarchuk's was the only dissenting voice as he propounded his own slogan, 'All power to the toiling people' and opposed 'the Bolshevik slogan "All Power to Soviets!" ' as long as those bodies were not 'remade and elected anew'. In short, what was the point of all the talk about 'the democracy' when it was still 'the class struggle' that was on the agenda, he asked, while the SR Piotr Beliaevsky protested the Bolsheviks labelling as 'petty-bourgeois' the eighty million 'toiling peasants' whom the SRs represented.[95]

With all four major factions moving their own resolutions, a commission was elected to draft a resolution that in the end proved acceptable to all but Yarchuk and some nine deputies who abstained. It did not, as had been requested, endorse the Central Executive Committee's resolution, but rephrased and sharpened it. Urging the need for a 'firm and strong revolutionary state power which is supported by the entire toiling revolutionary democracy', the Soviet promised its full support to 'those government measures' aimed at strengthening and broadening the revolution and defending the country. Requesting the Central Executive Committee to watch that the government did not deviate from the 8 July programme, the Soviet at the same time declared that 'for its part' it would itself rebuff all encroachments on the 'rights and activities of the legitimate organs of the revolutionary democracy' and that it continued to maintain its long-held position regarding 'the organization of power'. What the resolution did not do, though such had been the request, was to promise 'active support' to the government, nor did it endorse 'the socialist comrades' entry into the provisional government'.[96] But, in the circumstances, this was quite as far as the Kronstadt Soviet could go towards the Central Executive Committee without compromising its own long-standing and deep commitment to Soviet power.

Indeed, the formation on 24 July of the second coalition government, which dashed Smoliansky's and many a Kronstadter's sanguine hopes for a more radical government in which the Soviets would be the senior partner, coincided with a Bolshevik recovery and a leftward turn in the Kronstadt Soviet. Thus in the elections to the town Duma held on 26 July and based on universal as distinct from Soviet franchise, the Bolsheviks emerged as one of Kronstadt's two major parties. While 46,051 had voting rights, only 28,154 (i.e. 61%) voted, the SRs receiving 38.7% (10,900) and the Bolsheviks 36.3% (10,219). However, in Kronstadt proper, excluding the remote forts Ino (on the Finnish coast) and Krasnaia Gorka (on the mainland), with their heavy SR vote, the Bolsheviks received 9,027 votes compared with the 8,345 votes of the SRs and, even more significantly, of 4,550 sailor votes, 2,653 (58.3%) went to the Bolsheviks, with a mere 1,514 (33.3%) going to the SRs.[97]

Another Bolshevik triumph was the 27 July forced resignation of Foma Parchevsky, who had been a thorn in the Bolsheviks' side ever since his election as commissar of the provisional government at the end of May. The reasons given in the Executive Committee's resolution of non-confidence were his 'castism' – he had always insisted on occupying the chief commander's box in the theatre and on other occasions, and had perpetually quarrelled with the chauffeurs – that 'right from the beginning he did not and would not know his duties and work', and, finally, that he had consistently slandered Kronstadt and its Soviet in Petrograd and had thus undermined its authority there.[98] What brought matters to a head was Parchevsky's 20 July letter to *Rech'* in which he reiterated his policy that 'Kronstadt be in unison with Russia and under no circumstances form a state within a state', and complained that he and his policy had always been 'resisted by the Bolsheviks and the Anarchists'.[99]

None of the major parties in the Soviet was prepared to nominate a candidate to succeed him and when, in the end, Piotr Ediet was elected commissar, his party colleagues, the Menshevik-Internationalists, declared on 3 August that they were opposed 'in principle' to any of their comrades occupying the post of commissar of the provisional government and that they thus bore no responsibility for Ediet's activities in that post.[100]

So much for the prestige enjoyed in Kronstadt both by the provisional government and its elected representatives. Indeed, by the beginning of August there could no longer be any doubt that Kronstadt's Soviet system of government had survived intact and that it would continue to ignore the provisional government, perhaps less flagrantly, yet with as much impunity as it had prior to the July Days.

The Bolshevik party organization, too, had almost recovered its pre-July Days strength, thanks to the arrival of a group of very experienced party workers such as the veteran professional revolutionary Liudmilla Stal, Boris Breslav, Alexander Ilyin-Zhenevsky (Raskolnikov's brother) and Piotr Zalutsky, who replaced Raskolnikov and Roshal. With a loss of some 250, it still had about 3,000 members and its *Proletarskoe delo* which, with the reappearance of the Petrograd *Pravda* (now named *Rabochyi Put'*), had reverted to its local role, was published daily in 7,000 copies; of the two major clubs, Zemlia i Volia and Sovetskii, the latter was under Bolshevik influence if not outright control, and so were most of Kronstadt's fifty or so *zemliachestva*, associations and/or clubs of countrymen formed on a local, regional or ethnic basis.[101]

In the elections to the third Kronstadt Soviet held on 9 and 10 August the Bolsheviks received ninety-six seats, drawing even with the Non-Party group; the Left SRs received seventy-three (losing eighteen seats), the Menshevik-Internationalists received thirteen (losing thirty-three seats), while the Anarchists, for the first time, gained seven seats. Accordingly, the Executive Committee consisted of ten Bolsheviks, ten Non-Partyists, eight Left SRs, one Menshevik and one Anarchist; its chairman was the Bolshevik Lazar Bregman, while his deputies were the Non-Partyist Lamanov and the Left SR Genadii Pyshkin. The Left SR Shurgin was elected chairman of the Soviet, his deputy being the Bolshevik Lebedev.[102]

The Bolsheviks, in alliance with the Left SRs, had made sure that Lamanov, their severe critic in the aftermath of the July Days, would no longer be Kronstadt's number one, but they were apparently unable or unwilling to prevent his election to the chairmanship of *Izvestiia*'s editorial commission.[103]

As distinct from the May elections to the Soviet, the SR and Menshevik losses in August were the gain of the Non-Partyists, who increased their seats from sixty-eight to at least ninety-six, and the Anarchists, rather than of the Bolsheviks. Disappointment with the Menshevik and SR parties, who were identified with the odious provisional government, was on this occasion translated into non-party sovietism and anarchism, rather than sympathy or support for the Bolshevik party whose ruthless party-mindedness and crafty role in the July Days was still resented.

Moreover, Lenin's move in the wake of the July Days to scrap the Bolshevik war-cry 'All Power to Soviets' and write off the Menshevik

and SR controlled Soviets as 'organs of collaboration with the bourgeoisie' (a decision he announced and argued in his pamphlet *On
Slogans*, printed and published in Kronstadt), sowed confusion and
consternation among Kronstadt's Bolsheviks. It was no easy matter
to explain to the party's rank and file and to Anchor Square crowds,
who took pride in Kronstadt's soviet power, that 'All Power to
Soviets' had suddenly ceased to be a good thing for Russia at large.[104]

It thus fell to the Non-Party group which, within a week of its
electoral victory, had turned into the Union of Socialist Revolutionaries–Maximalists,[105] to take up the slogan 'All Power to Soviets'
and to develop it into a full-blown Soviet ideology. Kronstadt's
newly declared SR-Maximalists were singularly well equipped for
the task. Anatolii Lamanov, their leader, was known to have opposed
the July demonstration and, seconded on the *Izvestiia* editorial
board by the Non-Partyist Nemm, who was its secretary, was in a
favourable position to give ample newspaper coverage to their
views, even though they had to be passed by three major Soviet
factions represented on the editorial board. Moreover, with the
arrival some time in May of Arsenii Zverin and Grigorii Rivkin,
Kronstadt acquired some of the outstanding founders and leaders of
Russian SR-Maximalism who may well have been responsible for
transforming the Non-Party group into the Kronstadt Union of
SR-Maximalists.

Starting out in 1906 as a small radical faction of the party of
Socialist Revolutionaries, the Maximalists were so anti-parliamen-
tarian that the SRs excluded them for having adopted 'anti-parlia-
mentarism as a dogma'; so opposed were they to political parties
that they called themselves the *Union* of SR-Maximalists; so anti-
bourgeois and anti-capitalist that they called for an immediate
urban and agrarian social revolution in Russia entailing the 'socialization of power, of the land and of the factories' and the establishment of a 'republic of toilers'. Most important of all, drawing their
inspiration from the Paris Commune and from the 'maximal
socialist' Peter Lavrov, they saw in urban Soviets and rural communes the main elements of a federal structure of local and regional
Soviets crowned by a central Soviet, in which all Soviet deputies
would be subject to direct elections, continuous accountability and
instant recall. It was a Soviet ideology par excellence which the
Maximalists brought into the February revolution and to Kronstadt.

Speaking in the Soviet and writing both in Kronstadt's *Izvestiia*

and in *Trudovaia respublika*, the joint weekly publication of the
Petrograd and Kronstadt SR-Maximalists, as well as in pamphlets,
Zverin, Rivkin, Lamanov, Ippolitov (secretary of the Kronstadt
Union of SR-Maximalists) and one contributor who signed himself
A.M. (very probably Rivkin), propounded a simple view of the
world, advancing ideas as to how it might be changed and made a
better world 'in which the toiling people would be masters', by way
of those very Soviet institutions which the Russian revolution had
created.

They saw the world divided into a large majority of simple folk
and toilers – workers, peasants, soldiers and sailors – whose labour
'created all wealth' but who had been kept 'in material, spiritual and
political dependence', condemned to 'obey and carry out orders'
while a minority of 'all sorts of parasites', 'robbers' and 'vampires'
were landowners, the bourgeoisie, the generals and the officers.[106]
However, now that tsardom had been overthrown by the toilers, the
'cunning and cruel . . . clever and well-educated bourgeoisie' was
scheming to rob them of the fruits of their revolution, so that the
'fat banker' and the 'huckster' would rule.

To prevent that happening and to put an end, once and for all, to
'the kingdom of lies, deception and darkness', the Russian revolution,
they urged, must be a *social* revolution, abolishing private property,
'the root of the evil', and transferring 'all power, land, factories and
plants to the toilers' who were, in turn, to be organized in a 'toilers'
republic' based on the Soviets and the committees which they themselves had created. The Russian revolution would thus prove that
the 'unwashed, filthy, uncombed and semi-literate people' – the
'grey muzhik and the swarthy worker, the soldier and the sailor' –
could administer the state, legislate and rule *and* turn 'the learned,
educated and cultured' into 'their servants, the punctual executors
of their will'.[107]

These views admirably fitted the experience of the Kronstadters
who, having turned the tables on their betters, took fierce pride in
the Soviet power which they had created. Indeed, Arsenii Zverin's
simple and pure Soviet ideology may well have appealed to their
hearts and minds in a way that the Marxist rhetoric and party
jargon of the Bolsheviks could not, especially after Lenin had shorn
it of its Soviet component in the aftermath of the July Days.

Denouncing Kerensky's order to disband the Central Committee
of the Baltic Fleet, which he castigated as the presumptuous attempt

of 'one man' to 'annul our will, the will of the entire fleet', Zverin, speaking in the Soviet on 8 July, extolled the 'elective principle' as the creative heart of the Russian revolution:[108]

The elective principle is the foundation of our people's revolution, of our people's state power and of our popular organizations. What distinguishes our revolution from others is that it has class organizations of the toilers . . . In our Soviets of Workers' and Soldiers' Deputies, army, ship, factory and plant committees, each and every representative is responsible to his electors and when he ceases to implement their will, they are obliged to remove him . . .

Conscious of if not obsessed by the failure of the French revolution of 1789 to transfer power to the toiling people which had 'shed its blood' in the struggle for 'justice and liberty',[109] Zverin, Rivkin and their comrades were convinced that the Russian revolution would succeed where all preceding revolutions had failed. As Zverin urged in the Kronstadt Soviet on 17 July, when addressing a soldiers' delegation from the northern front:[110]

No other revolution has so far found the organizational forms of the emancipation of labour. Only the Russian people – not because of its special merits but because of its special historical circumstances – has found the saving form, and that is the local Soviet. What is the essence of these Soviets, and why do the bourgeois, and even some who call themselves socialists, hate them with all their heart though they dare not say so openly? The reason is that into these Soviets are elected grey and ignorant people who remain all the time under the control of their electors . . . for tomorrow they may elect others to represent their interests. In these Soviets is invested the power of the entire people. Our Soviets do not operate according to the constitutional laws of the bourgeoisie, whereby they elect those whom they have never seen, trusting them merely because they belong to a certain party. That trust has always been misplaced, and, if there are constitutional-ists here, then I challenge them to prove that any deputy in France or America or here in Russia ever justified the hopes of those who elected him.

While in Zverin's 'toilers' republic' most of the 'full people's power' would be vested in local Soviets, 'in Petrograd as well as in Kronstadt', matters which were 'beyond the capacity of any one district or town' would be dealt with by the central government. Elected by the All-Russian Congress of Soviets – the national legislature – the central government would serve as its executive. Indeed, when the Congress of Soviets convened, it would have the force of a Constituent Assembly:

The workers, peasants and soldiers will assemble from all over Russia and with the right to make decisions on everything, for they are not creating a *burzhui* republic, but a toilers' republic, and that is the aim of our revolution. Should we not achieve that, then we shall lose all, power and land, to the bourgeoisie.[111]

While Lamanov, Zverin and Rivkin were shaping Kronstadt's Soviet ideology in a manner designed to rally 'the entire toiling people' around inclusive, unifying Soviets rather than divisive parties, A.M., a frequent contributor to Kronstadt's *Izvestiia*, was busy creating the religion of a toilers' revolution.

He had made his *Izvestiia* debut in May in debate with Piotr Ediet, who had lashed out against the radical rhetoric of Anchor Square, warning against its 'voluntarist, extreme elements'. Relying on the subjective revolutionary will, they took no account of objective revolutionary realities, 'promise pie in the sky and give only words, words, words', Ediet sneered. Finally, he wrote, laying down his Marxist law:

Revolutions are not made; they *occur*. They are not created; they *proceed*. The revolution is an impersonal process subject to the iron laws of historical necessity. To *understand* a revolution is to win it; to divert it from its even course – is almost certainly to betray it.[112]

A.M. promptly took him to task:[113]

A law! An iron law! It is curious how fortunate the bourgeoisie is in this unjust world: it has riches, strength and even objective scientific laws on its side! It is only the toiling people who lack good laws, only their heroic, purposeful enthusiasm that turns always into up-in-the-air Don Quixotism! Laws! . . . Perhaps laws are called 'iron' because their material manifestations are, as it were, made of metal – bullets, bayonets, machine-guns!

Worse still, while the bourgeoisie 'despite its faith in the impersonal process' dreams of a heroic saviour, of a Napoleon, its scholars lecture an exhausted mankind:

You want happiness, your suffering is intolerable, you want to put an end to tears, to children's tears, to the groan of the famished, to the insolent laughter of the executioner?! Wait, madmen, look first! The iron laws do not permit that! . . . Suffer – revolutions are not made, revolutions occur!

Yet despite A.M.'s spirited reply, the 'minimalist' *and* determinist Ediet seems to have had the last word in this debate: in his rather conciliatory reply, he invited all maximalist 'word-mongers' to take the 'road of construction and creative work' in the Soviet and for its threefold task, 'the consolidation of the revolution's gains, achieving peace, and giving the country a Constituent Assembly'.[114]

Four months later, and a great deal more impatient and angry with all those 'minimalists' who presumed to urge 'self-restraint' on the desperate popular masses, A.M. exclaimed: 'We are hungry! We freeze and we suffer from exhaustion! We are ignorant and have no schools or museums! We are the poorest and most backward nation in Europe! And now we are asked to "restrain ourselves" even more!'[115]

A.M. himself certainly knew no self-restraint, and his expectations from the 'imminent socialist revolution' were truly boundless. Since the bourgeoisie had 'disgraced itself', the 'toiling people' – the 'heirs of bourgeois society' – were destined by fate to carry out all 'the best and noblest ideas of humanity' such as 'reason, justice and virtue'. Now that the 'dawn of revolution' had broken, and 'the sun of reason was rising', the popular masses, that 'greatest accumulation of energy', would create culture on an unprecedented scale and, opening countless schools, universities, museums and theatres, would free 'the genius hidden in the souls of the millions' to 'soar high'. If mankind could produce its Platos, Edisons and Raphaels even under conditions of oppression, then in that free society based on the 'foundations of socialization' which the revolution would usher in, there would be millions more scholars, philosophers, inventors and saints.[116]

To A.M. the revolution far transcended 'the struggle of the exploited against their exploiters'; its content and significance were moral and rational; it was nothing less than 'a liturgy of light, the joyous struggle for the Kingdom of Truth, Reason and Man'.[117] Thus, it must be as moral, enlightened and non-violent as possible, its eyes set always on the great achievements of spiritual progress as on that 'pillar of fire which led the Israelites'; for otherwise, it could easily degenerate into a 'mutiny of rebellious slaves', or share the fate of the great French revolution which had been disgraced by Marat and Robespierre who destroyed the 'holy cause' and paved the road for Bonaparte.[118] In order that such perversion of the great ideas of the revolution and of socialism did not occur, the revolutionary democracy and its 'Kronstadt vanguard – pride and glory of the revolution' must, he urged, be on ever-vigilant guard.[119]

Taking Soviets for granted, A.M., in common with most SR-Maximalists, was greatly impressed with French syndicalism, seeing the syndicates as 'institutions of social transformation on communist foundations' working towards the 'collectivist society of the future', rather than as mere organs of class struggle. Favourably comparing syndicalism's respect for culture and civilization with the cultural relativism and nihilism of anarchism,[120] A.M. nevertheless thought the syndicalists had gone too far in totally rejecting political parties. What was needed was a harmonious fusion of French syndicalism with some Russian party spirit; with that proviso, A.M. felt he could commend French syndicalism to his Kronstadt readers: 'It is undeniable that in syndicalism, with its faith in progress, in rationalism, and . . . in the freedom of the individual, there throbs a real creative life which is cramped neither by party spirit nor by slogans, for syndicalism is the ideology of the producers.'[121]

Kronstadt's Soviet ideology of toilers and 'producers', shaped by the Non-Party–SR-Maximalists in the aftermath of the July Days, reached its apogee in the revolutionary upswing and enthusiasm engendered in reaction to the mutiny led by General Lavr Kornilov, commander-in-chief of Russia's armed forces, against the provisional government. On 26 August, at the head of the 'Wild Division' of Caucasian mountaineers, Kornilov marched on Petrograd (and against Kronstadt, which figured high on his list of objectives) to clear but the Soviets and assume power. Slandered Kronstadt was now asked to come to the rescue of Petrograd: in an urgent cable to the Kronstadt Soviet, the Central Executive Committee of Soviets (with the assent of Kerensky) requested the despatch of a task-force of between three and five thousand fully-armed soldiers and sailors, commanded by their officers and equipped with provisions for three to four days, 'for the protection of the Central Executive Committee of Soviets of Workers', Soldiers' and Peasants' Deputies, of the revolution and of the democratic republic'.[122] Though there was no mention of the provisional government, its evacuation to the 'safety' of Kronstadt was seriously considered.[123]

The enemy, traitorous generals, tsarist officers, cossacks, counter-revolutionary bourgeoisie, all alleged to have been involved in the Kornilov putsch, was certainly as odious as could be to the Kronstadters. Indeed, one of General Kornilov's first objectives was, naturally enough, to 'liquidate the Kronstadt fortress' and evacuate and disperse its garrison.[124] Kronstadt, for its part, responded to Petrograd's desperate call for help by immediately despatching a strong task-force and issuing an impassioned 'Appeal', written by Anatolii Lamanov in the heightened language of SR-Maximalism:[125]

The traitors of the fatherland and of the revolution thought our revolution was already half-strangled and poisoned by their insinuations and slander and that all that was needed was one final blow to put an end to liberty. But the revolution is not dead! It is alive with the unity of the revolutionary forces straining forward once again to push the wheels of history! Together, comrades, let's make the wheels turn faster towards the victory of the toiling masses! Do not permit it to stop halfway, as happened not so long ago. Once the revolution is on the move again, let us, all together, as one, rally to its defence and development, to the creation of the new life! The time has come for the toilers to become the masters and creators of their own future, the future of socialism. Forward! Long live the Republic of Toilers!

In the same vein and using the same lofty revolutionary prose, Lamanov turned again, both during and shortly after the Kornilov crisis, to appeal to 'you toilers, you creators of wealth . . . you, and you alone who create all the necessities of life', defining for them the social and political aims of the revolution – the 'complete emancipation of labour, with labour's right to the full product of its toil!' and the establishment of a 'genuine revolutionary state power' with 'Soviets and Committees' in which the 'true toiler' will be the 'sovereign master and creator of all the country's life', his prayer being: 'May the Kingdom of Free Labour come! May there be a Republic of Toilers!'[126]

More prosaic and down-to-earth, but in the same spirit of non-party and all-inclusive 'toilers' ' unity – *pace* the Kronstadt Bolsheviks and their renewed and vicious campaign against the leaders of the Petrograd Soviet – was the Kronstadt Soviet's friendly and generous cable replying to the Central Executive Committee of Soviets on 28 August: the 'entire Kronstadt garrison' was ready at the first call of the Executive Committee to rush to 'the defence of the revolution' and put Kronstadt's 'entire military forces' at its disposal, At the same time, and on the insistence of Lazar Bregman and the Bolsheviks, the Central Executive Committee was asked to do all it could to ensure the release of the Kronstadters arrested in July, so that 'in these days of danger and fears for the fate of the revolution, they will be in our midst'.[127]

The same conciliatory spirit of fulsome cooperation with the Central Executive Committee marked the beginning of the Kronstadt Soviet's 29 August session, and 'prolonged applause' greeted a report that Iraklii Tseretelli had said that 'this was no time for coalitionism, but rather for radical and thorough action', and that Victor Chernov had then promptly embraced him.[128]

At this point, Ivan Flerovsky, Raskolnikov's successor in Kronstadt and no less consummate a politician, went into action to put an end

to the fraternal, non-party exaltation that characterized the Kornilov
Days in Kronstadt, and notably its unconditional support of the
Central Executive Committee. Invited by the session chairman
Konstantin Shurgin to review the 'current situation', he defined the
abortive Kornilov putsch as an attempt at a 'bourgeois counter-
revolution' and dismissed the Directory – Kerensky's new supra-
party rump government (both Kadet and socialist ministers had
walked out) – as an experiment in 'supra-class state power' bound,
in the Russian situation of heightened class struggle, to hang in the
air and collapse. In Russia it was only a class dictatorship that was
possible and, this being so,

Kronstadt must play its part in the construction of the new state power.
We must send our own representatives to the Central Executive Committee
[in Petrograd] to press the wishes of revolutionary Kronstadt. Together
with our military forces, we must send political forces. We must throw the
weight of our influence into the scales.

Right on cue, the Bolshevik Mikhail Lebedev, speaking in support
of Flerovsky, then proposed that Kronstadt send delegates to the
Central Executive Committee, and it was decided that five, one each
from the Soviet's five political factions, including the Anarchists, be
sent off; but since the new Anarchist faction refused to name their
delegate, only four were elected: the Bolshevik Ivan Flerovsky, the
SR-Maximalist Ivan Rybakov, the Left SR Aleksei Rudnev and the
Menshevik Ivan Kukanov.

At this point, Flerovsky proposed that the delegates be provided
with an 'Instruction' (*nakaz*) which he had already prepared. Its
preamble was nothing less than the Kronstadt Soviet's declaration
of equality, if not of independence, vis-à-vis the Central Executive
Committee:

The Kronstadt Soviet of Workers' and Soldiers' Deputies, as an organ
standing resolutely on guard over the revolution, deems it its duty and right
at a time of acute dangers to the revolution to send its delegates to the
Central Executive Committee . . . for the purpose of joint cooperation and
enjoying the status of members with equal rights in the Central Executive
Committee.[129]

The 'Instruction' itself[130] amounted to a fully fledged Bolshevik
programme: it demanded the total democratization of the army,
with counter-revolutionary generals being removed and replaced by
others elected by soldiers and officers, and the restoration of revolutionary soldiers' organizations as the sole means to secure democratic

discipline; all repressive measures, and the death penalty first and foremost, were to be abolished; the estates of the landowners were to be transferred to peasant committees; the eight-hour day was to become law, while 'organizations of democratic control' over factories, plants and banks were to be set up in which the representatives of the workers predominated; also demanded was a declaration of the rights of nations to self-determination, the immediate convening of the Constituent Assembly, the annulment of all secret treaties, and the drawing up of democratic peace proposals.

While the preamble of the 'Instruction' asserted Kronstadt's equality with the Central Executive Committee, its postscript asserted that the 'only way' these demands could be realized was by 'breaking with the capitalists, completely liquidating bourgeois counter-revolution, and transferring power in the land to the revolutionary workers, peasants and soldiers – this is the only course whereby the country and the revolution may be saved from collapse.' In short, the Kronstadt Soviet urged the Central Executive Committee of Soviets to adopt the Bolshevik post-July Days solution to the problem of power, which deliberately ignored the Soviets, when, in lieu of the hallowed call of 'All Power to Soviets', it demanded the transfer of power to 'the revolutionary workers, peasants and soldiers'.

True, the SR-Maximalists found the 'Instruction' too 'party-minded' and particularly objected to the inclusion of the demand for workers' control over industry, one of their main bones of contention with the Bolsheviks. Instead, they held that workers should be encouraged to seize the factories and plants and manage them themselves, rather than merely exercise control over production and distribution while leaving ownership and management untouched. But with both Left SRs and Menshevik-Internationalists supporting it, the 'Instruction' was carried overwhelmingly and 'with applause', and Flerovsky even felt confident enough to propose that it be printed and distributed as 'the platform of our Soviet', thus clinching both his own and the Bolshevik victory.

It is difficult to ascertain what reception the delegates and the 'Instruction' received in the Central Executive Committee, but Kronstadt's military aid was certainly appreciated and duly acknowledged by its chairman Nikolai Chkheidze who, writing on behalf of the Central Executive Committee, thanked the Kronstadt Soviet for the contribution its task-force had made 'in ensuring the tranquillity of the Petrograd population during these alarming days'.[131] He concluded with an expression of confidence that the activities of both the Kronstadt Soviet and the Central Executive Committee would 'proceed in solidarity' in the future, too. Yet with the Kronstadt Soviet's 'platform' now so Bolshevik that it no longer urged the transfer of power to Soviets but instead to 'revolutionary workers, peasants and soldiers', for Lenin all but a euphemism for the Bolshevik Party itself, such confidence was bound to be misplaced.

Even more Bolshevik was the 'Instruction' that Kronstadt's delegate Ivan Flerovsky was to take to the Democratic Conference of organizations of the 'revolutionary democracy' – Soviets, socialist parties, trade unions, cooperatives and municipalities – due to meet in Petrograd between 14 and 19 September. Organized by the Central Executive Committee, the Conference's chief purpose was, in the words of its invitation, to 'pronounce the final word' on that 'strong revolutionary authority' which Russia so badly needed;[132] and it was this very question of power that was on the Kronstadt Soviet's agenda on 7 September.[133]

The Bolsheviks came prepared with a fully drafted 'Instruction' and Liudmilla Stal opened the debate urging that in this 'turning point of the revolution' Kronstadt's delegate and his 'Instruction' must state 'clearly and firmly' that 'we are against coalitionism'. The Bolsheviks' solution to the political crisis, as they expressed it in their 'Instruction', was the establishment of a government made up of 'representatives of the revolutionary proletariat and of the peasantry', and in the same breath, 'the immediate convocation of the Constituent Assembly'. Since Soviets were not as much as mentioned, the SR-Maximalist spokesmen, Grigorii Rivkin and Sergei Kudinsky, insisted that it was only 'the entire toiling people of Russia' who had the right to decide the question of power, for such a matter could not be left to 'a few democratic organizations'; a Congress of Soviets must therefore be convened immediately to express 'the opinion of the whole of toiling Russia', particularly since the Democratic Conference, heavily weighted towards cooperatives and municipalities, would give 'decisive influence' to the moderate socialists who favoured coalition governments rather than to the workers of Kronstadt, Petrograd and Moscow.

The perennial debate on the nature of the Russian revolution centred this time around the 'Instruction's' demand for 'workers' control over production and distribution'. The SR Aleksei Rudnev (speaking for himself only) opposed workers' control, advancing the familiar Menshevik argument that Russia was technologically backward and uneducated, its industry dislocated and, were one to oust all those 'not in tune with the democracy', take power, and perforce 'confiscate capital' and make a social revolution, 'one would make a mess of it': 'We in Kronstadt do, it is true, have the right to speak of a social revolution; but Kronstadt is not the whole of Russia. Russia is vast and has 170 million peasants who do not know what a social revolution is, understanding it only as simple grabbing.'

If workers' control was too much for the moderate Rudnev, it was too minimal a goal for the SR-Maximalists Ippolitov and Rivkin, committed as they were to a fully fledged social revolution which would transfer both power and 'the land, factories and plants' to 'the toiling people'. It was precisely because industry was run down, so Rivkin argued, that workers' control would be most convenient for Russia's capitalists who were 'more parasitical' than their counterparts in industrially developed countries. It made no sense to rest content with transferring the landowners' estates to the people's ownership while leaving urban capitalist ownership untouched, and merely setting up workers' control over it.[134]

Agreeing that the Russian bourgeoisie was already 'counter-revolutionary', the Bolshevik spokesmen, Stal and Flerovsky, insisted that Russia was still too backward to make a socialist revolution unaided:

Our revolution is the prologue to world revolution; that was its great significance and the guarantee of its success. It can be victorious only if supported by the West; the [revolutionary] conflagration spreading to the West will mark the beginning of the social revolution and then our own revolution too will become a social revolution . . .

But Rivkin only sneered at such Bolshevik 'minimalism' and dependence on revolution in the West: 'If Russia is so backward that it cannot make a social revolution unless the West makes one, then perhaps we should wait until the West too presses the demand for the power of Soviets of Workers' and Soldiers' Deputies and all the rest!'[135]

When the vote was taken, the Bolshevik draft of the 'Instruction' as moved by Liudmilla Stal received 144 votes against 72 votes for Rivkin's draft, with five abstentions.[136] It was clearly a run-of-the-mill Bolshevik document,[137] all but identical with the resolutions regarding the Democratic Conference passed by such Bolshevik-dominated Soviets as that of Kiev (on 8 September) and Petrograd (on 11 September).[138] Each and every amendment proposed by the SR-Maximalists was rejected: thus they suffered round defeat on workers' control (they wanted it connected with socialization), the self-determination of nations (which they urged should be universal rather than merely pertaining to Russia), and the convocation of a Congress of Soviets (which they championed over the Constituent Assembly). The sole peculiarly Kronstadt component of the 'Instruction' was its self-righteous postscript:

We remind you that we in Kronstadt wanted to realize these measures we now propose to you some two or three months ago. Must we still wait for some Don Cossack uprising, or another Kornilov-like putsch! We say we must forestall them! It is up to you to create a united revolutionary front and a state power that will enjoy the confidence of the country![139]

If internally, that is in the Soviet, in its *Izvestiia* and in Anchor Square, Kronstadt continued to speak the pluralist language of radical left-wing socialism and to be governed by a coalition of left-wing socialist parties among which the Bolsheviks were most of the time the senior, but sometimes only a major, partner, the outside world had an altogether different view of it at the Democratic Conference where it appeared with an 'Instruction' couched in the stereotyped language of Bolshevism, and represented by the Bolshevik Ivan Flerovsky.

The final consolidation of Bolshevik leadership in Kronstadt's left-wing alliance came in the wake of the Democratic Conference's failure to solve the problem of power and prevent the formation of another weak coalition government with Kerensky as Prime Minister.

Flerovsky presented the Soviet with his report on the Democratic Conference on 26 September, in a session[140] marked by the formation of a radical-left consensus and bloc which accepted Bolshevik leadership in the revolutionary conquest of power now that the Bolshevik party had again embraced and championed 'All Power to Soviets'.

Dismissing such moderate socialist leaders as Dan, Liber and Gots for seeking their social base in 'propertied rural Russia', Flerovsky made a special point of denouncing the Menshevik-Internationalist leader Martov for his desperate last-minute effort to save the Democratic Conference from collapse. In appealing for a vote in support of the compromise resolution (which clearly ruled out the Kadets as coalition partners), Martov had furnished more than ample proof for Flerovsky that 'at the decisive moment, half-hearted leaders will always forsake the only correct path'. All that the Conference had achieved, in his view, was a dismal 'makeshift coalition government' with a Kadet programme, bearing moral responsibility only to a 'democratic Pre-Parliament'. But, he went on, that Pre-Parliament would in turn be diluted by the co-option of 'propertied elements' confronting a 'democracy' split into Bolsheviks and Left SRs on the left, confused SRs and Kadets on the right, and a dwindling group of Mensheviks in the middle.

Having thus driven home the Conference's abysmal failure and painted an even gloomier prospect for the future, Flerovsky then struck home with a defiant resolution which (except for its strident verbiage) proved acceptable to all factions ranging from the Menshevik-Internationalists on the right to the Anarcho-Syndicalists on the left. Only the fire-eating Bleikhman and his few Anarcho-Communists, scorning 'words and resolutions', dissented. Demanding direct action, Bleikhman reminded his listeners, who perhaps preferred to forget, that it was Kronstadt that had shown Russia how to make a 'real revolution', imposing 'permanent terror and the permanent vision of death and of revolution on the reactionaries'. At this point, even Yarchuk had had enough and, telling Bleikhman not to waste his time 'talking from his rostrum', challenged him rather to 'take the axe and chop heads!'

Yarchuk was particularly pleased with Flerovsky's radical resolution and his commitment to a 'merciless . . . social revolution' and congratulated him on having at last thrown his Marxism overboard, for 'it is only when the Bolsheviks make common cause with the left-wing that there will be victory'. Pleased, too, was the Left SR Grigorii Smoliansky who thought Flerovsky's proposals acceptable to 'all the left-wingers'. Nevertheless, he warned against Flerovsky's and the Bolsheviks' orientation and reliance on revolution in the West:

Comrades, we must not be carried away by what happens in France and some other countries; nor do we have much cause at present to rely on the revolutionary spirit, on the devotion to the socialist banner of the Western proletariat, and of the democracy of the West, no matter how much we would like to. The only thing we can rely on is faith in ourselves and in the strength of the All-Russian revolutionary democracy.

Together with Rivkin, Smoliansky objected to the coarse and strident language of Flerovsky's draft: 'When we speak in the name of an authoritative institution such as the Soviet, we must speak calmly, using language which will both win respect and give proper expression to our own feelings of confidence and dignity.'

But Flerovsky remained unmoved. 'When we steer our course towards world revolution', he told Smoliansky, 'the only respect we need is that of the revolutionary democracy!' 'You'd better measure your dignity by the respect of your enemies, as Nietzsche puts it', retorted Smoliansky, and a high-powered commission was set up to revise and reformulate the resolution:[141]

The new coalitionist provisional government is a union of patent Kornilovites and 'leaders of the democracy' conducting a policy of compromise that is, in practice, irresponsible and traitorous to the Russian revolution.

The Kronstadt Soviet of Workers' and Soldiers' Deputies regards that government as an obvious organ of bourgeois counter-revolution that will, by exacerbating the financial and economic crisis, push the country into civil war, thus betraying both it and the revolution to the international bourgeoisie's strangling and plunder.

Kronstadt's garrison and workers are determined not to give any support whatsoever to this treasonous government.

Only the Soviets of Workers', Soldiers' and Peasants' Deputies, and they alone, can organize the state power of the revolution.

The Kronstadt Soviet insists on the immediate convocation of [a congress of Soviets of] Workers', Soldiers' and Peasants' Deputies.

Long live the revolutionary Soviets! Long live the Russian revolution! Long live the world social revolution!

Not for nothing was the *Rech'* to define this declaration as Kronstadt's 'second secession' from Russia.[142]

Its publication, on 26 September, barely preceded Kerensky's last, futile attack on Kronstadt and the Baltic Fleet on the eve of the naval battle in the Moonzund Straits of the Gulf of Finland. In his Order of 29 September,[143] he singled out the Kronstadters for their repeated refusal to part with the guns emplaced in their forts:

It is time to come to one's senses and stop playing, wittingly or unwittingly, into the hands of the enemy. The men of Kronstadt have already reached the point where, at a critical hour, not all the means of defence are in their place . . . the native land . . . will not forgive thoughtlessness or intentional betrayal.

While it is difficult to decide whether the repeated requests to remove ten heavy guns from Kronstadt to forward positions in the

Moonzund Straits were a *bona fide* and desperate move in anticipation of the naval battle, or merely part of a plan to dismantle the troublesome Kronstadt fortress which according to General Brusilov 'has now lost its strategic significance',[144] the Kronstadters had no doubt whatever that what was aimed at was the liquidation of their Red Kronstadt. So much for their trust in the Naval Command.

The Soviet debated Kerensky's Order of 29 September in its session of 3 October.[145] After a short discussion, a long-winded and repetitive Appeal to Comrades and Citizens drafted by Flerovsky was adopted.[146] Rejecting Kerensky's insinuations as 'malicious' and 'contemptible', it retold the story of Kronstadt's maltreatment at the hands of Tseretelli and the bourgeois press in May and June, from which 'Red Kronstadt' had emerged untarnished, 'firm and uncrushable, the citadel of the revolution'. It also cited Kronstadt's heroic role in the Kornilov Days (the July Days were not so much as mentioned) when 'that very same Tseretelli was forced to drain the bitter cup of humiliation' and recognize Kronstadt's sailors and soldiers as 'the revolution's most reliable sons'.

If Kronstadt was now under attack for not permitting the disarming of 'the citadel of the revolution', the Appeal continued, it would continue to stand firm just as its sailors and soldiers would continue to die for the glory of the revolution in times of danger. 'Long live the Russian revolution! Down with the traitors to the country and the revolution! Down with those who slander the vanguard of the Russian revolution!' it concluded, with the usual flourish.

Whatever pride the Kronstadters may have taken in their devotion to the revolution and in that aggressive unity of purpose and mind which marked their Soviet's deliberations during the four weeks that preceded the October revolution, both their Resolution of 26 September and Appeal of 3 October were nevertheless tantamount to a declaration of war on the provisional government. And indeed, it was clearly in that spirit that Liudmilla Stal told the Kronstadt Soviet on 29 September[147] that the time was at hand to transfer power to the Soviets. 'Our task is the overthrow of this government of civil war', she said, while Parchevsky later noted that some three to four weeks before the October revolution Kronstadters were already 'speaking openly about the imminent uprising'.[148] That this was no empty talk can be gauged from the streamlined reorganization of Kronstadt's Military-Technical Commission which, set up to meet the emergency of the Kornilov putsch, had mobilized and transported Kronstadt's task-force to Petrograd efficiently and with despatch.

By 10 October, its reorganization completed, the Military-Technical Commission faithfully reflected in its composition both the political balance of the Kronstadt Soviet, as well as its broad ideological unity. Thus it consisted of six members of the Executive Committee (two Bolsheviks, two Left SRs, one SR-Maximalist and one Anarcho-Syndicalist), and fifteen representatives of the political parties, five being Bolsheviks, four SR-Maximalists, four Left SRs, one Menshevik-Internationalist and one Anarcho-Syndicalist. Thus of the Commission's twenty-one members only seven were Bolsheviks, while both its chairman and its secretary were Left SRs.[149]

The Commission's task was defined as the mobilization of Kronstadt's military resources in coordination with all such public and political organizations as 'advocate the transfer of power to the Soviets' for 'united action at the moment of decision'.[150]

Much of the business and executive power of the Soviet and of its Executive Committee seems to have passed to this Commission and by 3 October there were already complaints of poor attendance at the Soviet's sessions, so that at the end of each session 'only chairs, and neither workers' nor soldiers' deputies' were to be seen.[151] When roll-calls and the publication of the names of absentees in *Izvestiia* proved of no avail, it was decided on 17 October to hold only one instead of two sessions a week.[152] On 13 October, when Kronstadt's delegate to the Congress of Soviets of the Northern Region, the SR-Maximalist Sergei Kudinsky, sought to illustrate the 'firmness' of Kronstadt's Soviet power, it was the Military-Technical Commission that served as his point of reference, for 'not one decree is carried out unless it has the Commission's approval', he pointed out.[153]

Both the Bolshevik *Proletarskoe delo* and the Soviet's *Izvestiia* played their own part in preparing Kronstadt for the 'approaching crash'[154] and the 'imminent showdown';[155] thus *Izvestiia* informed its readers that 'the whole of Europe stands on the brink of famine; mutinies have broken out in Germany . . . England, France and Italy, too, are filled with dynamite. At this critical moment, the torch of the Russian revolution may well ignite the powder-keg that is Europe.'[156] Another *Izvestiia* editorial[157] had recourse to a different metaphor that increased the crescendo even more:

From abroad come groans and curses, and the torrent of the people's indignation is swollen to bursting point. How little more is needed to make it overflow and course over the entire world in a flood of proletarian revolution. It is the Russian proletariat alone that history has now placed at the head of the growing international movement which can provide the last decisive spur, and it will give it by way of its revolutionary government of Soviets of Workers' and Soldiers' Deputies. Long live the government of peace, of Soviets!

It was an attentive, quiet and singularly unanimous and determined Kronstadt Soviet that met on 23 October to hear Ivan Flerovsky and Efim Yarchuk report 'on the situation in Petrograd' and to take the final decision for the October revolution. Trotsky, chairman of the Bolshevik-dominated Military Revolutionary Committee which had prepared the uprising, had briefed Flerovsky and ordered him to return to Kronstadt immediately since 'events are moving so fast that everyone must be at his post'.[158] Flerovsky reported that the Petrograd garrison had moved from 'the realm of debate to the stage of action' and that the Military Revolutionary Committee now placed great store in 'the forces of revolutionary Kronstadt'. The 'explosion' for which they had been waiting in 'these last few weeks' was now before them 'in all its reality', and what was at issue was no longer a 'political', but a 'technical matter': 'The time for words, elucidations, appeals and psychology is over, and the time for the final showdown and the last battle to decide the future of the revolution is upon us . . . Now it is the turn of our military-technical organ . . . to give the instructions and the orders.'[159]

Flerovsky was seconded first by Konstantin Shurgin, who took up the slogan 'the time for words has passed, now is the time for deeds', and then by Yarchuk, who called on each and every man present to go to his unit or workshop and there explain 'what is happening' for now 'practically everything is at stake'.[160]

For once there was no debate, no resolution or declaration, merely silent, unanimous approval and agreement. Some eighteen commissars were elected to flank the commanders of units and commandants of forts and then, as if to sum it all up, came the little speech of Krasavin, a sailor from the minelayer *Amur*, who, reporting the ship's arrival from Helsingfors, declared that his vessel and its 'armed might' was at Kronstadt's 'disposal, as needed'.[161]

The turn of the Military-Technical Committee and of the commissars had indeed come when, next morning, the front page of

Kronstadt's *Izvestiia* boldly carried the 'Instruction' issued during the night to all military units, crews and forts, ordering them to obey only such orders as were duly signed by the committee, and to accept orders from the commanders and fort commandants only if these were counter-signed by the commissars attached to them.[162]

Thus Kronstadt's sailors, soldiers and workers, many of whom had learned to see themselves as 'revolutionaries, body and soul', were now fully mobilized *and* at the disposal of the Bolshevik leaders of the Petrograd Military Revolutionary Committee, 'our revolutionary staff' as Flerovsky termed it, and ready at its call 'to proceed anywhere where our forces are needed'[163] to transfer all power to the Soviets.

5

All Power to Soviets

Late in the evening of 24 October came the eagerly awaited telephone call from the Military Revolutionary Committee (MRC) summoning 'the armed forces of Kronstadt to come at dawn to the defence of the [Second] Congress of Soviets' which, convened the next day, was to give official Soviet sanction to the seizure of power.[1] Lazar Bregman and Nikolai Gorelnikov, the chairman of the Executive Committee of the Kronstadt Soviet and of its Military-Technical Commission, immediately ordered Kronstadt's expeditionary force, 'ships, units, detachments, crews and their commanders', to proceed to Petrograd 'in defence of the revolution and in support of the Revolutionary Committee, and in accordance with its orders'.[2] They also radioed a message 'TO ALL' that 'The Petrograd Soviet is in danger' and that 'military cadets, together with other dark elements', were preparing an attack.[3]

When the morning of 25 October came, Ivan Flerovsky, Kronstadt's number one Bolshevik and its liaison with the Petrograd MRC,[4] had good reason to feel proud and exhilarated when, together with Yarchuk, he reviewed the force of some 5,000 heavily armed sailors and soldiers (3,825 sailors and 943 soldiers) in Anchor Square and watched them board the ships and landing craft.[5] Yarchuk remembered the floating banners proclaiming 'All Power to Soviets in the Localities!' and 'The Land – to the Peasants! The Factories – to the Workers!' and the final words of his own short speech: 'Long live the social revolution!'[6] Flerovsky, for his part, recalled 'trembling with exaltation'; never before had he felt 'so strongly the ties that bound me to that mass of faces and eyes', until, at last, he managed to utter a few words to fit the occasion:

Comrades, events unprecedented in our history and in that of the whole world are now upon us. We are about to make a social revolution. We are going to overthrow the power of capital. To us has fallen the greatest of good fortunes – to fulfil the fervent dreams of the oppressed.

There was no applause; no shouts of approval or joy; just silence, and hugs, kisses, handshakes, and 'tears glistening in many eyes'.[7]

When the Kronstadt flotilla, led by the minelayer *Amur* with Ivan Flerovsky aboard, arrived in the Neva in the early afternoon of 25 October, it received a triumphal welcome from the sailors of the *Aurora* and, to shouts of hoorah, the band struck up. Vladimir Antonov-Ovseenko greeted the Kronstadters on behalf of the MRC: 'There is the Winter Palace . . . We must take it.'[8]

Eagerly awaited, the 'pride and glory of the revolution' was the only major outside military force to appear in time to support the Petrograd garrison in the seizure of power. The psychological impact of the Kronstadters' imminently expected arrival was already to be sensed in the afternoon of 24 October. John Reed, the left-wing American journalist and chronicler of the October revolution, walking along the Nevsky Prospect, noted the effect on a crowd of soldiers milling around the Kazan cathedral when one of a passing group of sailors shouted, 'Kronstadt is coming!' 'It was as if in 1792, in the streets of Paris, some one had said: the Marseillais are coming!'[9]

The Kronstadt contingent's military contribution to the insurrection on 25 October is difficult to isolate and assess since, immediately upon disembarkation, the entire force was put 'at the disposal' and 'under the command' of the MRC. But the Kronstadt sailors certainly made up a sizeable proportion (nearly 40%) of the 10,407 Baltic sailors,[10] the Bolsheviks' 'main active and loyal force',[11] who played so 'decisive a role' in the events of that day, and they are known to have occupied the vital bridges over the Neva, the Smolny Institute, the Petropavlovsk fortress and the Marinsky Palace, after they had closed and dispersed the Council of the Republic (the Pre-Parliament).[12] Certainly, they distinguished themselves in the storming of the Winter Palace and the arrest of the provisional government; thus, the Kronstadt *Proletarskoe delo*, in its special edition of 26 October, reported proudly:[13]

KRONSTADTERS IN THE FRONT RANKS

The Winter Palace is taken! Our comrades, the sailors of the Artificers' School and the Torpedo Detachment, armed with rifles, marched fearlessly in the front ranks against machine-gun fire! Honour and glory to the Kronstadt comrades! As fighters and defenders of the proletarian revolution, they have threaded a fresh garland in the never-withering wreath of honour!

Fresh Kronstadt contingents of some 3,000 soldiers, sailors and urgently needed naval gunners were rushed to Petrograd on 28 and 29 October and again covered themselves in glory during the decisive battles of the October revolution, for Gatchina, Tsarskoe Selo, Krasnoe Selo and the Pulkovo Heights.[14]

Altogether some 8,000 Kronstadters went out to make the 'social revolution', returning to a hero's welcome home on 3 November when their flotilla put in to Kronstadt's harbour. The red flag – 'the sacred banner of the International' – was ordered to be flown from the mast and stern of every ship and at the mast of the Naval Telegraph, while massed bands struck up to receive the men as they disembarked at the Petrovsk Pier.[15] Only days had passed, yet because of its proximity, its dedication to the October revolution, *and* its complete subordination to the Petrograd MRC, Red Kronstadt had already become the latter's major reservoir of crack troops, technical personnel, guns, shells and even food supplies.

Thus, on 27 October, when Gatchina had been taken by Kerensky's troops and Lenin began to fear for Petrograd, it was as a matter of course that he asked Fiodor Raskolnikov to ring Kronstadt and, when no contact could be established, sent him there the next morning with the urgent request to despatch 'without delay, a strong detachment armed with machine-guns and artillery'.[16] Next day, Nikolai Podvoisky, chairman of the MRC, ordered both Boris Donskoi, commissar of Fort Ino, and the Kronstadt Military-Technical Commission to send 'immediately 3,000 armed men, with artillery, to Petrograd, to be at the disposal of the Military-Revolutionary Committee'.[17] Both orders were, of course, implemented forthwith.

So loyal and safe a stronghold was Kronstadt, that the MRC immediately turned its notorious prisons into a major receptacle for 'counter-revolutionaries' such as captured officers, cadets and gardemarins (naval cadets), speculators, food-hoarders, persons accused of sabotage, and sundry other political opponents, including the editors of *Narodnoe slovo*.[18]

As early as 27 October, Feliks Dzerzhinsky, acting on behalf of the MRC, ordered that all those members of the disbanded Tsentroflot (the naval section of the Petrograd Soviet) who refused to 'assist in the work of the consolidation and salvation of the Russian revolution', i.e. to cooperate with the new government, be sent to Kronstadt. Two days later the men captured during the suppression of the uprising of the cadets of Petrograd's military school were, on the orders of the MRC itself, also sent there.[19] Only a few days later, E. K. Drezen, a member of the MRC, visited Kronstadt to 'ascertain the conditions under which the cadets and the gardemarins are kept', and, while there, acted together with the Kronstadt Executive Committee in appointing Ivan Gerasimov, a member of the Kronstadt Military-Technical Commission, as 'commissar for Kronstadt prisons'.[20]

Lenin, for his part, as chairman of the Council of People's Commissars, instructed the MRC on 10 November 'immediately' to arrest all speculators, hoarders and saboteurs, and keep them, 'pending trial by a military-revolutionary court, *in the Kronstadt prisons*'.[21]

The discipline of the Kronstadters was so far trusted that during the 'vodka riots' early in November, when crowds smashed into the Winter Palace wine-cellars and got themselves drunk, Anatolii Lunacharsky, People's Commissar for Education, begged the Soviet that 'in order to protect the art and historical treasures of the Hermitage and the Winter Palace from destruction' they should grant permission for 'the vast quantities' (some three million bottles) of wine, vodka and spirits stored in the wine-cellars of the Winter Palace to be shipped to Kronstadt since, 'there, their safety and inviolability can be guaranteed'.[22]

Kronstadt's reputation was finally made when, late in November, the sailors of the *Gangut* promised places 'in the Kronstadt prisons' to all 'pseudo-socialists who cling to the coat-tails of the bourgeoisie'.[23]

Yet, in common with the sailors who had dealt with the cadets during the 'cadet uprising' at the end of October 1917, the Kronstadt Soviet, in its session of 14 December 1917, indignantly protested against the transformation of the 'Free City of Kronstadt' into a 'Sakhalin the Second'.[24] Their October revolution was intended to turn the whole of Russia, and possibly the entire world, into a Soviet republic *à la* Kronstadt.

Indeed, many a non-Bolshevik Kronstadter, who had with gusto participated in or welcomed the October seizure and transfer of power to the Soviets, woke up on the morrow of that revolution to the hard fact that the government of People's Commissars elected at the Second Congress of Soviets was entirely Bolshevik and that the Menshevik and SR delegates to the Congress had walked out in protest against the insurrection and seizure of power.

By 29 October, an unsigned editorial in Kronstadt's *Izvestiia* was already lashing out against those socialists who, 'blinded by party-spirit', were immediately prepared to wash their hands of the revolution because its 'initiative' had been Bolshevik. Since the revolution's fate was now tied up with the Bolsheviks, it pointed out, they would have to choose between its 'victory or its defeat', there was 'no middle road'.[25] Another unsigned editorial, on 31 October, laboured hard to explain away the awkward truth that the October revolution had put the Bolsheviks in power:

Those who made the revolution had no intention of transferring all power to one left-wing party alone. In overthrowing the provisional government, the aim was to place power in the hands of the Soviets, but, since many 'socialists' then criminally deserted the Congress of Soviets, the Bolsheviks were compelled to take it into their own hands.[26]

Not surprisingly, when the Kronstadt Soviet assembled on 29 October to hear Yarchuk's and Rivkin's reports on events in Petrograd and on the Congress of Soviets,[27] to which they, together with Flerovsky, had been Kronstadt's delegates, the question of the 'construction of power' and its Bolshevik outcome stood squarely in the centre of a debate in which spokesmen of all political factions participated. It may well have been Kronstadt's last major debate on power.

Yarchuk's first concern was to refute all accusations that Kronstadt's sailors had behaved 'brutally' in Petrograd, and this overriding interest somewhat coloured his report of one of the major events in the October revolution. Speaking with vivid immediacy, he singled out the sailors of the Artificers' School for their exemplary restraint in the face of severe provocation during the assault on the Winter Palace: when shot at by the loyalist Women's Battalion after they had broken through the gates, they nevertheless laid no finger on those 'who had then fallen back on the feminine tactics of tears and hysterics'. Nor would 'our Kronstadters' kill the cadets after they had captured them 'with bombs in their hands'. They had merely disarmed them and then taken them to the Petropavlovsk fortress. When, following the arrest of the entire government in the Malachite Hall of the Winter Palace, the ministers Tereshchenko and Konovalov had asked for tea and cigarettes, the sailors readily supplied their needs and even engaged them in conversation; true, in the beginning, some had strained to 'finish them off', but others had held them back, shouting, 'If you are so seething with anger, slap them round the head, but don't touch them with your bayonets; they're in

our hands now, and we're going to deliver them to the Petropavlovsk fortress!' Although Yarchuk fully expected 'screams about
atrocities', history, he said forcibly, would record how the Kronstadters had 'treated their enemies'.

He had been greatly impressed with the Congress of Soviets: it
was no 'talking-shop', but did everything with despatch and
enthusiasm. 'Here, it is clear, are people who know their minds and
will act decisively'. As a Kronstadter, he took special pride in the
role the Soviets had played in the seizure of power and in that
Congress which had proclaimed 'All Power to Soviets!'

Raising the awkward question, which had already troubled him
greatly at the Congress,[28] as to how he, an anarchist, could accept
and support a Bolshevik government of People's Commissars,
Yarchuk declared that he did not belong to those who 'quarrel with
history' because it presumed to 'confound their teachings'; rather,
he felt it would be 'a crime' in 'so decisive a moment' not to be with
the toilers in their 'desperate struggle for emancipation'. Moreover,
whatever his past disagreements with them, the Bolsheviks had
convinced him all along that they 'meant business' and, when the
crucial moment came, they 'did not disappoint me, for they did
fight'.

Yarchuk knew his Kronstadters and was well aware that his
description of the 'exemplary order' and discipline which he had
observed in Petrograd would impress and convince:

I have never seen such order in Petrograd. The Nevsky looked like an
army camp, with camp-fires burning. Every motor-car was stopped and
passed only after its permit had been checked. I doubt if any other revolution
has seen such order. With terrible hand-to-hand fighting raging near the
Winter Palace, we got out at midnight on the left bank, and I was astounded
to see lights on in the houses, and people having dinner as if nothing were
happening in town. An uninitiated person would have thought all was well:
the tram-cars were running, and people sat at their tables eating and talking
peacefully! The soldiers and Red Guards were on their best behaviour . . .
when we made the round of the town, we found there had been no excesses.[29]

Yarchuk's delight in the orderliness of the October revolution may
seem strange in an anarchist, but he had become a Kronstadter, too,
by now.

It was on the Congress of Soviets and its 'construction of power'
that Rivkin now dwelt in his report.[30] Kronstadt, he said, had good
reason to 'triumph' now that its early battle-cry 'All Power to
Soviets!' was realized and the Congress of Soviets had assumed

power. If the Bolsheviks happened to be in the majority at the Congress, this by no means meant that in future 'the minority could not become the majority', and it was really the combined fault of the Mensheviks, SRs and Left SRs that 'power went to the Bolsheviks':

While a section of the right-wing [parties] walked out, the Left SRs made their own entry into the government conditional on the formation of a united democratic government consisting of all trends . . . small wonder the Bolsheviks found themselves alone in power as the natural result of the refusal of the others to join that power.

This, said Rivkin, was why the Council of People's Commissars was 'one-party'. But then it was a mere 'accident': the Congress had not 'decreed' it, and none of the Bolsheviks had 'insisted on it'. Moreover, now that the Soviets had assumed power, the 'old divisions' between defensists and internationalists, minimalists and maximalists, Bolsheviks and Mensheviks were bound to disappear: 'When power belongs to the Soviet . . . it is obvious that the toiling people must defend their country which is at war', and the word 'defensist' had thus lost all meaning.

In future, it would be 'capabilities' rather than political 'factions' that would be decisive. Now that the Congress had assumed the power, it should be organized 'like the Kronstadt Soviet' which 'is divided into commissions' in charge of various branches of activity, 'together constituting power in Kronstadt'. Such an organization of power would attract 'many more talents', for it would enable 'every socialist', regardless of the party or faction to which he belonged, to work in the central administration 'together with the toiling people, and not apart from it': 'What we have said and what Kronstadt has said, too, that power should be in the hands of the toiling people, that only Soviets which are above party . . . can unite all the revolutionary forces, and that only non-party organizations can give victory to the toiling people, all this is true.'

With that credo and plea for all-inclusive socialist unity Rivkin then went on to move the SR-Maximalists' resolution 'on the construction of power'.[31]

The Kronstradt Soviet urges that the very history of the great Russian revolution, and the contribution made to its success by the formation and the activity of the Soviets, has proved that the toiling masses can be victorious only when they act together as one front.

While welcoming the decision of the Second All-Russian Congress of Workers' and Soldiers' Deputies regarding the transfer of power to the

Soviets, and while declaring its full support of the power of commissars
authorized by the Congress, [the Kronstadt Soviet] deems it a natural
conclusion of the Congress's decisions that collectives be formed out of the
Central Executive Committee of Soviets in which all parties represented at
the Second All-Russian Congress of Soviets shall participate. The Kronstadt
Soviet regards it as the duty of all thinking revolutionaries to rally to the
Soviets of Workers', Soldiers', and Peasants' Deputies as the authoritative
organs of the revolution for the sake of governing and defending the country
and the revolution and for the immediate convocation of an All-Russian
Congress of Peasants' Soviets in view of threatening counter-revolution.

Konstantin Shurgin, speaking on behalf of the Kronstadt Left
SRs, fully endorsed Rivkin's resolution. Urging that 'All Power to
Soviets' was not meant to give power to one particular party,
Shurgin expressed fear lest the 'deep split' caused by the walk-out
of the Mensheviks and SRs lead to 'disaster'. The Left SRs therefore
demanded that all those who had been 'delegated' to the Congress
now share in the power.[32]

Announcing Bolshevik support for Rivkin's resolution, Liudmilla
Stal urged that the Soviet now halt the debate and honour the
memory of 'Kronstadt's fallen brothers' by singing the Funeral March
('You fell in the fatal fight'), and then reaffirm, by 'solemn oath',
that they would pursue the liberation of the toiling class to 'the
end'.[33]

Only then, with the Soviet now psychologically prepared, did she,
as was her wont, launch a vicious attack on those Menshevik and
SR 'traitors who presume to call themselves socialists'. While the
whole of Western Europe 'learns from us and creates Soviets', that
'unprecedented awesome union of the broad masses', 'these gentlemen, the Gots, the Libers and the Dans', had, she barked out, 'spat'
at the Soviets, dismissing them as a mere temporary 'scaffolding' for
the revolution: 'They will never create a majority! Rivkin says that
they should have submitted to the majority since one day they might
themselves become the majority. No! They will never be the
majority! They will never enjoy the confidence of the masses! The
only support they draw on comes from the petty bourgeoisie.' That
the counter-revolution was on the march did not bother them, she
charged. All they feared was the progress of bolshevism. Yet
bolshevism was not a party but 'the programme of all the toiling
classes, of the revolutionary democracy itself'. True, the People's
Commissars appointed at the Congress were all Bolsheviks, but that
had happened because 'the others were afraid to take power'. Even

now, real power was still vested in the Central Executive Committee and the Congress of Soviets, for the commissars were not 'firmly seated ministers', but remained responsible to these bodies and could easily be dismissed or re-elected by them. 'All Power to Soviets', as understood by the Bolsheviks and 'the other left-wing parties', would be realized only when in all localities, 'in every rural district, and in every townlet', the Soviets take power into their hands.[34]

While Yarchuk, Rivkin, Shurgin and their political factions seem to have swallowed their doubts and misgivings regarding the Bolshevik government that emerged from the October revolution, the small group of Menshevik-Internationalists in the Kronstadt Soviet were in no two minds about it. Their spokesman, A. Ermansky, a veteran revolutionary and Menshevik whose recent arrival in Kronstadt had been intended to rescue its shrinking organization of Menshevik-Internationalists,[35] stunned his listeners when he rejected the October revolution as a 'military mutiny'.[36] With a frankness amounting to a staggering lack of tact, he told an audience of highly politicized and activist sailors, soldiers and workers that the Russian revolution of 1917 rested largely on the 'soldier masses' which, he very much regretted to say, were politically 'inexperienced', rather than on the urban proletariat, 'politically the most advanced, the boldest and the most enlightened' section of Russia's popular masses. Moreover, he went on, the soldier mass had seen this revolution, made 'by force of their bayonets', as a 'social revolution' for the 'immediate realization of a socialist order', and it was this view that had fatally narrowed the revolution's social base precisely at a time when it was a broad 'democratic revolution' that was on the Russian agenda, for it was that type of revolution alone that could raise its culture and people to that high level which alone would make socialism possible.

Denied an extension of time to finish his speech, and amidst 'tumult, whistling and shouting', Ermansky then moved quite a provocative resolution.[37] Denouncing the seizure of power by 'military conspiracy' as 'senseless, irresponsible and fateful', and criticizing its timing – two weeks before the scheduled elections to the Constituent Assembly and on the eve of the Congress of Soviets – it rejected the Bolshevik government thus established by the 'violent seizure of power by a minority' as illegitimate and doomed. Urging that its liquidation now be immediately negotiated, the Menshevik-Internationalist resolution went on to press for a new 'homogeneous

democratic government', exclusive of 'propertied elements', to be
set up by agreement between 'all democratic organizations'. This
'democratic' government was to be charged with crushing counter-
revolution, convening the Constituent Assembly, embarking on
peace negotiations, transferring privately owned large estates to the
land committees and regulating the economy.

Not surprisingly, it was Yarchuk who warded off this unexpected
attack on Kronstadt's left-wing Bolshevik-led coalition and its role
in the October revolution.[38] With his usual witty and biting aplomb,
he took issue with Ermansky's fears of a social revolution and of its
narrowing base. There were some 400 capitalists all-told in America,
he said, while the rest of the population formed a broad democratic
base, yet there was no revolution in sight there. As for Ermansky's
contempt for a soldiers' revolution, those who had made it were
'yesterday's workers and peasants' whom the war had torn from
Russia's darkest corners, dropping them, dressed in army-greatcoats,
in places where 'thought quickens and one learns to understand
things better'. Nevertheless,

you presume to label our revolution a military mutiny! The slogan 'All
Power to Soviets!' may not suit you, but it certainly fits the Kronstadt Soviet
and we will permit no one to appeal against it. Ours is a very simple
prescription: all one has to do is to take what is here on a small scale in our
Soviet and in the Executive Committee and build it on a larger scale and
it will work there too.

Dealing with Ermansky's taunt that in reality 'the Bolsheviks had
seized power for themselves', Yarchuk argued that the majority had
supported them and all that he, Ermansky, could do now was to
oppose them and prove 'their theory wrong', and thus, perhaps, one
day, win over the majority. It was futile, however, to appear before
the Kronstadt Soviet with a discussion as to whether the Russian
revolution was social, bourgeois, or something in between. Even
were Ermansky to be given two hours instead of his allotted fifteen
minutes of speaking time, he 'would not convince us':

That's why we have an Anchor Square, and if you thought we were wrong,
why didn't you go there? Perhaps then the sailors might not have gone out
to fight for a social revolution. That's what you should have done! But
instead you came when they had already gone, it was not to them that you
went, but here to us! And you thought that if only you could speak for
another fifteen minutes, you would convince us!

At this point Ermansky interrupted to accuse Yarchuk of advancing a narrow 'provincial point of view' at a time when the Russian revolution was 'on the eve of disaster': 'I shall be more than glad if what I have said proves to be nonsense and if, when you meet me in the future, you can look me straight in the eye without a blush . . . I don't say this with a light heart, and I say it only that Kronstadt may know . . .'[39] Kronstadt's sailors did indeed note his prophecy of doom and promptly christened him 'Ermansky the Jonah'.[40]

When the motion was finally put, Rivkin's resolution was passed with 201 votes, against only eight cast for Ermansky's resolution. It was perhaps a sign of the times that Shurgin, chairman of the Soviet, should have angrily and sadly described the pandemonium that greeted Ermansky's speech and resolution as 'something which has never before happened here, where until now we have always listened quietly and, by way of questions and answers alone, taken issue with the opinions expressed'.[41] To cap all, at the end of the session there came the complaint of the Left SR Georgii Pupuridi who, returning from Petrograd with a copy of the Left SR *Znamia truda* in his hands, had been manhandled by a group of Bolsheviks. In the teeth of obstruction by the Bolshevik spokesmen Solomon Entin and Liudmilla Stal, he pressed on with a resolution exhorting 'workers, soldiers and sailors to treat one another with patience and have no recourse to the law of the fist'.[42] While it is true that this resolution was passed by eighty-three votes, as against seventy-five for Stal's counter-resolution, it is equally true that the incident demonstrated the extent to which the notorious 'customs of the [Bolshevik] Vyborg District' and its intolerance towards all non-Bolshevik brands of socialism had, with the October revolution, also spread to Kronstadt.

While the adoption, on 29 October, of Rivkin's resolution 'on the organization of power' marked Kronstadt's acceptance of the October revolution, the decisions of the Congress of Soviets, and the Bolshevik Council of People's Commissars that it had elected, Kronstadt also stipulated that, as a 'natural conclusion' of the decisions of the Congress, power be more widely shared and that 'parties that have their representatives at the . . . Congress . . . should participate'. This would certainly include the Left SRs and the SR-Maximalists and other left-wing groups and possibly even the Mensheviks and the SRs, should these return to the Congress, while Shurgin, on behalf of the Left SRs, had gone so far as to urge that all 'delegates' be included, implying that this referred even to those who had walked out on the Congress. Indeed, during the debate of 29 October Ermansky had already referred to negotiations[43] for the creation of an inclusive socialist coalition government ranging 'from the Bolsheviks to the Popular Socialists' already afoot under the auspices and pressure of the Railwaymen's Union, the *Vikzhel*, while next day a radio message was received from the ship's committee of the battle cruiser *Oleg* that 'all socialist parties are trying to form a bloc. Everyone is in good spirits.'[44] A similar spirit was in evidence in Kronstadt's *Izvestiia* of 31 October in which an unsigned editorial stressed the 'abnormality' of a government of one left-wing party and called rather for 'the unification of all forces dedicated to the revolution', and for the 'unity of the democracy'.[45]

Kronstadt's Bolsheviks, however, shared neither the optimism of the *Oleg*'s sailors nor the craving for unity of Kronstadt's *Izvestiia*, and the *Golos pravdy* of the same date warned that the 'agreement' and the coalition of 'all socialist parties' demanded by the Railwaymen's Union would be bound to lead to 'the most disastrous consequences for our revolution'.[46] Thus it was in a despondent mood and in the shadow of the failure of the *Vikzhel* negotiations due to the intransigence of the Bolshevik leaders Lenin and Trotsky and of a majority of the Bolshevik Central Committee (a minority resigned in protest) that the Soviet resumed its debate on power, on 2 November.[47] A bitter and even more aggressive than ever Zverin told the Bolsheviks 'publicly' that they had made a 'colossal mistake' in pushing their 'party leaders' to the fore. Instead, they should have shown that they were 'not fighting for the Bolshevik party, but rather for the power of the Soviets', even though their party was large and had the support of the proletariat and of a large section of the peasantry. For the power of the Soviets was not the power of 'this or that party . . . not of Lenin and Trotsky' but that of the toiling people and its 'true representatives', and these may well be 'inconspicuous people', but they were nevertheless good practical workers who had proven themselves to the full. He and the SR-Maximalists opposed a government based on parties, and stood for a 'purely functional Soviet government', for parties were divisive, while Soviets united, and the experience of the Kronstadt Soviet was the proof: 'Had it not united us, we would long ago have split into several camps.' Therefore, 'Down with parties! Long live the Soviet of Workers', Soldiers' and Peasants' Deputies!'

Zverin envisaged a Soviet authority whose 'central organ' would consist of the representatives of the provincial Soviets with the latter elected because they had become known as 'experienced, practical workers' rather than as 'theorists and orators'. It was they who would form the 'genuine Soviet state power' that would direct the country's social and economic life.

But even Zverin, though disappointed, declared he would not press his point against the Bolsheviks at a time of struggle against the 'counter-revolutionary' Committee for Salvation of the Fatherland and the Revolution, and he trusted that the Bolsheviks, who had so far 'fulfilled their promises', would eventually also 'correct their mistakes'.[48]

Anatolii Lamanov too reasoned with the Bolsheviks, reminding them that 'it was not the party that made the [February] revolution, but the people', and that the revolution's success had been secured when Soviets expressing 'the general will of the people' had been organized. Soviets, as such, did not pursue party interests, nor were they wedded to any particular (party) programme, but they did need 'perfect political and economic liberty'.[49]

In a similar vein, the Kronstadt organization of Left SRs in its declaration of 2 November 'insisted'[50]

on the speediest possible formation of a homogeneous socialist government drawn from all sections of the revolutionary democracy represented at the Congress. Responsible to the Central Executive Committee of Soviets, such a government alone will be capable of taking the country out of the bloody impasse created by the most recent events.

In the end, the Kronstadt Soviet issued a declaration to the Central Executive Committee of Soviets which was identical with the Bolshevik resolution (with Left SR amendments) adopted by that body itself on the night of 1 November.[51] Thus, the Kronstadt declaration,[52] too, laid down such 'conditions for an agreement' as would end any further negotiations with SRs, Mensheviks or even Menshevik-Internationalists towards the formation of a broadly based socialist coalition government, while making the Congress of Soviets the 'sole source of power', and the government of People's Commissars responsible to the Central Executive Committee of Soviets.

With Rivkin, Zverin and Lamanov and Kronstadt's Left SRs prepared, for the sake of Soviet state power, to accept, albeit reluctantly, a Bolshevik government, hoping that it would eventually become less Bolshevik and increasingly more Soviet, their own hapless role was soon inadvertently spelt out to them by a visitor from Petrograd. On 14 November, only some twelve days after Zverin had lashed out against the single-party-mindedness of the Bolsheviks, it fell to Lamanov, chairing the meeting of the Soviet, to welcome Ieronymus Yasinsky, an elderly and sedate man of letters, very lately turned Bolshevik and now a member of the party's propaganda section for the Baltic Fleet. With the tactless zeal of a convert, Yasinsky treated the Kronstadters to a panegyric on the Bolshevik party and its 'recent successes'. Defining a Bolshevik as 'a citizen who truly comprehends his sublime calling', he then turned to his Soviet audience, saying, 'Since many of you here are Bolsheviks, may I, through you, salute the great Russian party, the Communist party of Bolsheviks!' One wonders what Lamanov (and the non-Bolshevik majority) must have felt as he went through the motions of greeting the 'famous writer' on behalf of the Kronstadt Soviet.[53] For, as far as they knew, Kronstadt and their Soviet had not been taken over by Yasinsky's 'Communist party of Bolsheviks'. In fact, as Parchevsky remembered[54] and as one Krasnogorsky observed regretfully in Kronstadt's *Izvestiia* of 19 December 1917: 'In Kronstadt itself there was no October revolution; there were no radical changes in that order which had evolved since the March Days', in the process of 'safeguarding a maximum of freedom' against all encroachments, notably those of Kerensky.[55]

Indeed, although Kronstadt's sailors had stormed the Winter Palace and struck fear into the Nevsky Prospect, in Kronstadt itself, as *Soldatskaia pravda* reported, the October Days passed 'very quietly' and the city remained as orderly 'as before'.[56] In fact, Kronstadt experienced no terror or violence before June 1919 and the mutiny of its Krasnaia Gorka Fort.[57] Whether in revulsion against the blood-bath of 1 March 1917 or out of fear of becoming a 'new Sakhalin', Kronstadt's *Izvestiia* on 1 November 1917 exhorted its readers:

The bloody shadows of Robespierre and Marat must not darken our revolution. We must set an example of humanism, for we fight for the peace of the nations. We stand against bloodshed in general and needless bloodshed in particular. Let every soldier remember that we are not the gendarmes of Nicholas the Bloody! Let no drop of wantonly shed blood torment our consciences![58]

It was the same spirit that inspired Anatolii Lamanov to jump to the defence of the civil servants on 2 November, when the Kronstadt Soviet debated the strike of government officials[59] in protest against the Bolshevik takeover and the Bolshevik sailor Aleksei Pavlov urged that they be 'cast overboard!' Pleading that these 'toilers in state institutions' first be shown 'the true path', Lamanov proposed that should they then still 'throw in their lot with the bourgeoisie', the Soviet should deal with them 'honestly' and 'push them aside'. The country was in need of ability, he argued, and 'there are not that many talents' that they could be so lightly discarded. In that vein and in language that is unmistakeably Lamanov's, the Kronstadt Soviet appealed to state employees 'To rally closely to the side of the workers and the peasants in the building up of the kingdom of labour . . . and with their help consolidate the revolution's achieve-ments for the benefit of all toilers.'

Yet there was some repression: the Trudovik newspaper *Trud i zemlia* which had been a thorn in the flesh of the Kronstadt Soviet ever since its showdown with the provisional government in May 1917, closed down with No. 180 on 26 November 1917, but that may have been as much due to the Sovnarkom decrees of November 1917, which made advertising and paper allocations a state monopoly, as to local initiative.[60]

More radical, and with the edge directed against Kronstadt's small middle class, was the series of revolutionary decrees issued by the Kronstadt Soviet in December 1917 and January 1918. Thus, a graduated tax for warm clothes for the army, ranging from 52 to 360 roubles, was levied on 'the bourgeoisie', netting some 40,000 roubles which were given to the Third Army.[61] Private ownership of 'immobile property, houses and land' was abolished; all pharmacies, banks, picture theatres, baths and printing shops were socialized; on 31 January 1918 the municipal Duma was dissolved because, as the decree put it, of 'revolutionary necessity' and the need for 'economy in manpower and resources'. Finally, compulsory militia service was introduced for all citizens aged between eighteen and fifty, including priests.[62] The Soviet's refusal to exempt Russian orthodox priests from conscription into the militia aroused wide-spread resentment and serious opposition. The workers of at least two workshops and of the Construction Department of the Kronstadt fortress are reported to have held angry meetings to protest against this 'affront to the priestly dignity' at a time when, it was alleged, 'not one Jewish rabbi, Mohammedan mulla, Roman Catholic priest or German pastor' had been conscripted by the Executive Committee of the Soviet which 'consisted wholly of the heterodox'. This protest, and other agitation which fastened on the Soviet's refusal to grant financial assistance to Kronstadt's churches, notably a grant-in-aid to the naval cathedral choir, was accompanied by rumours that the Soviet planned to turn the churches into 'picture theatres and a circus'.[63] The hot-headed and anti-clerical Alexander Brushvit published a sharp reply in the Kronstadt *Izvestiia*: 'On Believers, Non-Believers and Black Hundreds'.[64] Patiently explaining why the Soviet could not maintain religious establishments, and why the church must be separated from the state, and illustrating his point with an account of how a local priest had refused to give his illegitimate *and* unbaptized baby boy a proper burial, Brushvit then lashed out against all those 'Black Hundreds' who remained 'immune to persuasion':

Woe to all you who have lost your epaulettes, your superfluous houses' pharmacies, picture theatres, baths and printing shops! Woe to you who no longer control all those pumps with which, since the creation of the world, you have drained the people's sweat and blood! Beware! Was the fear driven into you on 1 March so little that you now want more? Have you already forgotten that lesson, decked yourselves in new plumes, spread your little wings, and poised yourselves ready to fly again? Beware! For you will fly no further than the Naval Investigation [Prison]! The people's Soviet power knows where the shoe pinches, and how to cure you! Gentlemen Black Hundreds, do you understand?

His threats were given teeth the next day when the Kronstadt Soviet, 'striving towards the destruction of all survivals of the bourgeois order', reiterated the duty of all citizens, including priests, to serve in the town militia. The salaries thus saved, the Soviet urged, could be better spent on cultural–educational matters; moreover, professional, salaried militia-men were bound to turn, *horribile dictu*, into policemen. In the very same session, the Soviet also decreed 'the arrest and trial before a revolutionary court of all those who in future engage in counter-revolutionary propaganda against Soviet state power'.[65]

This ferocious bluster may have intimidated some, though only one deacon and the arch-priest Sergei Putilin (but he soon abandoned the priesthood and may have joined the SRs) agreed to serve; yet it did not prevent the religious question from intruding time and again into the Soviet's deliberations throughout December 1917 and January 1918. Indeed, some deputies themselves were said to have been involved in the religious protest movement, while the entire SR-Maximalist faction counselled moderation and warned that account must be taken of grass-root protest. They were, however, outvoted by ninety-one to fifty in a roll-call vote, when they came up against the combined weight of the Bolsheviks and Left SRs.[66] Lamanov's forebodings were well founded: as late as 19 February 1918, the Executive Committee of the Soviet admitted, in its Appeal to the Citizens of Kronstadt, that all warning measures had been exhausted, yet Black Hundred agitation on the religious question continued. It therefore decreed that 'no sermons on political subjects be preached from church pulpits' and the Department of Justice was empowered to arrest, fine and deport from Kronstadt all those guilty of counter-revolutionary agitation 'without distinction of rank'.[67]

And as for the socialization measures, initiated by Kronstadt's radical populist bloc of SR-Maximalists, Left SRs and Anarcho-Syndicalists, they were far less dictated by class hatred and fear of Black Hundred agitation than by the almost desperate pursuit of that 'revolutionary creativity and initiative' deemed necessary to enable Red Kronstadt to maintain itself as that 'model corner which loyally guards the revolutionary flame'.[68] So strongly was this felt that, during the 7 December debate on the socialization of houses, Lamanov urged the Soviet to pass the project and thus make Kronstadt a revolutionary pace-maker whence the message would 'spread all over Russia'.[69]

Passed by the combined vote of the SR-Maximalists, Left SRs and Anarchists, in the teeth of Bolshevik and Menshevik opposition, the decree ordered the transfer without compensation of all houses and land situated in the area of Kronstadt to the Central Housing Commission of the Kronstadt Soviet. The Housing Commission was to be underpinned and assisted by a large network of elective house committees entrusted with fixing and collecting rents from tenants (including former houseowners), and defraying therefrom all expenses for water, lighting, heating, cleaning, garbage removal and wages for yard-porters and chimney-sweeps. The remainder was to be handed over to the Housing Commission to cover the cost of repairs and the maintenance of incapacitated former houseowners who had hitherto lived on rents.[70]

Artemii Liubovich and the Bolshevik faction in the Kronstadt Soviet, acting apparently on instruction from Petrograd, had consistently though deviously obstructed the housing decree; fastening on the roughness of the draft, they were promptly and brusquely told by its author, Yarchuk, that he had not been engaged in writing 'a work of literature'. Rivkin, however, tried to conciliate and convince the Bolsheviks: 'You know, once it is socialists who have framed the project and socialists who guard the interests of the toilers, it follows that the workers will not be hurt when your Soviet state power tackles the problem in cooperation with the Housing Commission and the house committees.'[71]

Not surprisingly, the Bolsheviks remained unconvinced. Outvoted by ninety-nine to seventy-four votes, and failing even to have the project deferred for further discussion, they and the Mensheviks walked out in angry protest, to the cheerful applause of the radical populist majority, now truly feeling its revolutionary muscle and shouting derisively, 'They have united, at last!'[72]

Having thus failed to convince the 'Marxists', the Soviet presented its decree on housing in an appeal 'To the Toilers of the City of Kronstadt' on 20 December 1917. What was at stake, the appeal claimed, was nothing less than the abolition of the 'worst form of the exploitation of human labour' whereby a worker's family could be evicted into the street by a 'parasitical houseowner' and people had to live in humid cellars and garrets while good apartments stood vacant. The appeal ended with a blowing of revolutionary trumpets: 'Long live the rallying of the toilers around the Soviets! Long live Soviet state power! Long live the toilers' revolution!'[73]

It was into this still euphoric post-October Kronstadt, bent on its socialization spree, that Fiodor Chaliapin came on 17 December 1917, accompanied by the pianist V. Maratov and the cellist E. A. Volf-Izrael, to give a concert which, scheduled for the 28 October, had been deferred because of the October revolution.

Some ten to twelve thousand Kronstadters, the largest indoor audience Chaliapin said he had ever had, are reported to have crowded into the Naval Manège. He ended the concert singing the Marseillaise in French and, at the crowd's special request, then sang with it the 'Dubinushka'. 'It was a truly majestic spectacle', said Chaliapin. It was also a great moment for Anatolii Lamanov who had chaired the concert-meeting and now presented Chaliapin with a red-ribboned garland, thanking him on behalf of Kronstadt's citizens and their Soviet for his visit and concert at a time when all, 'including artists', banded together to serve the people, 'their sole sovereign master'. Chaliapin was 'deeply moved' and, speaking briefly in reply, urged the 'indispensability of knowledge for the people'. Quoting his own experience of 'sorrow and suffering', he told the vast mass of Kronstadters: 'Without knowledge – life is unmitigated horror', therefore, 'Study!' and, underlining his message, donated the concert's very substantial takings, some 10,276 roubles, to the Executive Committee of the Kronstadt Soviet for 'cultural–educational purposes'.[74]

Chaliapin's visit and the singing of the 'Dubinushka' gave moving expression to the Kronstadters' post-October elation:

> And the day came, and the people awoke
> And straightened its mighty back
> And, reaching for a truly sturdy club,
> Made for squire and tsar, priest and lord.
> Heh, dear stick, let's heave,
> Heh, green stick, you'll do it,
> Together let's pull and push and heave!

This was the high point of Kronstadt's Soviet power and democracy. The socialization of 'all the survivals from the bourgeois order' brought private land, houses, shops, pharmacies, saunas, printing presses and banks under the Soviet's control, and, by the decree of 31 January 1918, all functions, personnel, property, assets, obligations and debts of the municipal Duma were transferred to the Soviet, significantly expanding its local power and administrative responsibilites.[75] Yet, as Liubovich, speaking for all deputies, put it during the debate on reorganization, while the Soviet was 'the local power', it lacked 'the apparatus of power'. Instead, he lamented, it had 'those innumerable commissions in which we are drowning'. Repeatedly, speakers noted during the debate that the Soviet's role, which had been pre-eminently political in the pre-October period, had now become overwhelmingly economic and social.[76]

The new urgent challenge was driven home to Kronstadt's Executive Committee on 14 December 1917, when an elderly woman burst into its session beseeching the Soviet 'to feed her, otherwise she would die of hunger'. While the Executive Committee solved her immediate problem by decreeing that she be allowed meals in the Naval Assembly, the move prompted the Bolshevik Boris Molodtsov to sneer that the Soviet was becoming 'an almshouse'.[77] In the ensuing debate, Kronstadt's old-age homes, almshouses, crèches and orphanages, formerly administered by the municipal Duma, the church or private philanthropy, were revealed as overcrowded and neglected. The Soviet, seeing itself as the local 'state organization', had no alternative but to accept responsibility for social welfare, and to reorganize all philanthropic institutions under a single Soviet authority.[78]

In that spirit and in the light of 'the experience of the last two months of organic work', the Soviet commissioned the Left SR N. Pobedonostsev to prepare a project for the reorganization of the Soviet and its institutions. The draft 'Project of the Fundamental Principles of the Organization of and the Elections of the Soviet of Workers' and Soldiers' Deputies of the City and Fortress of Kronstadt' was presented to the Soviet plenum on 4 January 1918. Debated, amended, and adopted on 21 January, the Project provides a full statement of the objectives and organizational structure and principles of the Kronstadt Soviet between January and June 1918.[79]

The Project's ideological preamble defined the Soviet as 'the class organization of the entire toiling population of the city of Kronstadt' striving towards its 'complete political and economic emancipation'. But, it continued, emancipation must not lead to 'the creation of new privileges', but rather to the 'equal rights and obligations of all people'. The people's power and its organization of economic and political life aimed at 'the complete destruction of any form of class domination'. The organizational principles of the Soviet as 'the local power' sought 'a maximum of decentralization', while its 'rational coordination' and economy of resources would make it 'unconditionally unitary'. Similarly, while the Soviet franchise was to be restricted to 'toiling people only', elections were to be 'strictly democratic'.

The Project's major innovation was the creation of a permanent administrative apparatus. This abolished its proliferating network of close to forty control, operative and special purpose commissions, and replaced them with seventeen permanent departments (or ministries), staffed by permanent, salaried employees, and each headed by a chairman-in-charge, flanked by an elected specialist commission to control, advise and assist him. All chairmen were to be elected by the plenum of the Soviet to the Executive Committee, there to head a particular department for which they remained responsible and accountable to the Soviet's plenum. The chairman of the Executive Committee was to be responsible and accountable to the Soviet for the performance of all seventeen departments as a whole.

The debates show Soviet unanimity for replacing the indeterminate commissions with permanent departments and for electing individual members to the Executive Committee to take personal responsibility for the particular departments. These members were further required to have special qualifications and aptitudes for the job in accordance with the 'principle of personal responsibility' on which great stress was laid by the Project's author. There was also general agreement that departmental chairmen should have quali-fied salaried staff in accordance with their needs, and budgetary provisions were made for defined, established positions. Indeed, great play was made of a member of the Executive Committee who, chairing the Commission for Combating Drunkenness, *himself* went to smash a cache of liquor bottles and, in the process, got himself drunk. Malicious rumour then had it that 'the entire Executive Committee indulges in drunken orgies'.

But there was acrimonious debate about the political, as distinct from the professional, qualifications required of departmental chairmen. In the past (at least since May 1917, when the Kronstadt Soviet's original constitution had been drafted), election to the Executive Committee and to the commissions had been by party slates and in proportion to the party factions' strength in the Soviet. Now, Lamanov and his SR-Maximalists saw in the adoption of new criteria of professionalism the longed for chance to strike a blow against party-mindedness. Lamanov thus moved that the sole criterion for eligibility to the Executive Committee, and hence to chairmanship of a department, must be 'the practical aptitude of the candidates'. Party slates, he urged, should be kept out of the elec-tions and non-party Soviet deputies should have a fair chance of election to Soviet offices. The Soviet, he said, had never suffered from 'a dearth of party people, but rather from a shortage of men capable of doing a job'. The masses, in his view, did not prefer a candidate 'because he was a Bolshevik or a Menshevik, but because he was a decent man who could be trusted.' Countering Pobedono-stsev's argument (and that of his Bolshevik allies) that were it not for party slates 'a worker who belonged to the Black Hundred' could slip through, Lamanov urged that this could be checked and prevented at the base assembly level by party collectives or cells. Put to the vote, Lamanov's motion was passed by eighty-two to sixty-eight votes, in the teeth of angry Bolshevik opposition, with Piotr Smirnov shouting, 'That can't be!' while Bregman insisted on a re-count by roll-call. It was only thanks to the Left SRs, who rallied in defence of the Project, their brainchild, and who were anxious to retain the Bolsheviks' support, that a compromise formula was adopted by eighty-seven to nineteen votes. This stipulated that account be taken of both 'the political side and the practical suitability' of the candidate for a particular office. But this 'compromise' was no more than a sop to Lamanov. In practice it was rendered meaningless by point seven, which governed the election of the Executive Committee (the body including the seventeen chairmen of departments) and its praesidium, and determined that these would be 'proportional to factions' and thus controlled by party slates. True, the 'specialist commissions' assisting (and controlling) the chairmen of the departments were to be 'as much as possible specialist', yet it seems very likely that party political considerations remained important.

All socialist parties recognized as such by the Soviet (the moderate Popular Socialists or Trudoviks had, on the motion of Bregman, been refused recognition as early as September 1917) had the right to send one delegate each to the Executive Committee. But while formerly, and regardless of their numbers, parties had sent three delegates each to the Soviet, over and above their elected deputies, now the number of those they could nominate was to be proportional to the size of their faction. This arrangement seems to have been a compromise between Bregman, who would not give representation on the Executive Committee or in the Soviet to a party which had no deputies or faction in the Soviet, but who was defeated on this by forty-seven to forty-two votes, and Lamanov, who protested against this 'violence perpetrated against minorities'.

A major innovation, arousing considerable controversy because of the basic constitutional question it raised, was the decision, passed only by sixty-six to forty-five votes, with five abstentions, to make the praesidium of the Soviet identical with the praesidium of the Executive Committee. The chief function of the Soviet praesidium was to convene and lead the Soviet's sessions, and to represent it and do its business between sessions. But the praesidium of the Executive Committee had quasi-governmental functions, the chief of which was to ensure that the Soviet's decisions and decrees were implemented, to direct and coordinate the work of its own seventeen departments, and to be accountable to the Soviet plenum for the Executive Committee as a whole. Hitherto the offices of chairman and deputy chairman of the two bodies had been kept separate, and so manned as to reflect and balance the strength of party factions in the Soviet. Thus, the proposed creation of a single praesidium gave rise to what may well have been Kronstadt's major constitutional debate, of particular interest since it does not seem to have been argued strictly on party lines. True, the question of the separation of powers had already cropped up briefly in the aftermath of the July Days, when Lamanov (then chairman of the Executive Committee) had censured Raskolnikov (then deputy chairman of the Soviet) for having arrogated to himself executive powers during the night of 4 July when he issued directives to Kronstadt's military commanders in the name of the Executive Committee. But it was only now that the Kronstadt Soviet tried to come to grips with the intractable problem of separating its legislature from its executive. How would the dozens of Soviet deputies elected to executive posts or commissions (commissioners were generally forbidden to serve on more than one commission at the same time) reconcile their legislative and control duties with their role as executives? Was 'the Soviet to consist of bureaucrats?' asked the Left SR Barzdain. 'I hold a post in the militia, but am also at the same time a member of the Soviet, and as such ought to control that post.'

Yet while Lebedev and Lamanov accepted as a fact of life that the Soviet's legislative, executive, political and economic functions and activities were 'inextricably bound up', Brushvit denounced this as 'the root of the evil', which must be removed if Kronstadt wished to live up to its no longer deserved reputation as 'the best organized and functioning Soviet'. His prescription was for a 'strict separation' of 'legislators' (Soviet plenum), 'holders of authority' (praesidium and Executive Committee), and 'executives' (chairmen of departments). That 'separation' could be realized and the Soviet thus rescued from ignominiously becoming an assembly of 'bureaucrats' if all deputies elected to executive posts immediately relinquished their seats in the Soviet and gave up 'a right to control and call to account to which they are not entitled'. Their place in the Soviet plenum would be filled by newly elected representatives of their own base assemblies. The Soviet, while having no executive functions, would thus be able to exercise control over departmental chairmen through the 'initiative and control commissions' attached to the respective departments.

Not surprisingly, Bregman and Liudmilla Stal pounced on both Brushvit and Barzdain for presuming to call Soviet office-bearers 'bureaucrats', while the humourless Bregman insisted that 'a deputy elected by his workshop continued to be its representative regardless of whether he is a talker or a practical worker'. Brushvit found himself isolated when Liudmilla Stal dismissed his concern with the constitutional problems of Soviet democracy as 'just so many fine words', sneering at his 'stale, bourgeois truth, all learned by rote', on the separation of powers, as entirely irrelevant. 'Our aim is the transformation of our economic life', she insisted, and *that* required 'an efficient Soviet', equipped with departments, chairmen-in-charge, and commissions attached to them 'working under the Soviet's direction'.

With Kronstadt's constitutional debate thus stifled at birth, it is not surprising that both the Project and the debate on it ignored the crucial question of the Kronstadt Soviet's relations with Russia's new central organs of power, notably the Council of People's Commissars. This may well have been because Kronstadt, left to enjoy its self-government, had no particular reason to seek a clear definition. More important still, given the strongly decentralist views of Kronstadt's Left SRs, SR-Maximalists, and Anarchists, as compared with the hyper-centralist views of the Bolsheviks, this was bound to become a divisive issue, as Liudvik Grimm found on 14 December when, quite innocently, he complained about 'the torrent of decrees from Petrograd that showers down on Kronstadt as from a horn of plenty' with no one knowing whether what they received was a fully fledged decree, a mere draft of a decree, or just a discussion paper. Since, as he urged, 'we cannot turn a deaf ear on the decrees of the People's Commissars, as we did with Kerensky', a commissar should be elected to liaise with the government in Petrograd, and a registry of decrees should be kept by the Executive Committee. The Bolsheviks were immediately up in arms, protesting vehemently against such 'impermissible sarcastic asides against the central power', and their resolution against the election of a liaison commissar was barely carried by sixty-one to fifty-seven votes. It was only in June 1918 that the question of Kronstadt's relations with the central government was again raised, but by then it had become a major and vital issue in the debate on the draft of Russia's first Soviet constitution which subordinated local Soviets, such as Kronstadt's, to the 'corresponding higher organs of Soviet power', that is the central government, and ended the virtual autonomy of the 'Free City of Kronstadt'.

While there was general agreement on the structure and powers of the seventeen departments which, like those for finance, procurements, supply and distribution, housing, medical services, sanitation, industry, construction and repairs, fuel supply, labour, culture and education, the military, including Red Guards and the fire brigades, and public welfare, all combined the functions of government ministries with municipal departments, the Department of Justice alone caused some debate. Its Investigation Commission was instructed to investigate 'dispassionately' all crimes, and hand over cases of public misdemeanour (such as the drunkenness of four members of the Executive Committee) to the Department's Court of Public Conscience (which publicly reprimanded the four and deprived them of the right to public office for the following twelve months); more serious matters, ranging from contempt of court to homicide and counter-revolution, were to be passed to the Department's Revolutionary Tribunal; and the inevitable Commission to Combat Drunkenness became as much a special section of the Justice Department as Kronstadt's prisons.

Liubovich wanted the Investigation Commission, which was only permitted to make house searches and arrests with warrants issued by the Executive Committee, to be invested with 'much more executive power', so that it could, for example, 'totally root out all gambling'. But it was Lamanov who really let fly when he urged that prisons be replaced by penal workhouses which, in 'the era of toil', would provide criminals 'corrupted by the old order' with healthy conditions for correcting themselves, while the incorrigible, being mentally ill, would be placed in hospitals. Lamanov's plea proved irresistible and Kronstadt's notorious prisons were renamed 'Workhouses of Imprisonment' (Rabochie doma zakliucheniia).

Yet Kronstadt's judicial institutions were seen as transient, needed only so long as 'the entire population of Kronstadt has not learned to live without crime'. But the time would come when, so the chairman of the Investigation Commission insisted, 'there would be no crime or violence'. But that time was certainly not at hand in March 1918 when the praesidium of the Executive Committee ordered the arrest of the entire Investigation Commission on suspicion of having taken bribes, the price that had been exacted for a person's life having been fixed at 15,000 roubles.[80]

Yet regardless of the naive optimism of some of the debates, the Project was distinguished by a new, hard-headed understanding of the exigencies of organization, professionalism and politicization, a far cry from the early Utopian trust in the capacity of the 'grey muzhik and the swarthy worker, the soldier and the sailor' to rule and administer the state without the help of a bureaucracy. The reorganization of Kronstadt's Soviet had its clear parallel in the electoral instructions to the cells of all parties and non-party groups of the 'toiling collectives' (the new name for base assemblies), which urged them to spell out for the benefit of the electors 'the areas and branches of public life for which the proposed candidate was qualified'.

The new insistence on the personal responsibility of departmental chairmen and the employment of salaried personnel may have been a straw in the wind pointing to Lenin's move, in April 1918, to one-man management and the employment of 'bourgeois specialists'. Yet the unifying thread running throughout the debate was Kronstadt's deep and unswerving commitment to the elective principle and to the responsibility and accountability of all executives to the Soviet assembly. This certainly remained unchanged.

It was that reorganized, mature Kronstadt Soviet of early 1918 which Georges Gurvitch (soon to become one of the founders of French sociology) singled out in his report to the Central Executive Committee of Soviets. It was, he wrote, 'a model of Soviet organization', particularly remarkable for the 'exemplary scheme of its departments'.[81] There is no reason to quarrel with this appraisal, especially when comparing Kronstadt, as Gurvitch did, with other Soviets of early 1918. Yet Gurvitch entirely overlooked one necessary condition for Kronstadt's singular success as a Soviet democracy: the existence there of vigorous political parties which, through 'collectives' or cells in the base assemblies and factions in the Soviet plenum, jealously ensured that Soviet elections would be genuine and clean. Moreover, with the praesidium, Executive Committee, executive posts and commissions all manned in accordance with the strength of the various political factions in the Soviet, Kronstadt's Soviet democracy was invested with the advantages of a coalition government resting on an all but wall-to-wall parliamentary base.

This system could function only as long as all parties represented in the Soviet abided by its rules as defined in the Project's Instructions for Elections. Kronstadt's Bolsheviks, notably Liubovich, strongly supported the Project, so much so that Pobedonostsev, its grateful author, bestowed on 'the Bolsheviks of the Leninist persuasion' (together with the Left SRs, the SR-Maximalists and the

Anarchists) the honourable title of 'Socialist Revolutionaries', though only 'in the broadest sense of the term'.[82]

But were Kronstadt's Bolsheviks likely to continue satisfied with their minority status in Kronstadt when, in Russia at large, they were the ruling party? Indeed while the radical populist coalition of Maximalists and Left SRs held sway, albeit precariously, *within* Kronstadt and its Soviet, *externally* Kronstadt was a loyal stronghold of the Bolshevik regime. In the November 1917 elections to the Constituent Assembly (boycotted by the Maximalists and contested by the SRs in an undifferentiated general list only), the Bolshevik candidates Lenin and Pavel Dybenko received some 80.3% of the Kronstadt sailor vote (62.2% of those eligible cast their votes), 85.3% of the soldier vote (69.3% voted) and 68.2% of the civilian vote. Altogether out of 58,585 who did vote, 46,248 voted Bolshevik.[83] More importantly, Kronstadt served the Bolshevik regime as a major source of reliable crack troops and special task-forces. Beginning with Feliks Dzerzhinsky and Nikolai Podvoisky's requests of 4 November 1917 for Kronstadt sailors to guard the Smolny Institute and the Tauride Palace, the seats of the Council of People's Commissars and of the Central Executive Committee of Soviets, and throughout the remainder of 1917 and most of 1918 and 1919, a steady stream of demands for sailors and special task-forces reached the Kronstadt Soviet; they ranged from that of the Petrograd Soviet of 5 November 1917 for some five hundred of the 'most politically conscious comrades to regulate food supply, take food cargoes to their destination and put an end to the pilfering of grain and food cargoes', to Vladimir Antonov-Ovseenko's urgent appeal in early January 1918 for a large detachment of Kronstadt sailors to leave for the Don river area, there to reinforce the front against General Aleksei Kaledin, ataman of the Don Cossacks, and boost its morale.

When, on 10 December, Antonov-Ovseenko asked the Supreme Naval College to send to the south 'urgently and immediately' a detachment of some 120 'smart, very literate and energetic' intelligence officers, Pavel Dybenko turned to Kronstadt as a matter of course, asking for 120 'properly dressed and equipped' men.[84] Likewise, when Commissar Grigorii Evdokimov was to take a special task-force of Arkhangelsk sailors to Siberia, he requested 'a group of a hundred staunch Kronstadt comrades' to stiffen it.[85]

On 11 January 1918 the Kronstadt Soviet debated Antonov-Ovseenko's urgent appeal for an additional large force to be sent

south against Kaledin. Yarchuk, who together with Aleksei Pronin
and Stepan Bogomolov had commanded the first Kronstadt detachment sent there late in December 1917, gave warm support to the
request:

You cannot imagine how they welcome the Kronstadters everywhere! At
meetings, in the Soviet, they always let Kronstadters speak out of turn.
They must be sent there to boost the morale . . . Our Kronstadters terrify
Kaledin! You've probably heard what happened in Debaltsev? There
were just six of ours there when two of Kaledin's troop trains began to fire
at the station, and the moment they saw a sailor's ribbon, they took fright
that the sailors were there and turned back . . .

Yarchuk begged the Soviet to send a detachment whatever its size:
for

It is not important how many are sent; what matters is that the news
should spread: 'The Kronstadters are coming!' When we sent agitators, all
the newspapers reported that a detachment of 3,000 Kronstadters was on
the way, and even before our agitators arrived, Kaledin abandoned three
stations.

The Soviet found such pleading irresistible, and a detachment of
some 600 Kronstadters, commanded by the Left SR Karl Kallis who
had distinguished himself during the October revolution, left for the
southern front on 19 January 1918.[86]

Kronstadt sailors also played an inglorious role in the dissolution
of the Constituent Assembly. By 21 November 1917 the Executive
Committee of the Kronstadt Soviet was ordered by Pavel Dybenko,
People's Commissar for Naval Affairs, to keep 7,000 sailors 'on full
alert' for the anticipated opening of the Constituent Assembly on
26 November. That false 'alert' was followed by a meeting of some
20,000 'soldiers, sailors, workers and peasants' in Kronstadt's Naval
Manège on 3 December, where, after they had heard a report by
Fiodor Raskolnikov, now commissar for the navy, on the perform-
ance of the Soviet government, they resolved to support only a
Constituent Assembly that was 'so composed as to confirm the
achievements of the October revolution' and would be free of
'Kaledinites and leaders of the counter-revolutionary bourgeoisie'.[87]

Two days later, Anatolii Lamanov, who as an SR-Maximalist was
no great lover of bourgeois parliaments, used the columns of
Kronstadt's *Izvestiia* to juxtapose 'the Constituent Assembly and the
Soviets', taking the independent left-wing *Novaia zhizn*' to task for
'deceiving the people' by placing exaggerated hopes in the Con-

stituent Assembly. Arguing that there was no way of knowing how its deputies would address themselves to the task of building the 'new foundations of revolutionary Russia', Lamanov claimed that the toilers, who had by their labour 'created everything by which society lives', had the 'inalienable right', should the deputies act against their interests, to say to them: 'Out with you, unworthy ones!' But, he cautioned, that 'mighty word' should be uttered through the 'authoritative organs' of the Soviets. It thus followed that the toilers must strengthen the Soviets with deputies who were staunchly dedicated to their cause, for only powerful Soviets were capable of 'securing the final and irreversible victory of labour over capital'.[88]

The 'weak-willed, weak-nerved, rootless' and 'too clever by half' intellectuals of *Novaia zhizn* were again denounced by Kronstadt's *Izvestiia* which, on 20 December, castigated that 'boarding-school for virtuous, politically innocent young ladies' who 'pine away for the Constituent Assembly' as for a 'betrothed bridegroom'.[89] Kronstadt and its *Izvestiia* had indeed travelled a long way since the spring of 1917 and its own early enthusiasm for the Constituent Assembly!

On the eve of the opening of the Constituent Assembly, on 5 January 1918, the Kronstadt Soviet, at Dybenko's request, sent a detachment of some 600 sailors to Petrograd and the Tauride Palace, enjoining them before they boarded the landing craft to 'fulfil their revolutionary duty'.[90]

When at last the Assembly opened, Pavel Dybenko, himself a veteran Kronstadt sailor and the representative of the Baltic Fleet, spoke for its sailors and cursed it, exclaimin'g: We recognize Soviets only! Our rifles and bayonets will serve only the Soviet state and it alone! As for the rest – we are against them, down with them all!'[91] It fell to Fiodor Raskolnikov to lead the walk-out of the Bolshevik faction from the Assembly, but not before he had denounced its SR majority as 'counter-revolutionary' and threatened to put the 'final decision' on its fate into the hands of 'Soviet state power'. That fate was finally sealed when the Kronstadt sailor Anatolii Zhelezniakov, of Durnovo Villa notoriety and now commander of the Tauride Palace guards, ordered the members of the Constituent Assembly to get out 'because the guards are tired'.[92]

Whatever doubts some Kronstadters may have had about that praetorian exploit, it was no less a personage than Anatolii Lunacharsky, the People's Commissar for Education, who put their minds at rest. Arriving next morning in Kronstadt 'where it feels so good' to preach the new gospel of 'proletarian culture' which would blossom forth with 'the full splendour of its inner beauty and the untapped riches of the Russian character', Lunacharsky baldly condemned what had been an overwhelmingly *socialist* Constituent Assembly as 'the hope of all propertied elements', ranging from the Kadets and their SR allies to 'all Black Hundred scoundrels'.

Indeed, 'universal franchise', as 'the experience of Western Europe and America' had shown, 'preserved the bourgeois order'. But, 'a miracle has happened in Russia' and 'the people's genuine will' had found its expression in the representatives of the twenty million 'conscious elements of the masses' who had rallied to the Soviets. The role of parliaments would now devolve on Soviet congresses – their 'democratism is beyond doubt'.[93]

It was in this spirit that, in its session of 11 January 1918, the Kronstadt Soviet celebrated the demise of the Constituent Assembly and the transfer of its authority and 'business' to the Third Congress of Soviets (where Kronstadt was represented by the Left SR Konstantin Shurgin – with 157 votes – the SR-Maximalist Grigorii Rivkin – 147 votes – and the Bolshevik Fiodor Pervushin – 109 votes).[94] Liudmilla Stal rejoiced in 'the unimaginable ease with which the Constituent Assembly . . . a survival of the old order . . . has been sent packing' and proposed that Kronstadt greet the Third Congress of Soviets as 'that Constituent Assembly of the toiling masses' which 'would give a real push to our construction of a socialist order'. Seconding her, Anatolii Lamanov stressed the international significance of the Congress of Soviets: 'We observe that the revolution is spreading abroad. The world conflagration engulfs the entire globe, and we have come to a point at which the bourgeois order has outlived itself. In this Congress we greet the victorious beginning of the world revolution', and it was in that spirit that Lamanov's draft greeting was approved by the Soviet.[95]

By June 1918 Kronstadters had so strongly assumed the role of the Soviet state's special task-force that during the mutiny of the Torpedo Division in Petrograd at the end of June a force of 600 sailors was sent there on the orders of the command of the Baltic Fleet to occupy the area of the Obukhov Plant which had been put under martial law, and, as Sergei Saks, a member of the College of the People's Commissariat for the Navy, reported on 4 July 1918, 'they restored order in a most energetic way; that is, with their imposing looks they quickly convinced the Torpedo Division that they had acted wrongly and made them obey the orders of the Naval Command'.[96]

But the Soviet authorities may have gone too far in their enthusiasm for Kronstadt sailors. On 23 September 1918, Ivan Flerovsky, the general commissar of the Baltic Fleet, complained to Efroim Skliansky, a member of the College of the People's Commissariat for War, that 'the very best and most reliable elements' had been taken away from Kronstadt and from the fleet in general and begged for a short period of grace so that new cadres could be trained by the old hands.[97]

Internally, it was not for want of trying that the Kronstadt Bolsheviks put up with the dominant SR-Maximalist–Left SR coalition in the Soviet during the first six months of the post-October period. On 19 December 1917 Liubovich followed up the Bolshevik walk-out from the Soviet of 7 December by demanding the enlargement of that body by the election of additional members, and, when narrowly defeated by eighty-five to seventy-eight votes, seems to have forced new elections to the Soviet late in January 1918.[98] While these elections significantly changed the party balance in favour of the Bolshevik faction (from 96 to 139 deputies) as against sixty-four SRs, fifty-six Maximalists, twenty-one Non-Partyists, fifteen Anarchists and six Mensheviks,[99] they still saw the Left SR Pokrovsky triumph over the Bolshevik Bregman by 140 to 119 votes in a secret ballot for the chairmanship of the Soviet. True, of the three deputy chairmen elected (Bregman, Grediushko and Lamanov), all but the last were Bolsheviks, but that did not placate the Bolshevik faction. From *Golos pravdy* came Piotr Smirnov's open attack on 'the swamp', i.e. the coalition of Left SRs and Maximalists, for outdoing one another in profuse professions of dedication to 'the socialist revolution', while doing their very best to turn the Soviet into a 'foul talking-shop rather than assisting in the 'reorganization of the Soviet'. What irked Smirnov most was that the Left SRs, whose voting strength was only half of that of the Bolsheviks, had presumed to enlist the entire 'swamp' to have their candidate elected and that the latter would not resign, even though the Bolsheviks – who were 'almost a majority' – had declared that they had no confidence in him. 'A ministerial crisis is in the offing' was the ominous conclusion of an article which served notice that the Bolsheviks would press for new elections and for domination.[100]

Insult was added to injury when, on 7 March 1918, the Soviet elected its three delegates to the Fourth Congress of Soviets: Anatolii Lamanov was elected with 124 votes and Yarchuk with 95 votes, but the Bolshevik Liubovich came only third with a mere 79 votes.[101]

The mounting tension between the Bolsheviks and their erstwhile Left SR allies burst into the open on 7 March 1918 during the Soviet's debate on the treaty of Brest-Litovsk which Soviet Russia and Germany had signed on 3 March. Throughout January and February, Kronstadt's Left SRs, like their party comrades all over Russia, had vigorously denounced this 'annexationist, shameful and disastrous' separate peace with 'imperialist Germany'. Indeed, on both 30 January and 21 February 1918 (when Germany resumed hostilities and its 'obscene' peace terms became known), the Kronstadt Soviet had adopted a Left SR resolution (by ninety-five to sixty-five votes, with thirteen abstentions) rejecting the German conditions as tantamount to 'the subjugation of toiling Russia' and calling for an 'armed uprising against all oppressors' in defence of 'the social revolution'.[102]

The rival, and defeated, Bolshevik resolution sought to justify 'Brest-Litovsk' as 'a last desperate move' to halt the 'treacherous onslaught' of German imperialism on the proletarian revolution. A mass meeting, chaired by Lamanov, in the Naval Manège on 22 February, gave popular endorsement to the Soviet's stand and rejected both the moderate Bolshevik resolution and a more radical one moved by a group of workshops which condemned the 'surrender' of the Soviet government and called for a 'partisan war in defence of the homeland and of the revolution'.

During the debate of 7 March, the Bolsheviks, notably Liubovich and Entin, defended the Brest-Litovsk treaty against its opponents' 'blind faith' in a revolutionary war which would have to be waged by 'exhausted masses' and by an army which had 'ceased to exist'. It was nothing less than an 'irresponsible gamble' with the very existence of the Soviet republic, they said. Yarchuk's call for the 'arming of women and children' as 'our only way out', and Brushvit's appeal to and trust in the heroic deeds of 'valiant men', only strengthened Liubovich's argument. The more serious call of the Left SR G. Kvar for the creation of a united socialist front for a revolutionary war, entailing the cessation of terror 'against other parties', was seconded by the Anarchist Kliuchev who, for good measure, accused the Bolsheviks of signing the treaty so that they 'could save their strength for hangings and firing squads' and thus 'strangle the revolutionary spirit'. But Entin promptly charged 'Chernov, the bourgeoisie and the Mensheviks' with having adopted a revolutionary war as a 'provocation' intended to 'restore the Constituent Assembly and their own power'. To that accusation, those who had made common cause with the Bolsheviks in dispersing the Constituent Assembly and against Chernov and the Mensheviks had no answer.

When the vote was taken, the Soviet decisively reversed the stand taken in January and February. Whether this was due to intensive Bolshevik party pressure (the Bolsheviks insisted that ballot papers carry signatures and be published), to Liubovich's impressive rhetoric, or simply to the SR-Maximalists' decision to leave it to the individual members' consciences (as four-fifths of 'their faction', and those close to grass-root opinion, were convinced that Russia 'cannot wage war'), the Bolshevik resolution was carried by 101 to 58 votes, with no less than 27 abstentions and 7 invalidated votes (illegible signatures). While the bulk of the vote against the treaty came from the Left SRs and the Anarchists, it included a few SR-Maximalists, such as Lamanov, and at least two Bolsheviks (Ivan Kolbin and A. Kabanov).[103]

Brushvit, angry as ever, then declared that his Left SR faction did not regard this Soviet as representative and would withdraw from it. Voting on his motion for new and 'speedy' elections, eighty-eight supported Brushvit, forty-five voted against, and ten abstained. But before they had time to walk out of the hall of the Naval Assembly, Brushvit and his Left SRs were treated to a threatening speech by the Bolshevik V. Kiveisha (soon to become chairman of the local Cheka) who, shaking his fist at them, shouted,

Now, when the revolution is imperilled, you grind Soviet power under your heel. People who truly agonize over the perilous moment do not abandon their posts . . . If the Brushvits have assembled together here to engage in sabotage, then I say they have no place here and the small group which remains here will take arms against them.

Pandemonium broke loose as Kiveisha was shouted down, while his supporters applauded him equally loudly. Lamanov, then in the chair, angrily rang his bell and at last made himself heard. 'This is no place for threats, they are unworthy of revolutionaries! The threatening fist is not the argument of a revolutionary!' The walk-out was complete when Solomon Entin and a good number of Bolsheviks also left the hall in protest.[104]

Though a majority of the Soviet voted against new elections, their hand was forced when, at the next session of the Soviet on 22 March, a mere 104 delegates turned up. Elections were at last held on 1 April, but they only made matters worse for the Bolsheviks (at Lenin's suggestion, since March 1918 renamed Communists) who, with 53 deputies (out of 183) were still the largest party. But they now confronted a coalition of forty-one SR-Maximalists, thirty-nine Left SRs, fourteen Menshevik-Internationalists, ten Anarchists, and twenty-four non-partisan deputies. True, Lazar Bregman was now elected chairman of the Soviet, but Fiodor Pokrovsky was voted chairman of its Executive Committee and Lamanov deputy chairman. The new Soviet also elected chairmen of the seventeen departments which had replaced the vast network of commissions. Distribution of these posts seems to have been carefully balanced according to party strength: thus the Bolshevik Liubovich headed the Political-Agitational Department, but the SR-Maximalist Lamanov was in charge of the Cultural-Educational Department. Similarly the very important Military Department was headed by the Left SR Liudvik Grimm and the Control Department by the Menshevik Tsygankov, while the equally important Departments of Finance and Justice were headed by the Bolsheviks Yakov Ilyin and Stepan Grediushko.[105]

The continuing, though precarious dominance of the radical populist coalition asserted itself on 18 April when, by a vote of eighty-one to fifty-seven, with fifteen abstentions, the Kronstadt Soviet denounced the Moscow Soviet's repressive measures against the Anarchists.[106] Early in May 1918, in another show of strength the Soviet adopted an outspoken anti-German resolution calling for 'decisive armed resistance by all revolutionary elements against German expansionism' and instructing its Military Department to take 'most energetic' steps to prepare Kronstadt for defence in coordination with the Petrograd Military Staff.[107]

Kronstadt's bolshevization and the destruction of its multi-party Soviet democracy was not due to internal developments and local Bolshevik strength, but was decreed from outside and imposed by force.

It began in earnest on 14 June 1918, the day when Martov and the Mensheviks (on trumped-up charges of abetting White counter-revolution), together with the Right SRs, were expelled from the

Central Executive Committee of Soviets – the All-Russian Soviet 'parliament'. Provincial Soviets, including Kronstadt, followed suit. As Ivan Flerovsky, now general commissar of the Baltic Fleet, reported with satisfaction from Kronstadt, thanks to the sailor deputies who were 'almost all Bolsheviks', the Menshevik and Right SR deputies had now been 'removed from the Soviet!'[108]

It has been impossible to ascertain the role of the Kronstadt Left SRs and SR-Maximalists during the purge of their Menshevik and Right SR fellow deputies, except for that taken by Alexander Brushvit. On 20 June 1918, he is on record as having urged the Soviet plenum that party representation on the Executive Committee be confined only to those factions which 'stand on the platform of Soviet power', otherwise 'all sorts of Mensheviks may get in'. There was no point in 'molly-coddling these Mensheviks and Right SRs; we'll chop their heads if ever that should be necessary'.[109]

Ironically, it was in that very same session that Kronstadt made a final stand for its autonomy and (already clipped) Soviet democracy when it debated the 'Instruction' (*nakaz*) for its delegates to the Fifth Congress of Soviets,[110] the last at which Kronstadt was duly represented by the leaders of its three major political factions, the Bolshevik Bregman, the Left SR Pokrovsky, and the SR-Maximalist Lamanov.

The chief bone of contention in this debate was nothing less than the place of local Soviets, such as Kronstadt, within the framework of the Soviet state. The question had been heatedly debated during the spring of 1918 in connection with the drafting of the first Soviet constitution and its debate and adoption at the Congress of Soviets (4–9 July 1918). On this issue, as on many others since April 1918 when the Left SRs and the SR-Maximalists had moved so closely together that they seriously considered fusion,[111] the two factions stood together for the decentralization of government and for the autonomy of local Soviets against those Bolshevik centralizers who were determined to subject them to 'the corresponding higher organs of Soviet state power'.[112] Thus the common 'Instruction' which Fiodor Pokrovsky and Anatolii Lamanov were to take with them to the Congress on behalf of their factions urged the decentralization of the country's government.[113]

The Left SR Alexander Brushvit, the main speaker in the debate in support of the decentralist 'Instruction', argued the case for local Soviet autonomy with passionate conviction, quoting the success of

Kronstadt's Soviet democracy in which the executive, as he asserted with satisfaction, was under the effective control of the body politic. To illustrate his point, he proudly reminded members of the Executive Committee of 'the storm that had broken out' when they once tried to receive fifty pairs of galoshes for themselves 'out of turn' and of how quietly they had climbed down, hanging their heads in shame: 'This is the reason why there is such exemplary order here where our public life throbs deep within the masses. And note, *that* is something you will find hardly anywhere else. The masses are alert and watch what the leaders are up to . . .' Brushvit then argued fervently and bitterly against centralization and 'government from above' and against 'commissars sent from the centre' when it was 'emissaries who are needed' to come and teach. If that was 'the only way' to govern revolutionary Russia and 'plant socialism from above by centralist methods' then, he concluded, 'they had better close shop and admit that Russia has not yet grown up for socialism'.[114]

Brushvit's song of praise to Kronstadt's Soviet democracy turned to elegy later that month when his Left SRs too were expelled from the Soviet and excluded from all committees and responsible posts, as decreed by the Fifth Congress of Soviets on 9 July and the Fifth Congress of Sailors of the Baltic Fleet on 27 July 1918. That purge followed the 6–7 July abortive Left SR uprising against the Bolsheviks' brutal anti-peasant food requisitioning policies and their adherence to the 'obscene' Brest-Litovsk peace treaty with 'German imperialism'. The only Left SRs to survive the purge were those who publicly dissociated themselves from their Central Committee and condemned its desperate attempt to provoke war with Germany by such terrorist acts as the assassination of the German Ambassador Count Mirbach in Moscow on 6 July 1918.[115] The Kronstadt Soviet's Left SR faction does not seem to have survived this purge. Indeed, it was the Kronstadt sailor Boris Donskoi who on 30 July 1918 threw a bomb which killed the German commander General Eichhorn in Kiev. He was helped by the Kronstadt Left SR intellectual Grigorii Smoliansky and Irina Kakhovskaia, a frequent visitor in 1917 to the Kronstadt Left SRs and to Anchor Square.[116]

With the expulsion of the Left SRs in July 1918, complete Bolshevik domination of the Kronstadt Soviet was finally achieved. The Sixth Congress of Soviets in November 1918 saw Kronstadt represented for the first time by two Bolshevik delegates, Mikhail

Martynov and Choderain, and by them alone.[117] Elections to the Kronstadt Soviet in January 1919 returned seventy-three Communists, ninety-one Communist sympathizers, twenty-two non-partisans, one Menshevik (in November 1918 the Mensheviks were readmitted to Soviet elections), and one described as 'in sympathy with the Maximalists'.[118]

I have not been able to ascertain the result of the elections held in the summer of 1918, shortly after the purge of the Left SRs, but that early election was held up as an example, during the election campaign of January 1919, of the time when 'sailors, workers and Red soldiers sent representatives to the Soviet who held high the banner of Communism'.[119]

Soviet electors who emulated that example in January 1919 continued to do so in July 1919, when they returned ninety-seven Communists, eighty-four Communist sympathizers, fifty non-partisans and one lone SR-Maximalist,[120] Anatolii Lamanov (but he left the Maximalists in December 1919 and became a Communist party candidate).[121] The story was repeated in February 1920 when 52,700 registered Soviet electors returned 211 Communists and Communist candidates, 25 non-partisans, two Mensheviks, one SR, and one Armenian socialist (Dashnaktsiutiun).[122]

It is difficult to decide how much of the vote reflected genuine support for the Communist party. In the extreme and polarized conditions of the civil war, the Communist party alone stood for and was identified with Soviet power, and even Martov and the Mensheviks recognized it as the 'defender of the very foundations of the revolution' against White-Guardist counter-revolution and foreign intervention.[123] But how much of it was due to outright pressure, plain intimidation and manipulation?

Certainly, Kronstadt's *Izvestiia* (now edited by Solomon Entin) gave Soviet electors no choice but that of voting Communist. Its 16 January 1919 'Election Appeal' warned against 'White Guardists who have tried to infiltrate the sailor and Red soldier milieu', there 'to foment trouble over food shortages'. This plot had been foiled, the Appeal assured electors, and 'Russia has been proclaimed a war camp' in which 'a merciless struggle against those who directly and indirectly abet the enemy has begun'. 'Firm revolutionary discipline has successfully been established in Kronstadt's army and navy', the Election Appeal reported.[124]

In the same vein, only more brutally (coming so soon after the

June 1919 mutiny at the Kronstadt fort of Krasnaia Gorka and the uncovering of an officers' conspiracy in Kronstadt), the *Izvestiia* of 17 July 1919 ran an editorial telling electors that they were not voting for 'representatives of parties, but for representatives of classes'. The choice was between the 'Communists – the representatives of the class of toilers' and 'the representatives of capital – the hordes of 'glittering officers', their lackeys and all sorts of Constituent Assembly-mongers'. Therefore, *Izvestiia* harangued: 'Let all honest toilers, all who see in Soviet power their own power, send honest and staunch defenders of the toilers' interests into the Soviet. Red Kronstadt shall remain, as always, loyal to the proletarian banner, and shall send its true representatives – the Communists – into the Soviet.'[125]

Moral persuasion and outright pressure were solidly underpinned at the base assembly level. Here, the actual voting took place, supervised by electoral commissions which were *now* composed of one representative from the Soviet's 'organizing commission', one representative of the local (base assembly) committee (but these committees were altogether abolished late in January 1919), and, most importantly, one representative of the local Communist party cell (collective).[126] In the past, that is before July 1918, it had been precisely the various parties' local cells which had jealously watched and prevented the manipulation of elections of Soviet deputies by any of their rivals. Now it was only the representative of the local Communist party collective who, together with the representative of a solidly Communist Soviet, supervised and controlled the elections.

With the multi-party system eliminated by July 1918, the Soviet plenum became virtually a single Communist party 'faction', and elections to its executive offices assumed a perfunctory character, their outcome being a foregone conclusion. Thus, on 2 February 1919, the newly elected Soviet had on its agenda 'the election of departmental chairmen'; but the protocols laconically record that the Soviet's chairman, Mikhail Martynov, 'proposed on behalf of the Communist faction [*sic!*] the following comrades' who were 'elected and confirmed unanimously', two being 'elected and confirmed', with some abstentions (in one case six, in the other eight).[127]

The liquidation of Kronstadt's multi-party Soviet democracy was completed with the gradual emasculation and subsequent destruction of its rich grass-roots democracy of base committees in workshops, factories, plants and army and naval units. These were replaced at the base by a growing network of Communist party collectives responsible only to the party committee. Scores of commissars flanked and supervised both the military and naval commanders and the 'specialist' factory managers, overseeing the entire garrison and fleet and the vast majority of Kronstadt's factories and workshops which worked for and were controlled by the defence establishment.

The process began in earnest on 14 May 1918 with the *appointment* of Ivan Flerovsky as general commissar of the Baltic Fleet and chairman of its Council of Commissars, a body which replaced the disbanded elective Central Committee of the Baltic Fleet.[128] Flerovsky promptly appointed brigade commissars to whom all ships' committees were subordinated, deprived the committees of the right to sign on sailors and, if he did not actually initiate it, certainly backed the 25 July decision of the Conference of Sailor-Communists to 'cover the entire Baltic Fleet and its shore units with collectives of Communists which will be connected with all local and regional organs'. Shortly thereafter, the Communist-dominated Fifth Congress of Sailors of the Baltic Fleet decreed the expulsion of the Left SRs from all ship and base committees and subordinated the ships' committees to the party collectives by vesting the 'guarantee' for the suitability and performance of the committee's chairman in the collective itself, subject to the approval of the general commissar.[129]

Naval democracy was finally destroyed on 18 January 1919 when Trotsky, chairman of the Military Council of the Republic, decreed the abolition of all ships' committees, the appointment of commissars to all ships, and the setting up of revolutionary tribunals to maintain discipline, a function previously vested in elected 'comradely courts'.[130]

The liquidation of the *komitetshchina* – the once much-vaunted system of committees elected by and responsible to the rank and file base assemblies – in both Kronstadt's military and civilian establishments seems to have been completed by March 1919. It was then that the Second Conference of Kronstadt Communist Party Collectives made it imperative that party collectives be set up in 'all enterprises, institutions, units etc.' with three or more party members.[131]

The 'Instruction to the Collectives' issued by the Conference on 2 March ensured that all collectives, which were to include party members and sympathizers, would be under the direct and constant control of the party committee. The committee alone approved (or vetoed) the recruitment and exclusion of the collectives' members and the 'responsible organizers' and 'bureaux of three' elected by each collective. The 'responsible organizers' were required to attend weekly meetings convened by the party committee, the penalty for even a single absence without a good reason being exclusion, of which the collectives themselves were merely 'notified'. 'Responsible organizers' were further charged with filing a weekly report to the party committee on the collectives' activities, while a copy of the protocol of the collectives' weekly meetings had to be submitted for confirmation by the party committee.

The collectives' agitation, propaganda, recruiting and reporting activities were confined to the rank and file of their base units where they were exhorted to adopt 'undeviating vigilance'. But they had 'no right to interfere with the actions and orders of commissars and commanding staff'; on the contrary, they were told to 'assist and support the commissar'. Members of collectives were not entitled to any privileges or exemptions from their normal duties as 'workers, sailors or Red soldiers', nor to special consideration for any work or service misdemeanours. 'On the contrary', they were told, 'Communists will be subjected to severer penalties than non-Communists.'[132]

Communists were certainly singled out for special mobilizations. On 1 August 1918, when workers born between 1893 and 1897 were conscripted, *all* Communists, regardless of age and occupation, were called up, except those few regarded as indispensable for the running of local enterprises and of the Soviet and party apparatus, the motto being 'All Communists to Arms!'[133]

It was clearly no easy matter to be a rank and file party member. Candidates and members needed a high degree of identification with and devotion to Soviet power and its message of a new socialist world to submit themselves voluntarily to the onerous duties and rigorous discipline of a party collective. Small wonder that before the massive and relentless recruitment drives of the 'party weeks' in the latter part of 1919, Kronstadt's Communist party membership, thinned out by recurrent mobilizations, could be counted in hundreds rather than thousands.[134]

But Trotsky, bent on 'the constant and unflinching instruction, control and direction of the entire political life of the fleet', did not rely on base-level party collectives still close and responsive to the rank and file and democratically electing their own 'responsible organizers' and bureaux. The political department of the Baltic Fleet, or Politotdel, was Trotsky's answer; this was set up on 5 February 1919, and was followed on 22 February with the setting up of a political section (Politotdelenie) in Kronstadt, with Lazar Bregman as chairman.[135]

The first report of the Politotdel's activities up to April 1919, notably the work of its 'information section', suggests that its primary concern was the collection of information and data 'on the real political condition of the units of the Baltic Fleet'. This was achieved by way of weekly secret reports on units made by their commissars, information collected by its own functionaries who visited some sixty ships and shore units, and special intelligence reports supplied by the Cheka (the Extraordinary Commission for Combating Counter-Revolution, Sabotage and Speculation) on 'the political condition of some crews'. The Politotdel also systematically collected information on the suitability of the commissars themselves and brought them and the 'responsible organizers' of collectives together for the purpose of 'information, mutual understanding and the clarification of tasks in hand'.[136]

Whenever necessary, appropriate action was taken. Thus, when on 4 April 1919 the Kronstadt political section got wind of Left SR leaflets that had been distributed on the *Petropavlovsk*, it took steps leading to the discovery and arrest of the culprits, checked the mood of the crew and found it 'as satisfactory as before', and finally reported the incident to the Politotdel which, in its turn, passed it on to the Revolutionary-Military Council of the Baltic Fleet.[137]

The whole system of party control and surveillance over commanders and men by way of commissars and party collectives, and the coordination and consolidation of their activities by the Politotdel, was given sharper teeth by the establishment of the separate Kronstadt Fortress Naval Communist Battalion on 15 March 1919, two detachments of which were already in full training by 5 May 1919.[138]

While Kronstadt's spontaneous, free Anchor Square democracy may have lasted until July 1918 at the latest, by February 1919, if not earlier, mass meetings, now called 'meeting-concerts', were, thanks to the initiative of the 'section for agitation and propaganda' of the Politotdel, fully institutionalized. Organized by and proceeding under the auspices of the Politotdel these sailors' 'meeting-concerts' were held every second Sunday ('not more frequently') in Kronstadt's Engineers' College to serve 'the broad propagandization of the ideas of communism among the sailors, the exposition of the tasks of the present moment and the raising of the discipline of the naval personnel' – a far cry from the impromptu daily gatherings, the soap-box oratory and heated Anchor Square debates of 1917. A special feature of the new-style gatherings treated the sailors to an 'orators' section' on subjects ranging from the 'Anniversary of the Red Army', the 'Paris Commune', and 'The Proletarian Revolution in Hungary' to 'The Treachery of the Left SRs', while in the concert section sailor orchestras performed and entertained.[139]

'Central meeting-concerts' for all and general meetings of the entire fortress were also held occasionally. One such meeting, intended to mobilize Kronstadt for 'resistance to the enemy' and the sending-off of a task-force of some thousand sailors to the front, was held on 4 May 1919 in Anchor Square.[140] The 3 May telephone conversation in preparation for the meeting, held between Viacheslav Zof and the former Kronstadt sailor Alexander Baranov, both members of the Revolutionary-Military Council of the Baltic Fleet, is quite telling:[141]

Zof: Comrade Baranov . . . Tell me, do you think it is really necessary to convene a general fortress meeting in Kronstadt tomorrow?

Baranov: Yes, it can do no harm; but it would be a good thing if Grigorii Evdokimov [a leading fleet Bolshevik] and someone from the Petrograd party committee were there.

Zof: Saparov[142] has already promised; but we will probably get Evdokimov as well. So, contact the Kronstadt party committee, [L. K.] Artamonov [commandant of the Kronstadt fortress], [Ivan] Ludri [commissar of the Kronstadt naval base] and the Soviet institutions. Fix the time of the meeting, advertise it properly in the newspapers and I'll get the orators to Kronstadt for tomorrow's meeting: I'll let you have their names in a few minutes, but it would be a good thing if you also contacted [Moise] Lissovsky [editor of *Krasnaia gazeta*, leading party agitator and orator].

Baranov: Right, I'll see to it all and cable you the time of the meeting. Give me the names of the orators as soon as you possibly can.

Zof: All right, I'll cable.

The same organizing zeal must have gone into the 'central meeting-concert' held on 7 September 1919 to mark 'Soviet Propaganda Day'. After Alexander Baranov's 'stirring speech', the 'revolutionary mood' of the meeting's audience was summed up laconically in *Krasnyi baltiiskii flot*, the Politotdel's newspaper: 'The Red Kronstadters are unfailing fighters for Soviet state power.'[143]

No less stirring was Viacheslav Zof when (only a few months after the mutiny of Krasnaia Gorka Fort) he praised the loyalty of Kronstadt's 'Red Forts', writing in *Krasnyi baltiiskii flot*: 'Beware, you half-decayed parasites of the Old World! You Black Knights of the past! Hearken! Kronstadt's Red Forts are all on the ready to join battle on behalf of the great ideas of the working class, for a new, bright world, for the Kingdom of Toil!'[144]

A sailor-poet from the battleship *Petropavlovsk*, once renowned, if not notorious, for insubordination, threats to Kerensky and the provisional government, and the summary shooting of four of its officers during the Kornilov Days, used the same issue of the paper to tune his lyre to please the ears of the new masters – the commissars. Maksim Shkilenok's 'Red Song of the Brotherly Crew' saluted 'Red Kronstadt', with its 'battleships of Communards' steaming out to defend the 'Planet's Soviet' and, 'to the tune of Stenka Razin', Shkilenok went on to sing the praises of his tough, foul-mouthed master on the *Petropavlovsk*:

> Kolka Razin, our brave commissar,
> Always on the fo'c's'le ever on guard,
> A truly model Communard.[145]

Clearly, Trotsky was not alone in his admiration for the 'steely cast' of 'our commissars', that 'new Communist order of Samurais',[146] who had made such a clean sweep of Kronstadt's Anchor Square democracy.

Judging by the sparse reports of the Soviet's sessions published in its *Izvestiia* during 1919 and 1920, this body too was transformed: the dynamic parliament, which had thrived on polemics and debate, became a mere forum for the announcement and confirmation of resolutions and decisions and for exhortative oratory and mobilization. Whether the Soviet's agenda dealt with matters small or large, 'the return of cattle to cow-owners', the 'project of [collective] vegetable gardens', 'Left SR provocation', or revolutionary events in Germany, the protocols recorded no debate.[147]

Yet it was not Communist domination alone that ended the Soviet's traditions of lively debate and vigorous legislative and executive action. By May 1919, with the beginning of Yudenich's White

North-Western Army's advance towards Petrograd, Kronstadt was for the first time in the immediate front line of the civil war. A state of siege was proclaimed and much of the Soviet's business and its executive power now passed to the Kronstadt Committee of Workers' Defence. Elected by the Soviet on 7 May 1919 and given wide emergency powers, the Committee was chaired by Lazar Bregman and included some of Kronstadt's leading Communist party and Soviet functionaries such as the Soviet's chairman, Mikhail Martynov; his deputy, Ure Gertsberg; the commissar of the fortress, Yakov Ilyin; his deputy, Ivan Zherebtsov; the commissar of the naval base, Ivan Ludri; the secretary of the Communist party committee and chairman of the Revolutionary Tribunal, Dmitrii Kondakov; and Entin's successor as chairman of the combined departments of People's Education and the Press, Moise Lissovsky. Responsible directly to the Petrograd Defence Committee, these men made the vital emergency decisions and treated the Soviet plenum to *faits accomplis* and speeches of rousing exhortation.[148]

The session of 5 June 1919 was typical: with the White North-Western Army pushing towards Krasnaia Gorka, Kronstadt's mainland fort, it was the crucial question of the evacuation of the town's civilian population, notably its women and children, that was on the agenda. After Yakov Ilyin had explained the need to evacuate all non-combatant civilians, including the families of 'workers, sailors, and Red Army men', one deputy, Goncharov, reported that in his workshop 'people are worried about the evacuation'. He was promptly told by Mikhail Martynov, the Soviet's chairman, that since Kronstadt's surrender was out of the question, 'We shall only fight staunchly and decisively if we know that our near ones are out of danger', and that was the end of the debate, for now came the heroic rhetoric of Moise Lissovsky, Kronstadt's new spellbinder. In the Russia of 1919, with its broken-down transport, epidemics and famine, compared with which Kronstadt was a holiday resort, he promised the evacuees pie in the sky: 'You will be well looked after there, when you arrive at your destination. You will be given the opportunity to work honestly for your living and will not lack for anything; should you find that we have deceived and betrayed you, then put a bullet through our heads.'[149] Yet only a week earlier, on 28 May, Martynov had announced the decision to divide the evacuees into three categories: 'comrades, and those above suspicion', to be sent to the Don river area; 'not very reliable elements' to Kursk province; and 'completely unreliable bourgeois elements' to 'concentration camps'.[150]

But Lissovsky also promised bullets to 'the faint-hearted in our midst . . . lest they trouble us'. As for those to whom fell 'the great and noble task of defending Kronstadt', for them he conjured up the heroism and ever-lasting glory of the Paris Commune:

This is a historic occasion. Today we see the rebirth of the great days of the Convention and the Commune! Today we make our mark in history, for the glorious exploits of our heroic struggle will be written in letters of gold! Ours is a struggle till victory or death! Our children will be proud of their fathers.

'Prolonged applause' greeted Lissovsky, whereupon Martynov proposed that the session close with the singing of the Internationale: 'Let our enemies know that there is no dejection and cowardice amongst us!'[151]

Kronstadt's *Izvestiia* ran an editorial the next day, 'Glorious Evacuation', hammering the point that while other towns evacuated preparatory to surrender, Kronstadt was evacuating because it was 'preparing for battle'; it also served notice that 'only those who can defend it should stay on the Red Island, for in the eagle's eyrie there is room only for eagles. All others – out!' Yet in its modest information column, the very same issue of *Izvestiia* reported simply that 'many who registered for evacuation did not turn up' and 'the results are poor'.[152]

It was then that the Soviet decided on 'the immediate, compulsory evacuation of non-combatants such as women and children, and also of [some] workers, sailors, and Red soldiers, and of all untrustworthy elements'.[153]

By September–October 1919, 16,686 men, women and children had been evacuated to fourteen of the larger towns of central Russia and the Volga area. By September, only a mere 2,150 women and children were still registered as holding residence permits for Kronstadt. But by December 1919, some 5,500 or more had been repatriated or had drifted back on their own initiative, soon to be followed by thousands more. For in Kronstadt, unlike elsewhere in Russia, services were still maintained. Although the daily bread ration for non-workers and pensioners (children received an additional quarter pound of bread in school) had been reduced from one pound to three-quarters of a pound, citizens could still rely on the Soviet for that, if not more. Similarly, by the end of 1919

thousands of veteran sailors, who had served on the many fronts of
the civil war and in the administrative network of the expanding
Soviet state, had returned to the Baltic Fleet and to Kronstadt, most
by way of remobilization; others simply attracted by the better
living conditions and prestige of the Baltic Fleet.[154]

Kronstadt's tight and seemingly well-functioning Communist
system of organization, domination and control – Foma Parchevsky
complained bitterly that there was not even a black market in
Kronstadt[155] – was put to the test in May–June 1919, with the
advance towards Petrograd of General Yudenich's North-Western
Army. Even as that threatened, there came, on 13 June and in
anticipation of the Whites' approach, the mutiny of Krasnaia Gorka,
now Kronstadt's only mainland fort.[156] This was a terrible shock
to Kronstadt's Communist authorities, for, with the exception of a
detachment of sailors (two companies) and a Communist Company,
the entire Krasnaia Gorka garrison of some 1,300 defected, *including*
the commandant, Colonel Nikolai Nekliudov, the chairman of the
Communist party collective, Stepan Urban, and such veteran
Kronstadt Soviet stalwarts as the Left SRs Liudvik Grimm and
N. Priselkov. Many of the fort's gunners even went so far as to
boast that they were SRs and would 'overthrow the Bolsheviks as our
Central Committee has resolved'. Colonel Nekliudov's radio message
to Kronstadt and all its forts was simple: 'The commissarocracy has
been overthrown in the [Krasnaia Gorka] Fort. Come and join us!'
The Seraia Loshad' Fort did promptly join, but the garrisons in
Totleben and Rif did not, nor did they arrest their Communists
as Krasnaia Gorka had requested. Communists were arrested in the
Obruchev Fort but, while commandant Veselov wanted to join the
revolt, the other commanders there preferred to play a waiting
game and, when an ultimatum was received from Kronstadt, they
promptly freed the arrested party members, arrested the commandant and surrendered.

A worse shock was in store on 16 June when, after a supreme
military effort in which Kronstadt's sailors played a prominent
part, Krasnaia Gorka was recaptured. Practically the entire garrison
had joined the 'Whites', while some thirty leading Communists lay
murdered, among them Mikhail Martynov, the chairman of the
Kronstadt Soviet, Stepan Grediushko, the commander of the Communist Company, Fiodor Mitrofanov, the secretary of the local
Cheka, and Mikhail Artemov, a member of the Petrograd Revolu-

tionary Tribunal, who, prior to his execution, is reported to have exclaimed: 'Today it's you who shoot us – tomorrow we'll be shooting you!'[157] It was then that the terror came to Kronstadt.

True, there had been a Cheka in Kronstadt since the end of 1917 and its Naval Investigation Prison was notorious, but it operated chiefly as an extension of the Petrograd Cheka and dealt with opposition to the Soviet regime there, rather than with non-existent local opposition. As for the summary execution of some 300 officers in Kronstadt during the heyday of the Red Terror in the summer of 1918, it had apparently been 'directly prescribed' from Petrograd by Zinoviev himself.[158]

The terror began in all its fury on 15 June 1919 when Alexander Baranov, a member of the Revolutionary–Military Council of the Baltic Fleet, instructed the commissars Iakov Ilyin and Ivan Sladkov to purge the forts and batteries of 'all counter-revolutionary elements'. Next day, a drumhead court martial was set up, consisting of the chief of the Petrograd Cheka, F. D. Medved (chairman), the commissar of the *Petropavlovsk*, Nikolai (Kolka) Razin, and the chairman of the agitation-propaganda section of the Politotdel, Ivan Zhdanov.[159] Hardly any information is available on the 'radical purge' which this high-powered troika conducted, but Lazar Bregman did report laconically to the Politotdel on the 'Investigation, shootings and replacement' of the garrison of Obruchev Fort.[160] The cynical brutality behind that event was only fully revealed during the uprising of March 1921 when Kronstadt learned how on 16 June 1919 Nikolai Razin had lined up the garrison and ordered every fifth man, altogether fifty-five, to fall out ready to go on leave and how these men were then shot by Razin's detachment of Communist stalwarts in full view of their comrades.[161]

In Kronstadt itself, the Cheka uncovered and liquidated a conspiratorial anti-Soviet organization of officers, including Captain Alexander Rybaltovsky, chief-of-staff of the Kronstadt naval base, and the senior artillery officers Iuvenalii Budkevich and Kuprianov, and some members of the intelligentsia, while the families of these 'traitors' were arrested. 'Any form of sympathy for the arrested is tantamount to sympathy for treason!' declared the Appeal of the Defence Committee to the garrison and population of Kronstadt on 17 June 1919.[162] The Kronstadt *Izvestiia*'s editorial of 20 June, 'We Shall Square Accounts', openly espoused 'The Red Terror against the White Terror': 'No more magnanimity for the reptiles and their families! . . . we must teach them a lesson!'[163]

With all counter-revolutionaries liquidated and the rest of Kronstadt's 'bourgeois' population so intimidated that many members of the local intelligentsia, including Foma Parchevsky, escaped to the mainland,[164] an intensive drive was launched to recruit sailors, soldiers and workers into the Communist party. It was argued that stepped-up party work would make control over 'military specialists', i.e. command staff, 'more real and vigilant', but another reason for this move may have been the discovery on 8 July 1919 that there were a mere 132 Communists and 286 sympathizers in all Kronstadt's army units and forts.[165] This shrinkage in party numbers may have been largely due to the recruitment and mobilization of Communists for a host of military, political and administrative tasks, but it was also due to what tired party members, applying for 'exclusion from the party', and including in their number three *Petropavlovsk* sailors, called their 'political weakness'. They were promptly denounced by the bureau of the party executive as 'deserters from the party'. Coming in for special castigation was F. Zherebtsov, a former member of the Kronstadt Soviet *and* an assistant commissar who, it was claimed, was simply trying to wreak his vengeance for having been sacked from his position as assistant commissar and having failed to be elected to the bureau of the collective of the *Petropavlovsk*.

After the first local Party Week held in August, the Politotdel reported with satisfaction that there were now 160 Communists and 530 sympathizers in army units, apart from the 29 'responsible organizers' of the 29 party collectives and the 42 commissars. Naval units included 344 Communists and 788 sympathizers, apart from the 53 'responsible organizers' of the 53 party collectives and the 51 commissars.[166]

Party weeks and recruitment drives succeeded one another with great vigour in September, October, November and December, reaching a peak during the Party Week of 27 November to 2 December 1919 when, it was reported, 'sailors joined in droves' and in a few small ships 'the entire crew signed up for the party, often even including the command staff' (though the latter were eligible only after a trial period). Enthusiasm seemed so high that it was claimed that 'of the sailors it can definitely be said that two-thirds are members of our party', with the time not far off when 'the entire

Red fleet' will 'form one powerful Communist collective'. Of the
Red soldiers it was noted that 'almost a half' had become party
members and, since they were overwhelmingly of peasant background, this was seen as an index of the 'dramatic change' in the
peasantry's attitude to the Bolshevik regime. Yet even if these
claims were too rosy, by 1 March 1920 there were some 5,630 party
members among Kronstadt's 23,000 sailors and soldiers, with a
further 86 'responsible organizers' of the 86 party collectives and
some 80 commissars. Practically every third sailor and every fourth
Red Army soldier was a party member.[167]

As for the civilian population, the same 'brilliant results' were also
claimed among the workers, particularly among young workers and
women, although there was less success among the older workers.
Thus, by the same date, party membership had gone up to over
1,000 in a working population of some 13,000.[168]

The rapid transformation of Kronstadt's Communist party into
a mass organization made for its speedy bureaucratization. By the
end of February 1920 party collectives (with their membership
increased by up to seven times) were reorganized so that each was
now headed by a bureau of five, consisting of the 'responsible
organizer', the secretary, and three chiefs of sections and sub-sections.
The basic task of the collective was defined as the transformation of
'the young and new party members' into 'experienced, loyal and
energetic party workers'. General meetings were to be addressed by
'Politotdel speakers' on the party programme and Bukharin's and
Preobrazhensky's popular exposition of Bolshevik theory, the *ABC
of Communism*. Regular meetings of 'responsible organizers' and commissars were to ensure cooperation between the leading functionaries of units and ships.[169]

When it was found that both commissars and collectives presented
the Politotdel with weekly reports on their units that were too favourably slanted – due to 'not infrequent deliberate concealment of the
negative sides of the fleet's life, arising from the wrong-headed
desire to present their unit in a better light' – it was proposed that
commissars also file daily reports. Further, the collectives' weekly
reports were also to be duly signed by the 'responsible organizer',
the secretary and the head of each collective's agitation and information section, while staff commissars were to file fortnightly
reports, in lieu of monthly reports, on the 'condition of the commissars
under their command'.[170]

Thus, by June 1920, with the civil war won and the emergency over, Kronstadt's political section received daily reports 'on the political condition' of their units from the commissars, a weekly report from every collective, signed by its three leading functionaries, a fortnightly information and statistical report from commissars, and yet another fortnightly report on commissars from staff commissars. This incessant flow of reports was then processed and presented by Kronstadt's Politotdel (the upgraded Politotdelenie, or political section) in a report to Pubalt (the Political Administration of the Baltic Fleet), the new name given to the upgraded Politotdel of the Baltic Fleet after Raskolnikov's appointment as its commander-in-chief in June 1920.[171]

In short, the Bolshevik organizational structure, which had pushed out and replaced Kronstadt's and the Baltic Fleet's democracy, had – by 1920 – been turned into an elaborate system of controls, statistical accounting, and surveillance, in which the commissars and bureaux of the party collectives informed on the men and staff commissars in their turn informed on the commissars.

The massive administrative effort and sheer paperwork in this complex enterprise was truly staggering and apparently self-defeating. The Kronstadt Politotdel's fortnightly report to Pubalt for the period 1–15 January 1921 recorded the receipt of 385 daily, 58 weekly and 46 fortnightly 'political communiqués' filed by the commissars on Kronstadt's units and crews. But it also noted a *shortfall* of 348 daily, 10 weekly, and 5 fortnightly communiqués. In the same period, heads of the departments and sections of the Politotdel filed 165 daily reports on their own work, and 19 other reports. They also cabled Pubalt eleven daily reports 'on the condition of the units of the naval base and of the fortress', eleven daily reports on the work of the Politotdel, one fortnightly political report and one fortnightly political-statistical report.[172] All political activity had been reduced to the level of office correspondence, delegates to the February congress of the Baltic Fleet noted scathingly.

The lower echelons or rank and file party members were by now deeply resentful of that 'commissarocracy' which, in Kronstadt's naval and military garrison alone, had proliferated into a political department of 171 functionaries (by the end of 1920) with 92 commissars and 24 Politruks (political leaders in military units who were appointed to assist the commissar and were subordinate to him), in turn supported by 89 'responsible organizers', 89 secretaries, and 267 section-heads, all working within Kronstadt's 89 collectives (as at 1 July 1920).[173]

There were similar tensions between 'lower and upper echelons' in Kronstadt's (civilian) party organization and in its docks, plants and workshops. These were under the jurisdiction of the 'naval and military authorities' and were controlled by 'commissars, mostly sailors' who, as Lazar Bregman complained, took little notice of the powerless trade unions or the languishing Kronstadt Soviet. Indeed, as late as 1920 Menshevik influence was still felt among the workers of Kronstadt's large steamship plant and the 'Italian' go-slow strike, which took place there in the summer of 1920, was attributed to the work of that party's agitators.[174]

Raskolnikov's return to Kronstadt in June 1920, as commander of the Blatic Fleet, accompanied by his own retinue of commanders and commissars, did nothing to improve the situation; nor did his rigorous 're-registration' or purge of the party organization in September 1920 help matters.[175] Indeed relations between the rank and file and the senior functionaries of the party had become so strained that a conference of delegates of the party collectives of Kronstadt's naval and army units, convened at the end of November 1920, demanded the 'rigorous instruction of commissars and responsible party workers, and tight control over their activities', the revival of party organs, the recruitment of local party workers into the apparatus of the Politotdel, and something like a new party purge, but this time from below, so that: 'every party member be called upon to fight those unfit elements which, sadly enough, still linger on in our ranks even after the re-registration, catch them out, regardless of their positions, and throw them out like so much trash'.[176]

Raskolnikov had indeed travelled a long way since 1917 when, in January 1921, in an angry cable to the Central Committee of the party, he dismissed this critique as due to the machinations of Nikolai Kuzmin and Aleksei Kostin, his opponents in the controversy over the militarization of trade unions. They had 'artificially created a division between the united body of commissars and Politotdel functionaries on the one hand, and the mass of rank and file sailor-Communists on the other'. Further, they had – *horribile dictu* – aimed at 'the resurrection of the committee system' (*komitetshchina*) and those 'old anarchist tendencies' among the sailors which, with the 'greatest of difficulty', 'we have at last succeeded in weakening and neutralizing'.[177]

Kuzmin and Kostin, good commissars as they were, indignantly rejected the charges. On the contrary, they protested in a cable to the Central Committee sent on 19 January 1921 on behalf of an assembly of 3,500 'sailor-Communists', 'We are of the opinion that *komitetshchina* and the elective principle are inadmissible both in the navy and the army.' They professed their staunch adherence to 'iron military discipline' and 'unbreakable party discipline'. But perhaps they protested too much when claiming that 'there is not even one sailor to be found in the Red Baltic Fleet who has one good word for the committees'.[178]

For, two months later, when the Kronstadt sailors rose against the 'commissarocracy', it was to the 'committee system and the elective principle' that they looked, nostalgic for the golden age of Kronstadt's grass-roots democracy and its network of committees that the Bolsheviks, having used them, on their own admission and in the words of the Bolshevik Ivan Ludri, as 'a sharp weapon for the disintegration of the old navy'[179] and for the seizure of power, had then destroyed and scorned.

6

Kronstadt's third revolution

Kronstadt emerged relatively unscathed from the ravages of the civil war.[1] Despite recurrent mobilizations, which drained the naval base and the fortress of thousands of its sailors and soldiers, and the evacuations of 1919, which reduced its civilian population, by January 1921 there were still over 50,000 people, military and civilian, living in Kronstadt. Indeed, with the evacuation of the larger part of the Baltic Fleet from Reval and Helsingfors to Kronstadt in March and April 1918 (under the terms of the Brest-Litovsk Treaty), it had become the fleet's main base. Nor had the composition of its population greatly changed. Nearly 27,000 sailors and soldiers manned its forts and fortifications, its naval depots, and the battleships moored in the harbour, notably Russia's two remaining Dreadnoughts, the *Petropavlovsk* and the *Sevastopol*, while a work-force of some 13,000 was employed in its docks, naval installations and workshops, the steamship plant, sawmill and electrical station.[2]

Red Kronstadt was also regarded as a loyal stronghold of the Soviet regime and its Communist party, and its sailors, the renowned 'Red Eagles', had more than once been called to Petrograd to help in election campaigns, man roadblocks and quell mutiny, and were invoked as a praetorian threat to intimidate striking workers.[3] Despite the crisis in the Communist party at the end of the civil war, and the rigorous local purge conducted by Fiodor Raskolnikov in the autumn of 1920, the Communist party organization remained strong in Kronstadt, with some 2,900 full members and 600 candidate members.[4] Kronstadt also boasted a large and vigorous network of party schools and clubs, educational and cultural classes and groups, including theatre, art, music and literature, conducted by resident and visiting lecturers of the Politotdel.[5]

One reason for this impressive, almost lavish political-cultural activity may have been the need to keep the long-serving, energetic, intelligent and literate ratings of the inactive and decaying Baltic Fleet – many of them waiting impatiently for their overdue demobilization – busy and contented. Another – it was in all seriousness advanced by Mark Rudnyi, chief of Politotdel's cultural-educational section, in June 1919 – was to make the Red fleet into a 'Red school of communism'. Here, sailors would gain experience and knowledge, graduating as 'the Red instructors of the revolution' whose task would be 'to serve the fully fledged toiling order' of Russia's future as organizers, administrators and party workers.[6] Pubalt's ambition at the end of 1920, to reach out further and train cadres of 'revolutionary activists for abroad' and thus 'play an active role in the world social revolution', was only a short step away.[7]

In September and October 1920 the writer and party-lecturer Ieronymus Yasinsky visited Kronstadt to teach and also to examine naval recruits on their 'political literacy'. To him, Kronstadt looked 'tranquil, beautiful, neat and tidy, the houses kept in good repair, the parks green and the boulevards lined with ivy-covered walls'. His impression of the population was that it did not go hungry and that most people were kept busy doing something. Kronstadt's 'Red sailors' appeared to him 'serious and reliable, often good-natured and always courteous', a far cry from the swaggering dandy-sailors (*zhorzhiki*) 'with golden bracelets on their wrists' whom he had seen milling around in Petrograd on the Nevsky Prospect, in the Alexandrovsk park and in cinemas.

Yasinsky interviewed some 400 naval recruits drawn from the areas of the Kuban, Novorossiisk, Grodno, Vitebsk, Olonetsk and Petrograd, many of whom had come 'straight from the plough'. He was aghast to find that these confident-looking, reasonably well-fed and dressed lads, including a few party members, were politically ignorant if not illiterate, worlds removed from the highly politicized veteran Kronstadt sailors who had so deeply impressed him:

The recruits knew that Russia was a federal and socialist republic, though many could not explain the word 'federal'. They were aware that the Communist party existed and ruled, but only ten out of a hundred could even vaguely explain communism. To the tricky question as to who currently ruled Russia, it was only a rare bird who unhesitatingly and with conviction replied: 'the People'. There were a few mavericks who said: 'the commissars rule'. While all knew of comrades Lenin and Trotsky, they somehow could not distinguish between them. Asked who was the chairman of the Council of People's Commissars, the reply was often 'Trotsky and Lenin'. Some two or three frightened Ukrainian recruits begged: 'Let us off, we know nothing and we were never under Denikin.'

Yasinsky was apprehensive about the future when, 'sooner or later, Kronstadt's veteran sailors, who were steeled in the revolutionary fire and had acquired a clear revolutionary world-view, would be replaced by inexperienced, freshly mobilized young sailors'. Still, he comforted himself with the hope that Kronstadt's sailors would gradually infuse them with their 'noble spirit of revolutionary self-dedication' to which Soviet Russia owed so much. As for the present, he felt reassured that 'in Kronstadt the Red sailor still predominates'.[8]

Yasinsky's impressions were shared by Skoromnyi, a former sailor from the *Sevastopol* who was sent by the Politotdel to lecture to his former shipmates on the 'international situation'. He was impressed by the changes he noticed: 'the hull of the *Sevastopol* was freshly painted, the deck spick and span and orderly with plenty of bins for cigarette-butts and rubbish'. He rejoiced in the 'irreproachable discipline' of the *Sevastopoltsy* and the speed and despatch with which the crew assembled on deck after the commissar had given the order and the bugle had been sounded. He was also very much taken by the interest shown in lectures and in the 'educational and cultural courses', and he concluded his report with the recommendation: 'It would be good for other units and battleships to emulate the example of the crew of the *Sevastopol*, their craving for knowledge and their discipline.'[9]

Even allowing for considerable overstatement by propaganda-minded observers who came from decaying, starving and freezing Petrograd, Yasinsky's and Skoromnyi's accounts seem a reasonable summing-up of Kronstadt's good order and relative prosperity, certainly as compared with the rest of Russia.

Yasinsky's impression that the veteran politicized Red sailor still predominated in Kronstadt at the end of 1920 is borne out by the hard statistical data available regarding the crews of the two major battleships, the *Petropavlovsk* and the *Sevastopol*, both renowned since 1917 for their revolutionary zeal and Bolshevik allegiance. Of 2,028 sailors whose years of enlistment are known, no less than 1,904 or 93.9% were recruited into the navy before and during the 1917 revolution, the largest group, 1,195, having joined in the years 1914–16. Only some 137 sailors or 6.8% were recruited in the years 1918–21, including three who were conscripted in 1921, and they were the only ones who had not been there during the 1917 revolution.[10] As for the sailors of the Baltic Fleet in general (and that included the *Petropavlovsk* and the *Sevastopol*), of those serving on 1 January 1921 at least 75.5% are likely to have been drafted into the fleet before 1918. Over 80% were drawn from Great Russian areas (mainly central Russia and the Volga area), some 10% from the Ukraine, and 9% from Finland, Estonia, Latvia and Poland.[11]

One reason for the remarkable survival in Kronstadt of these veteran sailors, albeit in greatly diminished numbers, was precisely the difficulty of training, in war-time conditions, a new generation competent in the sophisticated technical skills required on Russia's ultra-modern battleships, and, indeed, in the fleet generally.[12]

Nor, as has so often been claimed, did new recruits, some 400 of whom Yasinsky had interviewed, arrive in numbers large enough to dilute or even 'demoralize' Kronstadt's Red sailors. As Evan Mawdsley has found, 'only 1,313 of a planned total of 10,384 recruits had arrived' by 1 December 1920 and even they seem to have been stationed in the barracks of the Second Baltic Crew in Petrograd.[13]

Kronstadt was well run and its population quite privileged and better supplied than the rest of Russia,[14] certainly far better than in neighbouring Petrograd. But when visiting their villages and home towns while on leave, its sailors and soldiers came face to face with the crying evils of the arbitrary, violent and disorderly rule of the commissars and Communists in the countryside. One early account which would have done Isaac Babel proud was that of the soldier I. Egorov who served in one of Kronstadt's forts. That Egorov's damning letter, style and spelling mistakes included, was at all published in Kronstadt's *Izvestiia* may perhaps be explained by its edifying conclusion, the conversion of this doubting Thomas to the true Communist faith by Kronstadt's spellbinder Lissovsky.[15]

Up to now I have not been a Communist or even a sympathizer as, for some reason, I had never had the chance to be in the company of real Communists or even to see them. When I went back to the village and worked there on the land after being demobilized, I had no chance to read any newspapers, and the only Communists I saw were those who lorded it over us in a manner never before permitted to any except the village policemen of tsarist days. Thinking that the high-ups permitted this, I could only wonder (knowing that Communists are also Bolsheviks) how the Bolshevik programme which I had been familiar with and endorsed in 1917 had changed. I tried hard to convince my villagers of the justice of the party, but what was my reward? I was shown up as a liar and a cheat when such

Communists appeared, and was almost ready to concede that we had again been duped, especially when I was remobilized and again saw the same type of Communists. The only difference between them was that our Communists (that is the village ones), proud of having been given revolvers and boasting of their power to requisition bread throughout the *volost'* [small country district], took the bread not from those they should have taken it from, but only from those who were not their friends, while the other Communists went on to the train and, sheltering behind the word 'requisition', robbed everyone of whatever took their fancy, but spared the speculators – and this fact was obvious. As luck would have it, I was posted to a fort where there were hardly any meetings or lectures, and so I didn't change my mind even though I knew from reading the newspapers that I should change my opinions about the Communists, yet I was so angry with such-like Communists as I had seen that I trusted nothing to do with political life. But yesterday, our comrade Lissovsky visited us and I must say that I was utterly swept away by his speech in which I couldn't catch so much as a single lying word (not as with other orators). Willy-nilly, the picture of past, present and future life and of the course of the revolution unfolded before me. Now I realize that the considerable injustice of the present moment that is perpetrated by such-like elements and that is similar to what was common under the old power will go on if we do not acquire consciousness, but fall again under the power of the bourgeoisie. And now, if I had the mighty voice of a giant, I would shout all over the world, Long live the power of the Soviet of Workers' and Peasants' Deputies! Long live Communists like comrade Lissovsky! Down with paper Communists!

Egorov's observations and grievances, as distinct from his conversion, were not exceptional. An analysis of 211 complaints that had arrived in the Complaints Bureau of the Politotdel of the Baltic Fleet by the end of 1920, many lodged by the crews of the *Petropavlovsk*, the *Sevastopol* and the minelayer *Narova*, has shown that the abuses of provincial authorities, the injustice of forced grain collections and illegal requisitioning provided the major focus of discontent.[16] 'Comrades heed my call!' one sailor wrote to the Bureau:

I am a sailor of the Red Baltic, serving in the fleet since 1914, I have stood up for the interests of the worker-peasant government and defended it against the onslaughts of all sorts of snakes . . . I appeal to you as defenders of truth . . . the district commissar K took away our sole remaining horse, and after that my father himself was arrested.

Examination showed the complaint to have been more than justified, the sailor's family having indeed been mistreated. A *Petropavlovsk* sailor, protesting the requisitioning of his family's cow, wrote to the Bureau on 21 November 1920:

Ours is an ordinary peasant farm, neither Kulak nor parasitical; yet when I and my brother return home from serving the Soviet republic people will sneer at our wrecked farm and say: 'What did you serve for? What has the Soviet republic given you?'[17]

Protests such as these were often prompted by the uninterrupted stream of letters the men received from their relatives, all complaining bitterly, with desperate cries for help, against the misdeeds of the local authorities. Passed from hand to hand, the letters were widely discussed and served to make the crews well aware of the state of affairs in the country.

New, and compounding that discontent in the latter part of 1920, was the growing resentment among rank and file party members in Kronstadt of the privileges and abuses of commissars, senior party functionaries and trade union officials who received special rations, allocations and housing,[18] and, dropping the concealment of the past, now quite openly enjoyed the good life. The rot seems to have set in with the return to Kronstadt in June 1920 of the newly appointed chief commander of the Baltic Fleet, Fiodor Raskolnikov, and his flamboyant wife Larissa Reissner. Setting up house on the flagship *Krechet*, they and their staff indulged in a feudal style of life, 'roast geese' and all, according to the tendentious memoirs of the émigré sailor Trofim Gonoratsky, whose account is corroborated by a former commissar of the *Gangut*[19] describing the 'three course meals' and, for good measure, the 'pounds of butter and rice and other good things' they consumed. The new set of commanders and party functionaries 'from the East' whom Raskolnikov brought with him from the Caspian Sea – he allegedly ousted nearly two-thirds of the old hands during the summer of 1920 – had also acquired a taste for comfortable living, good food and servants,[20] and, worse still, they had a penchant for 'advertising their well-being . . . openly before the very eyes of the sailor masses'. It was as if the new life style of the 'estate of commissars', which Martov noted in Moscow, had come to Kronstadt with Raskolnikov.[21]

Raskolnikov returned to Kronstadt after a distinguished career as commander of the Volga-Caspian Flotilla at the behest of Trotsky, his superior as People's Commissar for War and Navy. With the Soviet economy grinding to a halt and the party itself rent by faction and controversy, Raskolnikov's brief was the nearly impossible one of rebuilding the inactive and deteriorating Baltic Fleet and reorganizing its party apparatus.[22]

For even Kronstadt had been hit by the crisis. By December 1920, food stocks were so run down that the chief of the political section of the naval base reported 'discontent among the crews about pro-visions'.[23] The decline in party morale was clearly reflected in the steep drop in membership, from 5,630 party members in March 1920 to 2,228 by the end of the year,[24] many of them purged, but others having simply dropped out. Information on fifty-two members who were excluded or dropped out between 10 November and 6 December 1920 cites the following motives: 'fears his mistakes will give the party a bad name'; disagreement with the party's programme; tiredness; weakness of will; 'is upset by snide remarks of non-party members commenting on the party mess'; 'Communists don't get furlough' and might not be considered for demobilization; religious convictions; lives by black-marketeering.[25] Moreover, the over-whelming majority (88.1%) of party members were of recent vintage, having been recruited into the party only since October 1919, with 64% joining between October 1919 and January 1920, i.e. in the aftermath of the victory over Yudenich's North-Western Army, when the party's prestige had risen, and in the course of the relentless 'Party Weeks'. A mere handful only were pre-1917 'old Bolsheviks', 87 or 88 (3.9%) having joined the party during the period of the provisional government, and some 180 (8.1%) between October 1917 and January 1919. Ethnically, 89.4% were Russians, 2.8% Latvians, 2.6% Estonians, 2% Ukrainians, 1.1% Poles, while 2.1% belonged to twelve other nationalities.[26]

The situation in Kronstadt's civilian party organization was, if anything, worse: from a party membership of 1,000 in March 1920, the party had declined to 653 and 149 candidates by 1 January 1921, most of the loss due to drop-out rather than exclusion. Only three had joined the party before the February revolution of 1917, while a further sixty-one dated their membership to the period February to October 1917, with another 140 dating to the period between October 1917 and September 1919. But 449 (70%) were enlisted during the 'Party Weeks' of the latter part of 1919.[27]

Raskolnikov's vigorous drive for centralization, in particular his attempt to put the entire party apparatus of the Baltic Fleet, includ-ing that of the Petrograd naval base, under the control of the political directorate of the Baltic Fleet (Pubalt) which he had created out of the Politotdel, fell foul of Zinoviev, Petrograd's party boss, who regarded the party organizations of the Baltic Fleet as within his fiefdom. Moreover, Zinoviev, quite justifiably, saw in Raskolnikov the protégé of his rival Trotsky, and in his efforts to thwart him, found a staunch ally in Raskolnikov's deputy, the tough and blunt Nikolai N. Kuzmin, political commissar of the Baltic Fleet, who led the opposition to Raskolnikov within the fleet.[28]

By mid-January 1921 Raskolnikov was defeated, his attempt at reform a failure. The Second Party Conference of the Baltic Fleet held in mid-February 1921 put the final touch to Zinoviev's and Kuzmin's victory over him and his Pubalt when it denounced 'all forms of separateness' and recommended 'the incorporation of the Communists of the Baltic Fleet into the general party organization'.[29] The burial of Pubalt and Raskolnikov's departure from Kronstadt some time in February 1921 mark the collapse of the administration of the fleet and of its party organization.[30] Incredibly, unauthorized meetings of ships' crews were by then taking place behind the backs of their commissars, there being too few loyal rank and file party members left to nip them in the bud.[31]

In the very thick of the general crisis of War Communism and on the eve of large-scale workers' unrest in Petrograd, Kronstadt had shed party control. At the Second Party Conference of the Baltic Fleet on 15 February the veteran Kronstadt Bolshevik Vasilii Gromov, chief of the organizational section of Pubalt, sounded the warning that 'one must expect an uprising within two to three months should things continue that way.'[32]

When news of the strikes, lockouts, mass arrests and martial law in Petrograd reached Kronstadt on 26 February, the crews of the *Sevastopol* and of the *Petropavlovsk* held a joint emergency meeting in the face of protests and threats by their commissars, including Kuzmin. They elected a fact-finding delegation of thirty-two sailors which, on 27 February, proceeded to Petrograd and made the round of factories such as the Trubochnyi plant, the Laferme tobacco factory and the Baltic metal plant, as well as of some military units. They found the workers whom they addressed and questioned too frightened to speak up in the presence of the hosts of Communist factory guards, trade union officials, party committee men and Chekists. When, finally, a few did speak, they stuck to purely economic grievances and 'minimal demands'.[33] According to Petrichenko's account written five years later, there was one daredevil who took his life in his hands and said:

Since you are from Kronstadt with which they frighten us all the time, and you want to know the truth, here it is: we are starving. We have no shoes and no clothes. We are physically and morally terrorized. Each and every one of our requests and demands is met by the authorities with terror, terror, endless terror. Look at the prisons of Petrograd and you will see how many of our comrades sit there after being arrested in the last three days. No, comrades, the time has come to tell the Communists openly – you have spoken enough on our behalf. Down with your dictatorship which has landed us in this blind alley. Make way for non-party men. Long live freely elected Soviets! They alone can take us out of this mess![34]

The tenor of this speech, if accurately reported, was very similar to the propaganda line of the Mensheviks and the leaflet 'From the Russian Social-Democratic Workers' Party to the Starving and Freezing Workers of Petrograd!', drafted by Fiodor Dan, which was spread in one thousand copies and pasted on the walls of Petrograd on 27 February,[35] the day when the Kronstadt delegation made the rounds of Petrograd. It may well have influenced the famous *Petropavlovsk* resolution of the next day. The leaflet seized on the lack of political liberty as 'the central defect in our political system and in our government policy!' The only cure, the leaflet said, was 'freedom for all toilers' and, in particular, 'freedom of speech, freedom of the press, freedom to organize in parties, trade unions and cultural-educational societies'. But most important of all, it demanded 'new free elections to Soviets', free from 'all the machinations and coercion' which had earlier turned all elections into a 'pitiful comedy'.

Thus, and only thus could they make sure that the state no more be 'ruled dictatorially' by a Communist party that 'is closed, overstuffed with bureaucrats and divorced from the toiling masses' and ensure that it be '*in the hands of the toilers*'. Only thus, at last, would '*the workers' democracy* be truly realized'.[36]

On 28 February, the Kronstadt delegation returned from Petrograd and reported its findings to a general meeting of ships' crews chaired by Stepan Petrichenko, a senior naval clerk, and Piotr Perepelkin, a sailor-electrician and former Tsentrobalt member, on board the *Petropavlovsk*. The resolutions adopted there and then, after a lengthy and excited discussion in which the Communist leaders of the Kronstadt Soviet, Pavel Vasiliev and Andrian Zosimov, participated in a vain effort at blocking them, embodied the Kronstadters' understanding of the crisis and their critique of the Bolshevik regime:[37]

Having heard the report of the representatives of the crews sent by the general meeting of ships' crews to Petrograd to investigate the state of affairs there, we demand:

1. that in view of the fact that the present Soviets do not express the will

of the workers and peasants, new elections by secret ballot be held
immediately, with free preliminary propaganda for all workers and
peasants before the elections;

2. freedom of speech and press for workers and peasants, anarchists and
   left socialist parties;

3. freedom of assembly for trade unions and peasant associations;

4. that a non-party conference of workers, Red Army soldiers and sailors of
   Petrograd, Kronstadt and Petrograd Province be convened not later
   than 10 March 1921;

5. the liberation of all political prisoners of socialist parties, as well as all
   workers and peasants, Red Army soldiers and sailors imprisoned in
   connection with the working-class and peasant movements;

6. the election of a commission to review the cases of those who are held
   in jails and concentration camps;

7. the abolition of all political departments because no single party should
   have special privileges in the propaganda of its ideas and receive funds
   from the state for this purpose; instead of these departments, locally
   elected cultural-educational commissions should be established, to be
   financed by the state;

8. that all roadblock detachments [to prevent food smuggling] be removed
   immediately;

9. the equalization of the rations of all toilers, with the exception of those
   working in trades injurious to health;

10. the abolition of the Communist fighting detachments in all military
    units, as well as various Communist guards kept on duty in factories
    and plants; should such guards or detachments be needed, they could
    be chosen from the companies in military units, and at the discretion
    of the workers in factories and plants;

11. that the peasants be given the right and freedom of action to do as they
    please with all the land and also the right to have cattle which they
    themselves must maintain and manage, that is without the use of hired
    labour;

12. we request all military units, as well as the comrades *kursanty* (military
    cadets) to endorse our resolution;

13. we demand that all resolutions be widely published in the press;

14. we demand the appointment of a travelling bureau for control;

15. we demand that free handicraft production by one's own labour be
    permitted.[38]

Alarmed by the turn of events, the Communist authorities of
Kronstadt (i.e., the Executive Committee of the Soviet, as well as
the District Committee of the party), invited all army units, factories, workshops and Soviet institutions to a meeting to be held on
1 March in the Naval Manège at which Mikhail Kalinin, chairman
of the All-Russian Central Executive Committee of Soviets, would
address them.[39] The extent to which the Communist leadership,
both military (Politotdel) and civilian (District Committee of the

party and the Soviet) had misjudged the situation and become
paralysed can be gauged by the fact that they made no attempt
whatsoever to mobilize the party cadres,[40] an omission exploited by
Petrichenko and his friends in wresting the initiative and leadership
from them at the meeting.

This was not Kalinin's first visit to Kronstadt. Only a year earlier,
on 23 December 1919, the Kronstadters had celebrated the visit of
the 'All-Russian Elder' (*Starosta*) with a procession, a mass meeting
of some 10,000 sailors, soldiers and workers, flags, ovations, the singing of the Internationale and a special 'festive session' of the Kronstadt Soviet. In his eloquent response, Kalinin had congratulated
'glorious Kronstadt' and its 'world renowned' sailors on their 'continuous, socialist creativity' and ever-ready contributions to the
defence effort.[41]

The meeting of 1 March 1921 was larger: some fifteen to sixteen
thousand sailors, soldiers and civilians reportedly assembled,
huddled together in wintry, wind-swept Anchor Square.[42] But this
time, though convened by the authorities, the crowd was not controlled by them. There were no ovations, and no singing of the
Internationale. True, when Kalinin arrived, accompanied by
Nikolai Kuzmin and Pavel Vasiliev, chairman of the Kronstadt
Soviet, he was welcomed with military honours; yet the meeting
started on the wrong foot when Kalinin, having correctly gauged the
crowd's hostile mood, complained that he had lost his voice and
requested an adjournment to the Naval Manège so that he could
address an indoor meeting limited to sailors and Red Army soldiers.
He was promptly told by the protesting crowd: 'If you cannot speak,
there's no need anyhow, for you won't say anything new, and during
the last three years we've become so fed up with all that you've had
to say that it will be just sickening to listen to you.'[43] Whereupon,
Kuzmin rose to face a barrage of fierce condemnation of the Communist regime: 'roadblocks, hunger, cold, the war is over yet order
has not returned. Commissars and functionaries are cosy, but we
have been forgotten.' Calling for 'calm' Kalinin mounted the rostrum. He assured the audience that he too was a 'simple worker' and
pleaded with them to give 'the people's government' a chance to
repair the economy and not to believe the tales of 'whisperers behind
whose backs hide the SRs, the compromisers and the tsarist generals
with their *nagaikas*'. Then the heckling began: 'Drop it, Kalinyich,
you keep cosy all right' – the calls went up from all sides. 'Look at

all the jobs you have got, and you surely take rations for each of them!' a bearded soldier shouted from the crowd. Then came hostile slogans, a little speech: 'We have had enough of that life – prisons and executions without trial', and catcalls. There was so much shouting that Kalinin had to give up and leave the rostrum.[44] At that point members of the Kronstadt delegation regaled the crowd with descriptions of the 'horrors' perpetrated by the authorities in Petrograd.[45]

Undeterred, Kuzmin tried again, first warning the crowd that 'Kronstadt is not the whole of Russia and we therefore shall not take account of it',[46] and then in almost the same breath, he reminded them of Kronstadt's 'glorious pages'. But this time flattery did not work and a sharp voice cut in reminding Kuzmin of his ruthless past as a member of the Revolutionary–Military Council of the Sixth Army in the north:

'Have you forgotten how you had every tenth man shot on the northern front?!'
'Down with him! Down!' . . . the cries seethed all around.
Kuzmin tried to outshout them:
'We shot those who betrayed the workers' cause and shoot them we shall. As for you, you would have shot every fifth and not every tenth.'
'That's enough!', the shout went up, 'He gunned them down! You can't frighten us. We have seen it all . . . run him out of here!'[47]

After that debate and slanging match, Perepelkin, seconded by Petrichenko, moved the *Petropavlovsk* resolution, with the meeting, which must have been attended by a considerable number of Communist party members, approving it almost unanimously, only Kuzmin, Kalinin, Vasiliev and a few other party workers voting against. The meeting then decided to send a delegation of some thirty Kronstadters to Petrograd to explain their demands to the army units and factory workers there and to invite them to send a non-party delegation to Kronstadt. More important still, on the suggestion of Pavel Vasiliev who may have hoped thus to wrest the initiative from Petrichenko, the meeting resolved to invite all ships' crews, army units, the docks, workshops, trade unions and Soviet institutions to elect two representatives each and send them to a Conference of Delegates to convene the next day, 2 March, to work out procedures for the now due new elections to the Kronstadt Soviet.[48]

The night of 1 March was marked, certainly in all military units, by 'noisy and stormy debates and disputes' centring around the dramatic events of 1 March, the meeting in Anchor Square, the *Petropavlovsk* resolutions, and the imminent new elections to the Soviet. It was as if Kronstadt had suddenly shed the straitjacket of three years of Bolshevik rule and had again become its old argumentative self, the noisy debating society of 1917. Next morning, in that spirit, and freed from party instructions and pressures, the crews and army units, workshops and Soviet institutions elected their representatives to the Conference of Delegates, 'with the full sanction of the Kronstadt Ex[ecutive] Com[mittee]', as advertised in Kronstadt's *Izvestiia*.[49]

If the 1 March mass meeting in Anchor Square marked Kronstadt's escape from Communist control when, in the teeth of the senior Communist authorities present, it endorsed the *Petropavlovsk* resolution, the Conference of 303 elected delegates, meeting in the afternoon of 2 March in the Engineers' College and promptly electing a five-man praesidium consisting of Petrichenko, Yakovenko, Oreshin, Tukin, and Arkhipov, not one of whom was a Communist, institutionalized that emancipation, or rather 'secession', from Communist Russia.[50] Henceforth (and to the bitter end) that praesidium, with Petrichenko as chairman, there and then named the Provisional Revolutionary Committee and two days later, enlarged by ten more elected members to consist of fifteen members, became Kronstadt's effective executive or government. The Conference of Delegates which assembled again on 4 and 11 March to receive and debate the reports of the Revolutionary Committee and to propose measures and decrees, became for its part Kronstadt's interim Soviet or parliament.

Kuzmin and Vasiliev made a last-minute attempt on 2 March at the Conference to drive home to delegates the gravity of the situation of 'dual power' which they had created, and told them bluntly that if they wished for a showdown, they could have it: 'Communists will never voluntarily relinquish power and will fight it out to the end.' Kuzmin's threat was taken seriously and he, together with Vasilev and the commissar of the Kronstadt Battleship Squadron, Korshunov, was removed from the hall and arrested. With tempers rising, a heated debate followed regarding the status of those Communist delegates present (perhaps one-third). In the teeth of a protesting minority which demanded their arrest, the Conference decided that in view of their loyal behaviour during the confrontation with Kuzmin and Vasiliev, the Communist delegates be recognized as 'plenipotentiary delegates of units and organizations on a par with other [non-party] members'.[51]

The Conference then voted overwhelmingly for the *Petropavlovsk* resolution, thus giving it official sanction. In view of rumours that party loyalists were preparing armed resistance, the praesidium was then 'granted plenary authority to administer the town and the fortress' and requested to prepare the new elections to the Soviet 'so that the peaceful renewal and reconstruction of the Soviet system' could begin. A committee was immediately chosen to organize the new elections to the Soviet but what was apparently its first meeting was held as late as 11 March.[52]

The Revolutionary Committee, having set up headquarters on the *Petropavlovsk*, sent sailor squads to occupy and guard the telephone exchange, the headquarters of the Cheka, the arsenal, military headquarters, naval and military installations, all artillery positions, foodstores, bakeries and workshops. Thus by 9 p.m. on 2 March, the entire naval base and fortress, and all forts, with the notable exception of Krasnaia Gorka on the mainland (it had been renamed Krasnoflotskii after the mutiny of June 1919), were in its hands.

The takeover proceeded without resistance and without a shot having been fired, primarily because of that same paralysis and demoralization within the local Communist party organization which had already manifested itself at the Anchor Square meeting on 1 March and at the Conference of 2 March, when the numerous Communists present voted for the *Petropavlovsk* resolution, without even one speaking up to support Kalinin, Kuzmin and Vasiliev. As for outright party loyalists, leading functionaries such as Lazar Bregman and Andrian Zosimov were immediately arrested, while a group of some two hundred, led by the commissar Vasilii Gromov, and including eighty students of the Higher Party School and twenty Chekists, headed by the notorious Krishian Dulkis, made good their escape to Krasnaia Gorka.[53]

A major blow was dealt to the last remnant of party morale with the formation on 3 March of a collaborationist Provisional Bureau of the Kronstadt Organization of the Russian Communist Party (RKP), headed by the veteran Kronstadt Bolsheviks and functionaries Yakov Ilyin, Fiodor Pervushin and Andrei Kabanov, who, in a special 'Appeal', called upon local Communists not to sabotage the efforts of the Revolutionary Committee, but to remain at their posts and support the new elections to the Soviet.[54] Subsequently, with the demonstrative and advertised successive resignations from the party of some 497 members and the imprisonment of a total of 327 members, the Kronstadt party organization ceased to exist even as an opposition group.[55]

As for Kronstadt's senior military commanders, with little love lost for the Bolsheviks they seem to have willingly accepted the invitation of the Revolutionary Committee, extended to them during the night of 2 March, to carry on; thus they served as specialists and military advisers under the direct orders of the Revolutionary Committee and the close control of its revolutionary troikas that were soon elected by the rank and file in all army units and departments.[56]

Once Kalinin had brought back his first-hand report, the primary concern of the Communist authorities in Petrograd (Zinoviev) and in Moscow (Lenin and Trotsky) was to isolate Kronstadt from the mainland. An armoured train of loyal *kursanty* (officer cadets) was thus rushed to its chief supply base in Oranienbaum to overpower the First Naval Air Squadron there after it had endorsed the *Petropavlovsk* resolution,[57] while martial law was proclaimed throughout the Petrograd province. Patrols of the Peterhof Communist Battalion for Special Tasks guarded all roads leading over the ice to the mainland, to prevent Kronstadt agitators, newspapers and leaflets getting through. Thus, on 2 and 3 March, four *Sevastopol* sailors armed with 5,000 appeals and resolutions fell into their hands, while a few days later they captured another five agitators with 4,000 leaflets.[58] Once this was accomplished, an intensive and relentless propaganda campaign was mounted to isolate Kronstadt ideologically by discrediting it as a hot-bed of White-Guardist counter-revolution. The Bolsheviks fastened on the tsarist past of their own senior officers who were now cooperating with the Revolutionary Committee. They focussed their attack on the chief of artillery, Alexander Kozlovsky, a former tsarist officer who, after the February revolution, was Kronstadt's elected chief-of-staff, and, after the October revolution, had served the Bolsheviks so loyally that on 20 October 1920 the chief commander of the Baltic Fleet, Fiodor Raskolnikov, had awarded him a watch 'for courage and feat of arms in the battle against Yudenich'.[59]

Promptly on 2 March, an order of the Council of Labour and Defence (the old Defence Council), signed by Lenin and Trotsky, denounced 'the mutiny of the former general Kozlovsky', declared him an outlaw and branded the *Petropavlovsk* demands as a 'Black Hundred–SR resolution', while the Petrograd *Izvestiia* of 3 March went even further and immediately identified the very same Kozlovsky as 'the follower of Yudenich [*sic*!], Kolchak and other monarchist generals', who, aided by his 'henchmen–officers', had inspired Kronstadt's 'shameful double-faced game' and quickly assumed the leadership of the 'handful of *Petropavlovsk* mutineers'.[60] In the same vein, on 4 March an 'Appeal' by Zinoviev's Defence Committee of Petrograd denounced 'all these Petrichenkos and Tu[k]ins', meaning Kronstadt's Revolutionary Committee, as 'puppets who dance at the behest of the tsarist general Kozlovsky' and other 'notorious White Guards', and demanded the Kronstadters' unconditional surrender, or else 'you will be shot down like partridges'.[61]

Yet the Bolshevik leaders, certainly Zinoviev and Kalinin in Petrograd, knew exactly who Kronstadt's real leaders were and were equally well aware of their aims. Ivan Sladkov, commissar of the loyalist Krasnaia Gorka Fort, telephoning Stepan Petrichenko on the *Petropavlovsk* on 5 May, clearly distinguished between the sailors and the officers when he asked him: 'What are you going to do, you deluded blockheads, when the brass run off to Finland?' But the answer came quick as a flash, 'Red *Petropavlovsk* we were, and that we shall remain!' Even Zinoviev, who promptly instructed Sladkov to stop calling his old *Petropavlovsk* mates, distinguished between 'the rebels', or 'Petrichenkos', and the officers who 'assist them',[62] while Lenin on 15 March admitted that in Kronstadt 'they do not want the White Guards and they do not want our state power either'.[63] True, on 8 March at the Tenth Party Congress, Lenin had made great play of 'White Guards' and, while conceding that 'the Kronstadt sailors and workers . . . wanted to correct the Bolsheviks only on the matter of free trade' and thus aimed at a 'Soviet power, slightly changed or merely corrected', nevertheless accused the Kronstadters of serving in fact, regardless of their intentions, as 'the stepping stone and bridge for the White Guards'.[64] But Lenin's accusation did not really tally with the official line, which denounced 'Kronstadt' simply and brutally as a White-Guardist, anti-Soviet, counter-revolutionary rebellion.

This propaganda campaign was combined with a series of thorough security measures to ensure that Kronstadt was cut off and that no reinforcements and assistance could reach it until such time as a military offensive could be mounted. The sailor Gonoratsky remembered seeing a large group of some five hundred Kronstadt sailors herded into the Guards' Depot in Petrograd after Chekists had rounded them up on railway stations where they had been caught trying to make their way back from furlough.[65] Similarly, the *Petrogradskaia pravda* of 4 March reported the arrest by the Cheka of dozens of *Petropavlovsk* sailors, of the thirty Kronstadt delegates who had been sent to Petrograd, and of the families of Kronstadt officers, who were kept as hostages.[66] Nor would the Communist authorities take risks with the sailors of the Petrograd naval base, but rather kept them locked up in their barracks.[67] Gonoratsky was with them:

Our crew was fully assembled. No conversations whatever between sailors. The barrack was silent as the grave. Only Commissar Glukhov ran up and down the barrack like a caged lion, his eyes bloodshot. The *kursanty* were armed to the teeth, every one holding a revolver at the ready in his right hand, on the look out for any untoward movement. All depots were surrounded by machine-guns manned by Communists, and there were machine-gun emplacements near the store-room. The crew stood silent, but it was heart and soul with Kronstadt.[68]

The slander campaign and blockade of Kronstadt were combined with hurried concessions to the hungry Petrograd workers: road-blocks were lifted on 1 March, permission was granted to trade more freely, and the town received a sudden generous supply of meat, shoes and clothing. These measures proved so effective that by 4 March the commandant of the Petrograd Fortified District, Butlin, reported with satisfaction:

There have been no disturbances of the peace for the past two days and today one can notice a great change in our favour in the mood of both the workers and army units. We have cut off and blockaded Kronstadt, and it cannot hold out for long, even if we take no military action, for its reserves of fuel and provisions are limited.[69]

Kronstadt was tightly blockaded to the very end; save for one hundred bags of flour which the Russian Red Cross managed to get through and some medical supplies which the Finnish authorities let pass, all supplies were cut off.[70] Thus, as early as 17 March, when Ivan Oreshin and Nikolai Arkhipov, members of the Revolutionary Committee, were about to return from Terioki where they had tried to enlist the aid of the International Red Cross, they encountered the first columns of Kronstadt refugees moving towards Finland.[71]

While the Bolsheviks hypocritically denounced the Kronstadters'

demands and their attempt at the reorganization of the Soviet
system in Kronstadt as nothing but a camouflaged White-Guardist
plot, the Kronstadters themselves genuinely saw in their *Petropavlovsk* resolution a practical programme of reform of the Soviet
system from within. In fact it was nothing less than a blueprint for
a peaceful revolution: the removal of the Bolsheviks from power by
way of free elections to Soviets.

The *Petropavlovsk* resolution, together with its sequel, the more
explicit 'Appeal of the Revolutionary Committee to the Railwaymen' of 5 March,[72] demanded immediate new elections of 'all
Soviets and governments' by secret ballot based on 'equal franchise
for all – worker and peasant . . . so that the Russian people – worker
and peasant – could have their state power'. The assumption was
that free, secret and direct elections would prove a peaceful and sure
way to end the Bolsheviks' domination of the Soviets and of the
government, while the demand for 'equal franchise for all – worker
and peasant' was intended to abolish the Bolshevik differential
voting system which discriminated against the peasants in favour of
the workers: 25,000 urban working votes equalling 125,000 peasant
votes.[73] These elections were to be preceded by free propaganda, the
granting of freedom of speech and press to all workers and peasants,
the legalization of all left-wing socialist parties (presumably Left
SRs, SR-Maximalists, and Menshevik-Internationalists) and
anarchists, the restoration of freedom to trade unions and peasant
organizations and the abolition of all Bolshevik 'political departments' which were to be replaced by neutral, non-party 'cultural
and educational commissions'. Likewise all special Communist army
detachments and factory guards were to be abolished and 'all the
privileges of Communists' ended; this meant the destruction of the
entire network of Communist control within the armed forces,
cultural and educational life, factories and plants. In the same spirit
'all Chekas' were to be closed down, and the death penalty abolished,
while the criminal militia and the courts alone would be retained; all
political prisoners belonging to socialist parties, and workers,
peasants or soldiers imprisoned in connection with labour and
peasant protests, were to be released, while the cases of all those held
in prisons and concentration camps would be reviewed; thus was the
Communist police state and its terror apparatus to be dismantled.

In the economic sphere the resolution and the 'Appeal' were
mainly concerned with the 'disenserfment' of worker and peasant

and the breaking of the Bolshevik state monopoly over food supply. As for the worker: freedom of movement from one job to the other should be secured, Trotsky's notorious labour armies should be disbanded, workers should have the right to 'direct exchange of products with peasants', while peasants should be able 'to do as they please with all the land', provided that they did not employ hired labour; craftsmen should be able to practise their crafts freely but also use no hired labour. Measures designed to break the state's stranglehold over food supply and reorganize it on an equitable basis included: the removal of roadblocks preventing the free transportation of foodstuffs and their exchange, the equalization of rations, and, most important of all, free consumers' cooperatives 'so that the state could no longer play on the hunger of the worker'. The cooperatives were to have the right 'to purchase goods abroad' and thus eliminate the middle-man role of 'governmental speculators who amass millions from the workers' sweat' and 'for that purpose' workers' wages should be paid 'in gold and not in paper trash'.[74]

While in a situation of siege and blockade, the Revolutionary Committee could do no more than make food distribution more egalitarian and free the trade unions; but it certainly made a clean sweep of Communist domination and, during Kronstadt's sixteen 'days of liberty', gave it an effective government that adhered to its political programme and restored Kronstadt's Soviet democracy.

The composition of the Revolutionary Committee naturally enough reflected the leading role which the veteran sailors of the *Petropavlovsk* and the *Sevastopol* had played in the events of 28 February and 1 March. At least eight or nine of the fifteen members, including its chairman, the senior clerk of the *Petropavlovsk*, Stepan Petrichenko, were sailors or former sailors. Though Petrichenko had joined the navy as far back as 1912, he came to the *Petropavlovsk* only after the October revolution, joined the Communist party in August 1919, but seems to have left it sometime in 1920.[75] He was flanked by a veteran of the 1917 October revolution,[76] the telephone operator V. Yakovenko, who served as deputy chairman, and by the navigator F. Kilgast, who in 1917 had been a Menshevik member of the Kronstadt Soviet right from its establishment and the Soviet's representative to the town Duma.[77] The seaman-electrician from the *Sevastopol*, Piotr Perepelkin, was chairman of the Agitation Centre of the Revolutionary Committee; enlisted in 1912, he had been a firebrand activist in 1917 when he represented the *Sevastopol's* unruly ship's committee in June of that year and was arrested in the July Days as a delegate from Tsentrobalt.[78] Of the remaining sailor members of the Committee, for whom no further information is available, the artificer G. Ososov (enlisted in 1914) and the seaman S. Vershinin (enlisted in 1916) were from the *Sevastopol*, while the seaman-electrician F. Patrushev (enlisted in 1912) was from the *Petropavlovsk*. Though little is known about the senior artificer Nikolai Arkhipov, the fact that he was second deputy chairman of the Committee and accompanied Ivan Oreshin on his diplomatic mission to Finland suggests that he enjoyed Petrichenko's special confidence. All that is known of the senior medical assistant Kupolov is that he accompanied Vershinin on the night of 7 to 8 March to parley with the attackers and that he managed to escape and return to Kronstadt.

Ivan Oreshin, headmaster of the Third Trade School, one of the six civilian members of the Committee, stood out as the only intellectual on that body, and seems to have served as its 'Foreign Minister'. With the outbreak of the 1917 February revolution, Oreshin, a history teacher, was immediately elected chairman of Kronstadt's newly founded teachers' association and became a member of the Kronstadt Soviet and chairman of the municipal Duma. In 1917 he had been known as a popular lecturer and campaigned for a People's University in Kronstadt. Later, in March 1919, he founded Kronstadt's archive of 'printed and manuscript materials of the revolutionary epoch' and appealed to all citizens to deposit 'all revolutionary literature in the archive' and 'thus to render a great service to historical science and historical truth'. Politically he had been close to the SRs.[79]

V. Valk, foreman of Kronstadt's sawmill, was (together with Romanenko) in charge of the Committee's Department of Civil Affairs. A Menshevik since 1905, he is known from the Okhrana records for his unsuccessful attempt in March 1910 to set up a social-democratic military organization in Kronstadt. Valk too, had been a Menshevik member of the Kronstadt Soviet from its inception in 1917 and had served on its food supply commission, on the control commission attached to the captain of the harbour, and as a member of the provisional court.[80]

All that is known of Romanenko, watchman of the dry-dock, is that he was a veteran Kronstadter and a Menshevik and that, together with Valk, he had allegedly been active in Kronstadt's Menshevik underground.[81]

Other veteran Kronstadters included Tukin or Tulkin, a worker at the electro-mechanical factory and a Menshevik representative on the Soviet's finance commission in August 1917, who (after the arrest of the 'collaborationist' Communist Yakov Ilyin) was put in charge of food supply; Pavlov, a worker at the mines factory who was in charge of the Justice Department, and Baikov, transport chief of the Fortress Construction Department, who was in charge of the Transport Department.[82]

The Revolutionary Committee maintained contact with the entire population through its official daily newspaper, the *Izvestiia* of the Revolutionary Committee, which published its resolutions, appeals, orders and announcements, beginning with No. 1 on 3 March and ending with No. 14 on 16 March 1921, the eve of Kronstadt's fall.[83] Its three editors, Anatolii Lamanov, Sergei Putlin and V. Valk, were all veterans of the 1917 revolution. Anatolii Lamanov, who wrote its programmatic articles and gave the uprising its watchword, 'All Power to Soviets and not to Parties', may well be regarded as the chief ideologist of the Kronstadt uprising. Sergei Putilin, the *Izvestiia's* polemicist, satirist and jingle writer, was a defrocked priest (formerly of the Kronstadt naval cathedral) who, in 1918, had moved close to the SRs and taught Russian literature at the Communist party school during the civil war.[84] V. Valk, the third member of the editorial board, seems to have been in charge of the technical aspects of the paper's production.

A number of other 1917 veterans came to the fore: two of the three members of the 'collaborationist' Provisional Bureau of the Communist party had been prominent Kronstadt Bolsheviks in 1917 and party functionaries in the years of the civil war,[85] while its third member, Andrei Kabanov, had been a member of the Central Committee of the Baltic Fleet; S. Fokin, who now argued in the pages of *Izvestiia* for independent and powerful trade unions, had been an active member of the Kronstadt Soviet in 1917;[86] M. Roshchin, now chairman of the housing commission, had been a Bolshevik representative on Kronstadt Soviet commissions in 1917.[87]

Naturally enough, there were also veteran Bolsheviks, prominent in 1917, who strongly opposed the Kronstadt uprising: Lazar Bregman, who was secretary of the District Committee of the party and was one of the first Communists to be arrested, had been chairman of the Kronstadt Soviet at various periods during 1917 and 1918 and chairman of its Workers' Defence Committee; Ivan

Sladkov, one of Kronstadt's earliest Bolshevik activists, was now commissar of the Krasnaia Gorka Fort which immediately became a major centre in the attack on Kronstadt;[88] Vasilii Gromov, who had acquired some notoriety as Kronstadt's 'little tsar', led the early escape from Kronstadt of a group of two hundred party loyalists, and later headed a special unit in the assault on the fortress, being awarded the Order of the Red Banner for his part in the 'suppression of the Kronstadt mutiny'.[89]

While it would be going too far to suggest (without access to the relevant Soviet archives) that all the activists of the 1921 uprising had been participants of the 1917 revolutions, this certainly was the case with the 1,900 veteran sailors of the *Petropavlovsk* and *Sevastopol* who spearheaded it. It was equally true of a majority of the Revolutionary Committee, and of the intellectuals, Anatolii Lamanov, Sergei Putilin and Ivan Oreshin. Likewise, at least three-quarters of the 10,000 to 12,000 sailors – the mainstay of the uprising – were old hands who had served in the navy through war and revolution. True, most Communist party members among them were only of civil war vintage, the majority even of less than a year's standing, for early Bolshevik activists had been creamed off by frequent mobilizations and the expanding and far-flung Soviet and party apparatus.

The Revolutionary Committee, Kronstadt's interim government, exercised power through its wide network of revolutionary troikas. These were elected by the members of base organizations to replace the commissars, contained no Communists, and were the means by which all existing institutions such as Rabkrin (Workers' and Peasants' Inspection), Politotdel, the Garrison Club, Bureau of Trade Unions, workshops, factories, ships and army branches were brought under the effective control of the Revolutionary Committee. The revolutionary troikas were directly responsible to the Revolutionary Committee and served as the channels through which instructions were speedily transmitted downwards and their implementation reported back. The revolutionary troikas also kept a watchful eye on Communists who continued to be employed in institutions such as Politotdel or Rabkrin and thus neutralized their influence.[90]

The revolutionary troikas seem to have served as a stop-gap measure in the takeover of the existing Communist Soviet system pending new elections which were expected to return loyal non-party office-holders and functionaries, or until such time as new institutions had been set up to replace Communist institutions. Thus, when Rabkrin was abolished on 14 March and its functions transferred to the newly elected Council of Trade Unions which replaced the old Bureau of Trade Unions, Rabkrin's revolutionary troika too was abolished. The same happened when the Politotdel was abolished and its functions and property transferred to the Garrison Club. However, while the Council of Trade Unions as a newly elected and loyal institution was in direct contact with the Revolutionary Committee and had no revolutionary troika attached to it, the Garrison Club retained its revolutionary troika.[91]

If the Revolutionary Committee constituted Kronstadt's interim government, the Conference of Delegates was its revolutionary parliament, to be convened when important decisions had to be made and popular approval sought.

Apart from the stormy foundation session of 2 March which marked Kronstadt's formal break with the Communist regime, at least two more sessions of the Conference of Delegates were held, on 4 and 11 March. Though the published reports were unfortunately only bare summaries of the proceedings, they provide some insight into the workings of Kronstadt's revived Soviet democracy.[92]

During the session of 4 March, at which 202 delegates were present (had the Communist delegates present on 2 March been asked to stay away?), it was decided at the suggestion of Petrichenko to enlarge the Revolutionary Committee to fifteen members, and ten new members were then elected by an overwhelming majority from among twenty who stood for election. Petrichenko went on to report on the activities of the Revolutionary Committee, the state of military preparedness of the ships' crews and the garrison, the high morale of the population and the satisfactory state of food and fuel reserves (which he certainly assessed too optimistically). The Conference then resolved that all workers be armed and assume responsibility for the security and defence of the inner town, so that sailors and soldiers could be free to man the outer defences. It was also decided that elections should be held within three days to the governing bodies of the trade unions and to a newly founded Council of Trade Unions. Next came reports from sailors who had managed to break through the blockade and to return from Petrograd, Strelnyi, Peterhof and Oranienbaum, all of them unanimous in saying that the local population 'is kept by the Communists in complete ignorance of what is happening in Kronstadt', while rumours were being spread that 'a gang of White Guards and generals' was in control. This sad news is reported to have 'provoked general laughter' in the audience and a back-bencher's sarcastic comment: 'We have only one general here – the commissar of the Baltic Fleet Kuzmin – and he has been arrested.' On adjourning, the Conference adopted the watchword 'To Win or Die', which is reported to have characterized the general mood.[93]

The session of 11 March even more closely resembled the sessions of the Kronstadt Soviet of 1917. To keep delegates briefed and angry with the Bolsheviks' slander campaign, Petrichenko had the latest numbers of the Petrograd newspapers *Pravda* and *Krasnaia gazeta* distributed among delegates prior to the session which opened, even while 'the guns of our glorious floating fortresses [i.e. the *Petropavlovsk* and the *Sevastopol*] thundered', with a brief homage to the fallen 'Red eagles of Kronstadt', and concluded with an ovation to 'the defenders of Kronstadt'. In between came the prosaic business.

Item 1. Food supply: from the short report of the Revolutionary Committee and discussion, it appeared that the state of food supplies was 'entirely satisfactory', and the Conference resolved 'to regard the activities of the Rev[olutionary] Com[mittee] as correct and fitting'.

Item 2. Boots and underwear: the report that 280 pairs of boots had been requisitioned from jailed Communists for the benefit of bootless soldiers was greeted with 'thunderous applause' and shouts of 'Well done! Strip them of their sheepskins too!!!' The announcement made by the delegate from the sewing workshop that three thousand sets of underwear were ready for the use of 'first line fighters' was welcome news which was followed by Kilgast's appeal to delegates to solicit more footwear in their 'base organizations' (Putilin was listed in *Izvestiia* as having donated a pair of boots).

Item 3. Fourth anniversary of February revolution: in view of the military situation it was decided to defer festivities and 'celebrate the fall of the autocracy simultaneously with the overthrow of the commissarocracy'.

Item 4. Arrested Communists: some delegates suggested that jailed Communists be released 'on bail' as there were 'honest Communists' who had proved 'a model of dedication in the execution of their military duties', whereupon Petrichenko reminded delegates of treasonable acts committed by Communists such as Yakov Ilyin, Galanov and Gurev who, left at freedom and in their previous positions, had passed on vital information to the enemy. It was then decided that all arrested Communists should be kept in jail until such time as military operations had ceased and the situation had cleared up, but that the Revolutionary Committee should order no further arrests without prior consultation with the revolutionary troika of the relevant base organization.[94]

While such was the practice of Kronstadt's restored Soviet democracy, its ideology was expounded by Anatolii Lamanov, in the pages of the *Izvestiia* of which he had again become editor. He explained how and why the Soviet system established by the October revolution had been usurped and perverted by the dictatorship of the Communist party and invested Kronstadt's uprising with an all-Russian significance as the start of that Third Revolution which, restoring power to the Soviets, would create a genuine Soviet Republic of Toilers.

Lamanov was singularly well equipped for the task. He had taken an active part in the February and October revolutions and the civil war in Kronstadt; throughout the period of the provisional government and well into 1918 he was a member of the Executive Committee of the Kronstadt Soviet and for much of that time its chairman or deputy chairman, as well as the chief editor of its *Izvestiia*. He was also leader of the large self-consciously 'Non-Party' faction of the Kronstadt Soviet, and when, in August 1917, it turned into the Union of SR-Maximalists, he shared its leadership with Grigorii Rivkin and Arsenii Zverin, two of the most impressive and attractive leaders and theorists of SR-Maximalism who had turned Kronstadt into one of its major centres. The gentle, saintly and persuasive Rivkin seems to have had some considerable influence on Lamanov.

When Rivkin and Zverin left Kronstadt early in 1918 for Samara which had, by March of that year, become the major centre of SR-Maximalism in Russia,[95] Lamanov assumed leadership of the Maximalist faction in the Kronstadt Soviet which, in the elections held late in March 1918, had received no less than forty-one mandates, as compared with fifty-three Communists and thirty-nine Left SRs.[96] He was also deputy chairman of the Kronstadt Soviet and the most popular of its three delegates to the Fourth Congress of Soviets of March 1918, receiving 124 votes to the 95 gained by the Anarcho-Syndicalist Efim Yarchuk and the 79 that went to the Bolshevik Artemii Liubovich.[97] He was again elected in July 1918, and attended the Fifth Congress of Soviets together with the Left SR Fiodor Pokrovsky and the Bolshevik Lazar Bregman.[98]

Little is known of Lamanov's further political career, except that he remained a member of the Union of SR-Maximalists until the end of 1919, headed the Section of People's Education of the Kronstadt Soviet,[99] and that he was still contributing then to Kronstadt's *Izvestiia*, writing on education and advocating the introduction of a system of 'social security for working youth', so that 'the children of the toilers' – 'our successors' whose task it will be 'to build on and beautify the kingdom of toil' – will no more be disadvantaged.[100] In the same vein he argued for the establishment of a Workers' Technical College to educate the worker into a 'conscious and thinking producer' no more to be duped, enslaved and turned into 'a small ignorant cog in the production machine', but instead fully equipped to become 'the real master of life' and to manage the toilers' own 'factories, plants and general production'. Not surprisingly, as a student of technology himself Lamanov's educational ideal was the worker-technologist, 'the conscious creative individual who contributes the greatest possible benefit to the working collective' and who was totally dedicated to the building of a 'Soviet Russia of Toilers'.[101]

Lamanov's language and his inspiration were still very much those of Rivkin and SR-Maximalism and it is reasonable to assume that he fully well knew and very likely endorsed the critique levelled by his friends and mentors, Zverin and Rivkin, at the Bolshevik regime. When he left the Union of SR-Maximalists at the end of 1919, he did so, as he later claimed, solely in protest against its alleged terrorist attack on Communist party headquarters, subsequently exposed as a Cheka provocation.

The thrust of Maximalist criticism of the Bolsheviks before the October revolution and of Bolshevik dictatorship thereafter was directed at their *partiinost'* or party-centredness which, predicted the Maximalists, though founded to 'serve the interests of the toiling people', would, by the logic of general and sectional party interests as well the particular interests of its Central Committee and bureaucracy, eventually make the Bolshevik party 'run counter to the interests of the people'.[102] By April 1918 the entire front page of the Maximalist *Znamia truda* of Samara was given over to a denunciation of the Bolsheviks as 'commissarocrats',[103] while three months later the Council of the Union of SR-Maximalists called for the creation of 'a firm organizational basis' for the struggle against 'the commissarocracy'.[104]

The Maximalist critique grew fiercer in February 1919 with Zverin's systematic 'theses' denouncing the 'party dictatorship' and its policies of economic centralism and privileged groups, and demanding political and economic equality and the control by the 'toilers' of the entire administration:

either the social revolution is victorious in the political sphere as genuinely Soviet, with the dictatorship not of parties but of the toiling masses, with the self-organization of the toilers and the immediate realization of economic equality, or it perishes; together with it dies the world revolution.[105]

The Maximalists' watchword must therefore be 'Power to Soviets and not to Parties'. That slogan was so deeply felt that it was henceforth inscribed on the masthead of the *Maksimalist*,[106] where the very same Maximalist critique and message found more pungent expression in the first two of the 'Ten Commandments of the Soviet Citizen':[107]

1. Thou shalt have no other power than the power of free Soviets. Serve honestly and bow thyself down to one power only – the power of the Soviets which thou hast elected.
2. Thou shalt have no capitalist above thee, nor general, nor commissar, nor party committee, thou shalt not bow thyself down to them, nor serve them.

The third commandment, however, reaffirmed the Maximalists' support of the existing Soviet state:

3. Thou shalt, not merely in word, but in deed too, recognize Soviet state power, and support, strengthen and defend it against all enemies.

The tension existing between the first two commandments and the third, which at some time or other also characterized the entire non-Bolshevik left during the years of the civil war, beginning with the Anarchists, the Left SRs and the SR-Maximalists and ending with the Mensheviks, was bound sooner or later to snap. Thus, in December 1919 the Cheka arrested the entire Council of the Union of SR-Maximalists and many Maximalist leaders, including Rivkin and Zverin, all on trumped-up charges.[108]

In Kronstadt the tension between loyalty to the Soviet state and the demand for free elections to the Kronstadt Soviet broke dramatically with the confrontation of 1 March in Anchor Square when the Kronstadters adopted the *Petropavlovsk* resolution. It fell to Lamanov and *Izvestiia* to restate the Kronstadters' credo in the light of the new situation.

Lamanov who, after resigning from the Union of SR-Maximalists at the end of 1919, had become a candidate member of the Communist party some time in 1920, played no role in the beginning of the uprising; subsequently, he was never a member of its Revolutionary Committee and, unlike Sergei Putilin, may not even have been a delegate to the Conference. Nor does he seem to have held any official position and even his editorship of the *Izvestiia* was never made official. Yet his presence in the paper is strongly felt, beginning with a letter of 4 March announcing his resignation from the RKP and his return 'into the ranks of the Union of Socialist Revolutionaries–Maximalists whose watchword always was, is and ever will be "Power to Soviets and not to Parties"'.[109] It was with this letter that the 'All Power to Soviets and not to Parties' became the watchword of the Kronstadt uprising, used immediately in the first radio appeal of the Revolutionary Committee boomed by the *Petropavlovsk*'s powerful transmitter: 'To All . . . To All . . . To All . . .: Our cause is just: we stand for the power of Soviets and not parties';[110] it then appeared on the masthead of *Izvestiia*, was repeated in letters and articles, often in conjunction with the demand for freely elected Soviets, and became *Izvestiia*'s leitmotiv.[111] Lamanov expanded on it in a number of unsigned programmatic articles[112] which made a valiant attempt to justify the October revolution, to explain why the Soviet power, which the Kronstadters had helped to create, had degenerated into 'commissarocracy' so that a 'third revolution', of which the Kronstadt uprising was the 'courageous and confident' beginning, was needed.

Endorsed by Kronstadt's Revolutionary Committee, Lamanov's view of Russian history and his interpretation of the 'stages of the revolution', which owed a great deal to SR-Maximalism, became the official ideology of the uprising and, transmitted in slogans, messages and appeals, was wholeheartedly espoused as its own by Kronstadt's insurgent citizens. Stated in brief, Lamanov's argument ran thus. Having lived three hundred years under the 'tutelage' of the Russian police state, the 'oppressed people' had finally toppled the tsar's 'rotten throne' and both 'rich and poor Russia rejoiced in the freedom'. But the rich Russia of landowners and capitalists got the better of the poor Russia of workers and peasants, tried to bend its neck and strip it 'as before' of 'the fruits of its labour', without any longer sharing the spoils 'with the tsar and his myrmidons'. Meanwhile Kerensky led the Russian people 'slowly and surely' towards the Constituent Assembly, and while the rallying cry of that Assembly 'reigned supreme over the whole of Russia', the peasant was still without land and the worker was still exploited.

The Communist party, Lamanov conceded, had understood the mood of the masses and, with 'alluring slogans', had drawn the toilers into its camp and promised to lead them into 'the shining Kingdom of Socialism' which 'the Bolsheviks alone' knew how to build. Conscious of the threat of a 'new enslavement' posed by the power of the bourgeoisie, Russia's sailors, soldiers, workers and peasants, 'their patience at an end', had, in October 1917, shouldered the bourgeoisie aside. Seemingly, the toiling people had at last achieved 'its rights': the time of 'free toil on the land, in factories and plants' had come, and 'all power had passed to the toilers'. But that was not to be: 'teeming with careerists', the party of Communists had seized power, first removing from power 'the socialists of other tendencies', and then stealing the power from the peasants and workers, while claiming to rule 'in their name'. Then, with utter disregard for 'reason and the will of the toilers', they who had promised a 'free kingdom of toil' and a 'shining domain of socialism' instead created a 'bureaucratic socialism of slaves', with Soviets made up of party functionaries who 'vote obediently' according to the dictates of the party committee and its 'infallible commissars', with 'bureaucratic trade unions' which 'fettered workers to their benches' and turned labour into 'a new slavery, rather than a joy'; 'toiling peasants' were declared kulaks and 'enemies of the people' and were ruined so that they would labour on state farms, 'the estates of the new landlord, the state'. This system of 'bureaucratic socialism', Lamanov went on, was crowned by the terror of the Cheka which, in order to secure the privileges and carefree life of 'the new bureaucracy of Communist commissars and party functionaries', crushed 'all independent thought, all just criticism of the acts of the criminal rulers' by imprisonment or execution.

Thus Bolshevik communism, having drowned in blood 'all the great and shining pledges and watchwords of the toilers' revolution' had now turned into a 'commissarocracy plus firing squads' which, within three years, 'has completely put into the shade' three hundred years of tsarist autocracy. But now, at last, Lamanov rejoiced, the 'long-suffering patience of the toilers' had come to an end. Red Kronstadt, vanguard of the February and October revolutions, and now the first to overthrow the 'commissarocracy', had thus started the 'Third Revolution' against 'the dictatorship of the Communist party with its Cheka and state capitalism', fighting for a 'different kind of socialism', for a 'Soviet Republic of the toilers where the producer himself is the sovereign master and disposer of the product of his labours'.

The 'Third Revolution', transferring all power to 'freely elected Soviets', free from party pressure, and transforming the bureaucratic trade unions into 'free associations of workers, peasants and labouring intelligentsia', would, Lamanov predicted, set free the 'All-Russian *katorga*' and rouse 'the toiling masses of the east and the west': for it would serve as an example of 'new socialist construction' as opposed to the Communists' bureaucratic 'socialism in quotation marks'.

Sergei Putilin in his 'Kronstadt Jingles' spelt out their hopes and yearnings for equality, brotherhood and community:

> O what a bright morn is dawning:
> Trotsky's fetters we're now throwing off!
> And Lenin the Tsar we'll be toppling,
> As dictatorship comes crashing down!
> The toiler shall find a new freedom:
> Land and works will be labour's own.
> Free labour's the road to equality,
> To brotherhood now and for ever,
> So let's do it now, or we'll never![113]

Thus Lamanov and Putilin, their *Izvestiia* and its thousands of readers, sailors, soldiers and civilians alike, perceived their Kronstadt uprising as a Second Coming of the October revolution, the restoration of that Soviet democracy of which they had been robbed by the Communist party.

The Kronstadters' commitment to Soviet democracy was linked to a rejection of parliamentary democracy which they equated with 'the Constituent Assembly and its bourgeois regime', the *Uchredilka*. That rejection may have had its roots in the 1917 agitation of Maximalists such as Rivkin, Zverin *and* Lamanov, or of the Anarcho-Syndicalist Yarchuk, all of whom outdid one another in extolling the blessings of Soviets of toilers as compared with bourgeois parliaments. That view was certainly reinforced by an incessant stream of Bolshevik propaganda which, in December 1917 and January 1918, laboured the contrast between Soviets and *Uchredilka* and, in the years of the civil war, identified and discredited as the sworn enemies of Soviets all protagonists of the Constituent Assembly, such as Chernov and the Socialist Revolutionaries, with their 'Committee of the Constituent Assembly' (Komuch) (which they set up in Samara in May 1918), and the Kadets.

Moreover, the leaders of insurgent Kronstadt were appealing above all to a left-wing audience throughout Russia, including disillusioned Communists, in a vain bid to counter Communist propaganda which affixed a counter-revolutionary image to the Kronstadt uprising. They therefore also had very good practical reasons to advertise their staunch commitment to the Soviet system, and they did so by a deliberate retention of all the outward symbols of Soviet state power: the ubiquitous red flags, the Red Army star on the cockade of the chief-of-staff, and the use of the term 'comrade' in addressing one another. A Russian Red Cross representative who attended a meeting of the Revolutionary Committee on 12 March noticed a huge plaster bust of Lenin and a portrait of Trotsky in the Assembly Chamber and the use of a Communist seal on official documents. When he expressed his surprise and asked why Kronstadt had not replaced the seal, he was told they had not yet come round to dealing with it, and that 'it would serve the Bolshevik aim of raising a hue and cry regarding the White-Guardist intentions of the insurgents'.[114] How sensitive the Kronstadt leaders were to that Communist hue and cry can be gauged from the report of another Red Cross visitor: 'Kronstadt will admit no White political party, no politician, with the exception of the Red Cross. Only the Red Cross, and nothing but the Red Cross. Assistance must therefore be rendered most prudently, so as not to compromise Kronstadt in the eyes of the people.'[115]

Indeed, the Kronstadters were extremely resentful of all gestures of sympathy and promises of help coming from the White-Guardist émigrés. Their ire was roused when émigré newspapers such as *Obshchee delo* and *Rul'* rushed to acclaim the Kronstadt uprising as an anti-Bolshevik movement led by General Kozlovsky, thus playing straight into the hands of Bolshevik propaganda.[116] An early editorial in Kronstadt's *Izvestiia*, 'Gentlemen or Comrades', warned comrades against gentlemen, would-be 'fellow-travellers', who had applauded their 'great victory over the Communist dictatorship':

You are inspired with the fervent desire to restore the genuine power of the Soviets and with the noble hope of returning to the worker his free labour and to the peasant his right to dispose freely of his land and of the products

of his labour. But they hope to bring back the tsar's *nagaika* and the
privileges of the generals . . .

You need the overthrow of Communist power for peaceful construction
and creative work – they need it for the enserfment of workers and peasants.
Be on your guard. Do not let the wolves in sheepskin get near the captain's
bridge.[117]

There can be little doubt that the Kronstadters' devotion to
Soviet democracy was genuine. They believed they had learned from
their own experience to distrust elections which could not be controlled by the constituents at the lowest local level, such as the ship's
crew, the army unit, the factory floor and the village, and they
thought that once the stranglehold of the Communist party had been
removed, direct Soviet elections would be far more immune to
manipulation than nation-wide parliamentary elections where the
names of candidates unknown to the local voters appeared on party
lists.

The reporter of *Volia Rossii*, the SR newspaper published in
Prague, recorded the following interview with members of the
Revolutionary Committee who, after the fall of Kronstadt, had
escaped to Finland:[118]

'Tell me, why are you against the *Uchredilka*? You demand freely elected
Soviets, would not elections to the Constituent Assembly be held in the
same manner?'
'Ha-ha-ha', was the answer: 'elections to the *Uchredilka* inevitably mean
"lists" and "lists" mean that Communists will surely put through their own
people.'
'There would be secret ballots', I insisted, but they burst into laughter.
'For three-and-a-half years we have seen neither white bread nor secret
ballots, though both were promised to us. If we are to rid ourselves of the
Communists, if we are to have secret elections – [the answer is] Soviets in
every district, where people know one another and know whom they do
and do not wish to elect. Local Soviets will prevent that manipulation of
elections which the Bolsheviks have been so good at.'

A group of thirty professional officers from Kronstadt who are not
likely to have had any special love lost for the Soviet system insisted,
when interviewed in Finnish Ino where they had been interned, that
'the idea of Soviets elected by universal, equal and secret vote was
far more popular among the wide masses than the idea of the
Constituent Assembly'.[119]

The question of the Constituent Assembly was debated in the
Revolutionary Committee on 13 March following the arrival of an

emissary from Victor Chernov and the SRs, who promised military aid provided that Chernov be invited to Kronstadt as chairman of the Constituent Assembly and that the insurgents adopt the restoration of the Constituent Assembly as their maxim. A large majority spoke against, only Valk raising his voice in favour, while Petrichenko and Kilgast seem to have stalled.[120]

Even in the last desperate appeal of the Revolutionary Committee of 15 March 'To you, peoples of the world ... to you, Russian people who are scattered all over the world' asking for food and medical supplies, for moral and, perhaps, military assistance, there was only a slight diminution of Kronstadt's commitment to Soviet power:

We fight now for the overthrow of the party yoke, for the genuine power of Soviets, and may the free will of the people then decide how it wants to be governed . . . Do not tarry, nations of the world, lest history condemn you. You, too, Russian people, do not tarry, so that when your children ask you, 'Father, what did you do when blood was shed for the sacred freedom of the toilers of Russia?' you will be able to answer: 'I stood by them and helped them build a free Russia' . . . [121]

Kronstadt's rejection of the *Uchredilka* went hand in hand with suspicions of, if not contempt for, political parties. The maxim 'All Power to Soviets and not to Parties' was not directed solely at the RKP, the party par excellence. Indeed, some suspicion of all parties had been part of Kronstadt's political climate since the February revolution. In the five consecutive free elections to the Kronstadt Soviet in 1917–18, Kronstadters again and again made the 'non-party' group (in August 1917 it became the Union of SR-Maximalists) one of the three major factions in the Soviet, stronger than the Left SRs and almost as strong as the Bolsheviks. Its leader, Lamanov, as well as his friends Rivkin and Zverin, never tired of warning against parties and narrow party-mindedness. By March 1921, in the light of the pitiful performance of both the SRs and the Mensheviks and of the betrayal of the Bolsheviks, the Kronstadters' long-standing suspicion of political parties seems to have hardened into outright contempt: 'All political parties are bankrupt: there is not one that could satisfy either workers or peasants, and certainly not both', members of the Revolutionary Committee told the reporter of *Volia Rossii*.[122]

Moreover, even for party members, disillusionment with the Communist party bred disillusionment with parties in general. As Kurashev, a veteran sailor and former secretary of the Kronstadt

Soviet, now chief of the town's finance section, put it in his letter of resignation from the Communist party:

For the three years that I have been a party member, I have seen the full injustice of the higher echelons of the party which, infested with bureaucrats, have become estranged from the masses. I therefore discard the party label and have no intention of henceforth joining any other party; instead, I wish to work freely and honestly for the good of all the toilers of Soviet Russia, like any other honest citizen.[123]

Not surprisingly, contempt for political parties led to respect for trade unions. Indeed, linked to the belief that free elections would restore political power to the Soviets, which would again become (as in Kronstadt in 1917) the representative organization and government of the toilers, was the conviction that freely elected trade unions would restore economic power to the workers.

S. Fokin, an active member of the Kronstadt Soviet in 1917, had, as early as April 1917, called upon fellow workers to unite in an 'Eternal Union of Toil', marching together 'under the red banner of toil' into the 'Kingdom of Sacred Toil'.[124] Far more soberly, on 9 March 1921 he called simply for 'The Reconstruction of Trade Unions'.[125] He denounced 'the ruling party' which, aiming at a centralized Communist system with its commissars and political sections, had robbed the trade unions of their initiative and 'self-creativity', reducing them at best to the function of registering the numbers, skills and party affiliation of members and at transforming them, at worst, into a 'Communist gendarmerie organ shackling the toiling masses'. Now, with the fall of the Communist dictatorship, the trade unions must play a decisive role in the 'economic-cooperative construction' of the country and the cultural advancement of workers. For the Soviet Socialist Republic would be strong only when its government and administration passed into the hands of the toiling classes by way of 'regenerated trade unions'.

While Fokin's syndicalist views were merely a contribution to debate,[126] the 'regeneration' of Kronstadt's trade unions was begun almost immediately, on 4 March, with the resolution of the Conference of Delegates to hold new elections within three days for the secretariats of all trade unions and for the Council of Trade Unions; they also recognized the Council of Trade Unions (replacing the existing Bureau of Trade Unions) as the leading executive organ of workers, to be charged with maintaining constant and direct contact with the Revolutionary Committee.[127] Elections were apparently held on 7 and 8 March under the supervision of the revolutionary troika which controlled and watched the Bureau of Trade Unions.[128]

The real revolutionary change in the status and power of the trade unions came only on 14 March when the Revolutionary Committee decreed the abolition of the local Workers' and Peasants' Inspection (Rabkrin) as 'an institution which had been elected by the outgoing Soviet and which was now out of tune with the spirit of the times'. Its functions, notably that of 'workers' control' over civil, non-military enterprises, were transferred to the Council of Trade Unions.[129] Since the local Rabkrin, though nominally elected by the Kronstadt Soviet, had been a powerful institution of central government control over manpower, its recruitment and mobilization, the transfer of its functions to the Council of Trade Unions, or rather to a Council committee consisting of representatives from all trade unions, freed the unions from both the state and the local Soviet, and even somewhat strengthened them vis-à-vis their own Council. A practical illustration of the Council's new power was a decree of the Revolutionary Committee of 14 March which put it in charge of the reconditioning of the transport fleet, including the convening, under its auspices, of a technical commission to which representatives from all the enterprises concerned were to be invited to prepare estimates of the number of workers, the materials and the time needed to execute the work.[130]

The reorganization of trade unions was nipped in the bud with the fall of Kronstadt on 18 March; hence there is no way of knowing precisely what administrative role and economic functions the Revolutionary Committee intended to assign to the unions in the free, reconstructed Soviet system, though the direction in which it was moving is clear: that of democratizing and strengthening the unions and making them as independent as possible of the state.

There was then a great deal of truth in Ivan Oreshin's claim that 'in the two weeks' that Kronstadt was governed by its Revolutionary Committee 'they tried to put Soviet ideals into practice'.[131] Both elective and egalitarian principles were scrupulously observed. The Revolutionary Committee (the equivalent of the Executive Committee of the Kronstadt Soviet in 1917) had been elected by the Conference of Delegates (the equivalent of the Kronstadt Soviet of 1917) and reported back to it regularly, seeking approval of its activities and policies, even though, on 2 March, it had been given 'all plenary powers to administer the town and the fortress'.[132] The

Conference of Delegates had been elected by Kronstadt's body
politic at their places of work, in army units, factories, workshops and
Soviet institutions. Even the revolutionary troikas (the equivalent of
the commissions of the Executive Committee of 1917) were elected
by the base organizations, whereas the commissions of 1917 had been
elected by the Soviet. Likewise, the secretariats of the trade unions
and the newly founded Council of Trade Unions were both elected
by the entire membership of trade unions.

Thus Kronstadt's watchword 'All Power to Soviets and not to
Parties' was realized. True, left-wing socialist parties had been
declared legal but there are no signs they were actually revived, not
even the Union of SR-Maximalists 'into whose ranks' Lamanov had
announced his return. As for the Provisional Bureau of the RKP, it
seems to have become defunct after Yakov Ilyin, who had been left
in charge of supplies, was caught red-handed phoning vital information on the critical state of Kronstadt's food and fuel supplies to the
enemy in Krasnaia Gorka.[133]

With privileges abolished and all food rations, except those for
children and the sick, equalized, with all civil and economic affairs
placed on a war footing and administered by the Revolutionary
Committee, there was perfect equality in Kronstadt.

The serenity, high morale and unjustified optimism which seem
to have marked the mood in Kronstadt derived as much from an
overpowering sense of sudden unexpected liberation from a tight and
unjust system of domination, as from the experience of participating
as equals in the maintenance and defence of that new freedom. The
'enormous spiritual exaltation' which representatives of the Russian
Red Cross visiting Kronstadt on 11 and 12 March noted there[134]
lingered on in the accounts of Piotr Perepelkin and of a young Kronstadt worker who, after the fall of Kronstadt, shared their experiences
with Fiodor Dan in the Petrograd Prison of Preliminary Detention
(*Predvarilka*) before they were taken out by the Cheka and shot.
'Perepelkin recalled the inspired, spring-like atmosphere of Kronstadt; the children dancing in the streets, full of joy that they had
been delivered from the Bolsheviks, and then carrying food to the
positions; the brotherly relations between sailors, Red Army soldiers
and workers.'[135] In the same vein, the young worker remembered
'how everyone shared what he had to the last, and would willingly
do any work assigned to him' and that all could speak freely, 'even
the Communists'.[136]

For the benefits of Kronstadt's freshly restored egalitarian and free debating society were extended even to the 327 leading Communists, commissars and party loyalists who had been arrested and kept in jail. They received the same rations as ordinary Kronstadters and, according to the testimony of F. M. Nikitin, a Communist sailor who refused to make his peace with the new regime and was arrested, 'passed their time in general political arguments as to who was most to blame for what had happened, and . . . whose fault it was that the necessary measures against the mutineers had not been taken in time'.[137] They even managed to issue three numbers of a prison newspaper *Tiuremnyi luch kommunara* (Prison Light of the Communard), and to hold meetings chaired by the prison elder, ex-commissar Andrian Zosimov.[138] Indeed, the protocol of one such prison meeting and its request to permit Zosimov to travel to Moscow, so that he could inform the VTsIK (the All-Russian Central Executive Committee of Soviets) of 'the true state of affairs in Kronstadt', was even given serious consideration before being rejected by the Revolutionary Committee in its session on 13 March.[139] The worst that befell the imprisoned Communists was the confiscation, on 10 and 12 March, of their boots, sheepskins and great coats for the use of soldiers manning the outer defences.[140] Not surprisingly, some then thought that their final hour had come. Lazar Bregman's farewell message to his wife Mariia Pozdeeva on 10 March is telling:

Things are coming to a head. They have taken our boots today and I expect to be shot today. As for my personal feelings, I have forced myself not to think of the outside world and have cut myself off from everything. My heart has turned to stone. The news of the birth of our son has made me very happy. If they leave you [alive] – love him deeply, for me too, and make him into a Communist.[141]

Bregman's fears were unfounded. In its very first appeal to the people of Kronstadt on 2 March the Revolutionary Committee had stated its resolve that 'not one drop of blood be shed'[142] and it adhered to its pledge 'We do not take revenge' to the bitter end, more out of revulsion against the Bolshevik terror than anything else: 'We give all commissars, even the Cheka executioners, the same rations that we eat. True, we have refused to give butter to the commissar of the Baltic Fleet Kuzmin who said he cannot live without butter; but butter we give only to children and the sick.'[143]

The good-natured naivety in the behaviour of the Revolutionary

Committee was due, perhaps, to the ease with which the changeover had been accomplished and then welcomed by the vast majority of the Kronstadt population, and to the confidence given by control over a relatively inaccessible island fortress, and over Russia's last-remaining and formidably armed Dreadnoughts the *Petropavlovsk* and the *Sevastopol*. The Committee's conduct also owed much to the conviction that their truly Soviet cause was so obviously just that it must therefore be possible to convince every sailor, soldier or worker, even a Communist. Had not a majority of Communists repeatedly endorsed the *Petropavlovsk* resolution and loyally supported the uprising? No less than 784 party members had officially resigned from the party, among them persons of some standing who held command and administrative posts; resignations had also come from the intelligentsia, among them the Red Officer German Kanaev, the veteran schoolteacher and Communist activist Maria N. Shatel, and the judge, Allik. That naive confidence can be seen in Petrichenko's telephone conversation with the diehard Ivan Sladkov to whom he spoke as if he were still his old mate from *Petropavlovsk* days,[144] the misplaced trust that was put in Yakov Ilyin, and in Vershinin's quixotic horseback sortie to enemy *kursanty* put to flight during the night of 8 March whom he addressed thus:

Stop! Turn back, you sons of workers and peasants! The Soviet government oppresses you, the Communist dictatorship gives you nothing but oppression . . . I have come to you alone; you can do anything you like to me, but at the same time, we, the insurgent sailors, proclaim to you that we fight for a truly revolutionary power, against the Communists' violence and oppression, for a genuinely free power of Soviets.

The *kursanty* gave Vershinin short shrift and to the cry, 'You have told us enough of your tale', they pulled him from his horse and took him to headquarters.[145]

The same sanguine hope that, in the end, the Communist authorities would come round and negotiate with them, or that Petrograd would rise in support, seems to explain the strategy of 'passive defence' adopted by the Committee on 3 March. In so doing, they cavalierly ignored the advice of Major General Alexander Kozlovsky and his officers, who advocated an offensive strategy which would have despatched landing forces to the southern and eastern shores of the mainland, notably to Oranienbaum (where vast quantities of badly needed flour were stored) and to Sestroretsk; these, Kozlovsky thought, would create bridgeheads from which the

Kronstadters could push on towards Petrograd to join up there with the striking workers and the garrison.

But, constituting a relatively privileged and trusted group and a reservoir of elite shock troops in the Soviet system, and traditionally one of the least servile sections of the Russian people, the Kronstadt sailors failed to gauge the cowedness, political apathy and plain physical exhaustion of Petrograd workers. Dan noted how resentful and contemptuous the sailors he encountered in jail were of the Petrograd workers who 'would not support them and sold them down the drain for a pound of meat'.[146] Some captured sailors, when transported in chains on trucks through the streets of Petrograd to the place of execution, are reported to have sworn at groups of workers whom they passed.[147]

More than anything, the Kronstadt insurgents underestimated the vitality and unity of purpose of the Russian Communist party in the face of this threat to its monopoly of power, and, too, the strength of its hold over an atomized and exhausted Russia.

For in the end, it was the Communist party and the thousands of its members who volunteered 'for Kronstadt' that inspired, carried with it or just drove some 45 to 50 thousand troops into the final assault of 17 and 18 March that subdued insurgent Kronstadt. After the fiasco of the first attack on 8 March, Trotsky and the generals Mikhail Tukhachevsky and Sergei Kamenev realized only too well that ordinary Red Army soldiers, even when exceptionally well-fed and clothed,[148] were very reluctant and unreliable fighters against Red Kronstadt, although driven at gunpoint onto the ice and into battle by tough commissars such as Krishian Dulkis and Nikolai Razin.[149] Army cadets were mobilized and thousands of party members volunteered, including 279 delegates from the Tenth Party Congress, i.e., one-quarter of all delegates. In the Seventh Army alone, there were some 2,758 volunteers from party organizations in the major cities, and, at the time of the attack, the party element in ordinary units averaged between 15% and 30% and in crack units between 60% and 70%.[150] It is difficult to decide whether victory was achieved thanks to their intensive propaganda effort or to their personal example of courage and dedication: 'they simply went into the fire heedless of all precaution' and suffered up to 80% losses in dead and wounded.[151] The military historian S. E. Rabinovich, quoting the Red Army generals Mikhail Tukhachevsky and Vitovt Putna, goes so far as to claim that 'There was no other operation in the military history of the Red Army in which the presence and participation of specially mobilized members contributed so greatly to success as during the suppression of the Kronstadt mutiny of March 1921.'[152] 'There can be no Soviet power without the Communist party' was the message the Communist delegates preached before they went into battle. This was the party's final answer to Kronstadt's war-cry 'All Power to Soviets and not to Parties'.[153]

With the escape to Finland of some 8,000 soldiers, sailors and workers, including the majority of the Revolutionary Committee, the dispersal of thousands of Kronstadt and Baltic sailors to the Black and Caspian Seas and the Siberian Flotilla,[154] and the execution of many hundreds of other Kronstadt sailors and activists, including Lamanov, the story of Kronstadt's experiment in Soviet democracy ended in tragedy. It was symbolic that the old Kronstadt sailor Dybenko, now appointed military commandant of Kronstadt with the task of 'establishing a firm revolutionary order', should abolish the Soviet altogether and run Kronstadt with the assistance of a revolutionary troika consisting of tough old Bolshevik hands such as Bregman, Vasilev and A. I. Gribov. In an endeavour to erase all traces and memories of Kronstadt's golden age of Soviet democracy, he renamed its *Izvestiia* as *Krasnyi Kronshtadt*; the *Petropavlovsk* became the *Marat*, the *Sevastopol* the *Paris Commune* and Anchor Square became Revolution Square.[155] Soviets were not so much as mentioned except in the form of the adjective in *sovetskaia vlast'* (Soviet state power). The axiom that 'without Communists there could be no Soviet state power' was hammered at meetings of 'non-partyists', and at one such meeting (of the employees of the Food Supply Base) all present swore to be 'loyal sons of Russia' who would not allow themselves to be duped again by SRs and Mensheviks, but would go 'hand in hand with the Communist party'.

Those sailors of the *Petropavlovsk* whose lives had been spared swore at a solemn ceremony that they would 'give their lives' to rehabilitate themselves, to rebuild the Baltic Fleet and make its 'red flag fly so high that the proletariat of the whole world shall see it'. They made a humble beginning when they donated two hundred pairs of socks for the benefit of troops wounded during the 'liberation of Kronstadt' and one half of their monthly pay for a wreath in memory of 'the comrades who died during the capture of Kronstadt'.[156]

Finally, under the heading 'For Treason' Kronstadt learned that some twenty-six 'mutineers' who had been captured red-handed on

17 March had, after recovering from their wounds and being released from hospital, finally been tried and sentenced: twelve to death, including two former party members, the *Petropavlovsk* artificer O. Rykov and his fellow crewman the sailor Fedorenko; the remaining fourteen to various terms of hard labour. The accused Korakin is reported in *Krasnyi Kronshtadt* to have struck an 'aggressive pose' towards the Revolutionary Tribunal and, when asked by its chairman 'why he had gone against Soviet power', is quoted as having replied 'ironically': 'What difference does it make to us ignorant people what kind of power?'[157]

While Korakin, facing death, may no longer have cared 'what kind of power', the very same issue of *Krasnyi Kronshtadt* that reported the trial spelt out clearly in its editorial the 'fundamental features' of Kronstadt's restored 'dictatorship of the proletariat' during its 'initial phase': 'Restrictions on political liberty, terror, military centralism and discipline and the direction of all means and resources towards the creation of an offensive and defensive state apparatus.'[158] A prescription for counter-revolution if ever there was one.

7

Pride and glory of the Russian revolution?

Power and democracy were the fundamental questions which be-devilled Russia in the 1917 revolution, as they have ever since. The Kronstadters' attempt to solve them produced a bustling, self-governing, egalitarian and highly politicized Soviet democracy, the like of which had not been seen in Europe since the days of the Paris Commune.

Yet, not surprisingly, in the debate on and struggle for power which convulsed the Russian revolution, it was the Kronstadt Soviet's *power* that caught universal attention, notably that of Trotsky, Tseretelli and Lenin. But it was symptomatic of the revolution's tragedy that Kronstadt's singular and innovating achievement of Soviet *democracy* went largely ignored.

The despatch with which the spontaneously elected Committee of the Movement put down the savage outburst of class hatred and revenge was truly impressive. More impressive still was the speed, prudence and skill with which its successor, the Soviet of Workers' and Soldiers' Deputies, channelled the Kronstadters' revolutionary energies and egalitarian aspirations into the creation of a vast net-work of base assemblies, committees and trade unions, and, with their backing, established itself as an effective local authority. The Soviet's success in filling both the power vacuum created by the collapse and elimination of the Viren regime, and the institutional and cultural wasteland which it inherited, is more than remarkable. For, apart from some philanthropic, military-sporting and cultural-religious organizations, including no less than five societies for the struggle against alcoholism, chaired by Viren himself, his wife, some grey official, retired officer or priest,[1] there were no social, cultural or political clubs or trade unions to provide the creative setting for a local democratic intelligentsia in Kronstadt.[2] The town Duma, consisting largely of ennobled citizens, merchants, a few retired officials and a minority of petty bourgeois and others listed as 'peasants', was blatantly unrepresentative.[3] Small wonder that it was 'half paralysed' when the revolution struck, and in a 'depressed state' thereafter.[4]

Had it not been for some socialist activists, mainly instructors and petty-officers, a few socialist students and professionals, and the revolutionary socialist ideology which, despite Viren's tight *cordon sanitaire*, had reached the deeply disaffected garrison and the town's workers, the Kronstadt revolution could easily have degenerated into a drunken orgy and pogrom, more ferocious and destructive than that of October 1905, because so much more frustration, humiliation and deep class hatred had since accumulated. Indeed, many officers, gendarmes, police spies and officials owed their lives to their incarceration by order of the Committee of the Movement and to the constant vigilance of the Executive Committee of the Soviet thereafter.

It is against the background of the penny-pinching Viren regime, with all its social and cultural poverty,[5] its cruelty and sterility, that the creative achievement and civilizing promise of Kronstadt's February revolution must be viewed and assessed.

Did the 'model revolutionary order' of which Kronstadt's sailors, soldiers and industrial workers felt so proud really work? Most observers, including former provisional government commissars Pepeliaev and Parchevsky, seem agreed that in public order, personal safety, cleanliness, good repair and regular provisioning, Kronstadt was in much better shape than Petrograd. Pepeliaev's report to the committee of the state Duma on 27 May 1917 did, it is true, dismiss as 'naive' the Kronstadters' boast of having 'raised the defence capacity of the fortress'. He sneered at the proliferation of 'bureaucracy' under which 'trifling matters', earlier dealt with by unit commanders, were instead brought to the unit committee and then passed on to the Executive Committee of the Soviet for decision. But even Pepeliaev admitted that the fortress had not deteriorated.[6] Sympathetic observers, such as Nikolai Rostov and Philips Price, were deeply impressed with the dignity and business-like seriousness of the well-attended Soviet plenum debates. Fact-finding delegations from the Helsingfors Soviet, inspecting the plants and workshops of Reval and Kronstadt early in April 1917, reported – somewhat sanguinely – that in Kronstadt (as contrasted with Reval) 'productivity of labour had almost doubled compared with before the revolution' in the torpedo workshops, the electro-mechanical plant and other factories they had visited. And in June, Price, describing the factory committees and dock unions running Kronstadt's foundries and dockyards under the close control of the Soviet's operational commissions, concluded that they had reached a 'high state of efficiency'.[7]

As for the workings of Kronstadt's 'people's courts' and its Investigation Commission, information, and that sharply contrasting, has only been available to me for the latter. While Parchevsky remembered its proceedings as a travesty of justice, Evgenii Trupp, a member of the Commission, reported (*sic!*) its work to the *Delo naroda* as 'a daring experiment in the creation of revolutionary forms of justice'.[8] Still, it was only thanks to the Investigation Commission and its work that, by the end of June 1917 and despite very trying circumstances, most officers had either been acquitted and freed, or transferred to the Ministry of Justice in Petrograd to serve their sentences.[9]

But it was in its commune-like self-government that Red Kronstadt really came into its own, realizing the radical, democratic and egalitarian aspirations of its garrison and working people, their insatiable appetite for social recognition, political activity and public debate, their pent-up yearning for education, integration and community. Almost overnight, the ships' crews, the naval and military units and the workers created and practised a direct democracy of base assemblies and committees. Raised on them was the representative democracy of the Soviet, its Executive Committee and commissions. The elective principle was applied to all public offices. The office holders' accountability to their constituents was strengthened by the latter's right of instant recall and by the quarterly elections. The electorate was kept fully informed by Kronstadt's *Izvestiia* which published verbatim the proceedings of the Soviet and a register of votes cast there on crucial issues. Wage differentials were reduced to a minimum and all epaulettes and insignia of rank were abolished. A new-born and vigorous political and social culture of socialist parties, clubs and *landsmannschaften*, newspapers, lecture courses, public addresses, Anchor Square mass meetings and festive rallies enveloped and permeated Kronstadt's Soviet democracy.

Still, there were some limits to liberty and equality, even in the

'Free City of Kronstadt'. Thus, in the 14 April 1917 Soviet debate on
the question of labour mobility, fears for Kronstadt's skilled work
force won out over commitment to the 'principle of liberty'. True,
Lebedev denounced as 'serfdom' a system which legally tied workers
to their jobs, and could see nothing 'unpatriotic' in their seeking
better conditions elsewhere, since 'freedom can be defended anywhere'. But Ermoshchenko thought freedom could best be defended
in Kronstadt, 'the bulwark of Petrograd'. It was this latter view
which prevailed when the Soviet resolved that 'the transfer of workers
from Kronstadt to other towns is inadmissible'.[10]

Similarly, when a group of women volunteered for enlistment and
training in the workers' Red Guards during the Kornilov Days at
the end of August, the Soviet plenum, with utter disregard for the
lead given by the Executive Committee, for Bregman's dogmatic
appeal to socialist ideology, Yarchuk's historical reference to the
'heroic' women of the French revolution, and Lamanov's passionate
pleading, amidst laughter and uproar voted down his motion that
'women be admitted to the Red Guards on a par with men'. Neither
Yarchuk's threat that he would 'tell the women the whole story', nor
the desperate appeal of Shurgin, the Soviet's chairman, 'Comrades,
where is your equality?' could persuade them to reconsider the
matter at the next session.[11]

Yet while Kronstadt illustrates the working of Soviet democracy
in one particular locality, it tells little about the viability of a nation-
wide Soviet system such as the toilers' republic of federated communes advocated by Rivkin, Lamanov and Kronstadt's SR-
Maximalists. One necessary condition for Kronstadt's success may
well have been the open, free and pluralist society of the period of
the provisional government of 1917. Equally important was the
weakness of a central government that allowed Kronstadt virtual
autonomy, while at the same time underwriting its unilaterally increased wage bill and providing the supplies necessary to maintain
the base, the fortress and their civil establishment.[12] But most important of all was the continuing existence of active political parties
which contested (and jealously scrutinized) elections to the Soviet
assembly and insisted on the proportionate manning of the Soviet's
executive. They thus ensured that Kronstadt was virtually governed
(until June 1918) by a socialist coalition resting on a very broad
parliamentary base.

Thus, freeing themselves from the nightmare and servitude of an autocratic police state which, as the sailor Skobennikov put it, had taught them only to use their 'hands and feet', the Kronstadters proved convincingly the capacity of ordinary people to use their 'heads, too'[13] in governing themselves, and managing Russia's largest naval base and fortress.

Kronstadt's democracy was self-consciously egalitarian, but its body politic was confined to the mass of producers or 'toilers', and excluded members of the propertied classes, although in July 1917 they voted for and could be elected to the unimportant town Duma and, in November 1917, the Russian Constituent Assembly. Nor did this exclusiveness bother most Kronstadters. Indeed, inclusive democracy based on universal franchise, as compared with the exclusive democracy of the Soviet, was mentioned only once in the Kronstadt Soviet's recorded debates, when the Menshevik Pavel Malyshev wondered whether the Soviets, elected only by the 'revolutionary democracy', were in fact 'fully democratic'.[14] But none of his fellow deputies seems to have shared his doubts; on the contrary, they were convinced that their Soviet was more 'fully democratic' than a bourgeois parliament. Red Kronstadt, which understood its revolution as a turning of the tables both on the tsarist hierarchical order, its officer corps and bureaucrats, and on Kronstadt's own very small bourgeoisie, was fully satisfied with the clipped democracy of its Soviet. As the SR Kalabushev claimed, it represented 'almost the entire population', and that was quite good enough.[15]

Yet the Kronstadters' sovietism was not derived from any clearly defined social-political theory, nor was it conceived as an alternative to the parliamentarism of a future Constituent Assembly based on universal franchise. Its chief thrust was directed against the provisional government which Kronstadt denounced as lacking in revolutionary and popular legitimacy. Indeed, one of its accusations against the provisional government was precisely its repeated postponement of elections to the Constituent Assembly. In this sense, Kronstadt's sovietism, at least during the period of the provisional government, was pre-parliamentary. It turned anti-parliamentary only after the October revolution.

Even for such inveterate anti-parliamentarians as Zverin and Rivkin, the point at issue in the argument with the 'constitutionalists' was not universal franchise as against Soviet toilers' franchise. Their insistence was on Soviet deputies, responsible and responsive to the constituents, indeed 'punctual executors of their will', as contrasted with parliamentary deputies whom they castigated as too independent of and divorced from their constituents, and, so they claimed, invariably betraying their trust.

While the Kronstadt Soviet urged the speedy convocation of the Constituent Assembly, it does not seem to have given any thought to what relations should be between that future body and the existing Soviets acclaimed by all, with the notable exception of the Anarcho-Communists, as 'the sole parliament which expresses the will of the entire toiling people of Russia'. Kronstadt's vagueness on the subject was demonstrated in May 1917, when Raskolnikov, denouncing the provisional government and haranguing against a 'coalition ministry', proposed a government of Soviets 'headed by the people's Constituent Assembly' and was pressed no further on this hybrid; nor was the subject broached again.

But there was a truly dark side to Kronstadt's radical democratism. The insistent, almost obsessive desire to subject all executives, committee-men, Soviet deputies or members of the Executive Committee to the direct will and constant control of an active body politic made for the instability and weakness of both the Soviet and its Executive Committee. Indeed, it was precisely the flourishing grass-roots democracy that sometimes enabled popular, skilful and unscrupulous agitators such as Roshal, Yarchuk, and even Raskolnikov to subvert the institutionalized 'general will', as expressed by the Soviet's party system and its political balance. Making the rounds of the ships, military units, plants and workshops, and of Anchor Square's crowds, agitators could sometimes appeal directly to the electorate against too moderate or obnoxious Soviet deputies, and perhaps have them removed or made to change their votes. It was thus that they mobilized the 'masses' from outside against decisions of the Soviet in which they had been out-voted. True, in the April Days, Roshal's attempt at using mass pressure on the Executive Committee to reverse a moderate resolution of the Soviet failed, and he was promptly excluded. But on 25 May, he (or his associates) did succeed, by similar tactics, in forcing a faltering Executive Committee to rescind the agreement reached with Tseretelli and Skobelev. Similarly, it was only by mobilizing Anchor Square masses and the Bolshevized ships' crews and military units that Raskolnikov, bypassing the Executive Committee and the Soviet, brought off the supreme feat of organizing, under *Soviet* auspices,

Kronstadt's July Days expedition to Petrograd, where he made it serve open-ended *Bolshevik* aims.

But Roshal's and Raskolnikov's manipulative skills could only have brought Kronstadt's expeditionary force to Petrograd because, since June, its men had been ready for it, having been held back only at the last moment on 10 June. So far had matters gone that the Left SRs, the Bolsheviks' partners in the force, only walked out on them *after* the demonstration's detour to Bolshevik headquarters, when it became patently obvious that it had become a Bolshevik venture. Kronstadt's ready mobilization for the October revolution had little to do with Bolshevik manipulation. It was more than anything due to a broad Kronstadt consensus, embracing the entire Soviet's political spectrum, which regarded the overthrow of the weak and despised Kerensky government and the transfer of power to the Soviets as long overdue and voluntarily accepted Bolshevik leadership.

But despite the obvious limitations and defects of their egalitarian democracy, of which the Soviet deputies must have been well aware, Kronstadters were singularly lacking in self-doubt. Indeed, so confident were they in their vanguard role – Pepeliaev gaped at what he called their 'extraordinary conceit'[16] – and so proud of their exercise in self-government, that in summer and autumn they sent hundreds of special emissaries, liaison delegates and men due for home leave to many parts of European Russia. There, like Sergei Kudinski in the Soviet of Sormovo, they preached – far away from Kronstadt – the Kronstadt gospel of 'a Soviet which is the only master of all aspects of life . . . having all the power, revolutionary, political and economic'.[17]

Bolder still, in May and July 1917, they challenged Tseretelli's use of the Soviets to shore up a weak and faltering bourgeois government, and, in March 1921, rose against Lenin's and the Bolsheviks' emasculation of the Soviets and their cynical transformation into mere instruments of Bolshevik dictatorial rule.

To Tseretelli and the moderate majority of Mensheviks and Socialist Revolutionaries, Kronstadt was nothing but a hearth of Bolshevism[18] and a prime example of irresponsible anarchist 'experiments'. Worse still, Kronstadt was the first to challenge the 'united revolutionary power' of that coalition government which he had pledged himself to 'stand up for through thick and thin and support fully and unreservedly'.[19] The significance of the Kronstadt experiment in Soviet democracy was certainly lost on him. He preferred 'organs of local self-government' based on universal suffrage to Soviets representing the working masses alone. In his opinion, workers still lacked 'the organizational experience' required 'to take power and administer the state'.[20] He deeply resented the Kronstadters' persistent critique and demonstrative challenge to his policy of coalitionism, his 'reason of revolution' (*razum revoliutsii*). Indeed, he seems to have developed an intense dislike of Kronstadt, and particularly the 'elemental, rebellious' crowd that gave him a 'hostile, even though restrained' reception in Anchor Square during his visit on 24 May. Many years later, he still 'vividly remembered' the 'instinctive hatred and craving for revenge and violence' that greeted his censorious critique of their callous treatment of the imprisoned officers.[21] Nor did the Kronstadt crowd endear itself to his close friend Vladimir Voitinsky, the Petrograd Soviet's indefatigable trouble-shooter, who ran the gauntlet of Anchor Square heckling on 16 May 1917 and later remembered it as

degraded and demoralized by a *katorga*-like existence under tsardom, this crowd lacked proletarian class-consciousness. It had the psychology of a *Lumpenproletariat*, a stratum that is a danger to revolution rather than its support . . . material suitable for a rebellion *à la* Bakunin.[22]

Not so Nikolai Rostov. Both more sympathetic and more knowledgeable, as a Socialist Revolutionary neo-populist he had little time for the facile class analysis of the erstwhile Bolshevik-now-Menshevik Voitinsky. Rostov visited Kronstadt late in May and was deeply impressed.[23] But on 4 July, the panicky, trigger-happy Kronstadt expeditionary hosts' inglorious mêlée in the Liteinyi Prospect deeply shocked him. He visited Kronstadt again during the sobering up that followed the July Days, and was with the festive crowd that assembled on 19 July in Anchor Square to remember the Kronstadt uprising of July 1906 and to honour its martyrs:

The Kronstadt crowd! What it may still do to our revolution! Here it stands, in a compact mass, listening attentively, responding warmly. A good many are undoubtedly dedicated revolutionaries, and, like their comrades of yesterday, will probably be ready tomorrow to face death with equal dignity and exaltation. What a mighty bastion of revolution Kronstadt could be! Alas, when you scan this crowd, you feel bewildered, puzzled, have trouble in understanding it. Yet you very much wish to see this crowd stand in the camp of the revolutionary democracy, just as it stands now, there in Anchor Square.[24]

It was Tseretelli's and the moderate Soviet leaders' failure, and thus the tragedy of the Russian February revolution, that the Kronstadters' relentless critique of coalitionism was dismissed out of hand, while their novel experiment in Soviet self-government went unappreciated. Instead, the Kronstadters were written off as a mere Bolshevik and anarchist rabble, although Tseretelli and his associates knew full well that the Bolsheviks were in a minority there. Together, they thus abandoned what was still, as Rostov noted, an open-ended Kronstadt situation, surrendering it to the Bolshevik leaders in Petrograd who, right from the start, had been so deeply impressed with Kronstadt's 'special importance' that, as early as mid-March 1917, they had already sent some of their very best organizers and agitators there.

Worse still, the radical Kronstadt crowd prefigured the rising tide of radicalism that swept the urban masses of Petrograd in June–July, and rose again with renewed and greater vigour in September–October, alienating them from their Menshevik and Socialist Revolutionary leaders who had become fully identified with the coalition government, and driving them instead towards the Bolsheviks, with their 'All Power to Soviets' slogan. It was this that Voitinsky saw so clearly: 'that elemental, rebellious spirit, which in Kronstadt was already [in mid-May] boiling, seething and about to overflow, was only just beginning to flare up in the working-class suburbs of Petrograd'.[25]

But while Voitinsky either would not or could not act on his better knowledge, Tseretelli, standing, as Voitinsky put it, 'Like a captain on the bridge making policy',[26] may not even have wanted to notice the radical tide which made for 'All Power to Soviets'. Indeed, when later in his memoirs he pondered his Kronstadt experience and the failure of 'the democracy', it was its naive commitment to give 'unlimited freedom of propaganda' even to such elements as the Kronstadt Bolsheviks that he termed its 'basic defect' and 'greatest mistake'.[27] In short, the sole and simplistic lesson which Tseretelli drew in his Kronstadt chapter was regret at the 'democracy's' unwillingness, if not inability, to repress. Yet the Kronstadt sailors and soldiers who massed at the Tauride Palace on 4 July, shouting 'Tseretelli, Tseretelli!',[28] wished to remind him again, though more insistently and compellingly than in May, of his democratic mandate and duty to assume the power which the Kadet ministers had relinquished by walking out of the government on 2 July. Seeing the Soviet leaders so insensitive to their demands and so afraid of power – Fiodor Dan reportedly exclaimed, 'Shoot us down, but power we will not take!'[29] – the Kronstadters turned their backs on them, and, in the end, though a majority supported the SR-Maximalists and Left SRs, and many others were just non-party radical Kronstadt sailors[30] or Anarchists, they all threw in their lot with Lenin and the Bolsheviks. For they alone in Russia had the impressive organization and leadership, the active will and well-advertised determination to topple the discredited provisional government, holding out the promise of transferring 'All Power to Soviets' and making the Russian revolution into a social revolution.

There is little evidence to suggest that the Bolsheviks ever took the Kronstadt experiment in Soviet democracy more seriously than their Menshevik rivals, despite the praise lavished on the 'pride and glory of the revolution' for having assumed local power and provided both the example and the shock troops for the Bolshevik campaign of 'All Power to Soviets'. Even when, in May 1917, Lenin took up Kronstadt's cause against Tseretelli and the provisional government, defending it in the name of 'democratism', local self-government and elective offices, including that of the commissar, it was on Kronstadt as a pace-setter for Soviet *power* that he focussed, seizing on it to provide proof that in 'the localities' the revolution had overtaken Petrograd and had entered its 'second phase' which would transfer power to Soviets and to such institutions of popular sovereignty as the Constituent Assembly and organs of local self-government.[31] Thereafter, Kronstadt appears in his articles and private jottings together with Reval, Vyborg, the Baltic Fleet, and the troops in Finland, only as a forward base and recruiting ground for the seizure of power in Petrograd.[32]

If the Bolsheviks were too party-minded and absorbed in the business of seizing *power* and keeping it against all odds, the Mensheviks were too much obsessed with their bourgeois revolution to take note of Kronstadt's Soviet innovations. Indeed, of all the Russian 'Marxists', including the independent *Novaia zhizn'* group which stood somewhere between Menshevism and Bolshevism, it was only Ivan Bezrabotnyi (Manuilsky) in Trotsky's *Vpered* and Anatolii Lunacharsky in *Golos pravdy* who waxed panegyrical about the model democracy of the 'Kronstadt Commune'.[33]

Kronstadt's staunchest supporters were the neo-populist, non-Marxist radical left, the Left SRs, SR-Maximalists and Anarcho-Syndicalists. Visiting frequently, they found in its Soviet democracy the living prototype of their 'toilers' republic' of federated communes.

When, after the October revolution, Kronstadt became a major stronghold of Bolshevik Soviet power, its Soviet democracy, together with the naval democracy of the Baltic Fleet, was gradually whittled down until, in the end, it was contemptuously dismissed as some *komitetshchina* – misrule by proliferating committees. Small wonder that in March 1921, when the Kronstadt revolt burst on the Communist leadership assembled at the Tenth Party Congress to deal with Russia's economic crisis and the party's malaise, they saw in the Kronstadt programme and its demand for a renewal and reactivation of the Soviet system of democracy a simple and dangerous attack on Bolshevik power.

Moreover, a galaxy of Communist leaders and publicists, ranging from Trotsky, Nikolai Bukharin, Karl Radek, L. Sosnovsky, Emelyan Yaroslavsky in *Pravda* to Iurii Steklov in *Izvestiia*,[34] not to mention a host of smaller fry, rallied to a man in a vast and ugly propaganda campaign, aimed at the immediate ideological isolation and lasting delegitimation of Kronstadt's 'Third Revolution'. It was denounced as an ingenious White-Guardist plot, or at best as a petty bourgeois bridge to counter-revolution and restoration. Thus, unlike Tseretelli and his Soviet colleagues, as well as Kerensky and General Brusilov, who could not bring themselves or did not dare to take serious repressive action against the Kronstadters in 1917, Trotsky and the Communists did not falter when making good their threat to 'shoot them down like pheasants' in March 1921. Nor did they have to worry much about public opinion, certainly not among Communists. Even as severe a critic of party policy and leadership as the dissident Communist Alexandra Kollontai boasted at the Tenth Party Congress on 13 March 1921 that it was members of her Workers' Opposition faction who had been 'the first' to volunteer 'for Kronstadt' and thus 'to fulfil our duty in the name of Communism and the international workers' revolution'.[35]

The denunciation of Kronstadt continued unabated for months after its savage repression. As late as July 1921, Radek and Bukharin excelled in castigating the left and wayward Communist Workers' Party of Germany (KAPD) for having presumed to publish the left Dutch Communist Hermann Gorter's critical comment which rubbed in the point that it was the 'proletariat of Kronstadt' which rose 'against the Communist party' and had posed the awkward question whether the lesson to be learned was not that 'class dictatorship must replace the party dictatorship'.[36] There is not a shred of evidence to support the oft-repeated story that Bukharin, at the Third Comintern Congress, referred to the Kronstadters with sorrow as 'erring . . . true brothers, our own flesh and blood', whose revolt the Communists had been reluctantly 'forced to suppress'.[37] Nor is Bukharin likely to have thus publicly indulged his bleeding heart when savage denunciation of 'Kronstadt' had become a test of loyalty, if not a party ritual. Even spokesmen of the KAPD now hastened to dissociate themselves (and their theorist Gorter) from the Kronstadt *Aufrührer* (mutineers).[38] Indeed, at the Eleventh Party Congress, in March 1922, Trotsky used 'Kronstadt' to intimidate Alexandra Kollontai and the remnants of the defeated Workers' Opposition, identifying them, amidst applause, with 'the banner of Kronstadt – only Kronstadt'.[39] Small wonder that, in such an atmosphere of intimidation and repression, no serious analysis and party debate was possible.

While Radek and Bukharin cynically searched the foreign and White-Guardist press for 'exposures' that would provide 'a clear understanding of the social nature of the Kronstadt uprising',[40] Trotsky took recourse to facile sociology. He pointed to the alleged replacement of 'vast numbers of the revolutionary sailors' by such 'accidental elements' as 'Latvian, Estonian and Finnish sailors',[41] thus robbing Kronstadters of their glorious past and revolutionary credentials. While he never managed to live down his own gruesome role in the Kronstadt tragedy, he certainly did succeed in saddling its historiography with tendentious sociology.

Amidst the hysteria and cynicism of the Bolsheviks' reaction to 'Kronstadt', Lenin's immediate comments stand out as sober and honest. The Kronstadters, he conceded frankly, 'do not want the White Guards, and they do not want our state power either'. But their 'new power', regardless of whether it stood 'to the left of the Bolsheviks or slightly to the right', was doomed to a 'Crash' and bound to serve as a 'step-ladder', a 'bridge' to 'bourgeois counter-revolution'.[42]

In his private jottings, Lenin reached further, diagnosing the Kronstadt uprising as symptomatic of 'the political side, the political expression' of the economic crisis that beset Russian War Communism 'during the spring of 1921'. Lenin's 'lesson from Kronstadt' was double-pronged, and fateful in its historical consequences. 'In politics', Lenin noted, what was needed was 'a closing of the ranks', a tightening up of discipline 'inside the party', an insistence on 'the greatest firmness of the apparatus', the strengthening of a 'good bureaucracy in the service of politics', the stepping up of the 'implacable struggle against the Mensheviks, the Socialist Revolutionaries and Anarchists'. 'In economics', the Kronstadt episode, he thought, pointed to the need for 'the widest possible *concessions* to the middling peasantry', notably 'local free trade', in short, the New Economic Policy (NEP).[43] The Kronstadters' immediate and indignant protest of 14 March 1921, 'Kronstadt does not demand "free trade", but the genuine power of the Soviets',[44] was certainly lost on Lenin, single-mindedly bent as he was (as were all Bolsheviks, including Alexandra Kollontai!) on the maintenance and strengthening of the monopoly of power held by the Communist party. His decision to counter the Kronstadters' protest against the Bolshevik perversion of Soviet power with what Martov denounced as a new *Zubatovshchina* of 'purely economic concessions without a change in the political order'[45] marked a turning point, if not the terminal point, in the history of the Russian revolution. Lenin's response blocked what was still left of the revolution's political open-endedness, completed the formation of the highly centralized and bureaucratized single-party dictatorship, and put Russia firmly on the road to Stalinism.

In the very centre of that fateful historical decision, and of the tragedy of the Russian revolution, stood Red Kronstadt, its 'pride and glory'. Its sailors, soldiers and workers had enthusiastically enlisted in the front ranks of the October revolution and in the civil war, trusting that Soviet power would make the whole of Russia into one large Soviet democracy like their Kronstadt. Now it was they who found themselves in brutal confrontation with a Bolshevik power which had snuffed out their dream of egalitarian democracy and executed their Anatolii Lamanov as a 'counter-revolutionary'.

The *Krasnyi Kronshtadt* of 18 March 1921 trumpeted 'the return of Soviet power':

> Foiled are the Kadets' plots,
> Beaten their last black trump,
> Kronstadt lies at our feet,
> Adamantine is Soviet power![46]

Adamantine or not, it certainly made sure that prostrate Kronstadt would not rise again, and that its Soviet democracy would remain but an unfulfilled promise of the Russian revolution.

Notes

PREFACE

1 *Pravda o Kronshtadte* (Prague, 1921); N. Kornatovsky (ed.), *Kronshtadtskii miatezh: sbornik statei, vospominanii i dokumentov* (Leningrad, 1931); A. S. Pukhov, *Kronshtadtskii miatezh v 1921 godu* (Leningrad, 1931); Paul Avrich, *Kronstadt 1921* (Princeton, 1970); Evan Mawdsley, 'The Baltic Fleet and the Kronstadt Mutiny', *Soviet Studies*, vol. 24, no. 4, April 1973, pp. 506–21; S. N. Semanov, *Likvidatsiia antisovetskogo Kronshtadtskogo miatezha 1921 goda* (Moscow, 1973). For detailed bibliographies on the 1921 uprising consult Avrich, *Kronstadt 1921* and Kornatovsky, *Kronshtadskii miatezh.*
2 Evan Mawdsley, *The Russian Revolution and the Baltic Fleet: War and Politics, February 1917–April 1918* (London, 1978); Norman Saul, *Sailors in Revolt. The Russian Baltic Fleet in 1917* (Kansas, 1978); V. V. Petrash, *Moriaki baltiiskogo flota v bor'be za pobedu oktiabria* (Moscow–Leningrad, 1966); A. K. Drezen (ed.), *Baltiiskii flot v oktiabr'skoi revoliutsii i grazhdanskoi voine* (Moscow–Leningrad, 1932). Both Mawdsley, *Russian Revolution* and Saul, *Sailors in Revolt* contain excellent bibliographies on the Baltic Fleet.

I. A SAILORS' SAKHALIN

1 Estimate based on the statistical information in F. A. Timofeevsky, *Kratkii istoricheskii ocherk dvukhsotletiia goroda Kronshtadta* (Kronstadt, 1913), p. 127 and in V. V. Petrash, *Moriaki baltiiskogo flota v bor'be za pobedu oktiabria* (Moscow–Leningrad, 1966), p. 16.
2 L. T. Senchakova, *Revoliutsionnoe dvizhenie v russkoi armii i flote v kontse XIX-go nachale XX-go veka* (Moscow, 1972), p. 147.
3 A. K. Drezen (ed.), *Voennye vosstaniia v Baltike v 1905–1906gg.* (Moscow, 1933), pp. 25, 28; P. Z. Sivkov, *Kronshtadt: Stranitsy revoliutsionnoi istorii* (Leningrad, 1972), p. 147.
4 A. Drezen, *Revoliutsiia vo flote: Baltiiskie moriaki v vosstanii 1905–1906gg.* (Leningrad, 1926), p. 14.
5 R. [Fiodor] Raskolnikov, *Revoliutsionnyi flot* (Kronstadt, 1918), p. 4.
6 F. Kogan, *Kronshtadt v 1905–1906gg.* (Moscow, 1926), p. 8; Sivkov, *Kronshtadt*, p. 26; *Revoliutsiia 1905–1907gg. Dokumenty i materialy:*

Vysshiy pod'em revoliutsii 1905–1907gg. Vooruzhennoe vosstanie, noiabr'-dekabr 1905 goda (Moscow, 1953), Part 1, pp. 191, 846; Drezen, *Revoliutsiia vo flote*, p. 21.

7 Drezen, *Voennye vosstaniia*, p. 17.
8 *Ibid.*, pp. 17–18, 25–9.
9 *Vysshiy pod'em revoliutsii 1905–1907gg.*, Part 1, pp. 192–201; Drezen, *Voennye vosstaniia*, pp. 18–22; Kogan, *Kronshtadt*, pp. 9–13; Sivkov, *Kronshtadt*, pp. 27–9; G. Th. Tsivinsky, *50 let v imperatorskom flote* (Riga, 1923), p. 264; *1905 god v Peter'burge. Sbornik materialov*, issue no. 2 (Leningrad, 1925), p. 27.
10 L. Trotsky, *1905* (New York, 1972), pp. 166–8.
11 *Vysshiy pod'em revoliutsii 1905–1907gg.*, Part 1, p. 204.
12 Iu. Zubelevich (Dasha), *Kronshtadt v 1906 godu (vospominaniia revoliutsionera)*, 3 vols. (Kronstadt, 1917), vol. 1, p. 5; Drezen, *Voennye vosstaniia*, p. 101.
13 Drezen, *Voennye vosstaniia*, p. 101; Zubelevich, *Kronshtadt*, vol. 1, pp. 41–2, 44.
14 Drezen, *Voennye vosstaniia*, pp. 105–6, 108, 116; Zubelevich, *Kronshtadt*, vol. 3, pp. 86, 91.
15 Zubelevich, *Kronshtadt*, vol. 3, pp. 65–9; *Revoliutsiia 1905–1907gg. Vtoroi period revoliutsii: 1906–1907gg.*, vol. 2, Part 1 (Moscow, 1961), pp. 123–35.
16 'Kronshtadtskoe vosstanie 1906 goda', *Krasnyi arkhiv*, no. 4(77), 1936, p. 113.
17 N. Olshansky, 'Kronshtadtskoe vosstanie 1906 goda', *Krasnaia letopis'*, no. 5, 1922, pp. 199–200.
18 *Ibid.*, p. 197.
19 *Ibid.*, pp. 197–9; *Krasnyi arkhiv*, no. 6(43), 1930, pp. 166–7.
20 *Krasnyi arkhiv*, no. 6(43), 1930, p. 166; A. K. Drezen, 'Baltiiskii flot v gody reaktsii', *Krasnaia letopis'*, no. 4(31), 1929, pp. 39–40.
21 Drezen, 'Baltiiskii flot v gody reaktsii', p. 45.
22 *Krasnyi arkhiv*, no. 4(77), 1936, p. 113.
23 G. K. Graf, *Na 'Novike'. Baltiiskii flot v voinu i revoliutsii* (Munich, 1922), p. 291.
24 Gr. Kononov, 'Kronshtadttsy', *Moriak*, no. 11, 2 (15) September 1917, p. 242; Graf, *Na 'Novike'*, p. 291.
25 Pavel Dybenko, *V nedrakh tsarskogo flota* (Moscow, 1919), pp. 29–30.
26 Timofeevsky, *Kratkii istoricheskii ocherk*, p. 127; Petrash, *Moriaki baltiiskogo flota*, p. 16.
27 Quoted in A. Drezen, 'Baltiiskii flot v gody pod'ema', *Krasnaia letopis'*, no. 3(36), 1930, p. 145 and in K. F. Shatsillo, *Russkii imperializm i razvitie flota nakanune pervoi mirovoi voiny* (Moscow, 1968), p. 77.
28 Evan Mawdsley, *The Russian Revolution and the Baltic Fleet: War and Politics, February 1917–April 1918* (London, 1978), pp. 7, 157–9.
29 Petrash, *Moriaki baltiiskogo flota*, p. 21.
30 Quoted in M. A. Stoliarenko, *Syny partii – Baltiitsy* (Leningrad, 1966), p. 13.
31 Graf, *Na 'Novike'*, p. 363; Mawdsley, *Russian Revolution and Baltic Fleet*,

p. 2; Evan Mawdsley, 'The Baltic Fleet in the Russian Revolution', PhD thesis, University of London, 1972, p. 46.

32 *Mysli lichnago sostava o flote* (Kronstadt, 1913), issue no. 2, pp. 55, 108, 115.

33 Graf, *Na 'Novike'*, p. 363.

34 *Ibid.*, p. 355; Petrash, *Moriaki baltiiskogo flota*, pp. 31–2.

35 Timofeevsky, *Kratkii istoricheskii ocherk*, pp. 127–8.

36 Drezen, 'Baltiiskii flot v gody reaktsii', p. 72.

37 A. Drezen, 'Baltiiskii flot v gody pod'ema (okonchanie)', *Krasnaia letopis'*, no. 4(37), (1930), pp. 151–3.

38 *Ibid.*

39 Tomasz Parczewski, *Kronsztadt na tle rewolucji Rosyjskiej* (Warsaw, 1935), pp. 4–6.

40 Drezen, 'Baltiiskii flot v gody pod'ema', pp. 150–3.

41 *Ibid.*

42 Paris Okhrana Archive, Hoover Institution on War, Revolution and Peace, Stanford, XXIV K, no. 98558.

43 *Ibid.*, no. 1271.

44 Lenin to Maxim Gorky, 25 August 1912, V. I. Lenin, *Polnoe sobranie sochinenii*, 5th edn (55 vols., Moscow, 1958–65), vol. 48, p. 84.

45 A. L. Sidorov (ed.), *Revoliutsionnoe dvizhenie v armii i na flote v gody pervoi mirovoi voiny* (Moscow, 1968), pp. 315–16, 326–7.

46 A. K. Drezen, 'Armiia i flot v fevral'skoi revoliutsii', *Krasnaia letopis'*, nos. 1–2(46–7), 1932, p. 33; Sidorov, *Revoliutsionnoe dvizhenie*, pp. 318, 321, 323.

47 Iv. Egorov, 'Matrosy-bol'sheviki nakanune 1917 goda', *Krasnaia letopis'*, no. 3(18), 1926, p. 11.

48 *Ibid.*, pp. 12–13.

49 *Ibid.*, pp. 17–18.

50 *Ibid.*, pp. 20–9; *Krasnaia letopis'*, no. 4(19), 1926, pp. 68–76.

51 Sidorov, *Revoliutsionnoe dvizhenie*, pp. 378–87.

52 'Interesnyi istoricheskii dokument', *Izvestiia Kronshtadtskogo soveta*, no. 100, 20 July 1917.

53 *Ibid.*

2. THE FEBRUARY REVOLUTION IN KRONSTADT

1 Tomasz Parczewski, *Kronsztadt na tle rewolucji Rosyjskiej* (Warsaw, 1935), p. 15.

2 I. Zapisnoi, 'Svershilos', *Kotlin*, no. 52, 7 March 1917.

3 *Golos pravdy*, no. 27, 16 April 1917, quoted in P. Z. Sivkov, *Kronshtadt: Stranitsy revoliutsionnoi istorii* (Leningrad, 1972), p. 86.

4 Parczewski, *Kronsztadt*, p. 15; E. N. Burdzhalov, *Vtoraia russkaia revoliutsiia: Moskva, Front, Periferiia* (Moscow, 1971), p. 109.

5 O. L. D'Or, *Krasnyi chasovoi Kronshtadt* (Moscow, 1920), p. 6; A. P. Lukin, *Flot (russkie moriaki vo vremia velikoi voiny i revoliutsii)* (2 vols., Paris, [1933]), vol. 2, p. 182.

6 D'Or, *Krasnyi chasovoi Kronshtadt*, p. 6; *Baltiiskie moriaki v podgotovke i provedenii velikoi oktiabr'skoi sotsialisticheskoi revoliutsii* (Moscow–Leningrad, 1957), p. 20.

7 D'Or, *Krasnyi chasovoi Kronshtadt*, p. 7.

8 *Baltiiskie moriaki v podgotovke*, p. 20.

9 Quoted in S. S. Khesin, *Oktiabr'skaia revoliutsiia i flot* (Moscow, 1971), p. 42.

10 Parczewski, *Kronsztadt*, p. 16.

11 D'Or, *Krasnyi chasovoi Kronshtadt*, p. 6.

12 I. N. Kolbin, 'Kronshtadt ot fevralia do Kornilovskikh dnei', *Krasnaia letopis'*, no. 2(23), 1927, p. 135; the substance of Kolbin's account is confirmed by D'Or, *Krasnyi chasovoi Kronshtadt*, p. 7.

13 Egor Oreshnikov, 'Ispoved revoliutsionera', *Kotlin*, no. 61, 17 March 1917.

14 *Ibid.*; Kolbin, 'Kronshtadt ot fevralia do Kornilovskikh dnei', p. 137; *Baltiiskie moriaki v podgotovke*, pp. 20–1; *Izvestiia Kronshtadtskogo soveta*, no. 10, 30 March 1917.

15 *Baltiiskie moriaki v podgotovke*, p. 21; F. F. Raskolnikov, *Kronshtadt i Piter v 1917 godu* (Moscow, 1925), p. 24.

16 A. K. Drezen, 'Armiia i flot v fevral'skoi revoliutsii', *Krasnaia letopis'*, nos. 1–2(46–7), 1932, p. 55.

17 I. Zverkov, 'Istoricheskaia noch'' na 1 marta 1917g.', *Trud, zemlia i more*, no. 16, 10 May 1917; D'Or, *Krasnyi chasovoi Kronshtadt*, pp. 9–10; E. Yarchuk, *Kronshtadt v russkoi revoliutsii* (New York, 1923), p. 5; *Baltiiskie moriaki v podgotovke*; Kolbin, 'Kronshtadt ot fevralia do Kornilovskikh dnei', pp. 137–8; Parczewski, *Kronsztadt*, p. 25.

18 Arvid Drezen, 'Finlandiia i mestnye garnizony v 1906–7gg.', *Krasnaia letopis'*, no. 1(21), 1929, p. 121.

19 *Baltiiskie moriaki v podgotovke*, p. 48; Parczewski, *Kronsztadt*, p. 22.

20 Raskolnikov, *Kronshtadt i Piter*, p. 24; D'Or, *Krasnyi chasovoi Kronshtadt*, p. 10; G. K. Graf, *Na 'Novike'. Baltiiskii flot v voinu i revoliutsii* (Munich, 1922), p. 291.

21 As reported by G. Ivanov, chairman of the Investigation Commission of the Kronstadt Soviet, in *Kotlin*, no. 67, 25 March 1917; Parczewski, *Kronsztadt*, p. 25. However, Kronstadt's first commissar Victor Pepeliaev quoted a figure of fifty-one victims all told, A. K. Drezen (ed.), *Burzhuaziia i pomeshchiki v 1917 godu* (Moscow–Leningrad, 1932), p. 80.

22 Parczewski, *Kronsztadt*, p. 53.

23 *Kotlin*, no. 49, 3 March 1917; *Baltiiskie moriaki v podgotovke*, p. 48.

24 V. V. Petrash, *Moriaki baltiiskogo flota v bor'be za pobedu oktiabria* (Moscow–Leningrad, 1966), pp. 52–3.

25 Parczewski, *Kronsztadt*, p. 21; D'Or, *Krasnyi chasovoi Kronshtadt*, p. 10; A. Blinov, 'Pervye revoliutsionnye organy vlasti v Kronshtadte v 1917 godu', in S. F. Naida (ed.), *Voennye moriaki v bor'be za pobedu oktiabr'skoi revoliutsii* (Moscow, 1958), p. 136.

26 Parczewski, *Kronsztadt*, pp. 20–1.

27 N. Shaposhnikov, 'Soldatam i matrosam (1-go marta)', *Izvestiia Kr.*

soveta, no. 16, 7 April 1917; in a similar vein, the last lines of I. Zverkov's poem, 'Istoricheskaia noch' Kronshtadta na 1-go marta 1917g.', *Trud, zemlia i more*, no. 16, 10 May 1917:
> Hard to believe it: wide open are the prisons,
> The world is aglow with the light of liberty.
> All this happened on the First of March.

28 While in the cable which the 'Committee' sent on 2 March to the Duma Committee and to the Petrograd Soviet it referred to itself as the 'Provisional Kronstadt Committee of the National Movement', it signed the cable as the 'Kronstadt Committee of the National Movement', *Kotlin*, no. 49, 3 March 1917.

29 D'Or, *Krasnyi chasovoi Kronshtadt*, pp. 10–12; Blinov, 'Pervye revoliutsionnye organy vlasti', pp. 134–5.

30 *Kronshtadtskii vestnik*, no. 49, 3 March 1917, no. 51, 5 March 1917; Blinov, 'Pervye revoliutsionnye organy vlasti', pp. 134–6.

31 *Kronshtadtskii vestnik*, no. 51, 5 March 1917.

32 I. Zapisnoi, 'Svershilos''; 'Gorodskaia militsiia', *ibid.*

33 Quoted in Burdzhalov, *Vtoraia russkaia revoliutsiia*, pp. 111–12.

34 *Kronshtadtskii vestnik*, no. 49, 3 March 1917.

35 *Ibid.*

36 See the masthead of *Kronshtadtskii vestnik*, no. 51, 5 March 1917; *Revoliutsionnoe dvizhenie v Rossii posle sverzheniia samoderzhaviia* (Moscow, 1957), p. 623.

37 *Kotlin*, no. 49, 3 March 1917.

38 *Baltiiskie moriaki v podgotovke*, p. 22.

39 Drezen (ed.), *Burzhuaziia i pomeshchiki*, p. 74.

40 *Kotlin*, no. 51, 5 March 1917.

41 Drezen (ed.), *Burzhuaziia i pomeshchiki*, p. 75; Burdzhalov, *Vtoraia russkaia revoliutsiia*, p. 113; 'Postanovleniia sobraniia predstavitelei garnizona Kronshtadtskoi kreposti 3-go marta 1917 goda', *Kronshtadtskii vestnik*, no. 51, 5 March 1917.

42 *Kotlin*, no. 51, 5 March 1917.

43 *Kotlin*, no. 53, 8 March 1917, no. 54, 9 March 1917.

44 *Kotlin*, no. 55, 10 March 1917.

45 *Kotlin*, no. 52, 7 March 1917; *Revoliutsionnoe dvizhenie posle sverzheniia*, p. 384.

46 *Kotlin*, no. 53, 8 March 1917; *Revoliutsionnoe dvizhenie posle sverzheniia*, p. 384.

47 *Kotlin*, no. 55, 10 March 1917.

48 *Kronshtadtskii vestnik*, no. 54, 8 March 1917 quoted in Blinov, 'Pervye revoliutsionnye organy vlasti', p. 139; Burdzhalov, *Vtoraia russkaia revoliutsiia*, p. 115.

49 Blinov, 'Pervye revoliutsionnye organy vlasti', p. 142.

50 Skobennikov, 'Zhenshchiny organizuites'!', *Kotlin*, no. 57, 12 March 1917.

51 *Revoliutsionnoe dvizhenie posle sverzheniia*, p. 386.

52 *Kotlin*, no. 57, 12 March 1917.

53 *Kotlin*, no. 61, 17 March 1917.

54 *Kotlin*, no. 60, 16 March 1917.
55 Drezen (ed.), *Burzhuaziia i pomeshchiki*, p. 79; Burdzhalov, *Vtoraia russkaia revoliutsiia*, p. 117; A. Liubovich, 'Otzhivshee', *Izvestiia Kr. soveta*, no. 51, 21 May 1917.
56 *Kotlin*, no. 54, 9 March 1917; Sivkov, *Kronshtadt*, p. 96.
57 'V Kronshtadte', *Rech'*, no. 64, 16 March 1917.
58 Drezen (ed.), *Burzhuaziia i pomeshchiki*, p. 79; *Kotlin*, no. 72, 1 April 1917.
59 *Kronshtadtskaia iskra*, no. 22, July 1917.
60 Drezen (ed.), *Burzhuaziia i pomeshchiki*, p. 78.
61 *Kotlin*, no. 62, 18 March 1917; Burdzhalov, *Vtoraia russkaia revoliutsiia*, p. 114.
62 *Izvestiia Kr. soveta*, no. 15, 6 April 1917.
63 *Ibid.*, no. 1, 17 March 1917, quoted in Blinov, 'Pervye revoliutsionnye organy vlasti', p. 143.
64 Burdzhalov, *Vtoraia russkaia revoliutsiia*, p. 115.
65 *Kronshtadtskii vestnik*, no. 60, 15 March 1917; *Kotlin*, no. 67, 25 March 1917.
66 *Kronshtadtskii vestnik*, no. 58, 12 March 1917.
67 Iv. Egorov, 'Materialy o revoliutsionnom dvizhenie vo flote v 1910–1911gg.', *Krasnaia letopis'*, no. 5, 1922, p. 378; Ochevidets, 'Pervaia zhertva Baltiiskogo flota', *Moriak*, no. 8, 12 August 1917, p. 170.
68 *Revoliutsionnoe dvizhenie posle sverzheniia*, p. 256.
69 Drezen (ed.), *Burzhuaziia i pomeshchiki*, p. 79.
70 *Ibid.*
71 *Kotlin*, no. 67, 25 March 1917; *Izvestiia Kr. soveta*, no. 66, 8 June 1917.
72 Drezen (ed.), *Burzhuaziia i pomeshchiki*, p. 79.
73 *Izvestiia Kr. soveta*, no. 26, 20 April 1917.
74 Blinov, 'Pervye revoliutsionnye organy vlasti', p. 144.
75 *Izvestiia Kr. soveta*, no. 9, 29 March 1917.
76 *Ibid.*, no. 14, 5 April 1917.
77 *Kotlin*, no. 62, 18 March 1917.
78 Petrash, *Moriaki baltiiskogo flota*, p. 73; *Sed'maia (aprel'skaia) vserossiiskaia konferentsiia RSDRP (bol'shevikov)* (Moscow, 1958), pp. 125, 279; *Krasnaia letopis'*, nos. 5–6(56–7), 1933, p. 213; Blinov, 'Pervye revoliutsionnye organy', p. 142.
79 Evgorov, 'Materialy o revoliutsionnom dvizhenie vo flote 1910–11gg.', p. 381.
80 *Delo naroda*, no. 37, 30 April 1917.
81 N. Avdeev (ed.), *Revoliutsiia 1917 goda (khronika sobytii)* (vols. 1 and 2, Moscow–Petrograd, 1923), vol. 2, pp. 103, 219, 227; Vera Vladimirova (ed.), *Revoliutsiia 1917 goda (khronika sobytii)*, vol. 3 (Moscow–Petrograd, 1923), pp. 144, 177, vol. 4, p. 39; *Delo naroda*, no. 40, 4 May 1917.
82 For SR-Maximalist ideology see below, pp. 135–40.
83 *Izvestiia Kr. soveta*, no. 34, 29 April 1917; *ibid.*, no. 49, 8 May 1917, no. 160, 3 October 1917; N. Solntsev, 'K momentu', *Kommuna*, no. 6, September 1917; for an examination of the two wings of Russian

Anarchism in 1917, see Peter Gooderham, 'The Role and Influence of the Anarchist Movement in Petrograd, February–October 1917', paper presented to the Study Group on the Russian Revolution, January 1981.

84 *Izvestiia Kr. soveta*, no. 137, 3 September 1917.

85 A. Drezen, 'Baltiiskii flot v gody pod'ema', *Krasnaia letopis'*, no. 3(36), 1930, p. 149.

86 Sivkov, *Kronshtadt*, p. 85; Petrash, *Moriaki baltiiskogo flota*, pp. 46–7; Khesin, *Oktiabr'skaia revoliutsiia*, pp. 41–2; *Baltiiskie moriaki v podgotovke*, p. 20; *but* see David Longley, 'Some Historiographical Problems of Bolshevik History (The Kronstadt Bolsheviks in March 1917)', *Jahrbuecher fuer die Geschichte Osteuropas*, no. 4 (1974), pp. 494–514.

87 See the review of F. Raskolnikov's *Kronshtadttsy*, signed by a group of veteran Kronstadt Bolsheviks including P. Smirnov, D. Kondakov, A. Liubovich, A. Gertsberg, M. Pozdeeva and S. Entin, *Krasnaia letopis'*, nos. 5–6(56–7), 1933, p. 212.

88 *Ibid.*

89 F. N. Dingelshtedt, 'Vesna proletarskoi revoliutsii', *Krasnaia letopis'*, no. 1(12), 1925, p. 195; I. Gordienko, 'V Kronshtadte v 1917 g.', *Krasnaia letopis'*, no. 1(16), 1926, pp. 52, 54; also *Krasnaia letopis'*, no. 6(21), 1926, pp. 185–9; *Pravda*, no. 2, 7 March 1917.

90 B. Ia. Nalivaiskii (ed.), *Petrogradskii sovet rabochikh i soldatskikh deputatov: protokoly sasedanii Ispolnitel'nogo Komiteta i Biuro I. K.* (Leningrad, 1925), p. 13; *Kotlin*, no. 52, 7 March 1917.

91 Drezen, 'Armiia i flot v fevral'skoi revoliutsii', p. 273.

92 I. Zapisnoi, 'K momentu', *Kotlin*, no. 55, 10 March 1917.

93 Fiodor D., 'Kronshtadt', *Pravda*, no. 6, 11 March 1917.

94 'Postanovlenie Kronshtadtskogo soveta voennykh deputatov', *Kotlin*, no. 62, 18 March 1917.

95 A. K. Drezen (ed.), *Baltiiskii flot v oktiabr'skoi revoliutsii i grazhdanskoi voine* (Moscow–Leningrad, 1932), p. iii.

96 I. F. Kudelli (ed.), *Pervyi legal'nyi Peterburgskii komitet bol'shevikov v 1917 g.* (Moscow–Leningrad, 1927), pp. 52–3, 57.

97 Raskolnikov, *Kronshtadt i Piter*, p. 48.

98 *Kotlin*, no. 70, 30 March 1917.

99 *Izvestiia Kr. soveta*, no. 15, 6 April 1917.

100 R. Raskolnikov, 'Revoliutsiia i burzhuaziia', *Golos pravdy*, no. 24, 13 April 1917.

101 'Grazhdane matrosy, soldaty i rabochie!', *Golos pravdy*, no. 24, 13 April 1917.

102 R. Raskolnikov, 'Revoliutsionnyi Kronshtadt', *Pravda*, no. 23, 15 April 1917.

103 *Izvestiia Gel'singforskogo soveta deputatov armii, flota i rabochikh Sveaborgskogo porta v gor. Gel'singforse*, no. 21, 9 April 1917.

104 *Rech'*, no. 78, 5 April 1917, no. 81, 8 April 1917.

105 *Izvestiia Kr. soveta*, no. 22, 14 April 1917, no. 24, 16 April 1917, no. 25, 18 April 1917; Sivkov, *Kronshtadt*, pp. 145–6.

106 *Delo naroda*, no. 37, 30 April 1917.

107 *Izvestiia Kr. soveta*, no. 11, 1 April 1917.
108 *Ibid.*, no. 20, 12 April 1917.
109 *Volna*, no. 60, 13 June 1917.
110 *Izvestiia Kr. soveta*, no. 24, 16 April 1917.
111 *Ibid.*, no. 20, 12 April 1917.
112 Nik. Rostov, 'V Kronshtadte', *Izvestiia Gel'singforskogo soveta*, no. 75, 15 June 1917.
113 'Polozhenie o sovete rabochikh i soldatskikh deputatov', *Izvestiia Kr. soveta*, no. 37, 3 May 1917, no. 38, 4 May 1917; 'Instruktsiia po mestnym komitetam', *ibid.*, no. 40, 6 May 1917.
114 *Izvestiia Kr. soveta*, no. 69, 11 June 1917.
115 *Ibid.*, no. 71, 14 June 1917.
116 *Ibid.*, no. 119, 11 August 1917.
117 See 'Instruktsiia po mestnym komitetam', *Izvestiia Kr. soveta*, no. 40, 6 May 1917.
118 *Sverzhenie samorderzhaviia, sbornik statei* (Moscow, 1970), p. 191; *Revoliutsionnoe dvizhenie posle sverzheniia*, p. 633.
119 P. F., 'Pervye itogi', *Izvestiia Kr. soveta*, no. 24, 16 April 1917.
120 Philips Price, *My Reminiscences of the Russian Revolution* (London, 1921), pp. 39–40.
121 *Izvestiia Kr. soveta*, no. 69, 11 June 1917.
122 Rostov, 'V Kronshtadte'.
123 *Krasnaia letopis'*, nos. 5–6(56–7), 1933, p. 216.
124 A. Liubovich, 'Itogi', *Izvestiia Kr. soveta*, no. 30, 25 April 1917.
125 Price, *My Reminiscences*, p. 35.
126 *Rospisanie admiralov, generalov, shtab i Ober-Ofitserov grazhdanskikh i meditsinskikh chinov beregovogo sostava* (Petersburg, 1913), p. 42.
127 D'Or, *Krasnyi chasovoi Kronshtadt*, p. 16; Price, *My Reminiscences*, pp. 35–6.
128 D.I.K., 'Sotsial'naia revoliutsiia iz Kronshtadta', *Rabochaia gazeta*, no. 91, 27 June 1917.
129 *Izvestiia Kr. soveta*, no. 19, 11 April 1917.
130 *Izvestiia Kr. soveta*, no. 14, 5 April 1917, no. 34, 29 April 1917.
131 *Ibid.*, no. 33, 28 April 1917; Skobennikov, 'Znanie svet', *Izvestiia Kr. soveta*, no. 23, 15 April 1917.
132 V. Popeliavsky, 'Nuzhno kovat' svobodu', *Izvestiia Kr. soveta*, no. 20, 12 April 1917.
133 Antoshevsky, 'Strannoe iavlenie', *Izvestiia Kr. soveta*, no. 25, 18 April 1917.
134 *Golos pravdy*, no. 46, 10 May 1917.
135 *Bol'sheviki Petrograda v 1917 godu. Khronika sobytii* (Leningrad, 1957), pp. 259, 372; Sivkov, *Kronshtadt*, pp. 147–8; *Trud, zemlia i more*, no. 19, 14 May 1917.
136 'V Kronshtadte', *Rech'*, no. 168, 10 July 1917.
137 The session is reported in *Izvestiia Kr. soveta*, no. 30, 25 April and no. 31, 26 April 1917; see also A. Lamanov, 'Bor'ba i spokoistvie', *ibid.*, no. 28, 22 April 1917.
138 *Izvestiia Kr. soveta*, no. 30, 25 April 1917.

139 'Vlast' naroda', *Golos pravdy*, no. 30, 21 April 1917; see also Fiodor D., 'Kharakter russkoi revoliutsii', *ibid.*

140 *Revoliutsionnoe dvizhenie v Rossii v aprele 1917g. aprel'skii krizis* (Moscow, 1958), pp. 769–70.

141 *Ibid.*, pp. 760–1.

142 Raskolnikov, *Kronshtadt i Piter*, pp. 59–60.

143 *Izvestiia Kr. soveta*, no. 31, 26 April 1917.

144 *Vserossiiskoe soveshchanie sovetov rabochikh i soldatskikh deputatov* (Moscow–Leningrad, 1927), pp. 54, 289.

145 *Izvestiia Kr. soveta*, no. 19, 11 April 1917.

146 *Ibid.*

147 *Izvestiia Kr. soveta*, no. 35, 30 April 1917.

148 *Ibid.*

149 *Sed'maia (aprel'skaia) konferentsiia RSDRP*, p. 136.

150 *Izvestiia Kr. soveta*, no. 40, 6 May 1917.

151 *Izvestiia Kr. soveta*, no. 38, 4 May 1917.

152 *Golos pravdy*, no. 40, 4 May 1917.

153 *Izvestiia Kr. soveta*, no. 40, 6 May 1917; for the latter section of the debate published in no. 41, 7 May 1917 and not available to me, I have relied on the summary in I. Flerovsky, 'Kronshtadtskaia respublika', *Proletarskaia revoliutsiia*, no. 11(58), 1926, pp. 52–5.

154 Flerovsky, 'Kronshtadtskaia respublika', p. 55.

155 *Izvestiia Kr. soveta*, n. 44, 11 May 1917.

156 *Izvestiia Gel'singforskogo soveta*, no. 75, 15 June 1917.

3. THE KRONSTADT REPUBLIC

1 See the Declaration of the provisional government of 5 May 1917 as well as the statements of the Petrograd Soviet and of Iraklii Tseretelli, in R. P. Browder and A. F. Kerensky (eds.), *The Russian Provisional Government 1917* (3 vols., Stanford, 1961), vol. 3, pp. 1277–9.

2 *Izvestiia Kronshtadtskogo soveta*, no. 38, 4 May 1917; *Kotlin*, no. 52, 7 May 1917; D. N. Kondakov, 'Krepost' revoliutsii', in *V ogne revoliutsionnykh boev: Raiony Petrograda v dvukh revoliutsiiakh 1917g.* (2 vols., Moscow, 1967–71), vol. 1, p. 336.

3 *Izvestiia Kr. soveta*, no. 66, 8 June 1917.

4 *Ibid.*, no. 70, 13 June 1917.

5 *Ibid.*, no. 46, 14 May 1917.

6 A. K. Drezen (ed.), *Burzhuaziia i pomeshchiki v 1917 godu* (Moscow–Leningrad, 1932), p. 87.

7 *Ibid.*, p. 86; *Izvestiia Kr. soveta*, no. 50, 19 May 1917.

8 Drezen (ed.), *Burzhuaziia i pomeshchiki*, pp. 86–7.

9 *Izvestiia Kr. soveta*, no. 66, 8 June 1917.

10 The debate is reported in *Izvestiia Kr. soveta*, no. 54, 25 May 1917, no. 55, 26 May 1917, no. 56, 27 May 1917.

11 *Izvestiia Kr. soveta*, no. 56, 27 May 1917.

12 P. Golikov, 'Iz Kronshtadtskikh nastroenii', *Rabochaia gazeta*, no. 61, 20 May 1917.

13 The debate is reported in *Izvestiia Kr. soveta*, nos. 69–71, 11, 13 and 14 June 1917.

14 *Ibid.*, no. 48, 17 May 1917.

15 *Ibid.*, no. 69, 19 June 1917; F. F. Raskolnikov, *Kronshtadt i Piter v 1917 godu* (Moscow, 1925), p. 68; Golikov, 'Iz Kronshtadtskikh nastroenii'.

16 *Izvestiia Kr. soveta*, no. 70, 13 June 1917, no. 71, 14 June 1917.

17 *Ibid.*, no. 71, 14 June 1917.

18 A. Liubovich, 'Otzhivshee', *Izvestiia Kr. soveta*, no. 51, 21 May 1917.

19 *Golos pravdy*, no. 53, 19 May 1917, quoted in *Baltiiskie moriaki v podgotovke i provedenii velikoi oktiabr'skoi sotsialisticheskoi revoliutsii* (Moscow–Leningrad, 1957), p. 71.

20 A. Kh., 'Kronshtadtskaia respublika', *Trud, zemlia i more*, no. 28, 26 May 1917.

21 *Rech'*, no. 118, 19 May 1917.

22 'Prosim otvergnut' ', *Edinstvo*, no. 55, 3 June 1917; *Volna*, no. 57, 21 (8) June 1917; Vl. Blokhin, 'Kronshtadtskaia respublika', *Izvestiia Kr. soveta*, no. 67, 9 April 1918; P. Z. Sivkov, *Kronshtadt: Stranitsy revoliutsionnoi istorii* (Leningrad, 1972), pp. 188, 245.

23 *Birzhevye vedomosti*, no. 16254, 28 May 1917, no. 16256, 30 May 1917.

24 *Novoe vremia*, no. 14782, 20 May 1917.

25 Peregrinus, 'Kronshtadt: Vpechatleniia', *Delo naroda*, no. 57, 25 May 1917.

26 I. Vesenev, 'Kronshtadtskie tiur'my', *Novoe vremia*, no. 14786, 26 May 1917.

27 Robert Crozier Young, 'V Kronshtadtskikh tiur'makh', *Rech'*, no. 122, 27 May 1917.

28 Evgenii Trupp, 'Kronshtadtskie tiur'my', *Delo naroda*, no. 64, 2 June 1917.

29 Philips Price, *My Reminiscences of the Russian Revolution* (London, 1921), pp. 38–9.

30 *Izvestiia Kr. soveta*, no. 49, 18 May 1917.

31 N. Stroev, 'Lishit' Kronshtadt ognia i vody', *Novaia zhizn'*, no. 35, 30 May 1917.

32 Iu. Kamenev, 'Kronshtadt', *Pravda*, no. 62, 20 May 1917.

33 V. I. Lenin, 'Odin printsipial'nyi vopros', *Pravda*, no. 68, 28 May 1917, reprinted in Lenin, *Polnoe sobranie sochinenii*, 5th edn (55 vols., Moscow, 1958–65), vol. 32, pp. 218–21.

34 'Nabroski k tezisam resoliutsii o sovetakh', in *ibid.*, vol. 31, pp. 382–6.

35 Raskolnikov, *Kronshtadt i Piter*, pp. 68–71; F. Raskolnikov, 'Tov. Lenin i Kronshtadtskaia "Respublika"', *Krasnaia Letopis'*, no. 1(10), 1924, p. 49.

36 I. F. Kudelli (ed.), *Pervyi legal'nyi Peterburgskii komitet bol'shevikov v 1917 g.* (Moscow–Leningrad, 1927), p. 120.

37 Al. Ustinov-Bezzemel'nyi, 'Anarkhiia v Kronshtadte', *Zemlia i volia*, no. 50, 25 May 1917.

38 I. Bezrabotnyi,' O vol'nom gorode Kronshtadt', *Vpered*, no. 1, 2 June 1917.

39 N. Avdeev (ed.), *Revoliutsiia 1917 goda (khronika sobytii)* (vols. 1 and 2, Moscow–Petrograd, 1923), vol. 2, p. 200.

40 Pr-ov, 'Tsimmerval'd v gost'isakh u Kronshtadta', *Zemlia i volia*, no. 50, 25 May 1917.

41 Tomasz Parczewski, *Kronsztadt na tle rewolucji Rosyjskiej* (Warsaw, 1935), p. 40.

42 *Izvestiia Kr. soveta*, no. 51, 21 May 1917.

43 *Zemlia i volia*, no. 50, 25 May 1917.

44 I. Flerovsky, 'Kronshtadtskaia respublika', *Proletarskaia revoliutsiia*, no. 12(59), 1926, p. 128; Raskolnikov, *Kronshtadt i Piter*, pp. 72–3.

45 The session was reported in *Izvestiia Kr. soveta*, no. 76, 19 June 1917 and reprinted in *Proletarskaia revoliutsiia*, no. 12(59), 1926, pp. 153–8.

46 'Ot Ispolnitel'nogo Komiteta Kronshtadtskogo Soveta Rabochikhi Soldatskikh Deputatov', *Izvestiia Kr. soveta*, no. 53, 24 May 1917; *Proletarskaia revoliutsiia*, no. 12(59), 1926, p. 158.

47 *Rech'*, no. 119, 24 May 1917.

48 This account of the session of the Petrograd Soviet of 22 May is based on the reports published in *Novaia zhizn'*, no. 30, 24 May 1917; *Izvestiia Petrogradskogo soveta*, no. 73, 24 May 1917; *Rech'*, no. 119, 24 May 1917; Flerovsky, 'Kronshtadtskaia respublika', pp. 132–3.

49 See Raskolnikov, *Kronshtadt i Piter*, p. 68, also R. Raskolnikov, 'Kronshtadtskie dela', *Volna*, no. 43, 23 May 1917.

50 *Zhurnaly zasedanii Vremennogo Pravitel'stva*, no. 87, p. 66, 22 May 1917; I. G. Tseretelli, *Vospominaniia o fevral'skoi revoliutsii* (2 vols., Paris–The Hague, 1963), vol. 1, p. 414.

51 See Tseretelli's cables to the Executive Committee of the Petrograd Soviet and to the provisional government in *Rabochaia gazeta*, no. 7, 6 March 1917, no. 8, 7 March 1917.

52 *Izvestiia Petrogradskogo soveta*, no. 20, 21 March 1917, no. 29, 31 March 1917.

53 See Tseretelli's speeches of 3 April and 27 April 1917 in *Rechi I. G. Tseretelli* (Petrograd, 1917), pp. 21, 58, 60.

54 *Rechi I. G. Tseretelli*, p. 153; N. N. Sukhanov, *Zapiski o revoliutsii* (7 vols., Berlin–Petersburg–Moscow, 1922–3), vol. 3, pp. 419–20; Tseretelli, *Vospominaniia o fevral'skoi revoliutsii*, vol. 1, p. 142.

55 Raskolnikov, *Kronshtadt i Piter*, p. 71.

56 Tseretelli, *Vospominaniia o fevral'skoi revoliutsii*, vol. 1, pp. 418–19.

57 The debate was reported in *Izvestiia Kr. soveta*, no. 59, 31 May 1917, no. 60, 1 June 1917, no. 61, 2 June 1917 and reprinted in *Proletarskaia revoliutsiia*, no. 12(59), 1926, pp. 159–70.

58 For a report of the second (evening) session of 24 May 1917 see *Izvestiia Kr. soveta*, no. 62, 3 June 1917, no. 63, 4 June 1917 and reprinted in *Proletarskaia revoliutsiia*, no. 12(59), 1926, pp. 170–6.

59 Raskolnikov, *Kronshtadt i Piter*, p. 76.

60 *Zhurnaly zasedanii Vremennogo Pravitel'stva*, no. 88, 24 May 1917, p. 67; Tseretelli, *Vospominaniia o fevral'skoi revoliutsii*, vol. 1, pp. 422–3.

61 Vl. Voitinsky, 'Gody pobed i porazhenii: 1917 god', MS, pp. 132–3, Hoover Institution; Parczewski, *Kronsztadt*, p. 42; *Izvestiia Kr. soveta*, no. 55, 26 May 1917, no. 77, 21 June 1917.

62 For Parchevsky's interview of 30 May 1917 see 'Kronshtadt', *Rech'*, no. 125, 31 May 1917; *Novaia zhizn'*, no. 36, 31 May 1917.

63 *Rech'*, no. 122, 27 May 1917; Raskolnikov, *Kronshtadt i Piter*, pp. 76–7; 'Pobeda Kronshtadtskogo soveta rabochikh i soldatskikh deputatov', *Golos pravdy*, 26 May 1917, quoted in A. I-Zh., 'Bol'shevistskie gazety Kronshtadta i Gel'singforsa v 1917g.', *Krasnaia letopis'*, no. 3(24), 1927, p. 96 and in Sivkov, *Kronshtadt*, p. 197.

64 Raskolnikov, *Kronshtadt i Piter*, p. 77.

65 *Izvestiia Kr. soveta*, no. 55, 26 May 1917.

66 Voitinsky, 'Gody pobed i porazhenii', p. 136.

67 *Izvestiia Petrogradskogo soveta*, no. 76, 27 May 1917; Avdeev, *Revoliutsiia 1917 goda*, vol. 2, p. 209.

68 L. Martov, 'Kronshtadt', *Sotsialisticheskii vestnik*, no. 5, 3 April 1921; I. Deutscher, *The Prophet Armed: Trotsky 1879–1921* (London, 1970), p. 261.

69 *Pervyi vserossiiskii s'ezd sovetov rabochikh i soldatskikh deputatov* (2 vols., Moscow–Leningrad, 1930), vol. 1, p. 203; Voitinsky, 'Gody pobed i porazhenii', p. 136.

70 Avdeev, *Revoliutsiia 1917 goda*, vol. 2, p. 209.

71 Raskolnikov, *Kronshtadt i Piter*, p. 77.

72 The meeting was reported in *Izvestiia Kr. soveta*, no. 74, 17 June 1917, reprinted in *Proletarskaia revoliutsiia*, no. 12(59), 1926, pp. 177–81.

73 The text of the Appeal is in *Proletarskaia revoliutsiia*, no. 12(59), 1926, pp. 182–4.

74 E. Yarchuk, *Kronshtadt v russkoi revoliutsii* (New York, 1923), p. 7.

75 Nik. Ivan. Tupikov, 'Otboi', *Trud, zemlia i more*, no. 31, 30 May 1917.

76 *Izvestiia Kr. soveta*, no. 77, 21 June 1917.

77 *Zhurnaly zasedanii Vremennogo Pravitel'stva*, no. 94, 30 May 1917, p. 81; Parczewski, *Kronsztadt*, p. 45.

78 Vera Vladimirova (ed.), *Revoliutsiia 1917 goda (khronika sobytii)*, vol. 3 (Moscow–Petrograd, 1923), p. 1; *Izvestiia Kr. soveta*, no. 59, 31 May 1917.

79 *Izvestiia Kr. soveta*, no. 67, 9 June 1917.

80 P. Ediet, 'Pri osobom mnenii', *Izvestiia Kr. soveta*, no. 67, 9 June 1917.

81 This account of Kronstadt's part in the abortive demonstration of 10 June is based on I. Flerovsky, 'Iiul'skii politicheskii urok', *Proletarskaia revoliutsiia*, no. 7(54), 1926, pp. 60–7; also see *Baltiiskie moriaki v podgotovke*, p. 91.

82 *Novaia zhizn'*, no. 46, 11 June 1917.

83 *Golos pravdy*, no. 72, 11 June 1917, reprinted in *Baltiiskie moriaki v podgotovke*, pp. 89–90.

84 Sivkov, *Kronshtadt*, p. 218; Flerovsky, 'Iiul'skii politicheskii urok', pp. 68–9.

85 *Krasnaia letopis'*, nos. 5–6(56–7), 1933, p. 215.

86 *Izvestiia Kr. soveta*, no. 69, 11 June 1917.

87 'K tekushchemu momentu revoliutsii', 'Sladko pel solovei', 'O chem dumaet Tseretelli?', *Golos pravdy*, no. 71, 10 June 1917.

88 Voitinsky, 'Gody pobed i porazhenii', p. 127.

89 *Ibid.*, p. 126.
90 *Ibid.*, pp. 126–7.
91 *Izvestiia Soveta deputatov armii flota i rabochikh Abo-Olandskoi ukreplennoi pozitsii v gor. Abo*, no. 64, 18 June 1917.
92 *Izvestiia Kr. soveta*, no. 77, 21 June 1917.
93 Flerovsky, 'Iiul'skii politicheskii urok', p. 71; 'V Kronshtadte', *Novaia zhizn'*, no. 57, 24 June 1917.
94 *Rech'*, no. 144, 22 June 1917; Vladimirova, *Revoliutsiia 1917 goda*, vol. 3, pp. 100, 105, 108.
95 *Revoliutsionnoe dvizhenie v Rossii v mae–iune 1917g.* (Moscow, 1959), pp. 347, 416, 418, 421; 'Kronshtadtskie emissary', *Rech'*, no. 142, 20 June 1917.
96 A. Nemm, 'O samosudakh', *Izvestiia Kr. soveta*, no. 75, 18 June 1917; Evg. Trupp, 'V Kronshtadte', *Delo naroda*, no. 80, 21 June 1917.
97 The debate is reported in *Izvestiia Kr. soveta*, no. 84, 29 June 1917.
98 *Baltiiskie moriaki v podgotovke*, pp. 104–5.
99 *Zemlia i volia*, no. 77, 25 June 1917.
100 *Golos pravdy*, no. 83, 24 June 1917, quoted in *Baltiiskie moriaki v podgotovke*, p. 343.

4. THE JULY DAYS

1 N. Avdeev (ed.), *Revoliutsiia 1917 goda (khronika sobytii)* (vols. 1 and 2, Moscow–Petrograd, 1923), vol. 2, p. 200.
2 V. K. Medvedev, 'Kronshtadt v iiul'skie dni', *Istoricheskie zapiski*, no. 42, 1953, pp. 264–5; *Izvestiia Kronshtadtskogo soveta*, no. 84, 29 June 1917.
3 *Baltiiskie moriaki v podgotovke i provedenii velikoi oktiabr'skoi sotsialisticheskoi revoliutsii* (Moscow–Leningrad, 1957), p. 164; Medvedev, 'Kronshtadt v iiul'skie dni', p. 265.
4 *Izvestiia Kr. soveta*, no. 95, 14 July 1917.
5 *Ibid.*
6 M. L. Lurie, 'Kronshtadtskie moriaki v iiul'skom vystuplenii 1917 goda', *Krasnaia letopis'*, no. 3(48), 1932, p. 79.
7 *Baltiiskie moriaki v podgotovke*, pp. 164–5.
8 Lurie, 'Kronshtadtskie moriaki', pp. 93–4.
9 O. L. D'Or, *Krasnyi chasovoi Kronshtadt* (Moscow, 1920), p. 40; S. E. Vinogradov, *Flot v revoliutsionnom dvizhenii* (Petrograd, 1922), pp. 65–6.
10 Lurie, 'Kronshtadtskie moriaki', p. 94.
11 Medvedev, 'Kronshtadt v iiul'skie dni', p. 264.
12 *Izvestiia Kr. soveta*, no. 98, 18 July 1917.
13 V. V. Petrash, *Moriaki baltiiskogo flota v bor'be za pobedu oktiabria* (Moscow–Leningrad, 1966), p. 152.
14 *Baltiiskie moriaki v podgotovke*, p. 165; *Izvestiia Kr. soveta*, no. 95, 14 July 1917.
15 *Izvestiia Kr. soveta*, no. 98, 18 July 1917.
16 F. F. Raskolnikov, *Kronshtadt i Piter v 1917 godu* (Moscow, 1925), p. 117.
17 *Baltiiskie moriaki v podgotovke*, p. 166; Lurie, 'Kronshtadtskie moriaki', p. 81.
18 *Izvestiia Kr. soveta*, no. 95, 14 July 1917.

19 He concealed Liubovich's telephone request both in his report to the Kronstadt Soviet on 7 July and in his statement during his interrogation in the Kresty Prison on 14 July, *Izvestiia Kr. soveta*, no. 95, 14 July 1917; Lurie, 'Kronshtadtskie moriaki', p. 81.

20 Lurie, 'Kronshtadtskie moriaki', p. 81; Alexander Rabinowitch, *Prelude to Revolution* (Bloomington, 1968), p. 174; Leon Trotsky, *History of the Russian Revolution*, vol. 2 (London, 1934), p. 541.

21 Lurie, 'Kronshtadtskie moriaki', p. 81.

22 I. Tobolin, 'Iiul'skie dni v Petrograde', *Krasnyi arkhiv*, no. 5(26), 1927, pp. 42–3.

23 *Baltiiskie moriaki v podgotovke*, pp. 116, 166.

24 *Ibid.*

25 *Baltiiskie moriaki v podgotovke*, p. 167.

26 *Ibid.*

27 Petrash, *Moriaki baltiiskogo flota*, pp. 153–4; *Baltiiskie moriaki v podgotovke*, p. 349.

28 *Baltiiskie moriaki v podgotovke*, p. 154.

29 Lurie, 'Kronshtadtskie moriaki', p. 82.

30 Tobolin, 'Iiul'skie dni v Petrograde', pp. 44–5.

31 *Baltiiskie moriaki v podgotovke*, p. 168.

32 Lurie, 'Kronshtadtskie moriaki', p. 83.

33 *Baltiiskie moriaki v podgotovke*, p. 168.

34 *Novaia zhizn'*, no. 65, 5 July 1917.

35 *Baltiiskie moriaki v podgotovke*, p. 168; Rabinowitch, *Prelude to Revolution*, p. 182.

36 *Ibid.*

37 Rabinowitch, *Prelude to Revolution*, p. 182.

38 Petrash, *Moriaki baltiiskogo flota*, p. 155; *Izvestiia Kr. soveta*, no. 95, 14 July 1917.

39 *Baltiiskie moriaki v podgotovke*, p. 169.

40 Vera Vladimirova (ed.), *Revoliutsiia 1917 goda (khronika sobytii)*, vol. 3 (Moscow–Petrograd, 1923), p. 315; V. I. Lenin, *Polnoe sobranie sochinenii*, 5th edn (55 vols., Moscow, 1958–65), vol. 34, pp. 23–4; *Novaia zhizn'*, no. 65, 5 July 1917.

41 '3–5 iiulia, Vospominaniia b[yvshago] predsedatelia Kr. soveta t[ovarishcha] Liubovicha', *Leninskaia pravda*, no. 160, 16 July 1925.

42 I. Flerovsky, 'Iiul'skii politicheskii urok', *Proletarskaia revoliutsiia*, no. 7(54), 1926, p. 77.

43 *Izvestiia Kr. soveta*, no. 95, 14 July 1917.

44 *Ibid.*; Flerovsky, 'Iiul'skii politicheskii urok', p. 77; D'Or, *Krasnyi chasovoi Kronshtadt*, p. 42; I. N. Kolbin, 'Kronshtadt ot fevralia do Kornilovskikh dnei', *Krasnaia letopis'*, no. 2(23), 1927, p. 150.

45 Flerovsky, 'Iiul'skii politicheskii urok', p. 78; D'Or, *Krasnyi chasovoi Kronshtadt*, p. 43; Raskolnikov, *Kronshtadt i Piter*, pp. 124–5.

46 *Baltiiskie moriaki v podgotovke*, p. 127.

47 *Izvestiia Kr. soveta*, no. 95, 14 July 1917.

48 Raskolnikov, *Kronshtadt i Piter*, pp. 126–7; Flerovsky, 'Iiul'skii politicheskii urok', pp. 78–9; *Baltiiskie moriaki v podgotovke*, pp. 169–70.

49 D'Or, *Krasnyi chasovoi Kronshtadt*, p. 43; *Baltiiskie moriaki v podgotovke*, p. 170.

50 Alexander Zhenevsky, 'Arest V. Chernova v Iiul'skie dni 1917 g.', *Krasnaia letopis'*, no. 6(21), 1926, pp. 69–70; *Izvestiia Kr. soveta*, no. 95, 14 July 1917.

51 Quoted in Rabinowitch, *Prelude to Revolution*, p. 188.

52 Flerovsky, 'Iiul'skii politicheskii urok', p. 79.

53 N. N. Sukhanov, *Zapiski o revoliutsii* (7 vols., Berlin–Petersburg–Moscow, 1922–3), vol. 4, pp. 422–6.

54 Raskolnikov, *Kronshtadt i Piter*, pp. 129–30.

55 Flerovsky, 'Iiul'skii politicheskii urok', pp. 79–80; *Leninskaia pravda*, no. 160, 16 July 1925.

56 *Baltiiskie moriaki v podgotovke*, p. 170.

57 Tomasz Parczewski, *Kronsztadt na tle rewolucji Rosyjskiej* (Warsaw, 1935), p. 60.

58 *Izvestiia Kr. soveta*, no. 95, 14 July 1917.

59 *Proletarskoe delo*, 14 July 1917, quoted in Alexander Rabinowitch, *The Bolsheviks come to Power: The Revolution of 1917 in Petrograd* (New York, 1976), pp. 46–7.

60 Flerovsky, 'Iiul'skii politicheskii urok', pp. 83–5.

61 *Izvestiia Kr. soveta*, no. 107, 28 July 1917.

62 *Ibid.*, no. 126, 20 August 1917.

63 *Baltiiskie moriaki v podgotovke*, p. 170.

64 Raskolnikov, *Kronshtadt i Piter*, p. 137.

65 *Baltiiskie moriaki v podgotovke*, p. 170.

66 *Ibid.*, p. 171.

67 *Izvestiia Kr. soveta*, no. 92, 11 July 1917; F. Raskolnikov, 'V Iiul'skie dni', *Proletarskaia revoliutsiia*, no. 5(17), 1923, pp. 54, 77.

68 N. Rostov, 'Na iakornoi ploshchadi', *Rabochaia gazeta*, no. 115, 25 July 1917.

69 *Izvestiia Kr. soveta*, no. 106, 22 July 1917.

70 *Ibid.*, no. 92, 11 July 1917.

71 *Ibid.*, no. 106, 22 July 1917.

72 *Ibid.*

73 *Ibid.*, no. 95, 14 July 1917.

74 *Ibid.*, no. 98, 18 July 1917.

75 *Ibid.*, no. 95, 14 July 1917.

76 *Baltiiskie moriaki v podgotovke*, p. 131.

77 *Ibid.*, p. 142.

78 *Krasnaia letopis'*, no. 2(23), 1927, p. 154.

79 *Izvestiia Kr. soveta*, no. 95, 14 July 1917; Raskolnikov, *Kronshtadt i Piter*, p. 148.

80 *Izvestiia Kr. soveta*, no. 100, 20 July 1917.

81 Parczewski, *Kronsztadt*, p. 61; Sukhanov, *Zapiski o revoliutsii*, vol. 3, p. 180.

82 P. N. Lamanov, 'V Kronshtadte posle Iiul'skikh dnei', *Krasnaia letopis'*, no. 3(24), 1927, pp. 23–7.

83 *Ibid.*, pp. 27–34; Parczewski, *Kronsztadt*, pp. 63–9.

84 *Revoliutsionnoe dvizhenie v Rossii v iiule 1917g. Iiul'skii krizis* (Moscow, 1959), p. 418.
85 Parczewski, *Kronsztadt*, p. 65.
86 *Izvestiia Kr. soveta*, no. 95, 14 July 1917.
87 *Ibid.*
88 *Baltiiskie moriaki v podgotovke*, pp. 143–4.
89 *Izvestiia Gel'singforskogo soveta*, no. 103, 19 July 1917; Parczewski, *Kronsztadt*, pp. 67–8.
90 Flerovsky, 'Iiul'skii politicheskii urok', pp. 88–9.
91 *Baltiiskie moriaki v podgotovke*, p. 153.
92 *Izvestiia Kr. soveta*, no. 106, 27 July 1917.
93 *Ibid.*, no. 112, 3 August 1917.
94 Lenin, *Polnoe sobranie sochinenii*, vol. 34, pp. 2, 12, 17.
95 *Izvestiia Kr. soveta*, no. 112, 3 August 1917.
96 *Ibid.*, no. 108, 29 July 1917.
97 *Ibid.*; *Proletarskoe delo*, no. 15, 30 July 1917.
98 *Revoliutsionnoe dvizhenie v Rossii v iiule 1917g.*, p. 277; Vladimirova, *Revoliutsiia 1917 goda*, vol. 4 (Leningrad, 1924), p. 231.
99 *Rech'*, no. 170, 22 July 1917; Parczewski, *Kronsztadt*, pp. 69–71.
100 *Kronshtadtskaia iskra*, no. 3, 14 August 1917.
101 *Shestoi s'ezd RSDRP (bol'shevikov), Protokoly* (Moscow, 1958), pp. 77–8, 317–18; P. F. Zinchenko-Ostrovskaia, 'Kronshtadt revoliutsionnyi', in *V ogne revoliutsionnykh boev* (2 vols., Moscow, 1967–71), vol. 2, pp. 153–5.
102 Petrash, *Moriaki baltiiskogo flota*, pp. 186–7.
103 *Izvestiia Kr. soveta*, no. 123, 17 August 1917.
104 D. N. Kondakov, 'Krepost' revoliutsii', in *V ogne revoliutsionnykh boev*, vol. 2, p. 348.
105 *Izvestiia Kr. soveta*, no. 131, 26 August 1917.
106 The following brief exposition of some of the views of Zverin and Rivkin is based on [Nik.] Rivkin, *Priamo k tseli* (Petrograd, 1917); 'Prizyv pevtsa', *ibid.*, p. 16; A. A. Zverin, *Trudovaia sovetskaia respublika* [1917], (Moscow, 1918); Rivkin, *Taina demokraticheskoi respubliki* [August, 1917], (Moscow, 1918); *K rabochim, krest'ianam i soldatam* (Petrograd, 1917).
107 Zverin, *Trudovaia sovetskaia respublika*, p. 9.
108 *Izvestiia Kr. soveta*, no. 98, 18 July 1917.
109 Rivkin, *Taina demokraticheskoi respubliki*, pp. 5–6.
110 *Izvestiia Kr. soveta*, no. 101, 21 July 1917.
111 *Ibid.*
112 P. Ediet, 'Na rasput'e', *Izvestiia Kr. soveta*, no. 44, 11 May 1917.
113 A. M., 'K stat'e "na rasput'e"', *ibid.*, no. 46, 14 May 1917.
114 P. Ediet, 'O ponimanii revoliutsii', *ibid.*, no. 47, 16 May 1917.
115 A. M., 'Kadety', *ibid.*, no. 148, 19 September 1917.
116 A. M., 'Kultura', *ibid.*, no. 149, 20 September 1917; A. M., 'Dusha', *ibid.*, no. 153, 24 September 1917.
117 A. M., 'K momentu', *ibid.*, no. 138, 5 September 1917.
118 *Ibid.*
119 A. M., 'Trevoga dnia', *ibid.*, no. 139, 8 September 1917.

120 A. M., 'Frantsuskie sindikaty', *ibid.*, no. 151, 22 September 1917; A. M., 'Klass', *ibid.*, no. 155, 27 September 1917.

121 A. M., 'Frantsuskoe professional'noe dvizhenie', *ibid.*, no. 156, 28 September 1917.

122 *Baltiiskie moriaki v podgotovke*, p. 351.

123 N. Ia. Ivanov, *Kornilovshchina i ee razgrom* (Leningrad, 1965), p. 167.

124 *Ibid.*, p. 102.

125 *Izvestiia Kr. soveta*, no. 133, 29 August 1917.

126 A. Lamanov, 'Tekushchii moment i tseli revoliutsii', *Izvestiia Kr. soveta*, no. 136, 1 September 1917.

127 *Revoliutsionnoe dvizhenie v Rossii v avguste 1917g. Razgrom Kornilovskogo miatezha* (Moscow, 1959), pp. 492–3.

128 *Izvestiia Kr. soveta*, no. 134, 30 August 1917.

129 *Ibid.*

130 *Baltiiskie moriaki v podgotovke*, pp. 200–1.

131 *Izvestiia Kr. soveta*, no. 140, 7 September 1917.

132 R. P. Browder and A. F. Kerensky (eds.), *The Russian Provisional Government 1917* (3 vols., Stanford, 1961), vol. 3, p. 1671.

133 The protocol of the session of 7 September is in *Izvestiia Kr. soveta*, nos. 144–6, 13, 14 and 16 September 1917.

134 *Ibid.*, no. 144, 13 September 1917; see also no. 131, 26 August 1917.

135 *Ibid.*, no. 145, 14 September 1917.

136 *Ibid.*, no. 146, 16 September 1917.

137 *Ibid.*, no. 144, 13 September 1917.

138 *Revoliutsionnoe dvizhenie v Rossii v sentiabre 1917g. Obshchenatsional'nyi krizis* (Moscow, 1961), pp. 157–8, 161–2.

139 *Izvestiia Kr. soveta*, no. 144, 13 September 1917.

140 The protocol of the session of 26 September is reported in *Izvestiia Kr. soveta*, nos. 156, 158, 159, 161, 164, 165, 28, 30 September, 1, 4, 7, 8 October 1917.

141 *Ibid.*, no. 156, 28 September 1917.

142 *Baltiiskie moriaki v podgotovke*, p. 226.

143 Browder and Kerensky, *Russian Provisional Government*, vol. 3, p. 1629.

144 *Petrogradskie bol'sheviki v oktiabr'skoi revoliutsii* (Leningrad, 1957), p. 332; *Baltiiskie moriaki v podgotovke*, p. 227.

145 *Izvestiia Kr. soveta*, no. 171, 15 October 1917.

146 For the text of the Appeal see *Baltiiskie moriaki v podgotovke*, pp. 231–3; for Flerovsky's authorship, I. Flerovsky, 'Kronshtadt v oktiabr'skoi revoliutsii', *Proletarskaia revoliutsiia*, no. 10, 1922, pp. 133–4.

147 *Izvestiia Kr. soveta*, no. 167, 11 October 1917.

148 Parczewski, *Kronsztadt*, p. 74.

149 *Izvestiia Kr. soveta*, no. 176, 21 October 1917; Petrash, *Moriaki baltiiskogo flota*, p. 245.

150 *Baltiiskie moriaki v podgotovke*, pp. 225–6.

151 *Izvestiia Kr. soveta*, no. 171, 15 October 1917.

152 *Ibid.*, no. 183, 29 October 1917.

153 *Baltiiskie moriaki v podgotovke*, p. 244.

154 'Skhvatka blizitsiia', *Proletarskoe delo*, no. 76, 13 October 1917.

155 'Nadvigaiushchiisia krakh', *Izvestiia Kr. soveta*, no. 174, 19 October 1917.

156 *Ibid.*

157 'Pravitel'stvo mira', *ibid.*, no. 176, 21 October 1917.

158 Trotsky, *History of the Russian Revolution*, vol. 3, p. 1070; Flerovsky, 'Kronshtadt v oktiabr'skoi revoliutsii', pp. 135–6.

159 *Izvestiia Kr. soveta*, no. 189, 4 November 1917.

160 *Ibid.*, no. 190, 5 November 1917.

161 *Ibid.*

162 'Instruktsiia', *Izvestiia Kr. soveta*, no. 178, 24 October 1917.

163 *Izvestiia Kr. soveta*, no. 189, 4 November 1917.

5. ALL POWER TO SOVIETS

1 Leon Trotsky, *History of the Russian Revolution*, vol. 3 (London, 1934), p. 1070; A. Baranov, 'Oktiabr'skie dni v Petrograde', *Piat' let krasnogo flota* (Petrograd, 1922), p. 246.

2 *Baltiiskie moriaki v podgotovke i provedenii velikoi oktiabr'skoi sotsialisticheskoi revoliutsii* (Moscow–Leningrad, 1957), p. 268.

3 *Ibid.*, p. 263.

4 I. Flerovsky, 'Kronshtadt v oktiabr'skoi revoliutsii', *Proletarskaia revoliutsiia*, no. 10, 1922, pp. 131, 136.

5 *Ibid.*, p. 138; V. V. Petrash, 'Sostav baltiiskogo flota i uchastie voennykh moriakov v oktiabr'skom vooruzhennom vosstanii', in *Lenin i oktiabr'skoe vooruzhennoe vosstanie v Petrograde* (Leningrad, 1964), p. 329.

6 E. Yarchuk, *Kronshtadt v russkoi revoliutsii* (New York, 1923), p. 28.

7 Flerovsky, 'Kronshtadt v oktiabr'skoi revoliutsii'.

8 Trotsky, *History of the Russian Revolution*, vol. 3, p. 1101.

9 John Reed, *Ten Days that shook the World* (New York, 1960), p. 96.

10 *Lenin i oktiabr'skoe vooruzhennoe vosstanie v Petrograde*, p. 329.

11 N. N. Sukhanov, *Zapiski o revoliutsii* (7 vols., Berlin–Petersburg–Moscow, 1922–3, vol. 7, p. 120.

12 *Baltiiskie moriaki v podgotovke*, p. 277.

13 Quoted in *Baltiiskie moriaki v podgotovke*, p. 282.

14 P. Z. Sivkov, *Kronshtadt: Stranitsy revoliutsionnoi istorii* (Leningrad, 1972), pp. 342–3; *Baltiiskie moriaki v podgotovke*, p. 319.

15 *Baltiiskie moriaki v podgotovke*, p. 325.

16 F. F. Raskolnikov, *Kronshtadt i Piter v 1917 godu* (Moscow, 1925), pp. 240–1.

17 *Petrogradskii voenno-revoliutsionnyi komitet, dokumenty i materialy* (3 vols., Moscow, 1966), vol. 1, p. 233.

18 *Ibid.*, vol. 1, pp. 176, 473, 532, 539, vol. 2, pp. 274, 335, 465, vol. 3, pp. 110, 175.

19 *Ibid.*, vol. 1, pp. 176, 281.

20 *Ibid.*, vol. 1, p. 436.

21 V. I. Lenin, *Polnoe sobranie sochinenii*, 5th edn (55 vols., Moscow, 1958–65), vol. 35, p. 89.

22 *Petrogradskii voenno-revoliutsionnyi komitet*, vol. 2, pp. 187, 222–3, 245–6, 497, 519.

23 *Armiia i flot rabochei i krest'ianskoi Rossii*, no. 12, 5 December 1917.

24 Yarchuk, *Kronshtadt v russkoi revoliutsii*, p. 32; *Izvestiia Kronshtadtskogo soveta*, no. 5, 9 January 1918.

25 'Izmenniki revoliutsii', *Izvestiia Kr. soveta*, no. 183, 29 October 1917.

26 'Koalitsiia demokratii', *ibid.*, no. 185, 31 October 1917.

27 The protocols of the session of 29 October are in *Izvestiia Kr. soveta*, no. 185, 31 October, no. 186, 1 November, no. 187, 2 November, no. 188, 3 November 1917.

28 See Flerovsky, 'Kronshtadt v oktiabr'skoi revoliutsii', p. 146.

29 *Izvestiia Kr. soveta*, no. 185, 31 October 1917.

30 *Ibid.*, no. 186, 1 November 1917.

31 For Rivkin's resolution see *Izvestiia Kr. soveta*, no. 185, 31 October 1917.

32 *Ibid.*, no. 186, 1 November 1917.

33 *Ibid.*

34 *Ibid.*

35 Yarchuk, *Kronshtadt v russkoi revoliutsii*, p. 34.

36 *Izvestiia Kr. soveta*, no. 187, 2 November 1917.

37 For Ermansky's resolution see *Izvestiia Kr. soveta*, no. 189, 4 November 1917.

38 *Ibid.*, no. 188, 3 November 1917.

39 *Ibid.*

40 Yarchuk, *Kronshtadt v russkoi revoliutsii*, p. 34.

41 *Izvestiia Kr. soveta*, no. 187, 2 November 1917.

42 *Ibid.*, no. 188, 3 November 1917.

43 *Ibid.*

44 A. Shliapnikov, 'Oktiabr'skii perevorot i stavka', *Krasnyi arkhiv*, no. 9, 1925, p. 169.

45 'Koalitsiia demokratii', *Izvestiia Kr. soveta*, no. 185, 31 October 1917.

46 L. Stark, ' "Chestnaia" koalitsiia ili "vlast' sovetam" ', *Golos pravdy*, no. 99, 13 November (31 October) 1917.

47 For protocols of the debate see *Izvestiia Kr. soveta*, no. 198, 15 November, no. 200, 17 November, no. 201, 18 November, no. 202, 19 November, 1917.

48 *Izvestiia Kr. soveta*, no. 200, 17 November, no. 201, 18 November 1917.

49 *Ibid.*, no. 202, 19 November 1917.

50 *Znamia truda*, no. 63, 5 November 1917.

51 For the resolution of the Central Executive Committee see *Izvestiia Petrogradskogo soveta*, no. 214, 3 November 1917; James Bunyan and H. H. Fisher, *The Bolshevik Revolution 1917–1918* (Stanford, 1961), p. 197; as for the concession made to the Left SRs, see A. L. Fraiman, *Forpost sotsialisticheskoi revoliutsii* (Leningrad, 1969), p. 89.

52 The Kronstadt declaration is reprinted in *Znamia truda*, no. 71, 14 November 1917. I have had access only to part of the protocol of the debate in the Kronstadt Soviet on 2 November 1917 that preceded the declaration's adoption.

53 *Izvestiia Kr. soveta*, no. 209, 29 November 1917.

54 Tomasz Parczewski, *Kronsztadt na tle rewolucji Rosyjskiej* (Warsaw, 1935), p. 75.

55 V. S. Krasnogorsky, 'Revoliutsionnaia initsiativa', *Izvestiia Kr. soveta*, no. 225, 19 December 1917.

56 *Soldatskaia pravda*, no. 63, 28 October 1917.

57 For the Krasnaia Gorka mutiny of 13–16 June 1919 see below pp. 198–200.

58 V. Simsky, 'My ne dolzhny byt' Robespierami i Maratami', *Izvestiia Kr. soveta*, no. 186, 1 November 1917.

59 *Ibid.*, no. 202, 19 November 1917.

60 Vladimir Blokhin, 'Kronshtadtskaia pechat' 1917 goda', *Izvestiia Kr. soveta*, no. 234, 30 December 1917.

61 *Armiia i flot rabochei i krest'ianskoi Rossii*, no. 15, 8 December 1917; *Izvestiia Kr. soveta*, no. 6, 11 January 1918.

62 *Znamia truda*, no. 91, 9 December 1917, no. 113, 7 January 1918; P. N. Stolpiansky, *Istoriko-obshchestvennyi putevoditel' po Kronshtadtu* (Petersburg [1921]), p. 39; *Izvestiia Kr. soveta*, no. 23, 31 January 1918.

63 *Izvestiia Kr. soveta*, no. 5, 9 January 1918, no. 6, 11 January 1918, no. 8, 13 January 1918, no. 11, 17 January 1918, no. 17, 24 January 1918, no. 18, 25 January 1918; *Tserkovnye vedomosti*, no. 1, 5 January 1918 (I owe this reference to the kindness of Dr Michael Agursky).

64 A. Brushvit, 'O veruiushchikh, ne-veruiushchikh i cherno-sotentsev', *Izvestiia Kr. soveta*, no. 7, 12 January 1918.

65 *Izvestiia Kr. soveta*, no. 8, 13 January 1918.

66 *Ibid.*, no. 17, 24 January 1918, no. 18, 25 January 1918.

67 *Ibid.*, no. 27, 19 February 1918.

68 Krasnogorsky, 'Revoliutsionnaia initsiativa'.

69 Yarchuk, *Kronshtadt v russkoi revoliutsii*, p. 38; *Izvestiia Kr. soveta*, no. 234, 30 December 1917.

70 *Znamia truda*, no. 91, 9 December 1917.

71 *Izvestiia Kr. soveta*, no. 234, 30 December 1917.

72 *Ibid.*, no. 1, 3 January 1918.

73 *Ibid.*, no. 226, 20 December 1917.

74 'F. I. Chaliapin v Krasnom Kronshtadte', *Izvestiia Kr. Soveta*, no. 225, 19 December 1917.

75 *Izvestiia Kr. soveta*, no. 23, 31 January 1918.

76 *Ibid.*, no. 14, 20 January 1918.

77 *Ibid.*, no. 5, 9 January 1918, no. 6, 11 January 1918.

78 *Ibid.*, no. 7, 12 January 1918.

79 The following discussion is based on the *Osnovy organizatsii Soveta Rabochikh i Soldatskikh Deputatov* (Kronstadt, 1918) (published by the Kronstadt Organization of the Left SRs) and on the reports of the Soviet plenum debates published in *Izvestiia Kr. soveta*, no. 5, 9 January 1918, no. 6, 11 January 1918, no. 13, 19 January 1918, no. 14, 20 January 1918, no. 18, 25 January 1918, no. 20, 27 January 1918, no. 21, 28 January 1918, no. 22, 30 January 1918.

80 *Izvestiia Kr. soveta*, no. 50, 20 March 1918.

81 Quoted in Marc Ferro, *Des soviets au communisme bureaucratique* (Paris, 1980), pp. 168, 174.

82 *Izvestiia Kr. soveta*, no. 12, 18 January 1918.

83 Evan Mawdsley, *The Russian Revolution and the Baltic Fleet* (London, 1978), pp. 168–9, 205.

84 A. L. Fraiman (ed.), *Baltiiskie moriaki v bor'be za vlast' sovetov, noiabr' 1917–dekabr' 1918* (Leningrad, 1968), pp. 20, 61, 314, 71–2, 60.

85 *Petrogradskii voenno-revoliutsionnyi komitet*, vol. 1, p. 97.

86 Fraiman, *Baltiiskie moriaki v bor'be za vlast' sovetov*, pp. 317, 72, 318.

87 *Ibid.*, pp. 42, 49–50.

88 A. Lamanov, 'Uchreditel'noe sobranie i sovety', *Izvestiia Kr. soveta*, no. 214, 5 December 1917.

89 A.P.T., 'Liberaly novoi marki', *Izvestiia Kr. soveta*, no. 226, 20 December 1917.

90 Fraiman, *Baltiiskie moriaki v bor'be za vlast' sovetov*, pp. 68–9, 318.

91 L. S. Malchevsky (ed.), *Vserossiiskoe Uchreditel'noe Sobranie* (Moscow, 1930), pp. 33–4.

92 *Ibid.*, pp. 88–90, 110, 217.

93 Vladimir Blokhin, 'Proletarskaia kul'tura', *Izvestiia Kr. soveta*, no. 5, 9 January 1918, no. 7, 12 January 1918.

94 *Izvestiia Kr. soveta*, no. 3, 5 January 1918.

95 *Ibid.*, no. 22, 30 January 1918.

96 Fraiman, *Baltiiskie moriaki v bor'be za vlast' sovetov*, pp. 191, 194, 256.

97 *Izvestiia Kr. soveta*, no. 12, 18 January 1918.

98 *Ibid.*, no. 23, 31 January 1918.

99 Mawdsley, *The Russian Revolution and the Baltic Fleet*, pp. 164, 204.

100 P. Smirnov, 'Kronshtadtskii sovet', *Golos pravdy*, no. 23, 13 February 1918.

101 *Izvestiia Kr. soveta*, no. 43, 9 March 1918.

102 *Znamia truda*, no. 142, 26 February 1918; Yarchuk, *Kronshtadt v russkoi revoliutsii*, p. 46.

103 *Izvestiia Kr. soveta*, no. 31, 22 February 1918, no. 43, 9 March 1918, no. 44, 10 March 1918, no. 47, 14 March 1918.

104 *Ibid.*, no. 47, 14 March 1918.

105 *Ibid.*, no. 61, 22 April 1918, no. 52, 22 March 1918, no. 54, 24 March 1918; Fraiman, *Baltiiskie moriaki v bor'be za vlast' sovetov*, p. 161.

106 *Izvestiia Kr. soveta*, no. 77, 20 April 1918; Yarchuk, *Kronshtadt v russkoi revoliutsii*, p. 48.

107 *Znamia truda*, no. 203, 17 May 1918.

108 Fraiman, *Baltiiskie moriaki v bor'be za vlast' sovetov*, p. 188; L. Martov to Alexander Stein, 16 June 1918, unpublished letter, Nicolaevsky Collection, Hoover Institution.

109 *Izvestiia Kr. soveta*, no. 133, 2 July 1918.

110 *Ibid.*

111 Iu. I. Shestak, 'Bankrotstvo eserov-maksimalistov', *Voprosy istorii*, no. 1, January 1977, pp. 36–7; *Znamia truda*, no. 221, 7 June 1918.

112 *S'ezdy sovetov RSFSR i avtonomnykh respublik RSFSR*, vol. 1 (Moscow, 1959), p. 80.

113 Shestak, 'Bankrotstvo eserov-maksimalistov', p. 37.

114 *Izvestiia Kr. soveta*, no. 133, 2 July 1918.

115 *Piatyi vserossiiskii s'ezd sovetov rabochikh, krest'ianskikh, i kazach'ikh deputatov, stenograficheskii otchet* (Moscow, 1918), p. 247; Fraiman, *Baltiiskie moriaki v bor'be za vlast' sovetov*, pp. 207, 327.

116 W. H. Chamberlin, *The Russian Revolution, 1917–1921* (2 vols., New York, 1935), vol. 2, pp. 56, 126; Irina Kakhovskaia, *Die Attentate auf Eichhorn und Denikin: Erinnerungen* (Berlin, 1923), pp. 8–12, 46–9.

117 *Izvestiia Kr. soveta*, no. 249, 21 November 1918.

118 *Ibid.*, no. 21, 30 January 1919.

119 *Ibid.*, no. 16, 24 January 1919.

120 *Ibid.*, no. 166, 26 July 1919.

121 *Ibid.*, no. 296, 28 December 1919.

122 *Ibid.* no. 47, 28 February 1920.

123 Israel Getzler, *Martov* (Cambridge–Melbourne, 1967), p. 216.

124 *Izvestiia Kr. soveta*, no. 16, 24 January 1919.

125 *Ibid.*, no. 158, 17 July 1919.

126 *Ibid.*, no. 14, 21 January 1919.

127 *Ibid.*, no. 26, 5 February 1919.

128 Fraiman, *Baltiiskie moriaki v bor'be za vlast' sovetov*, p. 165; *Protokoly i postanovleniia Tsentral'nogo Komiteta Baltiiskogo flota, 1917–1918* (Moscow–Leningrad, 1963), pp. 64, 425.

129 Fraiman, *Baltiiskie moriaki v bor'be za vlast' sovetov*, pp. 195, 200, 204, 206–8, 327; I. M. Ludri, 'Sudovye komitety', in *Oktiabr'skii shkval* (Leningrad, 1927), p. 85.

130 A. L. Fraiman (ed.), *Baltiiskie moriaki v bor'be za vlast' sovetov v 1919 godu* (Leningrad, 1974), pp. 24, 28, 154.

131 'Instruktsiia dlia kollektivov priniataia 2-oi obshchegorodskoi konferentsii kollektivov v Kronshtadte 2-go marta 1919 goda', *Izvestiia Kr. soveta*, no. 52, 7 March 1919.

132 *Ibid.*

133 *Putevoditel' po Kronshtadtu* (Kronstadt, 1921), pp. 41–3.

134 Fraiman, *Baltiiskie moriaki v bor'be v 1919 godu*, pp. 167, 343.

135 *Ibid.*, pp. 24, 28, 154.

136 *Ibid.*, p. 50.

137 A. K. Drezen (ed.), *Baltiiskii flot v oktiabr'skoi revoliutsii i grazhdanskoi voine* (Moscow–Leningrad, 1932), pp. 174–5.

138 Fraiman, *Baltiiskie moriaki v bor'be v 1919 godu*, pp. 42, 191.

139 Drezen, *Baltiiskii flot*, p. 171.

140 Fraiman, *Baltiiskie moriaki v bor'be v 1919 godu*, p. 336.

141 *Ibid.*, p. 66.

142 The reference is most likely to Grigorii Safarov, a Petrograd party functionary.

143 *Krasnyi baltiiskii flot*, no. 47, 10 September 1919.

144 V. Z., 'Krasnyie forty', *Krasnyi baltiiskii flot*, no. 51, 24 September 1919.

145 Maksim Shkilenok, 'Krasnaia pesn' bratvy (na motiv Stenka Razina)', *ibid.*

146 L. Trotsky, 'Nashe voennoe stroitel'stovo i nashi fronti', speech delivered on 7 December 1919, in L. Trotsky, *Kak vooruzhalas' revoliutsiia*, vol. 2 (Moscow, 1924), Book 2, p. 7.

147 *Izvestiia Kr. soveta*, no. 26, 5 February 1919; no. 61, 20 March 1919; no. 1, 1 January 1919.

148 *Putevoditel' po Kronshtadtu*, p. 43; Fraiman, *Baltiiskie moriaki v bor'be v 1919 godu*, p. 69.

149 *Izvestiia Kr. soveta*, no. 123, 6 June 1919.

150 *Putevoditel' po Kronshtadtu*, p. 21.

151 *Izvestiia Kr. soveta*, no. 123, 6 June 1919.

152 *Ibid.*

153 *Putevoditel' po Kronshtadtu*, p. 45.

154 *Izvestiia Kr. soveta*, no. 129, 3 June 1919; no. 216, 25 September 1919; no. 296, 28 December 1919; A. S. Pukhov, 'Kronshtadt i baltiiskii flot pered miatezhom 1921 goda', *Krasnaia letopis'*, no. 6(39), 1930, p. 156.

155 Parczewski, *Kronsztadt*, pp. 88–9.

156 This account of the Krasnaia Gorka mutiny, 13–16 June 1919, is largely based on Lazar Bregman's report to the Politotdel of the Baltic Fleet of 28 June 1919, Fraiman, *Baltiiskie moriaki v bor'be v 1919 godu*, pp. 154–6.

157 *Velikaia oborona Krasnogo Petrograda v 1919 godu* (Leningrad, 1929), p. 53.

158 Parczewski, *Kronsztadt*, p. 75; Iu. Tsederbaum (Martov) to Alexander Stein, 25 October 1918, unpublished letter, Nicolaevsky Collection, Hoover Institution.

159 Fraiman, *Baltiiskie moriaki v bor'be v 1919 godu*, pp. 132, 134, 340.

160 *Ibid.*, p. 155.

161 'Tragediia forta "Krasnoarmeiskii"', *Pravda o Kronshtadte* (Prague, 1921), pp. 85–9.

162 Parczewski, *Kronsztadt*, pp. 101–2; Fraiman, *Baltiiskie moriaki v bor'be v 1919 godu*, pp. 136–7.

163 *Izvestiia Kr. soveta*, no. 135, 20 June 1919.

164 Parczewski, *Kronsztadt*, pp. 101–2.

165 Fraiman, *Baltiiskie moriaki v bor'be v 1919 godu*, pp. 167, 343.

166 *Ibid.*, p. 346.

167 Drezen, *Baltiiskii flot*, pp. 297, 312; Fraiman, *Baltiiskie moriaki v bor'be v 1919 godu*, p. 321.

168 Based on data in Pukhov, 'Kronshtadt i baltiiskii flot pered miatezhom', pp. 200–1.

169 'V krasnom baltflote', *Izvestiia Petrogradskogo soveta*, no. 46(538), 28 February 1920.

170 Drezen, *Baltiiskii flot*, pp. 321–2.

171 *Ibid.*; Pukhov, 'Kronshtadt i baltiiskii flot pered miatezhom', pp. 182, 177–81.

172 The Politotdel's report is quoted verbatim in S. N. Semanov, *Likvidatsiia antisovetskogo Kronshtadtskogo miatezha 1921 goda* (Moscow, 1973), p. 70.

173 Drezen, *Baltiiskii flot*, p. 299; Pukhov, 'Kronshtadt i baltiiskii flot pered miatezhom', pp. 182, 177–81.

174 Pukhov, 'Kronshtadt i baltiiskii flot pered miatezhom', p. 199.

175 *Ibid.*, pp. 187–8, 177–8.
176 *Ibid.*, pp. 179–80.
177 *Ibid.*, pp. 188–9.
178 *Ibid.*, pp. 190–1.
179 Ludri, 'Sudovye komitety', p. 87.

6. KRONSTADT'S THIRD REVOLUTION

1 This chapter tries to explore the continuity in personnel, ideology and institutions between February 1917 and March 1921. For the story of the uprising, the reader is referred to: Paul Avrich, *Kronstadt 1921* (Princeton, 1970); Leonard Schapiro, *The Origin of the Communist Autocracy* (London, 1955), pp. 296–306; W. H. Chamberlin, *The Russian Revolution, 1917–1921* (2 vols., New York, 1935), vol. 2, pp. 439–45.

2 Kronstadt's civilian population (28 August 1920 census) was 23,815; not included are 6,232 inhabitants who, on the day of the census, were listed as 'on the waterways and railroads of the Soviet Union'; the military population of the Kronstadt fortress and naval base numbered 25,527 soldiers and sailors and 1,423 officers and commissars; see A. S. Pukhov, 'Kronshtadt i baltiiskii flot pered miatezhom 1921 goda', *Krasnaia letopis'*, no. 6(39), 1930, pp. 180, 198, 200.

3 I. Flerovsky, 'Miatezh mobilizovannykh matrosov v Petrograde 14 oktiabria 1918g.', *Proletarskaia revoliutsiia*, no. 8(55), 1926, p. 236; A. L. Fraiman (ed.), *Baltiiskie moriaki v bor'be za vlast' sovetov (noiabr' 1917–dekabr' 1918)* (Leningrad, 1968), pp. 189, 191, 194.

4 N. Kornatovsky (ed.), *Kronshtadskii miatezh: sbornik statei, vospominanii i dokumentov* (Leningrad, 1931), pp. 13, 55; Pukhov, 'Kronshtadt i baltiiskii flot pered miatezhom', pp. 176, 180–1; A. S. Pukhov, *Kronshtadtskii miatezh v 1921 godu* (Leningrad, 1931), p. 50.

5 Pukhov, 'Kronshtadt i baltiiskii flot pered miatezhom', pp. 184–6; A. K. Drezen (ed.), *Baltiiskii flot v oktiabr'skoi revoliutsii i grazhdanskoi voine* (Moscow–Leningrad, 1932), pp. 313–16.

6 Pukhov, 'Kronshtadt i baltiiskii flot pered miatezhom', p. 185.

7 Mark Rudnyi, 'Instruktora revoliutsii', *Krasnyi baltiiskii flot*, no. 26, 28 June 1919.

8 Ier. Yasinsky, 'Kronshtadt', *Krasnyi baltiiskii flot*, no. 96, 23 September 1920; Yasinsky, 'Kronshtadtskie vpechatleniia', *ibid.*, no. 100, 2 October 1920.

9 Voenmor Skoromnyi, 'Na "Sevastopole" ', *Krasnyi baltiiskii flot*, no. 96, 23 September 1920.

10 S. N. Semanov, *Likvidatsiia antisovetskogo Kronshtadtskogo miatezha 1921 goda* (Moscow, 1973), p. 66.

11 See Pukhov, 'Kronshtadt i baltiiskii flot pered miatezhom' for data referring to the year of birth (rather than that of enlistment) of sailors serving in the Baltic Fleet as of 1 January 1921, which suggest that at least some 80% were veterans of the 1917 revolution; for similar conclusions see Evan Mawdsley, 'The Baltic Fleet and the Kronstadt Mutiny', *Soviet Studies*, vol. 24, no. 4, April 1973, p. 509.

12 Semanov, *Likvidatsiia Kronshtadtskogo miatezha*, pp. 65–6.

13 Mawdsley, 'The Baltic Fleet and the Kronstadt Mutiny', p. 509.

14 For details of the exceptionally good food rations received by both the military personnel and the civilian population of Kronstadt, notably the crews of the *Petropavlovsk*, the *Sevastopol* and the Training School Detachment who received special 'front-line rations', see Pukhov, 'Kronshtadt i Baltiiskii flot pered miatezhom', pp. 150–1.

15 'Iz pisem chitatelei' (signed *voennosluzhashchii* I. Egorov), *Izvestiia Kronshtadtskogo soveta*, no. 123, 6 June 1919.

16 Semanov, *Likvidatsiia Kronshtadtskogo miatezha*, pp. 61–9; [S.M.] Petrichenko, *Pravda o Kronshtadtskikh sobytiiakh* (n.p., 1921), p. 4.

17 Pukhov, 'Kronshtadt i baltiiskii flot pered miatezhom', pp. 165–6.

18 Kornatovsky (ed.), *Kronshtadtskii miatezh*, pp. 54, 56; *Pravda o Kronshtadte* (Prague, 1921), p. 156.

19 Pukhov, 'Kronshtadt i baltiiskii flot pered miatezhom', pp. 167, 187, 203; Trofim Gonoratsky, 'K vospominaniiam matrosa sluzhby 1914 goda', unpublished MS, Archive of Russian and East European History and Culture, Columbia University, New York, Notebook 10.

20 Pukhov, 'Kronshtadt i baltiiskii flot pered miatezhom', p. 187; *Pravda o Kronshtadte*, p. 145.

21 Martov to S. D. Shchupak, 26 June 1920, unpublished letter, Nicolaevsky Collection, Hoover Institution.

22 Mawdsley, 'The Baltic Fleet and the Kronstadt Mutiny', p. 514.

23 Pukhov, 'Kronshtadt i baltiiskii flot pered miatezhom', p. 150.

24 *Ibid.*, pp. 176, 180–1; Drezen, *Baltiiskii flot*, p. 297.

25 Pukhov, 'Kronshtadt i baltiiskii flot pered miatezhom', pp. 180–1.

26 *Ibid.*, p. 177; Mawdsley, 'The Baltic Fleet and the Kronstadt Mutiny', p. 509.

27 Pukhov, 'Kronshtadt i baltiiskii flot pered miatezhom', p. 201.

28 Mawdsley, 'The Baltic Fleet and the Kronstadt Mutiny', pp. 514–16.

29 Pukhov, 'Kronshtadt i baltiiskii flot pered miatezhom', pp. 194–6.

30 Mawdsley, 'The Baltic Fleet and the Kronstadt Mutiny', p. 518.

31 Pukhov, 'Kronshtadt i baltiiskii flot pered miatezhom', p. 193.

32 *Ibid.*, p. 196.

33 A. S. Pukhov, 'V Petrograde nakanune Kronshtadtskogo vosstaniia v 1921g.', *Krasnaia letopis'*, no. 4(37), 1930, pp. 110–11, 122; S. Petrichenko, 'O prichinakh Kronshtadtskogo vosstaniia', *Znamia bor'by*, nos. 14–15, December 1925–January 1926.

34 Petrichenko, 'O prichinakh Kronshtadtskogo vosstaniia'.

35 F. Dan, *Dva goda skitanii (1919–1921)* (Berlin, 1922), pp. 113–14; Pukhov, 'V Petrograde nakanune Kronshtadtskogo vosstaniia', p. 113.

36 Kornatovsky, *Kronshtadtskii miatezh*, p. 26; *Sotsialisticheskii vestnik*, no. 5, 3 April 1921.

37 A. S. Pukhov, 'Kronshtadt vo vlasti vragov revoliutsii', *Krasnaia letopis'*, no. 1(40), 1931, pp. 9–11.

38 *Pravda o Kronshtadte*, pp. 46–7.

39 Pukhov, 'Kronshtadt vo vlasti vragov revoliutsii', pp. 12–13.

40 *Ibid.*, p. 13.

41 A. L. Fraiman (ed.), *Baltiiskie moriaki v bor'be za vlast' sovetov v 1919 godu* (Leningrad, 1974), pp. 318–19.

42 Kornatovsky, *Kronshtadtskii miatezh*, p. 28; *Pravda o Kronshtadte*, p. 8.

43 A. Kozlovsky, 'Pravda o Kronshtadte', *Novoe russkoe slovo*, no. 76, 5 April 1921.

44 Pukhov, 'Kronshtadt vo vlasti vragov revoliutsii', pp. 13–14.

45 *Ibid.*, p. 14.

46 Petrichenko, *Pravda o Kronshtadtskikh sobytiiakh*, p. 7.

47 Pukhov, 'Kronshtadt vo vlasti vragov revoliutsii', pp. 13–14; Kozlovsky, 'Pravda o Kronshtadte'.

48 *Pravda o Kronshtadte*, pp. 10, 115.

49 *Putevoditel' po Kronshtadtu* (Kronstadt, 1921), p. 51.

50 Pukhov, 'Kronshtadt vo vlasti vragov revoliutsii', p. 27.

51 *Pravda o Kronshtadte*, pp. 116–17; Pukhov, 'Kronshtadt vo vlasti vragov revoliutsii', p. 27.

52 *Pravda o Kronshtadte*, pp. 45, 114.

53 Pukhov, 'Kronshtadt vo vlasti vragov revoliutsii', p. 30.

54 *Pravda o Kronshtadte*, pp. 50–1.

55 Kornatovsky, *Kronshtadtskii miatezh*, pp. 14–15

56 Petrichenko, *Pravda o Kronshtadtskikh sobytiiakh*, p. 9.

57 Kozlovsky, 'Pravda o Kronshtadte'; *Pravda o Kronshtadte*, pp. 92–4.

58 Pukhov, 'Kronshtadt vo vlasti vragov revoliutsii', p. 35.

59 Fraiman, *Baltiiskie moriaki v bor'be v 1919 godu*, pp. 322–3; *Baltiiskie moriaki v podgotovke i provedenii velikoi oktiabr'skoi sotsialisticheskoi revoliutsii* (Moscow–Leningrad, 1957), p. 166.

60 *Pravda o Kronshtadte*, p. 13; Kornatovsky, *Kronshtadtskii miatezh*, pp. 187–8; Peterburgskii, 'Pozornaia avantura', *Izvestiia Petrogradskogo soveta*, no. 47, 3 March 1921.

61 Kornatovsky, *Kronshtadtskii miatezh*, pp. 188–9.

62 *Ibid.*, p. 234.

63 *Desiatyi s'ezd RKP(b) mart 1921 goda. Stenograficheskii otchet* (Moscow, 1963), p. 414.

64 *Ibid.*, pp. 33–4.

65 Gonoratsky, 'K vospominaniiam matrosa sluzhby 1914 goda', notebook 10.

66 Kornatovsky, *Kronshtadtskii miatezh*, pp. 231–2.

67 *Pravda o Kronshtadte*, p. 175.

68 Gonoratsky, 'K vospominaniiam matrosa sluzhby 1914 goda', notebook 11.

69 Kornatovsky, *Kronshtadtskii miatezh*, p. 205.

70 Prof. G. F. Tseidler to President of Russian Red Cross, 20 March 1921, M. N. Giers Papers, Hoover Institution.

71 'Podrobnosti padeniia Kronshtadta', *Volia Rossii*, no. 169, 3 April 1921.

72 Unable to locate a full version of the 'Obrashchenie Revkoma k zheleznodorozhnikam', I have relied on the excerpts and paraphrase published in Pukhov, 'Kronshtadt vo vlasti vragov revoliutsii', pp. 46–9.

73 E. H. Carr, *The Bolshevik Revolution 1917–1923*, vol. 1 (London, 1950), p. 143.

74 Pukhov, 'Kronshtadt vo vlasti vragov revoliutsii', pp. 46–9.

75 Pukhov, *Kronshtadtskii miatezh v 1921g.*, pp. 76–7; Avrich, *Kronstadt 1921*, pp. 81–2.

76 Avrich, *Kronstadt 1921*, pp. 91, 178.

77 *Izvestiia Kr. soveta*, no. 32, 27 April 1917.

78 *Baltiiskie moriaki v podgotovke*, pp. 83, 134, 347; Dan, *Dva goda skitanii*, pp. 155–7.

79 *Kotlin*, no. 59, 14 March 1917, no. 72, 1 April, 1917; *Kronshtadtskii vestnik*, no. 56, 10 March, 1917; *Izvestiia Kr. soveta*, no. 70, 13 June 1917; Tomasz Parczewski, *Kronsztadt na tle rewolucji Rosyjskiej* (Warsaw, 1935), p. 33.

80 *Kronshtadtskii vestnik*, no. 59, 14 March 1917; *Izvestiia Kr. soveta*, no. 50, 19 May 1917, no. 124, 18 August 1917.

81 Avrich, *Kronstadt 1921*, pp. 94, 168.

82 Pukhov, *Kronshtadtskii miatezh v 1921g.*, p. 77.

83 *Izvestiia vremennogo revoliutsionnogo komiteta matrosov, krasnoarmeitsev i rabochikh gor. Kronshtadta*; all fourteen numbers were reprinted in full in *Pravda o Kronshtadte*, pp. 45–183.

84 *Kotlin*, no. 53, 8 March 1917; Pukhov, *Kronshtadtskii miatezh v 1921g.*, pp. 78, 93; Kornatovsky, *Kronshtadtskii miatezh*, p. 73.

85 *Izvestiia Kr. soveta*, no. 44, 11 May 1917, no. 70, 13 June 1917, no. 124, 18 August 1917, no. 173, 18 October 1917, no. 180, 26 October 1917, no. 61, 2 April 1918; *Baltiiskie moriaki v podgotovke*, pp. 191–3, 394.

86 *Izvestiia Kr. soveta*, no. 34, 29 April 1917, no. 50, 19 May 1917, no. 62, 3 June 1917; *Pravda o Kronshtadte*, p. 92.

87 *Izvestiia Kr. soveta*, no. 50, 19 May 1917, no. 60, 1 June 1917; *Pravda o Kronshtadte*, p. 149.

88 Kornatovsky, *Kronshtadtskii miatezh*, pp. 232–5.

89 V. V. Petrash, *Moriaki baltiiskogo flota v bor'be za pobedu oktiabria* (Moscow–Leningrad, 1966), p. 151; P. Z. Sivkov, *Kronshtadt: Stranitsy revoliutsionnoi istorii* (Leningrad, 1972), pp. 178, 252; Kornatovsky, *Kronshtadskii miatezh*, pp. 64–71; *Piat' let krasnogo flota* (Petrograd, 1922), p. 197.

90 *Pravda o Kronshtadte*, pp. 85, 97, 107, 132, 145, 148, 150; Petrichenko, *Pravda o Kronshtadtskikh sobytiiakh*, p. 15; Kozlovsky, 'Pravda o Kronshtadte'.

91 *Pravda o Kronshtadte*, pp. 85, 177.

92 *Ibid.*, pp. 56–7, 129–30.

93 *Ibid.*, pp. 56–7.

94 *Ibid.*, pp. 129–30.

95 G. Lelevich, 'Anarkho-maksimalistskaia revoliutsiia v Samare v mae 1918g.', *Proletarskaia revoliutsiia*, no. 7, 1922, pp. 141–2.

96 *Izvestiia Kr. soveta*, no. 61, 2 April 1918.

97 *Ibid.*, no. 43, 3 March 1918.

98 *Piatyi vserossiiskii s'ezd sovetov* (Moscow, 1918), p. 247.

99 *Pravda o Kronshtadte*, p. 59; G. F. Petrov, *Kronshtadt* (Leningrad, 1971), p. 273.

100 A. Lamanov, 'Mozhet li bit' obrazovanie privilegiei obezpechennykh?', *Izvestiia Kr. soveta*, no. 123, 6 June 1919.

101 A. Lamanov, 'Zadachi i stroitel'stvo trudovogo tekhnikuma', *Izvestiia Kr. soveta*, no. 201, 7 September 1919; A. Lamanov, 'Osmyslennost' truda zalog ego proizvoditel'nosti', *ibid.*

102 'Osnovy sotsializma', *Trudovaia respublika*, no. 11, 1 October 1917.

103 Lelevich, 'Anarkho-maksimalistskaia revoliutsiia v Samare'.

104 *Maksimalist*, no. 1, 1918, pp. 9–10 quoted in Iu. I. Shestak, 'Bankrotstvo eserov-maksimalistov', *Voprosy istorii*, no. 1, January 1977, p. 38.

105 'Tezisy doklada t. Zverina', *Maksimalist*, no. 11, May 1919, p. 19.

106 *Ibid.*; *Maksimalist*, no. 12, 1919, p. 1.

107 'Desiat' zapovedi sovetskomu grazhdaninu', *Maksimalist*, no. 11, May 1919, p. 7.

108 The relevant documents were published in *Maksimalist*, no. 14–15, March 1921, pp. 21–7.

109 *Izvestiia vremennogo revoliutsionnogo komiteta*, no. 4, 6 March 1921; *Pravda o Kronshtadte*, pp. 59–60.

110 *Pravda o Kronshtadte*, p. 65.

111 *Pravda o Kronshtadte*, pp. 68, 79, 97, 133, 141–2, 144, 146, 159, 176.

112 'Za chto my boremsia', 'Etapy revoliutsii', 'Sotsializm v kovychkakh', *Pravda o Kronshtadte*, pp. 82–4, 127–8, 173–4; English translations of 'What We Are Fighting For' and 'Socialism in Quotation Marks' are in Avrich, *Kronstadt 1921*, pp. 241–6.

113 'Malen'kii fel'eton. Kronshtadtskie chastushki', *Pravda o Kronshtadte*, p. 179.

114 'Kak nachalos' vosstanie v Kronshtadte', 12 March 1921, E. K. Miller Papers, Hoover Institution.

115 General Kliuev to General Miller, telegram 12 March 1921, Miller Papers, Hoover Institution.

116 'K Kr. vosstaniiu' letter to the editor signed I. (very likely Ivan Oreshin), *Volia Rossii*, 19 March 1921.

117 ' "Gospoda" ili "Tovarishchi" ', *Izvestiia vremennogo revoliutsionnogo komiteta*, no. 4, 6 March 1921; *Pravda o Kronshtadte*, p. 61.

118 'Beseda s Kronshtadtsami', *Volia Rossii*, no. 196, 6 May 1921.

119 Iurii Grigoriev, 'Dva dnia u Kronshtadtsev', *Novaia russkai zhizn*', no. 74, 2 April 1921.

120 Semanov, *Likvidatsiia Kronshtadtskogo miatezha*, p. 120; Avrich, *Kronstadt 1921*, pp. 124–5.

121 'Vozzvanie Kronshtadtsev', *Novaia russkaia zhizn*', no. 67, 23 March 1921.

122 *Volia Rossii*, no. 196, 6 May 1921.

123 *Pravda o Kronshtadte*, pp. 142–3.

124 S. Fokin, 'Prizyv', *Izvestiia Kr. soveta*, no. 34, 29 April 1917.

125 S. Fokin, 'Pereustroistvo soiuzov', *Pravda o Kronshtadte*, p. 92.

126 *Ibid.*, p. 92n.

127 *Pravda o Kronshtadte*, p. 57.

128 *Ibid.*, pp. 66–7.

129 *Ibid.*, p. 177.

130 *Ibid.*, p. 177.
131 'K Kr. vosstaniiu', *Volia Rossii*, no. 169, 3 April 1921.
132 *Pravda o Kronshtadte*, p. 43.
133 Kornatovsky, *Kronshtadtskii miatezh*, p. 228.
134 Kliuev to Miller, 12 March 1921, Miller Papers, Hoover Institution; D. D. Grimm to M. N. Giers, 15 March 1921, M. N. Giers Papers, Hoover Institution.
135 Dan, *Dva goda skitanii*, pp. 155–6.
136 *Ibid.*, p. 155; 'Bez komissarov', *Pravda o Kronshtadte*, p. 176.
137 Kornatovsky, *Kronshtadtskii miatezh*, pp. 87–8.
138 *Ibid.*, p. 77; Pukhov, *Kronshtadtskii miatezh v 1921g.*, p. 101.
139 *Pravda o Kronshtadte*, p. 153.
140 Kornatovsky, *Kronshtadtskii miatezh*, p. 77.
141 Aleksandr Zhenevsky, 'Pamiati tovarishchei pavshikh na postu: L. A. Bregman', *Krasnaia letopis'*, no. 1(16), 1926, p. 167.
142 *Pravda o Kronshtadte*, p. 45.
143 *Ibid.*, pp. 75, 106.
144 Kornatovsky, *Kronshtadtskii miatezh*, pp. 232–3.
145 *Ibid.*, p. 96.
146 Dan, *Dva goda skitanii*, p. 153.
147 'Svedeniia iz Petrograda ot 12 aprelia: Kronshtadt i otgoloski ego vosstaniia', Hoover Institution.
148 S. E. Rabinovich, 'Delegaty 10-go s'ezda RKP(b) pod Kronshtadtom v 1921 godu', *Krasnaia letopis'*, no. 2(41), 1931, p. 31.
149 *Pravda o Kronshtadte*, p. 147.
150 Semanov, *Likvidatsiia Kronshtadtskogo miatezha*, p. 161.
151 Kornatovsky, *Kronshtadtskii miatezh*, p. 247.
152 Rabinovich, 'Delegaty 10-go s'ezda', pp. 23–4, 37–8.
153 Leaflet of task-force of the delegates of the Tenth Party Congress, in Rabinovich, 'Delegaty 10-go s'ezda', p. 51.
154 Pukhov, *Kronshtadtskii miatezh v 1921g.*, pp. 178–9.
155 Avrich, *Kronstadt 1921*, p. 213; 'Rasporiazheniia krasnoi vlasti v Kronshtadte', *Krasnyi Kronshtadt*, no. 1, 18 March 1921, no. 42, 6 May 1921.
156 'Bol'she ne obmanut'!', *Krasnyi baltiiskii flot*, no. 37, reprinted in Kornatovsky, *Kronshtadtskii miatezh*, p. 250.
157 V. Mudrovich, 'Za izmenu – iz zasedanii Revtribunala', *Krasnyi Kronshtadt*, no. 42, 6 May 1921.
158 *Ibid.*

7. PRIDE AND GLORY OF THE RUSSIAN REVOLUTION?

1 *Kronshtadt na 1916 god. Spravochnaia kniga* (Kronstadt, 1916), pp. 59–71.
2 Tomasz Parczewski, *Kronsztadt na tle rewolucji Rosyjskiej* (Warsaw, 1935), pp. 4–7, 32.
3 F. A. Timofeevsky, *Kratkii istoricheskii ocherk dvukhsotletiia goroda Kronshtadta* (Kronstadt, 1913), pp. 132–3.
4 A. K. Drezen (ed.), *Burzhuaziia i pomeshchiki v 1917 godu* (Moscow–Leningrad, 1932), pp. 76, 78.

5 Parczewski, *Kronsztadt*, p. 5.
6 Drezen (ed.), *Burzhuaziia i pomeshchiki*, pp. 83–4.
7 Nik. Rostov, 'V Kronshtadte', *Izvestiia Gel'singforskogo soveta*, no. 75, 15 June 1917; Philips Price, *My Reminiscences of the Russian Revolution* (London, 1921), pp. 39–41.
8 Parczewski, *Kronsztadt*, pp. 53–4; *Delo naroda*, no. 74, 14 June 1917.
9 'V Kronshtadte', *Rech'*, no. 147, 14 June 1917.
10 *Izvestiia Kronshtadtskogo soveta*, no. 24, 16 April 1917.
11 *Ibid.*, no. 136, 1 September 1917.
12 Drezen (ed.), *Burzhuaziia i pomeshchiki*, p. 80.
13 Skobennikov, 'Grazhdanin Guchkov', *Izvestiia Kr. soveta*, no. 20, 12 April 1917.
14 *Ibid.*, no. 70, 13 June 1917.
15 *Ibid.*
16 Drezen (ed.), *Burzhuaziia i pomeshchiki*, p. 84.
17 *Revoliutsionnoe dvizhenie v Rossii nakanune oktiabr'skogo vooruzhennogo vosstaniia* (Moscow, 1962), p. 128.
18 'La république bolchevique de Kronstadt' is the heading of the Kronstadt section in the early French draft of Tseretelli's 'Souvenirs sur la révolution russe', unpublished MS, Nicolaevsky Collection, Hoover Institution.
19 *Pervyi vserossiiskii s'ezd sovetov rabochikh i soldatskikh deputatov* (2 vols., (Moscow–Leningrad, 1930), vol. 1, pp. 65–7.
20 *Rechi, I. G. Tseretelli* (Petrograd, 1917), p. 172; *Rabochaia gazeta*, no. 93, 28 June 1917.
21 I. G. Tseretelli, *Vospominaniia o fevral'skoi revoliutsii* (2 vols., Paris–The Hague, 1963), vol. 1, p. 415.
22 Vl. Voitinsky, 'Gody pobed i porazhenii: 1917 god', MS, pp. 125, 129, Hoover Institution.
23 Rostov, 'V Kronshtadte'.
24 N. Rostov, 'Na iakornoi ploshchadi', *Rabochaia gazeta*, no. 115, 25 July 1917.
25 Voitinsky, 'Gody pobed i porazhenii', p. 128.
26 Vladimir Voitinsky to Iraklii Tseretelli, 4 January 1930, unpublished letter, Nicolaevsky Collection, Hoover Institution.
27 Tseretelli, *Vospominaniia o fevral'skoi revoliutsii*, vol. 1, p. 426.
28 I. Flerovsky, 'Iiul'skii politicheskii urok', *Proletarskaia revoliutsiia*, no. 7(54), 1926, pp. 79–80.
29 A. V. Lunacharsky, *Byvshie liudi: ocherk istorii partii es-erov* (Moscow, 1922), p. 29.
30 D.I.K., 'Sotsial'naia revoliutsiia iz Kronshtadta', *Rabochaia gazeta*, no. 91, 27 June 1917.
31 V. I. Lenin, *Polnoe sobranie sochinenii*, 5th edn (55 vols., Moscow, 1958–65), vol. 32, pp. 218, 430.
32 *Ibid.*, vol. 34, pp. 383, 390.
33 Ivan Bezrabotnyi, 'O vol'nom gorode Kronshtadt', *Vpered*, no. 1, 2 June 1917; A. V. Lunacharsky, 'Kronshtadtskaia kommuna', *Golos pravdy*, no. 52, 18 May 1917.

34 *Pravda*, March–May 1921, nos. 57, 60, 62–9, 73, 75, 86, 89, 90, 110; *Izvestiia*, March 1921, nos. 50, 52, 54, 56, 68.

35 *Desiatyi s'ezd RKP(b) mart 1921 goda. Stenograficheskii otchet* (Moscow, 1963), pp. 300–1.

36 *Protokoll des III. Kongress der Kommunistischen Internationale (Moskau, 22 Juni bis 12 Juli 1921)* (Hamburg, 1921), pp. 190, 342, 564, 567.

37 Rafael Abramovitch, *The Soviet Revolution 1917–1939* (New York, 1962), pp. 202–3, 209; the passage attributed to Bukharin by Abramovitch is not to be found in the protocols of the Third Congress of the Comintern as he suggests, but is taken verbatim from André Morizet, *Chez Lenine et Trotski* (Paris, 1922), p. 71 and refers to a conversation Morizet had with an unnamed 'comrade'.

38 *Protokoll des III. Kongress der Kommunistischen Internationale*, p. 617.

39 *Odinadtsatyi s'ezd RKP(b)*, *Stenograficheskii otchet* (Moscow, 1961), p. 132.

40 K. R., 'Kronshtadt v osveshchenii beloi pressy', *Pravda*, no. 63, 24 March 1921; [Bukharin], 'Razoblacheniia g. Miliukova', *Pravda*, no. 110, 22 May 1921.

41 'Tov. Trotskii o sobytiiakh v Kronshtadte', *Pravda*, no. 57, 16 March 1921.

42 *Desiatyi s'ezd RKP(b)*, pp. 414, 33–4; Lenin, *Polnoe sobranie sochinenii*, vol. 43, p. 370.

43 *Ibid.*, pp. 367–71, 373, 383, 387.

44 *Pravda o Kronshtadte* (Prague, 1921), p. 151.

45 L. Martov, 'Kronshtadt', *Sotsialisticheskii vestnik*, no. 5, 3 April 1921.

46 *Krasnyi Kronshtadt*, no. 1, 18 March 1921.

Index